GLIKL

THE TAUBER INSTITUTE SERIES
FOR THE STUDY OF EUROPEAN JEWRY

Jehuda Reinharz, General Editor
ChaeRan Y. Freeze, Associate Editor
Sylvia Fuks Fried, Associate Editor
Eugene R. Sheppard, Associate Editor

The Tauber Institute Series is dedicated to publishing compelling and innovative approaches to the study of modern European Jewish history, thought, culture, and society. The series features scholarly works related to the Enlightenment, modern Judaism and the struggle for emancipation, the rise of nationalism and the spread of antisemitism, the Holocaust and its aftermath, as well as the contemporary Jewish experience. The series is published under the auspices of the Tauber Institute for the Study of European Jewry—established by a gift to Brandeis University from Dr. Laszlo N. Tauber—and is supported, in part, by the Tauber Foundation and the Valya and Robert Shapiro Endowment.

For the complete list of books that are available in this series,
please see www.brandeis.edu/tauber

GLIKL

MEMOIRS

1691–1719

EDITED & ANNOTATED
WITH AN INTRODUCTION BY
Chava Turniansky

TRANSLATED BY
Sara Friedman

BRANDEIS UNIVERSITY PRESS
Waltham, Massachusetts

Original Bilingual Yiddish-Hebrew edition published as
Glikl: Zikhronot 1691–1719 (Zalman Shazar Center, 2006).

Brandeis University Press
© 2019 Brandeis University
All rights reserved
Manufactured in the United States of America
Designed by Eric M. Brooks
Typeset in Garamond Premier Pro by Passumpsic Publishing

For permission to reproduce any of the material in this book,
contact Brandeis University Press, 415 South Street, Waltham MA 02453,
or visit http://www.brandeis.edu/library/bup.html.

Library of Congress Cataloging-in-Publication Data
available upon request
Cloth ISBN: 978-1-68458-005-7
Paperback ISBN: 978-1-68458-004-0
Ebook ISBN: 978-1-68458-006-4

5 4 3 2 1

IN MEMORY OF URI,

my beloved soulmate,

who was taken from me,

as Chaim from Glikl,

after thirty years of marriage

and who continues to

light up my life.

The publication of *Glikl*
was generously supported by
Valya Shapiro and
the Valya and Robert Shapiro Endowment.

The publication of *Glikl*
was made possible by the generous support of
the Fund for the Translation of Jewish Literature,
in loving memory of its founder and director,
Lucy S. Dawidowicz.

CONTENTS

ILLUSTRATIONS

ACKNOWLEDGMENTS

I spent many years editing, annotating, and translating Glikl's fascinating work, in the writing of which she found comfort following the death of her husband. Similarly to Glikl, this endeavor gave me solace after the loss of my husband.

My lengthy journey toward that critical annotated bilingual (Yiddish-Hebrew) edition of her memoirs published by the Zalman Shazar Center was an intellectual and emotional adventure. It involved constant, close, and intensive contact with friends, colleagues, and students, the staffs of libraries and archives, experts in an endless list of disciplines, all ready to answer my questions, share their knowledge, expertise, and wisdom generously and with devotion, and to help me understand the text and the world in which it was composed. My friend Erika Timm from the University of Trier in Germany, an incomparable expert in Old Yiddish language and literature, accompanied me closely during every stage of my work and graciously contributed a chapter elucidating Glikl's language. Throughout the entire journey, I benefited from the expertise and wise counsel of my good friends Jacob Elbaum and Ada Rapoport-Albert, who read large portions of the bilingual edition carefully and offered illuminating comments.

Here, in this English edition, I would like once again to express my deepest gratitude to this wonderful web of people who contributed sage advice, support, and friendship. This edition is the result of the initiative and devotion of my student and long-standing friend, Sylvia Fuks Fried, in cooperation with the Zalman Shazar Center for Jewish History and the Tauber Institute for the Study of European Jewry. I must thank again, from the bottom of my heart, my close friend Ada Rapoport-Albert, who read significant portions of the English translation and offered skillful solutions to problems that arose from an exacting comparison with the source. Marion Aptroot generously consulted on the thorny questions of suitable spellings of the panoply of names that appear throughout. Etka Liebowitz and

Aliza Berger-Cooper translated the footnotes. I am grateful to my student and devoted research assistant Rebecca Wolpe, for her invaluable assistance with various translations and meticulous treatment of the notes and bibliography. I am deeply indebted to the extraordinary translator, Sara Friedman, whose translation is inspiring, enlightening, and delightful. My esteem for her is immeasurable.

This edition was made possible through the generosity of the Fund for the Translation of Jewish Literature, administered by Neal Kozodoy, the Valya and Robert Shapiro Endowment at the Tauber Institute for the Study of European Jewry, and a generous gift from Laura S. Schor in support of the HBI Series on Jewish Women.

My sons Meir, Avner, and Elisha, my daughters-in-law, my grandchildren, and my partner Berty were a source of loving support and encouragement for which I am forever grateful.

CHAVA TURNIANSKY
Jerusalem, 2019

A NOTE TO READERS

In an effort to naturalize Glikl into English, we have chosen to use unique Hebrew terms such as *shammash* (synagogue assistant), *gabbai* (head of the communal apparatus), and *parnas* (lay leader of the community) rather than English terms like "sexton" or "beadle" that yield no additional understanding, or long strings of words to stand in for the one (like "lay leader of the community"). These terms appear unitalicized and are generally explained at first mention in the annotations at the bottom of the page of text.

By contrast, italics are used in the translation to indicate Glikl's quotations of Hebrew sources in Hebrew, biblical verses and sayings of the sages from the Midrash, Mishnah, and Talmud, as well as liturgy from the daily and High Holiday prayer books. The annotations include sources and explications as needed for all these instances, as well as for other allusions or references to Old Yiddish literature, moral and ethical writings, ritual practices, and historical figures and events. Individuals that Glikl mentions are identified and, to assist the reader, the panoply of immediate and extended family members are arranged in several family trees in the Appendix. Readers should refer to the map to locate Glikl's and her relatives' and acquaintances' domiciles, and situate her and others on their travels.

The spelling of the names of the many people who appear throughout these writings presents a particular problem for the English version of the work. Since we cannot always or entirely discern how these Hebrew and/or Yiddish names were pronounced in Glikl's times and environs, a simple transcription is rarely helpful. The use of the commonly known forms of Hebrew names in English (such as Moses for Moshe, Samuel for Shmuel, Samson for Shimshon, Eve for Chava, and the like) does not seem advisable, inasmuch as these forms introduce a foreign-sounding element into the text. For that reason, we chose in general to adhere to the modern standard Hebrew valence of the Hebrew names, hence, for example, Avraham,

Yakov, Chava, and Rivka (in accordance with Yiddish pronunciation, the accent always on the first syllable), rather than the Anglicized Abraham, Jacob, Eve, and Rebecca; and to follow the modern standard Yiddish valence of the Yiddish names, hence, for example, Glikl, Anshl, and Lipman, instead of the Germanized Glückel, Anschel, and Liepmann. The "ch" in Chaim and elsewhere is to be pronounced as a guttural sound as in "challah" (as is "ḥ" with an underdot, as well as "kh"); the sound of "ay" in Fayvesh is akin to "i" in "mine"; the "ey" in Beyle is akin to the "a" in "make."

Another editorial choice requires explanation. In the original, the Hebrew letter "resh," followed by an apostrophe and preceding a man's given name, may be an abbreviation for "Reb," a traditional Jewish title or form of address, corresponding to Mister, Sir, for a man who is not a rabbi, as well as an abbreviation for "Rabbi," a man with rabbinic ordination or scholarly status. We have chosen to use "Reb" throughout to indicate "mister," while "R." is used for those men who bear the honorific title and who are, in many cases, referred to by the acronym form of Moreynu veRabeynu Reb, rendered in our translation "our master and teacher R. . . ."

GLIKL

If this seventeenth-century Yiddish writer, born in Hamburg in 1645 and deceased in Metz in 1724, had seen the various renditions of her name in published versions of her work, she wouldn't have recognized herself. Not in the name Glikl Hamel, and even less in the more commonly used and far more aristocratic appellation Glikl *von* Hameln, since these epithets substitute the name of her birthplace Hamburg with that of her husband's Hamel, which became attached to his first name Chaim only after he had left the place and settled elsewhere (for what good is it to be called Hamel when you live in Hamel?). Furthermore, toponymical epithets were in those times used among Jews only for men, not for women. A woman's name reflected first of all her paternal kinship (in our case: Glikl *bas* Reb Leyb, the daughter of Mr. Leyb) and then, with marriage, her transition from her father's authority to that of her husband's (Glikl *eyshes* Reb Chaim Hamel: the wife of Mr. —), in which she remained even after his death (Glikl, *almones* Reb Chaim Hamel: the widow of —) as long as she did not remarry and become *eyshes* someone else. After her death, one or more of these epithets would be engraved on her tombstone and probably registered in the *Memorbuch* or memorial book of the community.

No less than by the strange name, Glikl would have been startled by the genre designations and titles given by scholars, translators, and publishers to her writing: *Zikhronot* or *Zikhroynes*, Memoirs or *Memoiren*, *Denkwürdigkeiten*, *Tagebuch*, Autobiography, "The Life of," and even "The Adventures of Glikl Hamel." She herself gave her book no name, no title, no genre definition. Failing to do so was most unusual in those days, when most Yiddish books were explicitly named by genre: *mayse* (story), *maysebukh* (storybook), *lid* (poem), *shpil* (play), *minhogim* (customs), *mesholim* (fables), *tkhines* (supplications). In the absence of a genre designation, the nature of the book was either implicit in the title, as in *Seyfer mitzves noshim* (book of commandments for women) and *Ḥamisho ḥumshey toyre beloshn-ashkenaz* (the five books of the Torah in Yiddish), or briefly described on the title page as in the case of the *Tsene-rene*, which was presented as a selection of commentaries on the weekly portions of the Torah.

Why then did Glikl refrain from giving her book a title or naming its genre? Was it only because she did not intend to have it published? Most Hebrew and Yiddish manuscripts — even if not directly intended for publication — were at that time given a title page or at least a title. But even later on, when Glikl's grandson supplied the copy his father had made from her manuscript with a regular title page, he too abstained from providing a title. He did adorn the page with a biblical verse in the conventional manner, but when referring to the work itself, called it simply "*haksav*" (the writing).

Not only did Glikl refrain from granting her book a title, but throughout her writing she avoided labeling it in any way or giving a name to what she was writing, referring to it only as "it," "this," "such," or "what I am writing." In Glikl's opening Hebrew sentence, "I began writing this in the year 5451 [1691]," a pronoun (*ze*), not a noun, is used to indicate the object of her writing, and this is the case whenever a name for her opus is required. The Yiddish pronoun *dos* ("this" or "that") appears mainly in short phrases such as "*dos vos ikh shrayb*" (lit. this which I am writing) and alternates with *zolkhes* and *dizes* (variations of "such," "that," and "this"), which Glikl uses even when revealing that she has already conceived the structure of her book: "I intend, God willing, to leave all this for you in seven little books, if God grants me life." — she says — "Therefore I think it would be most appropriate to begin with my birth." In most translations, the pronoun *dizes* in this sentence is left out, while its counterpart *zolkhes* turns into "*meine Lebenserinnerungen*," "my memoirs," "*mes souvenirs*," terms that have no equivalent whatsoever throughout the original. And indeed, what Glikl was writing was so utterly different from anything published and known in the Jewish world until then, that it is not at all surprising she didn't have a proper name for it.

Although current research has made significant contributions to the inventory of European Jewish ego-documents now available, it is still true that among the variety of genres in Jewish literature until the nineteenth century — whether in Hebrew or in Yiddish, the two languages of Ashkenazi Jewry — autobiographies or memoirs are quite a rarity, and written by a woman, all the more so. Among those works written by Ashkenazi women before the Enlightenment that have come down to us — all but one or two of them in Yiddish — no account of a personal life exists. Apart from private letters and the little poems a couple of young girls attached to the books they typeset at the family's printing shop, the few available women's writings comprise poems and prayers of various kinds, a sermon, and one major work, Rivka bas Meir Tiktiner's book of moral instruction, *Meynekes Rivke* (Rebekah's Nurse).

Only twice does Glikl mention concrete genre definitions concerning her own work, one of them in the negative: "*Mayne libe kinder*" — she says — "in writing this I do not intend to compose a book of moral instruction for you — I am not capable of that" and again: "Nor am I writing this as a book of moral instruction for you." This last remark, which is followed by her recurring explanation of the purpose of her writing — to drive away the melancholic thoughts in the long nights of her widowhood — concludes with a statement about the action she undertook for that purpose: "I therefore took it upon myself to record the events I still remember from the description of my youth, to the best of my knowledge and insofar as it can be done." In the original Yiddish sentence, in which a verb ("to write" or "to tell") is missing, Glikl may be indicating a literary genre, the *beshraybung*. Her immediate reservation, saying, "This is not to make an exception of myself or to set myself up, God forbid, as a pious woman," seems to imply that only exceptional individuals may be the subject of a *beshraybung*, an idea she most probably derived from her acquaintance with works thus entitled, like the *Beshraybung fun Aleksander Mukdon* (Alexander of Macedonia) that she mentions as the source of some of her stories. However, concerning her own book the term occurs only once, it refers to her youth only, and it may bear no direct implication to genre at all.

◆

"SEVEN LITTLE BOOKS"

Despite her reservations, Glikl proceeds to achieve her goal: to leave what she is writing in seven little chapters she calls "books" and to begin with her birth. But it is only in the second book that Glikl starts recording the

events of her life. What, then, does the first book deal with? Mainly her
spiritual world with her ideas and reflections on this world and the world
to come; on God and man; on the choice between good and evil; on the
misery of the righteous and the prospering of the wicked; on the meaning
of fate and suffering, and of sin and atonement; on the value of material
possessions; and on other such matters. Moral precepts and practical
instructions pertain to topics such as faith and trust in the Creator, love
of one's fellow man, study of Torah, honesty in trade, and the duties of
parents toward their children. This lengthy account of her meditations is
full of quotations from the Scriptures and other Hebrew sources, either in
their original language or in Yiddish translation, interlaced with proverbs,
aphorisms, anecdotes, parables, and above all — both short and long stories
of Jewish or non-Jewish origin, intended to illustrate and concretize whatever is being said. These features of the narrative are characteristic of most
of Glikl's other chapters as well.

The first book of Glikl's memoirs is, in fact, an introduction to her spiritual world, a kind of manifesto of the faith, beliefs, aspirations, motives,
and opinions of a God-fearing pious Jewish woman. However, its language
and style, the character of the elements of which the flow of contents is
made up, and the way in which these are interwoven with moral precepts
and guidelines, clearly reflect the conventions of popular Yiddish *musser-
literatur*, a didactic genre intended to teach the unlearned whatever they
are supposed to know in order to act, live, and behave as good Jewish men
or women should. It reached its heyday at the beginning of the seventeenth
century, before Glikl was born, but the fruits it bore then remained alive
during her lifetime and for many generations after she wrote her book.
Her awareness of, her familiarity with, and the importance she attributed
to this genre and to its edifying aims are clearly evident throughout her
writing, but her book as a whole is by no means a *musser-seyfer*, a book of
moral instruction. Glikl herself strongly refutes this possibility twice in the
first chapter, when she realizes the extent to which her writing resembles
the mentioned genre and its conventions. After elaborating on other, "real"
(meaning Hebrew) books of moral and spiritual instruction, which she
does not name, she specifically recommends to her children the two most
popular Yiddish works of this kind, the *Brantshpigl* and the *Lev Tov*, thus

adopting the most widespread conventional recommendation for Yiddish books (apart from the *Tsene-rene*).

But with one exception, Glikl's mentions of books of moral instruction all appear — and quite profusely — in Book One only, and for good reason, too, for if we were to remove from it just a few fragments, most of them concerning Glikl's explanations about her writing and some original thoughts on the relations between parents and children, Book One would in fact be a regular Yiddish *musser-seyfer* in miniature, with all its attendant features: the style and the language; the contents and the ideology; the kinds of topics discussed and the manner of discussion in the first person plural and not in the singular; the combination of criticism of certain aspects of actual conduct with precepts and guidelines for ideal behavior; and the way in which all these are interlaced with illustrative quotations, proverbs, aphorisms, and stories. Moreover, Avraham ben Shabtai Halevy ish Horowitz's well-known Hebrew book *Yesh Noḥalin*, a treatise written in the traditional form of an ethical will, which Glikl reports was orally translated to her into Yiddish, appears to have been the source of inspiration for most of the contents of this chapter (as well as for most moralizing passages elsewhere) and a model for some of its main stylistic features. Still, the first book of the memoirs not only introduces us to Glikl's spiritual world at the time of writing, but also suggests the modes and means by which this world was shaped: a considerable amount of varied reading, an intense exposure to a rich and multiform oral tradition, both complemented by the experiences and teachings of life.

Most of these insights are lost through the blatant omissions in the first German translation — and in the English, French, and Italian versions that followed it — which obliterated the greatest part of the first book, as well as many of Glikl's reflections elsewhere and most of the stories she wove into her writing. The first translator of Glikl's work into Hebrew removed the first chapter from its original site and placed it at the end. His reason for doing so was his belief that "[o]nly after the reader has read the six chapters of the memoirs and learned about the life of Glikl and her brethren will he be able to comprehend the contents of the chapter she placed at the beginning as an inevitable product of the events she witnessed and experienced" (Rabinovitz 1929, p. 5). In this he was, of course, quite right:

the first book is indeed the product of the experiences that preceded the writing. But it is precisely — but of course not only — for this reason that it should be left in its place. Pushing it off to the end alters the very nature of Glikl's reflections on her life and interferes with our view of them. It also distorts the specific character of her book by assuming a process that leads directly from the past to the present and culminates in the emergence of the well-formed personality of the author.

In fact, this mature personality is already present at the start of the memoirs. At this point the author is neither a child nor an adolescent, whose diary entries record her experiences from childhood to old age, but a mature woman, who in middle age begins to write her memoirs in which she looks back to her past from the vantage point of a lifetime of experience. There is, therefore, no way of tracing the formation of Glikl's personality through her reactions to the events of her life as they took place. Her memoirs can, however, bring home to us her ways of observing, remembering, analyzing, and interpreting these past events, and can allow us to contemplate her personality as it was at the time of writing, when a good part of her life was already behind her. For when Glikl first started writing her memoirs, she was a woman of forty-five, an age then considered much more advanced than today. Behind her lay her childhood and adolescence, her engagement at the age of twelve, her marriage to Chaim Hamel two years later, the birth of fourteen children, the upbringing and education of the thirteen that lived, the death of one of them at the age of three, the betrothal and marriage of four others, the death of her husband, and a short period of widowhood. To these domestic events we must add the incidents and occurrences that took place within the extended family and among the family's servants, neighbors and friends, acquaintances and business associates either in Hamel, where Glikl spent the first year of her married life; or in her birthplace Hamburg, where she lived most of the time; or else in one of the many other locations she visited in order to call on relatives or friends, to negotiate, arrange, or celebrate the marriages of her children, to do some business on her own, or to assist her husband in his trade. Her travels in times of peace and war, within Germany and abroad — to Amsterdam and Copenhagen — had already broadened her horizons and enriched her experience. Thus, the woman who sets about writing her memoirs is not only a mature personality shaped by the experience of forty-five years of life, but a person fully aware of herself and of her present status in life, conscious of her purpose in writing, quite knowledgeable about the form in which she wishes to shape her book, and determined to have her personal ideological manifesto precede the story of her life.

In the second book, where this life story begins, a significant transformation takes place and persists to the end. The collective "we sinful human beings," which prevails in the first book, gives way to a predominant individual: "I, Glikl." The characteristic eclectic principles of Yiddish *musser-literatur* and its illustrative devices continue to play an important role, but they are now most intimately linked to the story of the narrator's life. The moral instruction does not derive anymore from abstract principles, traditional thought, or common wisdom, but from concrete personal experiences, and it appears particularly in passages that sum up the lessons of everyday life in moralistic terms. The countless episodes, anecdotes, and descriptions of personal, family, and community affairs that do not directly provide, or intend to provide, moral instruction or practical guidance, and their like — as well as the story of the author's life and the prevalent first person — will not be found in a regular Hebrew or Yiddish book of moral and spiritual guidance.

Some of these features render it impossible to consider the "ethical will" (*tsavaat mussar*) as subtext or model for Glikl's work beyond the first book. That specific branch of *musser-literatur* — to which the aforementioned book *Yesh Noḥalin* belongs — is a particularly practical genre dealing mostly with the instruction of the basic ethical norms of conduct. Although the ethical will is often formulated in the first person, addressed to the author's son or children, and interlaced with examples and stories, it does not tell a life story, and therefore differs greatly from Glikl's work. Her writing differs greatly also from the personal wills that have come down to us from that time and geographical area: their main issue — the disposition of the inheritance — is often accompanied by some moralizing exhortations, ethical commands, and practical rules of behavior, probably in the same way these elements infiltrated even private letters and accompanied Glikl's recording of the events of her life. Her opus, however, as well as the mentioned wills, may only figuratively be considered ethical wills, for

they lack the most prominent essential feature of the genre and deal mainly
with matters foreign to it. There is, however, an underlying common intention: the wish to pass on to the next generation a sum of life experience, to
warn the addressees against frivolous deeds, and to show them the way of
righteous conduct in family life and in commerce, the proper behavior in
human relationships; in a word, to hand down to them a philosophy of life.
Glikl's decision to address the memoirs to her children is, of course, most
appropriate for an autobiographical work in which their parents play the
central roles.

"I was born, so I believe, in the year 5407 [1647], in the holy community
of Hamburg, where my pious, devout mother brought me into the world,"
says Glikl at the beginning of her life story—she is mistaken, however, for
the year was actually 1645—and she goes on to comment on the saying of
the sages: "*Better never to have been created than to have been created*," after
which the leaf in which she is likely to have described the household and
charity of her parents is the one and only missing leaf from the nearly two
hundred the manuscript comprises. However, this can hardly be the reason
for the fact that the period of the writer's formative years, her growth and
education, her evolvement from childhood into maturity—precisely the
topic that research of modern autobiography since Rousseau's *Confessions*
considers to be the key to and the quintessence of the genre—is almost
entirely missing from Glikl's memoirs. All we know about her own short
childhood—for a girl betrothed at the age of twelve and married at the
age of fourteen is evidently considered an adult—comes down to no more
than a few sentences: "I was born in Hamburg, but I heard from my dear
parents and others—I was not yet three years old when all the Jews of
Hamburg were served with an edict of expulsion and forced to move to
Altona," or, "It was in my childhood—I was about ten years old—when
the Swede went to war with His Majesty the King of Denmark. I cannot
write much news about it since I was a child and had to sit in ḥeder [tra-
ditional elementary school, lit. "room"]." And, while praising her father,
she remarks, "He gave his children, boys and girls alike, an education in
higher matters as well as in practical things." Did these higher matters include all the subjects of the contemporary curriculum for boys, or just a
few of them? And what do "practical things" mean: writing, arithmetic,

correspondence skills, household chores, bookkeeping basics, rudiments of trade? And what kind of ḥeder was it; who taught what to whom and for how long? Glikl does not provide any direct answers to these questions, but the form and content of her writing attest to her skills and disclose many of the sources of her knowledge.

Once Glikl decided to make her own birth the starting point of her memoirs, she had to make use of information she obtained from other people's experiences and recollections in order to cover at least the first years of her life, for which she could not possess the necessary personal memories. We cannot tell what this reservoir of information may have contained, but the elements from it that she chose to include in her book clearly point out that it was not at all her intention to focus here on herself. Not only does her book lack any concrete picture, however partial, of her early childhood, but it does not render any such depiction of her life up to her engagement at the age of twelve—well beyond the age at which personal recollection can scarcely be retrieved.

The subject matter of this part of her memoirs consists mainly of family occurrences (only seldom witnessed by herself), events in the congregation of Hamburg-Altona, and the figures of her direct ancestors. In dealing with all these topics, which are thoroughly and deeply interrelated, she often shifts to the past, two or three generations before her birth, touches on the foundation and history of the kehillah (community) into which she was born, and moves from her direct ancestors to other personalities related to them or to their community before she turns nearer to the present for an orderly outline of her husband's family and a concluding statement: "My dear children, I write this for you in case your dear children or grandchildren come to you one of these days, knowing nothing of their family. For this reason I have set this down for you here in brief, so that you might know what kind of people you come from." In doing this, she is, in fact, following a literary pattern, for genealogies and family or ancestral histories were in the seventeenth century a most common frame for autobiography.

As a result, Glikl presents us with a wide gallery of male and female figures, most of whom she never met, but whose images—construed from the stories she heard—still thrill and charm her at the time of writing no less than they did in childhood. Glikl's reticence about her own self in recording this chapter of her early life may well point to the fact that she ascribed little or no importance to the role of the self at this age, and was well aware of a total dependence on family and community before the emergence of a distinct, concrete, and self-conscious individual identity.

Most of the stories pertaining to real figures in this part of the book play a twofold didactic role: they present — by the exemplary character and deeds of the personalities described — well-defined ideals of behavior, and create a link between the young listener and the past of both the family and the community. In committing these stories to writing, Glikl shares the same aims. She also attests to the function and impact of a rich oral tradition, and displays, simultaneously, her evident awareness of an alternative method of transmission.

Some of the stories are no more than anecdotes, which, although their didactic purpose is not prominent, do depict vivid and fascinating episodes. Here is one example:

> Now, my father, of blessed memory, as I mentioned, before marrying my mother, may she live long, was married to another woman, by the name of Reytse, who was apparently an extremely talented person, a most capable woman who ran a large, respected household; she ultimately died without having any children with my father, of blessed memory. This woman already had an only daughter. In this way did my father, of blessed memory, gain — along with his first wife — a stepdaughter too, second to none in both beauty and deed. She spoke fluent French, which turned out one time to be most advantageous for my father, of blessed memory. For my father, of blessed memory, had received a pledge from a certain non-Jewish gentleman, valued at five hundred reichstaler. Well, after some time, this gentleman returned with two other gentlemen, seeking to redeem his pledge. My father, of blessed memory, suspecting nothing, goes upstairs to get the pledge. His stepdaughter was standing at the clavichord, playing the instrument so as to render the gentlemen's wait less tedious.
>
> The two gentlemen, who were standing near her, start conferring together: "When the Jew comes back with our pledge, we'll grab it from him without giving him the money and get out of here." They

were speaking French, never dreaming that the maiden could understand them. As my father, of blessed memory, comes back with the
pledge, she starts singing loudly [in Hebrew]: *"Beware! Not the
pledge! Today — here, tomorrow — gone!"* In her haste, the poor girl
couldn't express herself any better. So my father, of blessed memory,
says to the gentleman: "Sir, where's the money?" Says the man: "Give
me the pledge." Says my father, of blessed memory: "I'm not giving
any pledge; first I must have the money." One of the men then turns
to the others and says: "Fellows, we've been duped, the whore must
know French," and with that they bolted from the house, shouting
threats. Next day the gentleman returns alone, pays my father, of
blessed memory, the principal with interest, and redeems his pledge,
saying: "Useful for you — you invested wisely when you had your
daughter learn French," and with that he went on his way. (Book One)

Even a typical short passage like this touches on a series of issues and
invites a variety of observations. As to its literary aspect, the passage proves
the author's ability to render, in concrete and sharp detail, a story she remembers from childhood, and to vividly reconstruct situations and events
she did not witness. Her sensible use of direct speech, her subtle choice of
language — such as the use of the Hebrew-Yiddish word *mashkon/mashkn*
for "pledge" by both father and daughter compared with the German word
Pfand by the Gentile, or the gentleman's epithet *hur* (whore) for the young
girl compared with Glikl's term *bsule* (maiden) — and other manifestations
of stylistic sensitivity attest to her fine literary talents. The passage contains
incidental details on a variety of topics such as first, second, and childless
marriages, the fate of stepchildren, the education of girls, the money-
lending business and its dangers, the use of secret languages among Jews
and Gentiles, and even a line from a humorous popular song.

Despite the associative blend of individual portraits with descriptions
of community affairs intertwined with the author's personal opinions,
her stories and quotations, and despite the narration's rapid turning from
one topic to another, a basic blueprint for this chapter can be discerned.
Glikl's father, the first individual subject of the narration, is not only the
founder of the family: she ascribes to him the function of founder of the

community as well, which allows her to elaborate on the origins of both at once. The second central figure to appear is not her mother, as would be expected, but her maternal grandparents; and it is only after she describes the crucial incidents of their lives, especially her grandmother's, in some detail, that she turns to her parents' marriage, and then — but not before offering a moving description of her beloved grandmother's death — she moves on to her own wedding, an occasion for introducing her husband's paternal grandparents. The omission of any details about *his* maternal and *her* paternal grandparents seems to suggest a view on ancestry and pedigree based on gender, while the following meticulous orderly presentation of all her husband's brothers and sisters is clearly intended to praise their father, making no mention at all of their mother.

It is right after her wedding that we first hear Glikl's voice turning gradually from the passive to the active mode: "After my wedding, my father and mother returned home. I was a child of less than fourteen, and I had to stay alone, without my father and mother, in a foreign land, among strangers. But all this was not hard for me, since I enjoyed the generosity of my pious father-in-law, of blessed memory, and my late mother-in-law. They were distinguished people, most decent, and they maintained me extremely well, better than I deserved." For this same reason — she says after a brief comparison between *her* hometown and her husband's village — "I forgot Hamburg entirely," but no real impression of her life and experiences in Hamel is left before she states, "After my wedding I lived with my husband for a year in Hamel" and goes on to record the main events that followed: the young couple's moving in with Glikl's parents in Hamburg, the birth of their first child, and their moving to a house of their own. Glikl's voice in the first person grows louder and clearer and does not weaken when joined by the plural "we" (with no prevalence of "my husband and I" over "I and my husband"), with which it alternates constantly, according, of course, to the kind of "I" in question, as, for instance, in her statement, "When *we* came to Hamburg, *I* conceived immediately [italics added]."

There is no doubt about the central roles played by marriage and the independence of a home of her own in the emergence of Glikl's self-conscious individual identity and its consolidation into a partnership of two. Glikl's keen sense of partnership is clear from the start: "My husband, of blessed memory" — she recollects — "was very preoccupied with his business affairs; although still young, I did my part by his side. I do not write this to praise myself — my husband, of blessed memory, did not take advice from anyone but did whatever the two of us decided together." This sentence at the opening of the third book gives way to an orderly account of the attendants, agents, and partners in the family's business, and of a series of occurrences related to them. These initiate the long chain of variegated events, incidents, and episodes that Glikl selects from her memories of the thirty years of married life that preceded the death of her husband to make up the third and fourth books. She does indeed do her share by his side: not only is she frequently asked for her advice and opinion, but she herself interviews agents, inspects potential partners, drafts partnership agreements, keeps books, and is at the same time busy having, raising, and educating her children, looking for suitable matches and dowries for those who have reached marriageable age, and supervising a large and rich household. She appears to be an active equal partner in all decisions concerning family affairs as well as business matters. That is why no one wonders at the reply of her dying husband when asked about his will: "I don't know what to say. My wife, she knows everything. She should continue just as she was doing before." Glikl does much more than that: she takes on the business herself, puts into practice her remarkable financial expertise and her competence in commerce, develops new original enterprises, and sees the business grow and prosper under her sole management.

Even though Glikl explains right at the outset, time and again, that her writing was induced by her state of mind after the loss of her husband, she does not follow the common practice of other seventeenth-century women to focus primarily on the portrait of the devoted and adored husband, and to append to it, with appropriate modesty, a briefer portrait of themselves. It is in fact Glikl and *her* personal life story that take center stage. Her story does not begin with Chaim Hamel's entering her life, nor does it end with his leaving this world. The meticulous account of his death and its immediate aftermath appear at the beginning of the fifth book, but Glikl continues to record her memories of the subsequent events of her life, in what turns out to be about one-third of her written work: her widowhood, her second marriage, her move to Metz, the death of her second husband, and the years she lived under her daughter's and son-in-law's roof until she quit writing, for no explicit reason, about five years before her death. Even in these last stages — when her personal life grows less and less eventful, her references to Chaim Hamel become scarcer before they disappear altogether, and the writing begins to resemble entries in a diary — Glikl keeps on recording, as she had done before, a selection of episodes and occurrences from the private as well as from the public sphere.

It may be surprising how relatively few of the recorded episodes occur at home. Some of them depict Glikl's activities while her husband is away: taking care of the correspondence, keeping informed of his whereabouts, worrying and anxious about his health and safety, and awaiting his return. No mention is made here of children or household. Somewhat more frequent are episodes that focus on husband and wife at home. They illustrate the couple's mutual concern, support, and devotion in times of crisis, their ways of sharing joy and sorrow, their manner of discussing family and business matters. Although Glikl strives to provide an ideal portrait of her husband, she does not conceal their differences of opinion — at times she concedes to him, and at times she stands her ground — nor does she hide her occasional feelings of anger, resentment, or disappointment. The dialogues between husband and wife contained in some of these and other episodes display a reciprocal cordial and respectful manner of conversation notwithstanding the different modes of invocation involved: she addresses him by the formal and polite pronoun *ir*, while he addresses her by the familiar *du*, uses her name always in the diminutive (Gliklchen), and often calls her *mayn kind* (my child). We never hear *her* calling him by name, but in writing, his name Chaim is always prefixed by the title *reb* (mister).

Normal pregnancies and births are merely mentioned in their proper place within the chronological sequence of events, and only when they involve an irregularity — illness, danger, death, a miraculous recovery or a funny episode — do they become worthy of detailed description. Rarely a glimpse is offered at mother and child or children at home, and there is almost no reference to their growing up, their behavior, upbringing, and formal education. As a matter of fact, there are almost no substantial accounts to endorse Glikl's brief retrospective summary: "I gave birth every two years and worked hard, as one does with such a household full of children, may God protect them. I thought no one had a heavier load or worked harder at raising children than I did. But, fool that I was, I did not know how good I had it with my children sitting around my table *like olive saplings around your table."*

A relatively larger space is taken up by Glikl's accounts of her children's marriages. These focus regularly on the matchmaking process and the precise conditions of the engagement agreement (the *tno'im*), and conclude after a few, or more than a few, short or long observations regarding the wedding itself, with a variation of the same phrase: "Thus was the wedding concluded amid joy and gladness." All the children's marriages and weddings are mentioned (except for that of the youngest daughter), but here, again, only those associated with a remarkable event, or with particularly favorable or unfavorable circumstances, are described at length. The outstanding case is the marriage of Tsipor, the eldest daughter, which is narrated in meticulous detail from the first rumor about the amazing *shidekh* (match) to the wedding's finale, including the family's delightful journey to Amsterdam and then to Cleve, a full account of the noblemen present, a report of the pomp displayed and the foods eaten, and a retelling of several unusual incidents that took place during this unique social event.

Whoever seems to regard Glikl as a prototype of the *yiddishe mame* (Jewish mother) — whatever that meant then or means today — should bear in mind that she does not once mention most of her children ever again after their weddings, except for those who later passed away, in which case she records the death in two or three short sentences. As if she were following the popular saying *"Oys di oygn, oys dem hartsn"* (Out of sight, out of mind), Glikl does mention, and frequently at that, only those of her children she actually sees. Besides, there is no allusion at all to any grandchildren — not even to the offspring of the children she does see and mention — before she is over sixty-five years old and writing the last two chapters of her book. Whether the absence of any reference to her grandson Moshe's conversion to Christianity in London in 1711 is a consequence of this practice or stems from lack of information, her interest in her grandchildren — or in writing about them — seems to be almost nil.

Many of Glikl's most meticulous descriptions are devoted to the journeys she made with or without her husband or children, and to encounters and incidents that happened away from home, either on the way, by coach or aboard ship, in public lodgings, or at the houses of relatives and friends. Although her travels brought her hundreds of miles away from Hamburg, there is no reference whatsoever to the scenery that unfolded before her eyes during her trips, including the short excursions to the countryside she called *lust-shpatsir* or *lust-rayz*. She may express the pleasure and delight or the annoyance and irritation she experienced, register the relevant weather conditions, or conclude the description of the voyage with a precise account of its cost and duration, yet still not provide any concrete detail to form an image, however partial, of the places she saw.

In fact, there are very few mentions — never concrete portrayals — of material objects except for those included in the few descriptions Glikl provides of the most luxurious residences of court Jews and bankers she visited. Her accounts focus mainly on the event itself: on what she, the members of her extended family, and many other people did and said — often in direct speech — in the course of the events she chooses to record; on their behavior and relationships; on the decisions they make and the consequences. Her opinions and sentiments about the narrated events are at times open and outspoken, and at times more or less implied, even when she alludes to divine intervention and expresses her religious feelings.

Notwithstanding the fact that the narration revolves largely around people involved in the events, and we can see them act, hear them talk, and thus learn about them, no concrete details allow even for a rough outline of a face, a body, an appearance. Adjectives denoting nonphysical qualities (virtuous, pious, devout, righteous, honest, clever) or implying economic, social, or intellectual status (wealthy, distinguished, respected, prominent, learned, wise) abound, while those related to physical qualities are extremely scarce and nonspecific: "handsome," "beautiful," or "very beautiful" alternate with "intelligent," "wise," or "clever" on only rare occasions, including those concerning her own children. Regarding her husband — we don't even know his age, and only her recurring remark that they were both very young leads to the conclusion that he was not much older than she. Concerning Glikl herself, we have only vague notions of her physical surroundings — where did she write? in a room of her own? — and almost no notion of her appearance. In the course of a dangerous journey, she complies with her husband's request to remove her fine traveling dress and change into old rags instead. Asked by Reb Meir, a fellow traveler, "My dear Reb Chaim, why are you so worried? And why are you making your wife dress so hideously?" Reb Chaim replies, "God knows I'm not worried about myself or the money I'm carrying—it's the womenfolk I'm worried about, my wife and the maidservant." Says Reb Meir: "No need to worry; seriously, Reb Chaim, you are wrong about your wife—you should not have made her dress so hideously, nobody would have harmed her anyway." "My husband, of blessed memory," remarks Glikl, "was very angry at Reb Meir's joking and took it very much to heart." In this indirect but unique allusion to Glikl's physical appearance, *I* can visualize a good-looking woman, while other readers may envision just the contrary. Besides, I consider the mere narration of the episode as proof of Glikl's self-confidence and her sense of humor, which was not shared by her husband.

As in ego documents on the whole, one or more of a great variety of reasons, concepts, and intentions may have determined Glikl's choice of episodes to describe, figures to portray, issues to comment on, stories to incorporate into the narrative. One or more of a no lesser diversity of notions, considerations, and practices may have dictated her selection of narrative modes and devices, of details to be included or left out, her choice of language, her manner of expressing emotions, and so on. The extremely complex nature of memory and remembering, combined with the writer's wishes and intentions, her character and talents and much more, does not allow for more than tentative speculation. Moreover, our expectations of the autobiographical text are surely quite different from those of Glikl's contemporaries, who must have read such a text differently from the way we read it today. The prevailing literary conventions, as well as the character of her addressees, must have guided her writing in many ways. The attitudes, ideals, sensibilities, and interests of her time in general, of the Jewish people in particular, and of the socioeconomic group she belonged to are clearly and profusely imprinted in her memoirs. But in the end, it is Glikl's distinct personality, her personal view of her life and times, and her particular choice of what she wishes to record that form the structure of her book.

Many pages are devoted to lengthy and meticulous reports of commer-

cial affairs, financial activities, civil lawsuits, the ups and downs of part-
nerships, business enterprises, and entrepreneurs. Most accounts concern
directly Glikl's nuclear or extended family; a few concern other more or
less prominent wealthy individuals. Together they offer a thorough and
vivid insight into economic life and its conceptualization. Glikl's recurring
references to the assets and exact sums of money people own, pay, lend,
borrow, or allot for dowries may point not just to a constant worry, but
to a complete lack of inhibition in discussing these matters, as if it were
commonplace to do so.

In dealing with all these issues, Glikl often moves, as she does in her visits
and travels, from the private to the public sphere. Her sporadic allusions to
episodes of war and political conflicts are usually no more than background
accessories intended to substantiate the relation of other events concerning
herself, her family, or her acquaintances. On the other hand, her interest in
the behavior of the community and its leadership is mainly present at the
beginning—in her accounts of communal events that took place before
she was born—and at the end, when she is seventy and residing in Metz.
On this occasion, a rhetorical question—"Shall I write at length what
else is happening here, or whether the community is following the right
path?"—gives way to some short comments on the changes she witnessed
since she moved to the place, and to a meticulous account of a long and
tortuous dispute about the appointment of the chief rabbi. The account
that follows, of the tragic Shavuot incident in the synagogue, and the recording of a mysterious astronomical phenomenon at the end of the book,
are only two of a series of extraordinary or remarkable public, semipublic,
or quasi-public events Glikl cared to record. However different their character, their significance for the community, and the extent of their impact
on its members may be, they are all in fact sensational events, for there can
be no doubt about the public excitement they caused. Whether crimes or
disasters, trials or executions, the news about the self-proclaimed messiah
Shabtai Tzvi, or the case of the old widower who broke the promise he
made his dying wife to marry their young stepdaughter—they all become,
in Glikl's narrative, an integral part of the story of her life. Moreover, the
particular combination of the private and the public, the individual and
the communal in Glikl's writing renders not only a revealing image of a

woman's life and personality, but a fascinating portrait of an entire society and a whole period as well.

It is therefore not surprising that Glikl's untitled *"dos vos ikh shrayb"* turned out to be a singularly important social and historical document and at the same time one of the greatest literary achievements of Ashkenazi prose — in Yiddish or Hebrew — at least until the end of the eighteenth century. Although these appreciations have encouraged serious research — first and foremost that of Natalie Zemon Davis in her *Women on the Margins* — the memoirs themselves will convince the reader that it is not only their having been written by a Jewish woman of the seventeenth century, but their scope, their contents, and their character that make them unique.

Although a few autobiographies or memoirs — mainly in Hebrew and mostly unpublished at the time — had been written before, none can compare to hers in its comprehensive, colorful, and multiform character, its rich gallery of vividly depicted figures, its vibrant description of the period's fortunes and misfortunes and the family's joys and sorrows, its retrospective insight, and its intimate personal manner. And indeed, what Glikl was writing was so utterly different from anything published until then in Yiddish or Hebrew that it is not at all surprising she did not have a name for it.

WRITING, EDUCATION, LANGUAGE

One of this work's unique contributions is the singular insight offered by the writer's female perspective. Naturally she wrote about a range of matters and from perspectives that are rarely found in writings dating to her lifetime, most of which were penned by rabbis and scholars, leaders and community functionaries, or other central figures. As a woman, Glikl was a member of the silent majority whose voice is heard in the written word only on rare occasions; yet as a member of the socioeconomic elite, Glikl's voice is not representative of its female silent majority. Her upbringing, education, and way of life were certainly similar to those of other women of her station, many of whom are mentioned in her work, and thus they may have also shared her spiritual world. Yet, it is impossible to determine to what extent her personal world — including the breadth of her education,

FIGURE I
Bertha Pappenheim posing as Glikl in
"Portrait of Mrs. Glikl Hamel" by Leopold Pilichowski.
Original photo from collection of Alice and Moshe Shalvi.

the scope of her reading, her desire to express herself in writing, and her lin-
guistic-stylistic abilities — was also common to her female contemporaries
since only Glikl has left us such a comprehensive and complex composition.

Considering the limited and often misleading information available
concerning the education and spiritual world of Jewish women in the early

modern period, the modern-day reader of Glikl's work is likely to find the author's decision to write, or even her literacy, somewhat surprising. In fact, many — if not most — of her female contemporaries were literate; not only those of similar socioeconomic status. The very existence of a lively Yiddish literature offers clear evidence of this: indeed, women constituted the most significant portion of its intended readership. The considerable number of Yiddish private letters and other documents written by women of various stations — wives and daughters of rabbis, printers, community leaders and functionaries, large- and small-scale merchants, and many others — which have reached us demonstrate how widespread the command of Yiddish was among Glikl's female contemporaries. Moreover, a number of literary compositions penned by women — most of them from the learned elite — in the Ashkenazi cultural domain during the early modern period have survived. However, fundamental and obvious differences — from the scope of the work, its nature and its purpose, to the presence of the "self" — prevent a fair comparison of their works with Glikl's composition. Yet all these works were composed in the same language, Old Yiddish ("Western Yiddish"), in which Hebrew constitutes — as it does in Modern (or "Eastern") Yiddish — an integral organic component.

Rich in Hebrew elements and numerous quotations from the Hebrew scriptures, Glikl's language is likely to give the impression that she possessed a good command of the holy tongue and read Hebrew texts fluently. However, Glikl's own testimony, together with a comprehensive and thorough examination of the text, reveals that this was not the case; rather, her knowledge of Hebrew — even if indicative of an effort to learn the language — was rooted first and foremost in Yiddish, her spoken tongue. Recent studies have proven not only that most of the Hebrew words and expressions she employed in her written language were at the time active components of spoken Yiddish — indeed, most of them remain so today — but also that most of the quotations from the sources woven into her composition — mainly biblical verses and sayings of the sages — were a living and integral part of spoken Yiddish. Thus Glikl did not need to examine the Bible, Mishnah, Talmud, or other works in the holy tongue, nor read Yiddish books of moral instruction (*musser-literatur*), as scholars surmised in the past. She encountered most of the Hebrew elements of her language and the Hebrew quotations she employs naturally in the process of acquiring her spoken language, and certainly enriched this repository through intelligent listening within her Yiddish-speaking surroundings. Through her spoken language — concerning the world of her concepts and values, and the treasure trove of sources — Glikl acquired an entry into contemporary Yiddish literature; so too the range of Yiddish literary genres also served as an important source for her impressive erudition.

It is reasonable to assume that other women of her station had a similar education and that among them were others who, like Glikl, put ink to paper to tell the story — or episodes — of their life; yet only Glikl's work has reached us. It reveals a general picture, at the heart of which is the portrait of an individual: a woman similar to others of the same gender and status but at the same time made unique by her writing and her literary talent, who relates her life story, revealing her personal growth, an increasing sense of self, and the consolidation of her self-appraisal. Indeed, these constitute the foundation of Glikl's certainty in determining that her memoirs — and among them her introspection and even ruminations regarding questions of the utmost importance: good and evil, sin and punishment, human actions, and God's will — are indeed important and sufficiently interesting to warrant bequeathing them to future generations.

We cannot know whether the writing of her memoirs met the author's expectations, but the creative joy that is very much evident in her composition indicates that not only did writing serve as a relief and comfort but also gave her great pleasure, satisfaction, and fulfilment. Thus it is clear that in writing, Glikl responded to a creative talent that demanded realization; her grief at the disaster that beset her, her increasing desire for comfort, and her fear of melancholy initially motivated her to embark on this endeavor. At the same time, her work contains no indications that Glikl viewed her writing as a rare and unusual act; the lack of such signs apparently reveals that she was aware of similar compositions, written by other women, although these have not — or have not yet — reached us.

The brief entry on Glikl's death in the Metz Burial Society Register records only that Mrs. Glik [!], the wife of the deceased community leader Reb Hertz Levy, died and was buried with a good name on Thursday, the

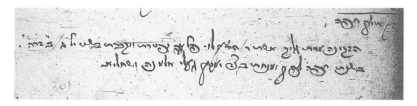

FIGURE 2
Entry on Glikl's death and burial, Metz Burial Society Register.
Jewish Theological Seminary of America (Ms. 5936).

second day of Rosh Hashanah of the year 5845, and she lies at the right side
of the widow Gelle.

Similarly, no mention is made of her writing or her composition in the
words of praise in the lengthier *in memoriam* to Glikl inscribed in the
Metz community's *Memorbuch*:

> May God remember the soul of the aged, important and pious
> woman Glikl, daughter of Judah Joseph of blessed memory from
> Hamburg, [. . .] for she was a housewife and was most wise in the
> trade of precious gems and also most learned in the rest of the re-
> spectable virtues, and all the days of her life behaved in the manner of
> pious women, doing good deeds for the living and the dead, and her
> words were pleasant to all people and she prayed with great devotion,
> never stopping for vain conversation. So too, her heirs gave charity
> to the poor in her name, may her soul be bound up with the chain of
> life, together with the souls of Abraham, Isaac and Jacob, and Sarah,
> Rebecca, Rachel and Leah, and with the souls of all the other pious
> men and women in the Garden of Eden, Amen. She passed away and
> was buried, with a good name, on the second day of Rosh Hashanah
> 5485 [September 19, 1724].

This standard format—the phrasing of which would certainly have
suited many of Glikl's female contemporaries of the same age and status
—notes, as was customary, the personal details of the deceased (her name
and the name of her father, place of birth, date of death and burial), with
the addition of only one unique characteristic (her wise dealings in the
trade of gemstones). This official record, similar to the few other "external"

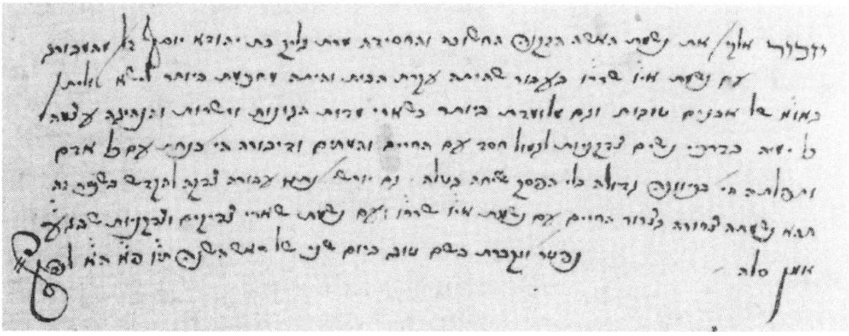

FIGURE 3

In Memoriam to Glikl, Metz *Memorbuch*.
Jewish Theological Seminary of America (Ms. 3670).

sources that directly mention Glikl, offers only a meagre contribution to
our knowledge about this woman and her times: it is most insubstantial,
making acutely evident the significance of her memoirs as a fascinating and
extraordinary historical source.

♠

GLIKL'S MEMOIR AS A HISTORICAL SOURCE

Although it was certainly not her intention, Glikl's memoirs are an invaluable historical source and contribute significantly to our knowledge
about the life and times of her generation. The historian must approach
it, however, with the caution appropriate for dealing with a literary, autobiographical composition. The work is not principally concerned with
relating historical facts for their own sake, but rather with a subjective,
experiential contemplation of them and an examination of their meaning;
it does not reflect the past as it was, but rather as the author perceived
and remembered it; its expression in writing is molded by many factors, in
particular the image of herself and her life that the writer sought to impart
to her addressees.

Naturally, most of the work describes events that affected the writer or
that occurred in her presence within narrow, intimate frameworks or wider
ones; these depictions enhance the portrait of life at that time, and eluci-
date the lived experience of Glikl and her contemporaries.

In addition, a significant portion of the composition concerns events that occurred during Glikl's lifetime in the public sphere, close to her or at some remove. Verifying the historical authenticity of the facts whenever possible reveals some mistakes and inaccuracies, most regarding dates or chronology, although these are insignificant when compared to the many accurate details in the work. Most of the facts about historical events, communal or otherwise, that Glikl mentions are accurate, even in instances where literary adaptation altered the details of an event or the nature of one of the personalities involved.

When describing events that occurred at times and locations outside the range of her personal experience and memories — for example, before her birth, during her early childhood, or before she became acquainted with her husband's family — Glikl obviously employed the memories of others, utilizing information from a second- or third-hand source. This she received in the form of anecdotes and stories circulating within the family or community, which were transmitted orally. Whether Glikl noted the matters as she remembered them being related, or adapted them using her talent, they are indeed simply anecdotes and oral stories. We cannot use them to assess the trustworthiness of the entire composition or to deem other facts reported therein true or false. Yet thanks to the details these anecdotes contain — concerning how the people of those generations regarded the world they lived in — and due to the very fact of their recording, these anecdotes and stories can shed light on the functions, trends, and behavior of oral transmission, as well as the transition from oral stories to the written word.

In her work Glikl combined many disparate elements into one composition, adapting and molding them in a personal and unique manner. This personal expression in fact offers an unusual perspective on the author and the ways in which she articulated her world in words, situating in the linguistic sphere an authentic and particularly revealing historical document. Works printed from the earliest days of Yiddish until near the end of the eighteenth century utilized a unified form of Western Yiddish, and this form of the language, almost unaffected by local developments, enabled the distribution of all Yiddish works throughout the entire Ashkenazi diaspora. This language also characterizes most manuscripts intended for printing. Although in manuscripts that were not intended for publication the living, spoken language is evident, there is no other work comparable to Glikl's text in terms of the range of content, the diversity of subject material, stylistic variety, the fluency of its discussion, or the extent to which direct speech is employed. Thus Glikl's work is doubtless a unique linguistic-historical document, extremely rare and fascinating.

For scholars of history, as well as researchers of language, literature, and literary history, the work of Glikl bas Leyb offers a true treasure trove of information and insights. For those not engaged in historical study, it promises a captivating and emotional reading experience.

PLACE AND TIME, COMMUNITY AND NEIGHBORS

All the places mentioned in Glikl's book can be easily pinpointed on a map of Europe, whether or not she or her extended family resided there permanently or temporarily, visited them, or passed through them while traveling. However, it is impossible to mark on a map the political borders between geopolitical administrative units of various kinds (church principalities including archbishopdoms, bishopdoms, and monasteries; secular principalities such as free cities and the properties of free knights); this is not only due to the multiplicity and variety of these units, but mainly because of the temporary nature of their existence and the alterations they underwent following changes in government, wars and annexations, unifications and secessions, and all the other events that occurred during the period described in Glikl's memoirs. The period she covers clearly ends when she stopped writing, following the description of the events that took place in 1719. However, as is the nature of memoirs, the narrative begins before the writer embarked on her literary endeavor. Glikl began writing her memoirs in 1691, and, despite declaring it her intention to begin the account with her birth, in 1645, her text offers a retrospective survey of her family and community history, stretching two to three generations before her birth. The general events that occurred in those generations, as in the entire composition, are not discussed but merely serve as background information,

FIGURE 4
Hamburg Stock Exchange.
Staatsarchiv Hamburg.

for the most part in a very limited fashion, to occurrences in the personal, familiar, and communal frameworks. These three frameworks become one living mass in the author's words concerning the generations that preceded her and in the few remarks about her community during the time of her writing.

A brief survey of the historical background provided by Glikl's work reveals the complex and changing status of the Jewish community in Hamburg and Altona—the towns in which Glikl was born, raised, and resided for most of her life—and how the community's status affected the lives of its members. During the seventeenth century, Hamburg was a blossoming free port and trade city (freie Reichsstadt), governed by a senate that represented the rich merchants; representatives of the priesthood and urban class were also involved in its decisions. A stock exchange had been active in the city since 1558, and in 1619 a central bank also opened its doors. In 1650, sixty thousand residents lived in Hamburg. Beyond the walls of the city to the west, "barely fifteen minutes away from Hamburg," according to Glikl, lay Altona. When the city's ruler died without progeny in 1640,

FIGURE 5
Altona.
Staatsarchiv Hamburg.

Altona passed to Denmark, and the Danish king sought to transform it
into a city to rival Hamburg.

The first Jews who settled in Hamburg were conversos from Portugal
who arrived at the end of the sixteenth century, returned to Judaism, and
founded a large and rich community that blossomed throughout the seventeenth century; this community began to decline toward the end of the
century due to economic restrictions and other limitations that led its
members to migrate. Ashkenazi Jews did not have the right to settle in
the city until the second half of the seventeenth century, unless they were
servants of Sephardi families. In contrast, from the end of the sixteenth
century, Ashkenazi Jews settled in neighboring Altona; and after Altona
passed to Danish rule in 1640, they received the right to establish a community in the city. Seventeen Ashkenazi families from Altona, including
Glikl's family, had been living in Hamburg since the 1620s, enjoying the
greater range of economic opportunities. Although their residence in the
city was based on private arrangements with the authorities, it was not
legal. In 1648 when Glikl, who was born in Hamburg, was three years old,
these families were ordered to leave the city. Most of the exiles returned

to Altona, which could not provide a livelihood for all its Jews — around forty households. They were thus forced to reside in Altona while earning their living in Hamburg, which was allowed under humiliating conditions.

The situation changed after the winter of 1657–1658 when, following the Swedish invasion of Altona, the Jews fled to the fortified city of Hamburg. The lobbying of the exiles, among them Glikl's father, now bore fruit: they received permission to settle in Hamburg, although as Jews under the protection of the Danish crown. Eighteen Ashkenazi families, living in Hamburg as servants in Sephardi households, joined their efforts to establish a community in the city. The Ashkenazi community grew quickly, by the end of the century outnumbering that of the Sephardi Jews: in 1680 there were around sixty Sephardi families, while the number of Ashkenazi families in 1696 passed three hundred; in this year the Ashkenazi Jews in Hamburg were granted official recognition. A small Ashkenazi community consolidated also in the neighboring town of Wandsbeck, which belonged, like Altona, to Denmark.

Due to the pressure of the Lutheran clergy, Ashkenazi Jews in Hamburg, residing on the "street" allocated to them, were not allowed to pray or bury their dead in the city. These actions were permitted in Altona, where their synagogue and cemetery were located; thus throughout the seventeenth century, their religious center was situated in the kingdom of Denmark. Prayer services were conducted secretly in homes in Hamburg — sometimes these passed off peacefully and on other occasions resulted in expulsions to Altona. The close link between the Ashkenazi communities on the two sides of the political border continued despite the internal tensions between them and the tense relations between the Danish crown and the Free City of Hamburg. In 1671 the Ashkenazi communities in Altona, Hamburg, and Wandsbeck united into one body, known as the Three Communities or the AHW Communities (according to the first letters of their names), under the leadership of the rabbi and rabbinical court in Altona. Within the framework of this body, which existed until 1811, the communities maintained their organizational independence.

Metz, where Glikl resided from the time of her second marriage until her death in 1724, is situated on the Moselle River in northeast France. Unlike Hamburg, a Jewish community had existed there since the early

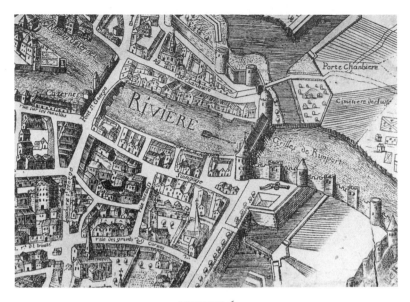

FIGURE 6
The Jewish Quarter, Metz, 1696.
Detail of "Plan releve et tres exact de la ville de Metz (1696),"
Cliché La Cour d'Or, Musée Metz.

Middle Ages, although the community Glikl joined was established at the end of the sixteenth century, and since then had received the protection of French kings (in Glikl's lifetime, Louis XIV and XV), enjoying a significant degree of religious and economic freedom. From the beginning of the seventeenth century, it possessed a synagogue and cemetery, and in 1700, when the city population numbered twenty-two thousand, twelve hundred Jews resided in the community.

In Metz, as in Hamburg-Altona, Glikl was related to the leaders of the community and the group of prominent figures in the socioeconomic realm. In her work, she provides a range of portraits depicting the economic and social activities of these circles in great detail. However, although she is punctilious in noting the title "parnas" (community leader, lit. "provider") with regard to everyone who held this position in her community or others, the community as an organized institution and a public entity takes center stage in her composition only at its very beginning and end: in her words about her forefathers and her childhood on the one hand, and on the other, when she writes, in her later days, about the community in Metz. In the space between these two extremes, the community has no real presence, peeking out from behind the scenes only in connection with a few dramatic events.

The community, in the sense of the ethnic group of Jews in Glikl's place of residence, is present as a self-evident entity in every instance of "we" that is not restricted to her family unit, whether or not this is juxtaposed with "them," "the others." These "others" (who are never referred to as "goyim" but only as "uncircumcised," "not members of the children of Israel," or "non-Jews") are usually portrayed as enjoying coincidental, although close and friendly, contact with Jews. These encounters occurred on the roads (officials, coachmen, and villagers; the owners of half-way inns and their guests; a soldier who accompanied Glikl and her husband at his master's orders, protecting them on a journey during wartime) and also in the city, at home and in its surroundings (merchants and money lenders, residents who offer Jews refuge or help them in times of disaster, bankruptcy officials, a Christian's maidservant, a Shabbes-frau serving in Glikl's house, a postwoman, a lawyer, and even members of the aristocracy who were invited to attend a Jewish wedding). When discussing "others" as a group, Glikl distinguishes carefully between subgroups (councilors, the urban classes, priests, merchants, craftsmen, sailors); some of these subgroups constitute what she calls "an evil crowd" — to her surprise, these people behave moderately in a time of crisis even though "when things are peaceful they stir up trouble and hatred of Jews."

Mentions of the various kinds of "others" are usually neutral, but are often accompanied by a positive tone of admiration or even veneration. By contrast, on many occasions, when describing the behavior of Jews among themselves — mainly toward her and her family — or in the framework of their functions as community leaders, her tone is negative, critical, and at times even enraged. Certainly this is merely a logical and necessary result of the fact that her life as well as her social and business contacts were mainly conducted within Jewish society. However, the difference between Glikl's depictions of the Jews and their lives in a non-Jewish environment and the parallel portrayals offered by historical research is surprising. Despite the atmosphere of hatred in which the Jews lived, the limitations imposed upon them and the constant harassments they suffered, as documented by scholarship, according to Glikl's memoir, she and her family enjoyed a great degree of freedom, peace, and security at home and on the road, in peace and in wartime. Aside from occasional expulsions, which became increasingly rare, from their places of residence, for the most part, she and other Jews faced the same urban dangers as non-Jews (wars, plagues and life-threatening illnesses, short life expectancy, armed robbery, and other dangers while traveling). On a few occasions, she reports events rooted in friction between the two population groups; even in those cases, her words tend to be considered and objective. This disparity offers one small example of the complex problems presented by what is known as "historical" writing in general and in particular "autobiographical" compositions.

FROM MANUSCRIPT TO PRINT
AND TRANSLATION

The original text in Glikl's handwriting has not been preserved, but two copies, both made by her youngest son Moshe, were passed down within the family from generation to generation, eventually finding their way in the late nineteenth century to the scholar David Kaufmann (1852–1899), who published the memoirs with some annotations in 1896. Since then, one of the copies went missing but for a small four-leaf folder, which is now held in the National Library of Israel (in Jerusalem). The other (virtually complete) copy is preserved at the Municipal and University Library of Frankfurt-am-Main. The title page attached to the complete manuscript reveals that the copy was made by Glikl's youngest son Moshe, then rabbi in Baiersdorf, while the title page was added in 1743 by Moshe's son Chaim. After his death in 1788, the manuscript came into the hands of his nephew Chaim, the son of his brother Yosef, who registered this fact on the title page while residing in Königsberg (see Figure 9). Other copies may well have circulated within the family, but they have not come down to us.

Glikl's work is known mainly in translation because the original was reprinted only once, and its original language, Old Yiddish, was no longer understood by the general public even at the time of its publication

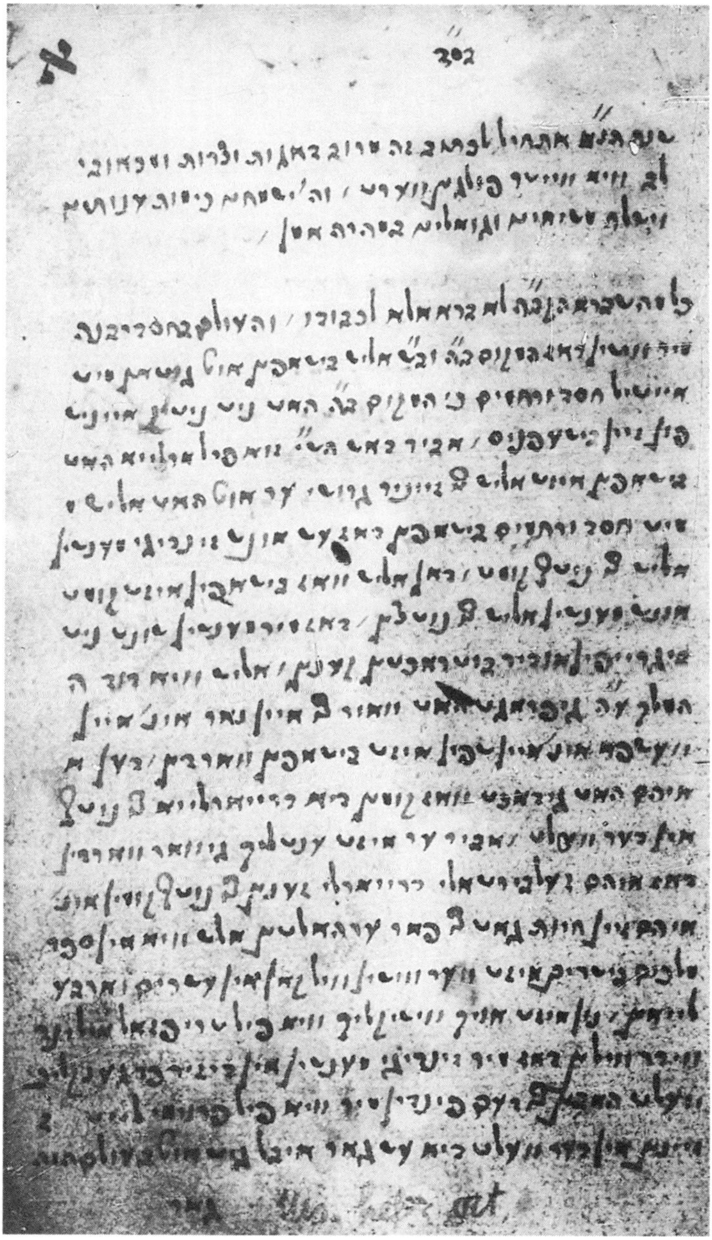

FIGURE 7

First page of the complete copy of the manuscript.

Universitätsbibliothek Johann Christian Senckenberg, Frankfurt am Main.

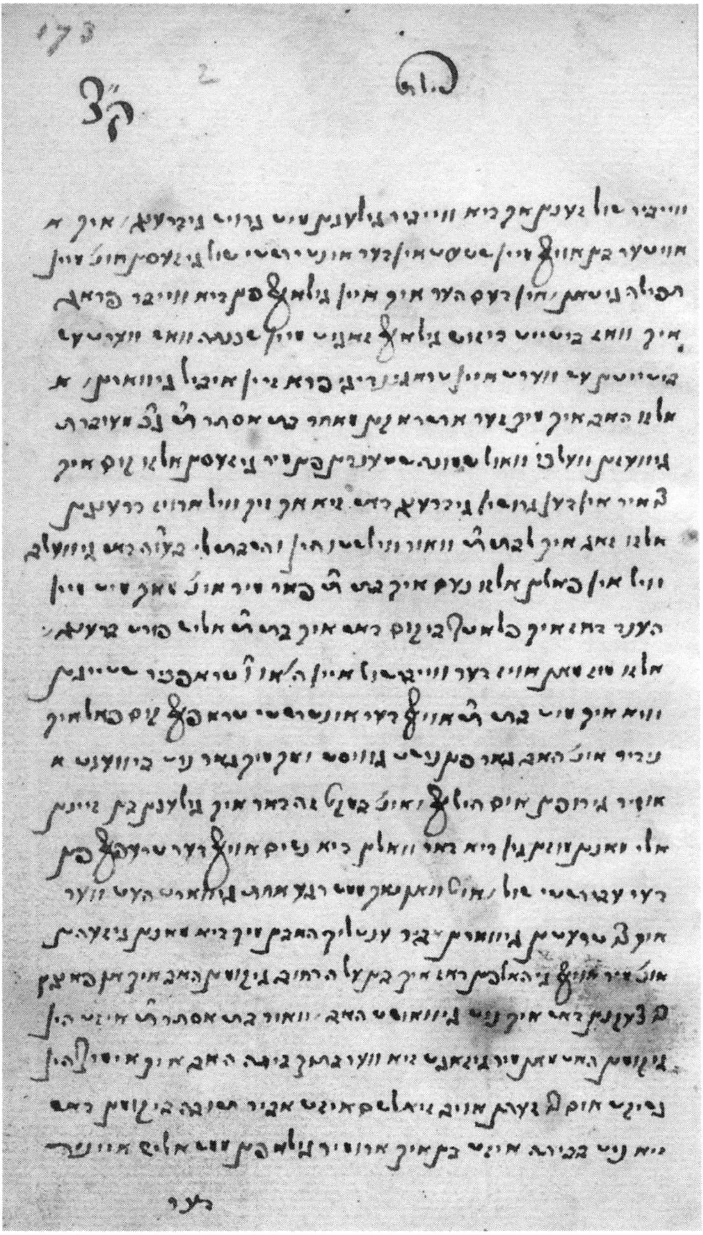

FIGURE 8

A page of the fragmentary copy of the manuscript.

Jewish National and University Library in Jerusalem.

by Kaufmann. A transcription (*Umschreibung*) into German was made by Glikl's relative, Bertha Pappenheim (1859–1936), who also posed as Glikl for the portrait of the author (see Figure 1) painted by the artist Leopold Pilichowski (1869–1933), but this *Umschreibung* was at the time intended only for the family. A subsequent annotated translation into German by Alfred Feilchenfeld emphasized biographical and historical events (to which he appended numerous important glosses), but omitted the author's reflections, along with many of her introspective contemplations and most of the stories she wove into her writing (only three of them appear in an appendix at the end of the book). Feilchenfeld's translation served as the basis for Marvin Lowenthal's abridged translation into English, which was later followed by translations into French, Italian, and Russian. The English translation by Beth-Zion Abrahams, the Hebrew translation by Alexander Siskind Rabinovitz, the Modern Yiddish translation by Dr. Yosef Bernfeld, and the Dutch translation by Mira Rafalowicz are for the most part faithful to the original Yiddish.

Glikl's work was enthusiastically acclaimed especially after it appeared in Feilchenfeld's German translation, and has since served many scholars as historical source for their specific studies in numerous and diverse topics. But it is only since the last two decades of the twentieth century, due to the growing scholarly interest in autobiography and the development of gender studies, that the work itself as well as its author have become the object of serious academic research.

ABOUT THIS EDITION

More than a century elapsed from the first publication of the original Yiddish text of the memoirs (Kaufmann 1896) to the second (Turniansky 2006), a careful and meticulous revised critical edition of the manuscript, annotated and accompanied by a Hebrew translation on facing pages, and a comprehensive introduction.

Although the bilingual Yiddish-Hebrew edition of the memoirs served as the basis for this English edition, this version is in fact a thoughtful adaptation for the English reader. It constitutes a full translation of the text,

renders in italics Glikl's Hebrew quotations from the Hebrew sources, and
retains the rich annotation of the bilingual edition, providing the reader
with biblical and rabbinic citations as well as historical, social, and cultural
background and sources. The reader with specialized interest in aspects of
the Yiddish language, its Hebrew components, its style, its idiomatics, and
so on, is referred to the bilingual edition where references to rare or hitherto unexplored Hebrew and Yiddish sources are also noted, and which
includes Erika Timm's enlightening linguistic analysis of Glikl's language.
Five family trees, informed by the memoirs themselves as well as external
sources, appear in the appendix to this English edition and serve as guides
to four generations of Glikl's extended family and her rich portrayal of
their lives.

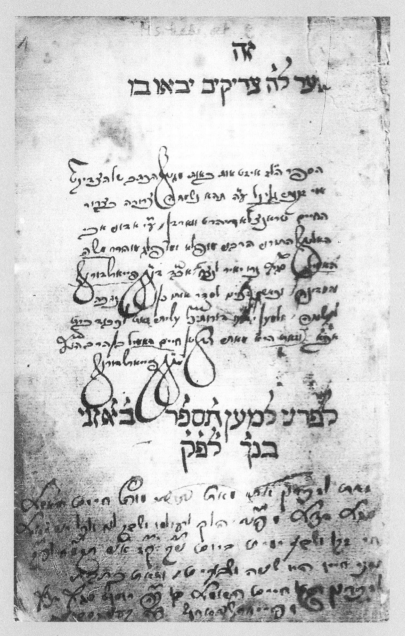

GLIKL

MEMOIRS

1691–1719

I begin writing this in the year 5451[1] with God's help, due to a surfeit of worries, troubles, and heartache, as will be told presently; and *may God give us joy as long as our afflictions*[2] and send our Messiah speedily, amen.

Everything that God, blessed be He, created, *He created for His own glory*,[3] *and the world shall be built upon lovingkindness*.[4] We know that God, blessed be He, in creating everything, acted only out of kindness and compassion, for He has no need of any of His creatures. But the creation of so many species of creatures is all for God's glory, blessed be He, and He created everything with kindness and compassion, to be of use to us sinful human beings. For everything that He created is of good use to us human beings, even if we cannot grasp this or understand it, like King David, of blessed memory, who asked what the purpose was of creating fools, wasps, and spiders, for he wondered of what use these three were in the world. But in the end he found that the three were of use to him in saving his own life,[5] with God's help, as described in the Book of Kings.[6] Anyone wishing to know can read in the *Twenty-Four*.[7]

Now, it is well known how much misery, distress, and aggravation we sinful human beings have in this transitory world. Moreover, we see how

1. 1691.

2. Cf. "Give us joy for as long as You have afflicted us" (Ps 90:15). For all the English translations of the Bible, see http://www.taggedtanakh.org unless otherwise noted.

3. Cf. "Everyone that is called by My name [and whom] I have created for My glory" (b.Yoma 38a and elsewhere). For all the English translations of the Babylonian Talmud [b.], see https://halakhah.com/.

4. Cf. "The world is built by love" (Ps 89:3).

5. As related in the *Alphabet of Ben Sira* 1544, pp. 24–25; see also Yassif 1985, pp. 237–239. For a comprehensive discussion of the tale, see Yassif 1985, pp. 71–76. Yassif cites the source from Midrash Psalms 34:123, which reads "foolishness" and not "fool."

6. The story is not in the Book of Kings (see n. 5). Moreover, the verse and matters the story seeks to clarify are not there, but rather in the Book of Samuel.

7. An accepted moniker for the Hebrew Bible owing to the number of its books.

many righteous men suffer greatly and live in this world in great misery. On
the other hand, we see too that many wicked men enjoy a life of pleasure
and wealth; they and their children are successful, while the God-fearing
righteous man and his children, poor wretches, suffer exceedingly. We may
wonder at this, asking how it can be so. For Almighty God is a righteous
judge. But I said to myself *this too is futile,*[8] for the deeds of God cannot
be grasped or fully understood. Our teacher Moses, of blessed memory,
yearned for this, saying "*Let me know your ways,*"[9] yet he never attained it.
We should therefore not dwell upon it. In any case, one thing is certain:
this world was created solely for the world to come. And that is also why
God, in His great kindness, created us in this world that is naught and transitory — so that, if we do good deeds and believe in God as we should, He
will surely bring us from this burdensome, tedious world to the eternal one
that is all serene calm, and all our suffering and pleasure in this world shall
last but a short time. A man's lifespan is fixed at seventy years,[10] fleeting and
quickly gone. So many hundreds of thousands never attain even that. But
the world to come — is eternal. *How abundant is the good that You have in
store for those who fear You.*[11] Happy is the man whom God, blessed be He,
rewards in the world to come, which is eternal and lasting, for all man's sorrows, worries, and misfortune in this world endure but a short time. Once
a man has borne all his sorrows, suffering, and misfortune, and his time
has come to die, he dies just like all those who live their whole life in great
luxury. In fact, the poor man, wretched creature, who has had nothing but
troubles and suffering his whole life, will certainly die at peace, *for that day
I had hoped,*[12] since the poor wretch was as good as dead every day,[13] he
put his firm trust in God to give him his reward in the world to come. He
believes that he has a large account with God in the world to come, since
all his pleasures and comforts in this world are all reserved for him in the
world to come, *when will I come to appear before God.*[14]

8. Cf. Eccl 2:21, 23, and more.

9. Cf. Exod 33:13.

10. Cf. "The days of our years are threescore years and ten" (Ps 90:10).

11. Cf. Ps 31:20.

12. This echoes "this is the day we hoped for" (Lam 2:16; see also Ps 25:5).

13. This echoes "the poor man is counted as dead" (Rashi's commentary on Gen 29:11 and elsewhere).

14. Ps 42:3.

For this reason I believe, as far as I can understand, that the poor man's death does not come upon him with so much hardship and suffering. This is not the case with the wicked rich man who enjoys all his wealth and property, experiencing nothing but abundance; he and his children are successful, and nothing stands in their way. But when his time comes to leave this world, he realizes how much enjoyment and pleasure he derived from this world, especially once he submits to soul-searching and, toward the end of his days, ponders over the good which God gave him in this world, though he did not serve God well or discharge his duties adequately. Certainly, once he recalls that he must now leave all his possessions behind and depart from this world in order to go to the other world, the eternal world, where he will have to relinquish his duties and give an account of himself and his deeds in this world — the journey will be harder and more bitter for him than for the wretched, poverty-stricken man. Why should I go on at length?

My dear children, I began writing this, with God's help, after the death of your pious father, since it afforded me some pleasure when the melancholy thoughts were upon me. I passed many sleepless nights in the throes of severe anxiety for we were *like sheep without a shepherd*[15] — as our faithful shepherd was no more, and I feared I would give way to melancholy thoughts, God forbid. So I would often rise in the night to spend the sleepless hours in this fashion.

My dear children, in writing this I do not intend to compose a book of moral instruction for you — I am not capable of that. Our sages have composed several such works, and we also possess our holy Torah where one can find everything and learn what is good for us and what will bring us from this world to the world to come; we may cling firmly to our beloved Torah. For example, a passenger ship is sailing at sea. One of the passengers goes to the stern and leans far over toward the sea. He falls overboard and is about to drown. Seeing this, the captain throws him a rope, cautioning him to hold on tightly to the rope so as not to drown. So too are we, sinful human beings, likened in this world to swimmers in the sea. We cannot be sure, even for the blink of an eye, that we will not drown. It is true that Almighty

15. Cf. Num 27:17; 1 Kgs 22:17.

God created us with kindness and compassion so that we might be totally without sin, but due to Adam's sin we are ruled by our baser nature.[16]

God, blessed be He, also created hordes of angels who all do His bidding. They have no baser nature. It follows that they do only good, without being commanded to do so. In addition, God created animals, birds, and other creatures who have only a baser nature and know nothing of doing good. Then God created us, human beings, in His image; we have an intellect like the angels do, yet He gave us human beings the choice to do our own will: to do evil, God forbid, or do good. But great, good, all-merciful God has thrown us ropes to cling to—our holy Torah—that cautions us so that we may not drown. Although we have the ability to do as we choose, God has written in His holy Torah everything we need in order to be righteous and do only good, like the angels. He also set out in the Torah the reward or punishment for observing commandments and for transgressions. *And I chose life.*[17] God forbid that we fail to serve our Maker and be swayed by evil thoughts, like stupid sheep that receive neither reward nor punishment in this world or the world to come. If we acted that way, God forbid, we would be much worse than animals. For an animal falls down and dies and is not obliged to give an account of itself; but wretched man is obliged, as soon as he dies, to give an account of himself before his Maker. It is therefore advisable for us human beings to settle our accounts while we are still alive; that is, we know well that we are sinful, ruled by our baser nature, for *there is not one good man on earth who does what is best and does not err.*[18] This is how one must behave: the moment one is guilty of the slightest transgression, it is necessary to express remorse and repent, as our sages have written in their books of morals, so that the transgression may be erased from the ledger, to be replaced only by mitzvot.[19] But when the sinner lives like an animal—not only does he do no good, he actually does all manner of bad—dying with his sins still upon him—oy, he will discover in the world to come that his ledger contains nothing but debts— these are his transgressions—while the facing page, where payment should

16. This is clearly based on Gen 3:22–24 and its commentaries.
17. Cf. "Choose life" (Deut 30:19).
18. Eccl 7:20.
19. For the possible sources, see Turniansky 2006a, p. 15, n. 50.

appear — that is, repentance and good deeds — is blank. Thus, sinner, you remain wholly liable, and with what will you repay your Maker who took such care to warn you?

Now, need I elaborate all the troubles and suffering that the sinner undergoes in his lifetime, and the bitter, anguished terror he faces, as well as the length of time it takes him to pay his debts in the world to come? But God, blessed be He, is so merciful that He collects His debts in this world. If we repay them one by one, that is, by *prayer, charity,*[20] *and good deeds*, a little at a time, in the appropriate manner, then we are able to repay our debts in this world since God does not wish us to bring about our own death through repentance — no, rather, everything in the appropriate manner, as our sages have written, and as is written in our Torah. And when one does in fact keep a balanced ledger in this world, the account will be in good order in the world to come; one is then able to approach one's Maker joyfully, for great God is compassionate.

For what does God, blessed be He, care if a person is good or, God forbid, wicked? It is due solely to His righteousness and compassion that He has done this for us, *as a father has compassion for his children.*[21] We are His children; God, blessed be He, is compassionate to us if we desire it. We pray *"As a father has compassion for his children."*[22] But God forbid if God had not been even more compassionate with us than a parent with a child. For a parent with a wayward child takes care of him and helps him two or three times. Finally, tiring of this, the parent spurns the wayward child and sends him away to fend for himself, even if he knows it will be the child's downfall. Although we miserable children are constantly sinning against our Father in heaven, every hour, every minute, yet our great, beneficent Father in heaven, in His infinite compassion, tells us when we are covered in sin. Then, when we call out to Him with all our hearts and repent of our sins, He takes us back much quicker than a father of flesh and blood would take back his wayward child.

20. Cf. "Repentance, prayer and charity avert the evil of the decree" (from the *Unetane Tokef* prayer; see Maḥzor Rosh Hashanah 2014, p. 170). For other sources, see Turniansky 2006a, p. 16, n. 51.
21. Ps 103:13.
22. This refers to the prayer "Today is the birthday of the world" from the Rosh Hashanah mussaf service; see Maḥzor Rosh Hashanah 2014, p. 244.

And so, my dear children, do not despair, God forbid, of repentance, prayer, and charity, for great God is most compassionate, *a God compassionate and gracious, slow to anger*[23] for the wicked as well as the righteous,[24] if they abandon their wicked ways and repent in time. Certainly every sinner must be as careful as possible not to sin anymore, for everyone knows what a serious transgression it is to sin against one's father, and how powerful is the commandment to honor one's father and mother. We must be all the more careful then not to arouse the anger of our Father in heaven who created us and our forefathers, for great, all-merciful God created us sinful humans naked. He gives us life, food, drink, and clothing; we receive all our needs from His holy, generous hand. We have no ability to judge whether one man's lot in this world is better than another's. People often receive their benefits in this world, while others — their benefits are reserved for them in the world to come. You can be assured that nothing escapes great, beneficent God. A righteous man, though perhaps he has not fared well in this world, can be assured that in the world to come his righteousness will bear fruit so that he will be rewarded with wealth, pleasure, everything that he lacked, the poor wretch, in this world, where he was forced to see the many wicked men in this world deriving much pleasure from all the good things in life — while the righteous man often lacks even enough bread to satisfy his hunger. If he accepts this with love, praising and thanking his Maker for everything, until, by dint of righteousness and patience, he is no longer distressed and can approach the Judge on high, that is when he will find out why it is that good men suffer in this world while so many haughty wicked men prosper. In this way he will realize how right he was to adhere to righteousness and devotion, and he will give praise to God above.

When God, blessed be He, causes something to happen to a person, it is all for the best, since we sinful human beings are wayward children whom great, gracious God wishes to chastise so that we become good children and servants of our gracious master and father. This is why He chastises us — that we may learn from His chastisement to follow in His path. For we are not worthy of all the good that Almighty God gives us; we are not

---

23. Exod 34:6.

24. Cf. b.Eruvin 22a and elsewhere. See also "God is long suffering towards the righteous and the wicked" (Rashi's commentary on Num 14:18).

capable of serving Him adequately to repay Him for all He does for us. These things are too numerous for me to write, but this we must know: everything that we have is from His great kindness and compassion, an unwarranted gift. But the punishments that are frequently meted out to us are due to our sins, happy is the person upon whom God brings suffering in this world.[25] Everything must be accepted with love, as you will read in the following story about a physician.

I found a story in the book by the gaon R. Abraham son of R. Shabtai Levy,[26] who wrote in his book of ethics: if God causes a person suffering and anguish, here is a very good potion.

There once was a king who had a physician, a learned man, and the king thought very highly of him. This doctor once did something against the king. The king was furious and ordered that the physician be thrown into the dungeon; that he be tortured with iron scourges on neck and legs; that he be stripped of his fine clothes and be given a coarse, prickly garment; that he be given nothing to eat except a small piece of barley bread and nothing to drink except a few sips of water. The king ordered the jailers to attend carefully to whatever the physician said, bidding them to return to him after some time to report what they heard the physician say. The jailers came back to the king and said: "We could not hear what the physician said, for he said nothing at all. We felt throughout that he was a man of great learning."[27]

After the physician had been imprisoned thus for a long time, the king sent for the physician's kin. The relatives came to the king in great distress, fearing for the physician's life and anticipating that the king would inform them of their kinsman's death. When they were brought to the king, he ordered them to go see their kinsman the physician in jail and speak with him; perhaps he would be willing to heed what they had to say. The relatives went to see the physician in jail and began speaking to him as follows: "Dear kinsman, we are most distressed to see you suffering so in jail where you are

---

25. Cf. "This the Holy One Blessed be He, brings suffering upon the righteous in this world, in order that they may inherit the future world" (b.Qiddushin 40b and elsewhere).
26. This refers to *Yesh Noḥalin* by R. Avraham ben Shabtai Halevy ish Horowitz, with glosses by his son R. Yakov. For the story cited, see *Yesh Noḥalin* 1615, p. 62b; and cf. Book Five, p. 255, n. 216.
27. This echoes "Silence is a fence for wisdom" (m.Avot 3:13).

tortured with iron scourges on neck and legs; instead of fine foods, all you get to eat now is a small piece of barley bread; whereas you used to drink fine wine, now you are given only a few sips of water. You used to be attired in velvet and silk; now we see you clothed in nothing but a coarse, prickly wool garment. This puzzles us extremely: despite all this, your appearance is unchanged, you are not haggard, you are hale and hearty. We find you now just as you were in your prime. We would like to know how you survive the torture and all of this unfazed, showing not the slightest sign."

The physician replied to his relatives: "Dear kinsmen, when I entered the jail I brought with me seven kinds of herbs; I mixed them well and pounded them very fine and prepared a potion, of which I drink a little bit every day. That is why my appearance is unchanged, I am not haggard, I am fit and can resist torture; I am quite contented." The relatives replied: "Dear kinsman, we beseech you to reveal the names of the herbs in your potion in case one of us should encounter such troubles and suffering as you have endured; that way we too will be able to prepare a similar potion and drink of it and not die of our suffering." Said the physician, "Dear kinsmen, I will tell you. The first herb is trust in God, who can save me from all my troubles and suffering—though they had been twice as terrible; God can save me from the king too, since the king's heart is in God's hands.[28] The second herb is hope and good advice I give myself—to resign myself to everything and accept all my trials with love. This good advice prevents me from despair. The third herb is acknowledging that I have sinned and that I am in jail, suffering and being tortured, because of my sins. Since all this is due to my sins, I myself am to blame. So why be impatient, why rant? As the verse tells us: 'Your iniquities have been a barrier between you and your God.'[29] And our sages too tell us: '*a person does not suffer except if he sinned*.'[30] The fourth herb is this: even if I grow impatient and cannot stand it anymore and rant against my suffering, what can I possibly do?

28. Based on the biblical verse "Like channeled water is the mind of the king in the Lord's hand; He directs it to whatever He wishes" (Prov 21:1); and cf. *Yesh Noḥalin* 1615, p. 62b). This also echoes "for he can do anything he pleases" (Eccl 8:3).
29. See Isa 59:2. Glikl cites the verse in its Yiddish translation.
30. Free Yiddish translation of "There is no suffering without sin" (cf. *Yesh Noḥalin* 1615, p. 62b). Cf. "There is no suffering without iniquity" (b.Shabbat 55a).

Will that change anything? It could have been much worse — If the king had ordered me put to death, I would have had to die before my time, then all would be lost; as King Solomon said: '*a live dog is better than a dead lion.*'[31] The fifth herb is knowing that God, blessed be He, is inflicting great hardship upon me for my own good, so that I can be cleansed of my sins in this world and gain life in the world to come, as the verse says: 'Happy is the man whom You discipline, O Lord.'[32] For this reason I rejoice in my suffering, and my rejoicing brings great good to the world, as is written: 'He who joyfully bears the chastisements brings salvation to the world.'[33] The sixth herb is: I rejoice in my portion,[34] and I praise God, blessed be He, and thank Him, for I might have been tortured even more with iron scourges, or been beaten and whipped, or had other bitter tortures worse than death inflicted upon me. I eat barley bread now; had the king so wished, he could have ordered that I be given no bread at all, neither barley nor wheat. Now the king allows me a few sips of water; had the king so wished, I would get nothing at all to drink. My clothes are of coarse, prickly wool now; had the king so wished, I would be obliged to remain quite naked in summer and winter, tortured until I'd pray in the morning for nightfall and at night — for morning.[35] For this reason I accept my suffering with love. The seventh herb is: '*God's salvation is as the twinkling of an eye,*'[36] meaning that God's aid can come in a moment, for God is compassionate and gracious, and He renounces punishment that He brings upon man.[37] God, blessed be He, can deliver us from our troubles and heal our pain. And so, my friends, these are the seven herbs I found and used. They have preserved my former

31. Cf. Eccl 9:4. Glikl cites the Hebrew verse and adds its Yiddish translation.

32. See Ps 94:12; see also b.Berakhot 5a and Rashi's commentary there. Glikl cites the verse only in Yiddish, not in the original Hebrew.

33. Cf. b.Taanit 8a.

34. Cf. "Who is rich? He who rejoices in his portion" (m.Avot 4:1) alluded to in Yiddish.

35. Cf. "In the morning you shall say, 'If only it were evening!' and in the evening you shall say, 'If only it were morning!'" (Deut 28:67), alluded to in Yiddish.

36. For the possible sources, see Turniansky 2006a, p. 26, n. 86. A variant of this idiom ("*in the* twinkling of an eye") appears in *Yesh Noḥalin* 1615, p. 63a.

37. Cf. "You are a compassionate and gracious God, slow to anger, abounding in kindness, renouncing punishment" (Jon 4:2); and also "He is compassionate and gracious, slow to anger, abounding in kindness." (*Yesh Noḥalin* 1615, p. 63a). Glikl cites the verse in Yiddish, not in the original Hebrew.

appearance and strength. Every God-fearing man must therefore accept willingly and joyfully the suffering that God inflicts, for suffering redeems one's body and acts in one's favor in the world to come, the eternal world; furthermore, man must trust his Maker to be beneficent in return for his faith." Thus ends this instructive story.[38]

Dear children, I do not wish to go on at length for fear of going too much into depth, as even ten books would not suffice. Read in *Brantshpigl*,[39] in *Lev Tov*;[40] or, those who can study — read in books of moral instruction,[41] you will find everything there. I ask this of you, dear children: have patience. God, blessed be He, has inflicted punishment upon you — accept it all with forbearance, and do not cease praying; perhaps He will have mercy. Who knows what is best for us sinful human beings: whether it is better to live in great wealth and enjoy this life to the full, spending our time enjoying the luxuries of this transitory world, or is it better that our Father in heaven, in His utmost kindness, keep us in this sinful world so that we turn our eyes heavenward always and call out wholeheartedly to our gracious Father, shedding scalding tears. In this way I am certain that our beneficent, faithful God will show us mercy and will lead us out of this long, sorrowful exile. His compassion is great, His kindness too. His promises to us surely will come to pass; we need only wait patiently.

My dear children, be good and honest; serve God our Lord with all your heart in good times as well as bad, God forbid. *Just as we say a blessing for a good hap, so should we say one for an evil hap.*[42] If God, blessed be He, causes something to happen to you, do not grieve inordinately; remember that all is His doing. If God, blessed be He, inflicts punishment upon you, causing

---

38. For a partial comparison of Glikl's story with the original, see Turniansky 1993, pp. 160–162; Turniansky 1994c, pp. 48–49; Turniansky 2004, pp. 129–131. The story appeared in Yiddish in a slightly different version in *Lev Tov* 1620, pp. 115a–116a.

39. *Sefer Brantshpigl* (*The Book of the Burning Mirror*) by Moshe Henochs Altshul of Prague (*editio princeps* Cracow 1597) was one of the most popular and widespread ethical works in Yiddish (see Zinberg 1972–1978, pp. 157–159). See also next note.

40. *Sefer Lev Tov* (*The Book of the Good Heart*) by Isaac ben Eliakum of Poznan (*editio princeps* Prague 1620), like *Sefer Brantshpigl*, enjoyed widespread popularity (see Zinberg 1972–1978, pp. 160–164). The recommendation to read both books together also appears in other sources.

41. Meaning books of morals in Hebrew, the reading of which, according to Glikl, requires a learning ability that is not necessary for reading the aforementioned Yiddish books.

42. Cf. b.Berakhot 48b; see also b.Berakhot 54a; m.Berakhot 9:5. For all the references to the Mishnah (m.), see https://www.sefaria.org.il/texts/Mishnah.

the death of your small children or close relatives, God forbid—do not grieve inordinately, for you did not create them. Great God who created them takes them back as He sees fit. What can a helpless human being do who must take that same path himself? Similarly, when God causes you to suffer financial loss—God above gives and takes away. Naked were we born and naked must we depart;[43] all our money will not do us any good. And so, my dear children, one must bear any loss or setback stoically, since none of all this belongs to us—it is but a loan. So what is there to be sorrowful about? Only for letting a day go by without observing the commandments, and certainly one should be sorrowful for committing transgressions, God forbid, for we human beings were created for the sole purpose of serving God, observing His commandments, and fulfilling what is written in our holy Torah: "*For thereby you shall have life and long endure.*"[44] In any case, it is no transgression for a man to toil to provide *well for his wife and children.* "*Who do right at all times*"[45] means: a man who is able to provide for his children and family—God also gives him the means of giving charity to the poor;[46] he is happy.[47] Such labor and toil are indeed a commandment, for our great Father in heaven, our sole God, has done everything with the greatest wisdom: a father loves his children, and close relatives too love each other, otherwise the world could not exist. Why should a person exert himself so much for his children? Surely a person can live contently without providing for his children and close relatives. But great, gracious God, in His infinite compassion, made it so that parents love their children and help them; the children, seeing this behavior in their parents, will follow their example with their own children. For example,[48] there once was a bird with three chicks who lived on the seashore. All of a sudden the bird

---

43. This echoes in the reverse order "Naked I came out of my mother's womb, and naked shall I return there" (Job 1:21). See also m.Avot 6:9.

44. Deut 30:20.

45. Cf. "Happy are those who act justly, who do right at all times" (Ps 106:3).

46. Cf. "Is it possible to do righteousness at all times? This, explained our rabbis of Jabneh ... refers to a man who maintains his sons and daughters while they are young" (b.Ketubbot 50a). The end is connected to the verse "he gives freely to the poor; his beneficence lasts forever" (Ps 112:9).

47. Apparently referring to the beginning of the verse cited in this Book, n. 45.

48. As far as I know, this is the earliest record of the story that follows. See Silverman-Weinreich 1988, pp. 24, 381–382, n. 12; Aarne and Thompson 1987, no. 244C*. For more references, see Turniansky 2006a, p. 31, n. 103.

perceives that a strong wind is blowing and the stormy sea is crashing upon the shore. Says the bird to its children: "We must fly away across the sea at once or we are lost." But the chicks could not yet fly. So the bird grips one of the chicks with its feet and flies over the sea. When they reach the middle of the sea, the bird says to his son: "See, my son, the hardships I must endure on your account, and how I risk my life for your sake. When I am old, will you be kind to me and provide for me?" Answers the chick: "My beloved father, just take me across the sea, and I will do anything you ask in your old age." Upon hearing this, the bird flings the chick into the sea to drown, saying: "This is what a liar such as you deserves." The bird then flies back to shore and picks up the second chick. When they reach the middle of the sea, the bird addresses the chick, repeating what he said to the first one. The second chick too promises to render every kindness to his father as the first had done, but the bird flings this one into the sea as well, saying: "You too are a liar." Then he goes back to shore and picks up the third chick. As he reaches the middle of the sea with the third chick, he says to him too: "See, my son, the hardships I must endure and how I risk my life for your sake. When I am old and can no longer move, will you be kind to me and provide for me as I am doing for you now?" Answers the chick: "My dear father, all you say is true; indeed you toil and worry much on my account. I must repay you for it, if possible, but I cannot promise it with any certainty. I can promise you only this: when I have young of my own, I will treat them as you have treated me." The father says: "You speak truthfully and wisely. I will spare your life and carry you across the sea." From this we learn that God inspires the reasonless birds to raise their young. We see further the following difference: parents bear the burden of caring for their children, raising them with such devotion, but if children had the same cares and hardships with their parents, they would quickly tire of it.

Let us now return to our point: people should love each other, as is written, "*Love your fellow as yourself.*"[49] Although this is a major point, it is rare these days to find one who truly loves his fellow. In fact, whenever an opportunity arises for a person to ruin another, it is seized gleefully. There

---

49. Lev 19:18.

is nothing surprising about parents loving their children. We see this with the insentient animals, who have their young and raise them until they can fend for themselves, whereupon the parents leave them. We human beings are better and wiser in this regard. Not only do we work hard to raise our children until they are old enough to manage without us—we human beings continue to worry about our children's well-being for as long as we live, though some might say: "Oh, why must I always be worrying about my children? Is it not enough that I raised them, worried about them, took pains to marry them off with good dowries, and made decent human beings of them? From now on, let them take care of themselves and feed themselves." That is certainly the right way, and definitely what is good and appropriate, for must a person be a slave forever? Yes, perhaps that is fair, and it might be the right way, as long as one's children and close relatives are provided for, with their lives going smoothly. But should the opposite happen, God forbid, what person with a wise heart would refrain from taking up the burden of his children and close relatives? *Rachel weeping for her children.*[50] *I am the man who has known affliction.*[51] There can be no doubt that our children's misfortunes grieve us more than do our own. Certainly, in my humble opinion, it would have been far less difficult for our father Abraham had the situation been reversed: if he were the one about to be sacrificed, instead of him sacrificing *his only son Isaac.*[52] *For who can bear exile from his country.*[53] Yet Abraham did it all for the love of God, blessed be He, asking no questions.

Even if we had no other exemplary act in the whole world, God forbid, this one would fully illustrate how we should serve God, blessed be He, with love, teaching us not to attach importance to material, transitory things. For great God gave us everything, and He may take it all away again if He so chooses. We can say nothing at all about His deeds. Many wicked men are happy in this world, as are many righteous men, and vice versa: many righteous men suffer in this world, as do many wicked

50. Jer 31:14.
51. Lam 3:1.
52. Cf. Gen 22:2.
53. Cf. "For how can I bear to see the destruction of my homeland" (Esther 8:6). Glikl's use of the word "homeland" fits the commentary "my homeland is my family" (Ramban's commentary on Gen 24:7) and similar ones that refer to Abraham's progeny.

men. Therefore, my dear children, this is best: serve God wholeheartedly, without deceit or hypocrisy, without showing one thing outwardly while secretly believing another, God forbid. Pray with conviction, fear, and awe, and do not talk of other matters when you are standing in prayer. Consider this a most severe transgression: to stand praying to our great Maker, then all of a sudden, in the middle of the most important prayer — to start discussing an entirely different matter with a flesh and blood interlocutor. Is God to be kept waiting while a person finishes chatting about his own affairs with his neighbor? Our sages have written about this at length, as I have mentioned. You can read about it and then study Torah, each according to his knowledge and ability, then apply yourselves to earning an honest living for wife and children, for this too is a major commandment. In particular, a person must conduct his business honestly with Jews and non-Jews alike, lest God's name be desecrated, God forbid. If one has money or goods belonging to another, he must guard them even more carefully than if they were his own, lest he come to wrongdoing or injustice toward any man. For this is the first question that we are asked in the world to come: Were you honest in your business dealings?[54] Even if a man has toiled much in this world and accumulated a fortune through theft and fraud, God forbid, using it to give his children large dowries and inheritances after his death — woe be to those wicked men who forfeit the world to come for the sake of their children's wealth, without knowing if this stolen fortune will remain in their children's possession; even if it does, it remains for a passing moment, not for eternity, so why sell the eternal in exchange for the temporary? If a high mountain of sand is to be moved, and the sand is removed bit by bit every day, there is hope that ultimately the entire mountain will be removed. But to forfeit eternity, God forbid — the world to come — this is something we must ponder; we are sure to regret it if we do not give it due consideration.

How nice it would be to live as is recounted in the chronicles of Alexander the Great:[55] In a certain country lived people who were considered wise

---

54. Cf. "When man is led in for judgment he is asked, Did you deal faithfully" (b.Shabbat 31a). Glikl cites this in Yiddish.

55. We do not know of any Yiddish work on Alexander the Great. Individual stories and entire works about him based on the ancient Hellenistic tradition were widespread, including in German

men; they cared nothing for the rest of the world and ate only what grew in nature. Likewise, they drank nothing but water; there was no hate or malice among them, and they wore no clothes. Alexander the Great, who, as is well known, conquered the entire world, heard much of the wisdom and lives of these people. He sent emissaries inviting them to come see him and make him their king and master. If they failed to do so, he would kill them all. They replied: "We go nowhere nor come anywhere, nor do we ever leave our country, for we love neither gold nor silver. We are content with what God gives and nature provides. Now, your king—seeing that we will not come to him—should he seek to come here and kill us, he can do so. For this he needs no special preparation, since we will not oppose him nor will we plead for our lives, for when we die—only then do we begin to live. But should your king want to come peaceably and learn our customs and our wisdom, we agree willingly."

The emissaries of King Alexander returned and recounted everything. King Alexander and his dignitaries promptly made the necessary preparations, then set out on the journey to the wise men's country. He remained there several days, receiving instruction in their wisdom, learning from them until he was exceedingly pleased. The king wished to make them great gifts, but they wanted nothing, saying: "We need neither fortune nor gold nor silver—nature provides enough." Said King Alexander: "Still, ask me for anything you like and I will give it to you." They all began clamoring: "O king, give us eternal life!" Said the king: "How can I give you this? I wish I could give it; if I had it, I would take it for myself." Said the wise man: "O king, see for yourself: you know that all your deeds, all your toil, the many nations and lands that you destroyed—all are yours only for a fleeting moment, not for eternity. What did you need it all for?" The king did not know what to answer, yet he replied: "That is how I found the

---

and Hebrew (see Turniansky 2006a, p. 38, n. 130). Several stories on Alexander appear in the Gemara (see b.Yoma 69a, b.Sanhedrin 91a, b.Tamid 31b–32b), which impacted upon the Midrash. Others were included in *Sefer Yosifon* or were added onto it (see Flusser 1981, pp. 54, 461–491, and the commentary, pp. 216–248; for other Hebrew versions of the story, see Davis 1995, p. 254, n. 193). Yiddish readers knew of stories about Alexander the Great primarily through the translation of *Sefer Yosifon* into Yiddish (*editio princeps* Zurich 1546) and from other works that have not come down to us, such as those that served as the source for Glikl's story presented herein (see next note). For another story about Alexander the Great, see Book Six, pp. 282–284.

world and that is how I must leave it. A king's heart cannot exist without acts of war."[56]

I do not recount this tale as truth; it may be a story told by heathens. I tell it here to pass the time and to show that there are people in the world who do not attach importance to wealth, putting their trust always in their Maker. We have other books of moral instruction, praise God, from which we can learn all good things. Nor am I writing this as a book of moral instruction for you. My sole purpose, as I said, was to stave off melancholy thoughts in the evenings and long nights: *Bitterly she weeps in the night.*[57] I therefore took it upon myself to record[58] the events I still remember from the description[59] of my youth, to the best of my knowledge and insofar as it can be done. This is not to make an exception of myself or to set myself up, God forbid, as a pious woman. No! In this world *punishments are too great to bear.*[60] I am a sinful woman, I am sad to say, chock-full of sins, every minute, every hour, every blink of an eye. There are very few sins that I have not committed. *For these things do I weep and my eyes flow with tears.*[61] I but wish I could weep and plead and repent adequately for my sins. But the suffering, on my own account and that of my children, my anxiety, due to my sins, that I would be left on my own to live with my orphaned children, as well as material matters — these prevent me from attaining the degree I aspire to. I pray to God my Maker to show mercy and put an end to all my sorrows and troubles, *for my inmost self must weep*[62] and *I drench my bed*[63] since we have *no one to rely upon save our Father in Heaven.*[64] For we human beings understand nothing of each other's sorrow; everyone thinks his own sorrow is the greatest.

56. Glikl's version of the story is different from the Hebrew and Yiddish versions mentioned earlier, n. 55: it is shorter; certain matters are omitted while others appear in a more detailed or in an altered form.

57. Lam 1:2.

58. "To record" is the editor's addition. The sentence in the original is missing the name of the act that Glikl "took upon herself."

59. Glikl uses the term *beshraybung*: literally a description. On the genre thus called in Old Yiddish literature, see Turniansky 2006a, p. 41, n. 141.

60. Cf. "My punishment is too great to bear" (Gen 4:13).

61. Lam 1:16.

62. Jer 13:17.

63. Ps 6:7.

64. Cf. m.Sotah 9:15 (beraita), "Upon whom can we rely? [Only] on our Father in Heaven."

A philosopher was once walking down the street. He met a good friend of his who began complaining at length of all his worries and troubles. The philosopher says to his friend: "Come, let us go up on the roof." They went up on the roof where they could see the houses of the entire city. The philosopher says to his friend: "Come, my friend, I will show you all the houses of the entire city; see, in this house there is this sorrow and that calamity; in the next house there is this suffering and that affliction." In brief, the philosopher showed his friend that every house in the city, every single one, had its own particular suffering and anguish. "Now, my friend, take your own suffering and anguish and fling them among the houses, then take one of these houses for yourself instead of your own suffering." But upon reflection, he realized that those houses too had tribulations equal to, if not greater than, his own. In the end he preferred his own lot. We see the same thing in the well-known proverb "The world is full of suffering; each finds his own."[65]

What can we do? If we turn to God, blessed be He, with all our hearts, he will not forsake us; He will come to our assistance and that of all of Israel, bringing *good tidings and consolation;*[66] *He will send the Messiah speedily, amen, may it be God's will.*

END OF MY BOOK ONE

---

65. See the proverb "Die ganze Welt ist voll Pein, jeder find't das Sein" (Tendlau 1860, no.752; Landau 1901, p. 58 [Pein]). For popular Yiddish versions, see Bernstein 1908, p. 203 [*pekl*]; Furman 1968, p. 308, no. 1282; Stutchkoff 1950, p. 498. For German versions, see Wander 1987, V, p. 159, no. 55; p. 571, no. 5. Glikl also introduces a somewhat different version of the story accompanying the proverb; see Book Four, p. 173, n. 154.
66. Cf. for example, Grace After Meals (Siddur 2016, p. 988).

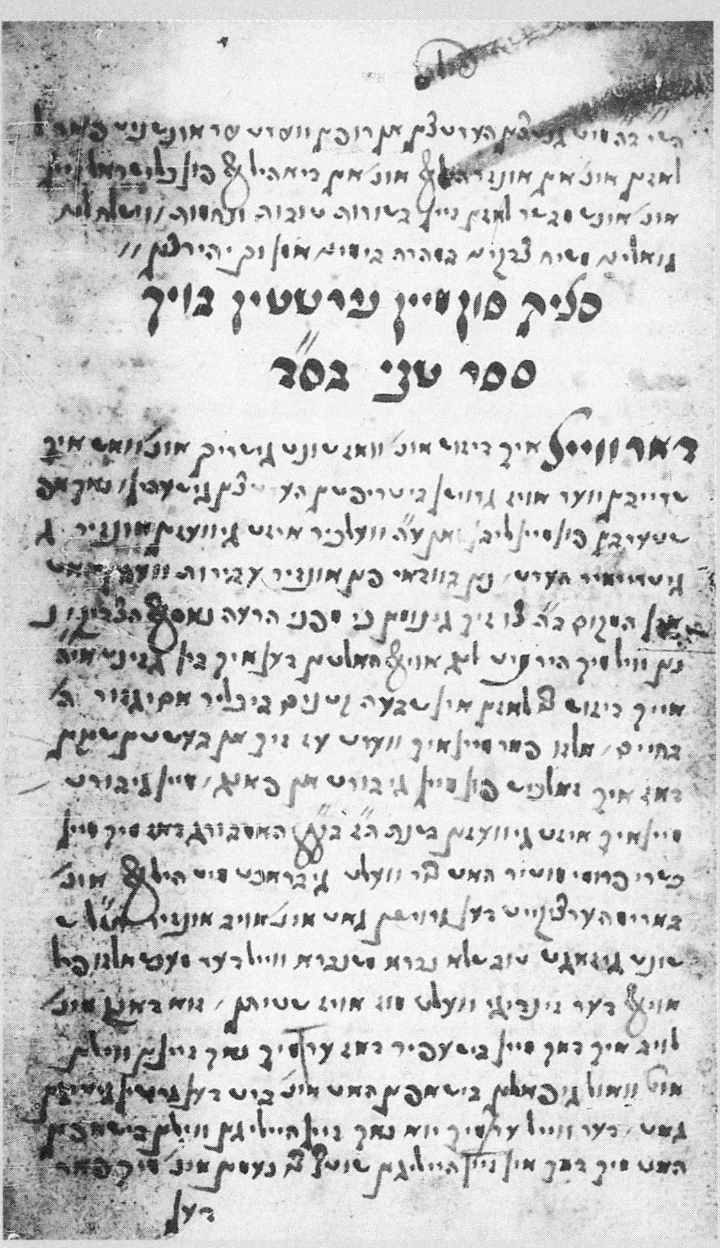

סליק פון דיין ערשטין בויך

ספר שני בס״ד

FIGURE 10

End of Book One and beginning of Book Two of the complete copy of the manuscript.

Universtätsbibliothek Johann Christian Senckenberg, Frankfurt am Main.

WITH GOD'S HELP

This, as well as what I have already written and what I am about to write, comes from a deeply grieving heart following the death of my dearest husband, of blessed memory, who was our faithful shepherd; surely God, blessed be He, took him to Him because of our sins, for *because of evil the righteous was taken away*.[1] I will not dwell on this at length here, since I intend, God willing, to leave all this[2] for you in seven little books, *if God grants me life*. Therefore I think it would be most appropriate to begin with my birth. I was born, so I believe, in the year 5407,[3] in the holy community of Hamburg, where my pious, devout mother brought me into the world, with the help of great God in His kindness. True, our sages observed, "*Better never to have been created than to have been created*,"[4] since one suffers so much in this sinful world; nevertheless, I thank and praise my Maker for creating me according to His will, as He saw fit,[5] and I pray to God, great and kind: since He did create me as He saw fit, to extend His holy protection over me.[6]

Anyone entering his[7] house hungry left with his hunger satisfied. He

1. Cf. Isa. 57:1.
2. Glikl avoids specifying what she is referring to, here and in the text that follows, preferring indirect references such as "that" or "this."
3. The stipulated Hebrew year runs from August 30, 1646, to September 20, 1647, but in fact Glikl was born sometime between August and October 1645, so she was not yet three in August 1648, when the Jews of Hamburg were served with the edict of expulsion (see this Book, n. 8); thus in 1699, she was fifty-four years old (see Book Six, p. 258, n. 19).
4. Cf. b.Eruvin 13b.
5. This echoes the blessing recited by women in the morning service: "who has made me according to His will." See Siddur 2016, p. 26.
6. At this point, a page is missing in the manuscript, in which Glikl probably discussed her father and his family origins and might also have mentioned his surnames "Pinkerle" and "Stade," which appear in other sources too (see Book Four, p. 174, n. 162).
7. Glikl is clearly referring to her father's house.

gave his children, boys and girls alike, an education in *higher matters as well as in practical things.* I was born in Hamburg, but I heard from my dear parents and others—I was not yet three years old when all the Jews of Hamburg were served with an edict of expulsion[8] and forced to move to Altona,[9] which belonged to His Majesty the King of Denmark,[10] who granted the Jews good privileges.[11] Altona was barely fifteen minutes away from Hamburg. There were some families living in Altona—about twenty-five households, and we had our synagogue and cemetery there. We lived in Altona for some time,[12] until appeals to the authorities in Hamburg were successful and the Jews of Altona were granted travel passes allowing them to enter the city and engage in commerce there. Each pass was valid for four weeks. The pass was granted by the mayor of Hamburg and cost one ducat. When it expired, a new one had to be obtained. However, the four weeks often turned into eight for those acquainted with the mayor or other officials. This made it very hard on people, poor things, since they had no choice but to go to the city all the time to earn their living; it was especially hard on the poorer people. Many often dared enter the city surreptitiously, without a pass. If the officials caught them they were arrested, and their release was achieved only with great difficulty and large sums of money. Early

8. The edict (August 16, 1648) declared that the Ashkenazi Jews from Altona who had settled in Hamburg during the previous two decades must leave the city by Passover 1649 (See Kaufmann 1896, p. 24, n. 2; Feilchenfeld 1913, p. 4, n. 3; Grunwald 1904, pp. 8–10; Marwedel 2001a, p. 47; Richarz 2001a, p. 17). The expulsion did not include the Ashkenazi Jews who served in the Sephardi community.

9. Altona was a town in Schleswig-Holstein on the right bank of the Elbe, close to Hamburg. In 1661 it became a city under the rule of Denmark, and today a neighborhood in Hamburg. On the Jewish community in Altona, see *Encyclopedia Judaica* 1972, vol. 2, cols. 779–780 and the introduction to this book.

10. Frederick III, King of Denmark, reigned 1648–1670.

11. These are the privileges that the King of Denmark, Christian IV, granted the Ashkenazi Jews of three communities: Hamburg, Wandsbeck, and Altona, in August 1641, thereby ratifying the privileges granted the Jews by the previous ruler, which allowed them to have a synagogue and cemetery, and established the obligatory tax Jews had to pay (see Feilchenfeld 1899, pp. 274–275; Grunwald 1904, p. 8; Marwedel 1976, p. 51, n. 89; Marwedel 1982, p. 186). On the legal status and community affiliation of Glikl and her family, see Richarz 2001a, p. 17.

12. While Glikl's description provides the main source for most of our knowledge about Jewish life in Hamburg and Altona, other sources corroborate details of her account (see Feilchenfeld 1913, p. 14, n. 3; Grunwald 1904, pp. 6–11; Graupe 1973, pp. 172–175; Marwedel 2001a, pp. 45–48; Marwedel 1982, pp. 186–187; and elsewhere).

in the morning, straight from the synagogue, these wretches would go into the city, and toward nightfall, as the gates were about to close, they would return to Altona; the poor things often risked their lives on leaving the city because of persecution by worthless thugs, until every woman, poor thing, gave thanks to God when her husband returned home safely. At that time there were not even forty-two households in Altona, including those who had moved there from Hamburg; while not wealthy, they all earned an honest living. One of the wealthiest men at that time was Chaim Fürst,[13] who had ten thousand reichstaler;[14] my father, of blessed memory, with eight thousand reichstaler; others had six thousand, and some had two thousand. But they all behaved politely to each other and lived together amicably, living a better life than the richest men today; even those who had only five hundred reichstaler to their name knew how to enjoy life and were contented, more so than today, when the rich are greedy, as is written: *Nobody dies with half of his desire gratified.*[15] In any case, I still recall that my father was a man of unparalleled piety, and had he not suffered so badly from the gout he would have achieved much more. Despite that, he succeeded in providing well for his children.

It was in my childhood — I was about ten years old — when the Swede[16] went to war with His Majesty the King of Denmark.[17] I cannot write much news about it since I was a child and had to sit in ḥeder.[18] We were living in Altona at the time, worrying endlessly, since it was an extremely cold winter — there had not been anything like it for fifty years. People called it "the Swedish winter."[19] The Swedes were able to gain access by all roads

13. On the wealthy Fürst family, see *Encyclopedia Judaica* 1972, vol. 5, col. 1010.

14. The reichstaler was the only stable monetary unit for currency conversion and comparison in the complicated mosaic of German-speaking countries, whose currencies included the taler, gulden, and mark.

15. Cf. Eccl. Rab. 1:32.

16. The term "the Swede" (der Schwede) includes the entire nation, army, and king, who terrified their opponents because Sweden was a strong and active military power in the seventeenth century.

17. This refers to the 1657–1660 war of Charles X Gustav, King of Sweden (1654–1660), against Friedrich III, King of Denmark (1648–1670). See Munck 1990, pp. 228–229; Feilchenfeld 1913, p. 17, n. 5; Feilchenfeld 1899b, pp. 276–277; Marwedel 2001a, p. 47.

18. Ḥeder is the elementary Jewish school. We have only a sparse amount of information on schooling for girls during this period, including that of Glikl. See Turniansky 1994a, pp. 46–57; Turniansky 2010.

19. The winter of 1657–1658 (see Richarz 2001a, p. 18).

since the roads were all frozen over. Suddenly, on the Sabbath, came the cry: the Swedes are coming! That was in the morning; we were still in bed. We all jumped out of bed — my goodness, without getting dressed, and all, children too, ran into the city to find shelter: some of us hid among the Sephardim, others among the burghers.[20] We remained there for some time, until my father, of blessed memory, interceded with the authorities, becoming the first Jew to return to live in Hamburg. Gradually, following further intercession with the authorities, more Jewish families were permitted to live in the city, whereupon nearly all the households moved to Hamburg,[21] except for those who were living in Altona before the expulsion and stayed there.

At that time, taxes paid to the authorities were very low. Each person would reach an individual agreement with those in charge. However, in Hamburg we had no synagogue or any other privileges;[22] we lived there only by the consent of the Council. Still, Jews would convene in a quorum for prayers in private rooms as well as they could, poor things. Although the councilmen had some knowledge of this, they willingly turned a blind eye, but if the clergymen found out, they would not tolerate it and we were driven out, alas, like frightened sheep, and forced to go pray in the synagogue in Altona. This would go on for a while until once again we would crawl wretchedly into our prayer holes. In this fashion we have intervals of peace in between expulsions to this day,[23] and I fear this will go on as long as we remain in Hamburg[24] and the burghers are in power. *May God, blessed be He, compassionate and kind, show us mercy and send our righteous Messiah soon and let us serve Him, blessed be He; may we be*

20. That is to say that some found shelter with Sephardi Jews and some among non-Jews (cf. Richarz 2001a, p. 18). On Sephardi Jews and their Hamburg community, see Ornan-Pinkus 1986; Grunwald 1902; Feilchenfeld 1898; Cassuto 1927; Kellenbenz 1958; Kellenbenz 1989; Studemund-Halévy 1991; Studemund-Halévy and Koj 1994.

21. On the return of the Ashkenazi Jews to Hamburg after their flight due to the war, see Feilchenfeld 1899, pp. 277–278; Grunwald 1904, pp. 10–12; Marwedel 2001a, pp. 47–48; Marwedel 1982, p. 187; Richarz 2001a, p. 18.

22. See this Book, n. 11.

23. On life between Hamburg and Altona, see this Book; see also Feilchenfeld 1913, p. 18, n. 7; Richarz 2001a, pp. 17–18.

24. Regarding Glikl's thoughts on this matter, cf. Feilchenfeld 1913, p. 18, n. 8; see also Kaufmann 1896, p. 27, n. 1.

pure of heart so that we may pray in our Temple in the holy city of Jerusalem, amen.[25]

They settled in Hamburg where my father, of blessed memory, did business in precious stones and other things, the way a Jew does — a little bit of this, a little bit of that. The war between Denmark and Sweden grew fiercer; the King of Sweden,[26] in a sweeping victory, conquered all the territory held by the king,[27] until he reached the capital, where the King of Denmark resided, and laid siege to it. The city nearly fell to the King of Sweden, but His Majesty the King of Denmark had extremely loyal subjects and advisors assisting him with money and provisions, until with God's help he was able to withstand the attack. All this most certainly comes from God, blessed be He and His name, who assisted him because he was a good, righteous king, God-fearing and devout, and we Jews were contented under his rule. Even though we lived in Hamburg, each head of household had to pay a tax of only six reichstaler, no more. After this, the Dutch came to the aid of the king, sailing their ships through the Sund Strait,[28] breaching the siege, and thus was there peace.[29] But the kings of Denmark and Sweden are always at odds with each other, although they are friends and marry into each other's families, yet they bear a permanent grudge against each other.

At that time, my late sister Hendlche[30] became betrothed to the son of our master and teacher R. Gumpl of Cleve[31] and received a dowry of eighteen hundred reichstaler — a very large sum at the time — no one in

---

25. This passage does not derive from any specific liturgy and appears to comprise a medley of formulaic prayer and blessings.

26. The King of Sweden was then Charles X Gustav (see this Book, n. 17).

27. From now on, King Friedrich III of Denmark (see this Book, n. 17) is referred to without mention of his name.

28. The Sund Strait is located between the Baltic Sea and the North Sea. See Feilchenfeld 1913, p. 20, n. 9; p. 17, n. 5.

29. For Glikl's account of the second stage of the war and its termination, cf. Feilchenfeld 1913, p. 209, n. 9.

30. Hendlche (or Hendele) is Glikl's eldest sister (see Family Tree A).

31. Mordechai Gumpl of Cleve (also known as Marcus Gompertz) belonged to the well-known Jewish banking family (see *Encyclopaedia Judaica* 1972, vol. 7, cols. 773–774). He initially lived in Emmerich and then in Cleve; he died in 1664 (see Kaufmann and Freudenthal 1907, pp. 9–13; Stern 1950, according to the index; Feilchenfeld 1913, p. 20, n. 10). On the relations between the Gompertz family and Glikl's, see Feilchenfeld 1913, p. 328; see also Family Tree D. Cleve (German Kleve, English Cleves) is a town in North Rhine-Westphalia.

Hamburg had ever given such a sizeable dowry. On the other hand, it was the very best match in all Ashkenaz; everybody praised the excellent match and the large dowry. But my father, of blessed memory, was occupied with his business affairs; he had firm faith in God, blessed be He, trusting Him to assist him in arranging respectable marriages for all his other children too. His conduct — the way he ran his household, his hospitality, and every single thing he did — in all these he was better than today's rich men who have thirty thousand of their own and more. He continued acting in this fashion until his dying day.

Shall I describe the wedding he held for my late sister and the important people who attended with my in-laws,[32] our master and teacher R. Gumpl and his family, what a holy man, may he rest in peace — I could never describe it adequately, but he was not like those who live in our times. So honest in his business affairs, such a lavish wedding — I cannot describe it properly, nor, most important, how much joy he brought the poor and needy.[33] May we find favor thanks to his good deeds. My father, of blessed memory, was not a very wealthy man, but, as I already mentioned, he trusted in God, blessed be He, and owed no man anything. Thus he made an honest living, sparing no effort to provide for his wife and children, with God's help. By now an elderly man, my late father, _crushed by pain and suffering_,[34] hastened to marry off his children. When my late father married my mother, may she live long, he was a widower. For over fifteen years he had been married. He and his first wife had no children, then she died, may she rest in peace, and after her death my father married my mother. She was an orphan, poor thing; my beloved, pious mother often told me about her poverty-stricken life as a fatherless orphan with her pious, devout mother, Matte, of blessed memory, whom I knew. There was not a more pious, devout woman than she, may she rest in peace.

My late grandfather's name was Reb Nathan of Ellrich,[35] of blessed

32. The term "in-law" applies to all relatives by marriage, not only to the parents and closest relatives of your husband or wife.

33. By following the custom of holding a lavish meal for the local poor and giving each one a coin (see Lewinsky 1975, p. 504).

34. See b.Berakhot 5a: "If the Holy One, blessed be He, is pleased with a man He crushes him with painful sufferings." This surely refers to his suffering from the gout (see this Book, p. 61).

35. Glikl's maternal grandfather; his last name refers to the city of Ellrich in North Thuringia.

memory, who lived in Detmold, a wealthy, well-respected man. In the end, when he was served with an edict of expulsion[36] and forced to leave with his wife and children, they went to Altona. At that time, fewer than ten families lived in Altona, and only then did Jews begin settling there. Altona belonged at that time to the Count of Schauenburg;[37] Nathan Spanier[38] was the first to gain permission for Jews to live in Altona. Altona and the whole district of Pinneberg[39] did not yet belong to the Danish crown, then the count died without an heir.[40] In this way, the district fell to the Danish crown. Everyone came to live there, one by one. This same Nathan Spanier settled his son-in-law our master and teacher R. Leyb[41] in Altona too. This same Reb Leyb was from Hildesheim, and although not wealthy he was an honest man, may he rest in peace; he made respectable matches for his children, as was the custom at the time. His wife, Esther,[42] of blessed memory, was a pious, extremely lively woman, very knowledgeable in business matters. Indeed, she ran the entire household, traveling regularly to the fair in Kiel[43] with merchandise, that is, she did not take much merchandise with her — people made do with little in those days. She was a good speaker, and *all who saw her admired her.*[44] The ladies of the Holstein

36. I could not find any information on the expulsion of the Jews from Detmold during this period.

37. The Count of Schauenburg: Ernst III (Graf von Holstein-Schauenburg) died in 1611 (on him and his treatment of the Jews, see Marwedel 1976, name index).

38. On Nathan Spanier, "lay leader of the Jews of Schauenburg," his position and activity in Altona until his death in 1647, see Duckesz 1915, p. 36; Marwedel 1976, esp. p. 49, n. 85; p. 50, n. 6, which also explores the details mentioned by Glikl. Spanier's daughter, Freyde, married Yosef Hamel, Glikl's father-in-law. Another daughter, Esther, married Leyb Hildesum, mentioned later (see also Family Tree B).

39. The district of Pinneberg (Grafschaft Pinneberg) is today a city west of Hamburg. On the details mentioned here, see Marwedel 1976, pp. 42–43.

40. Otto VI, Graf von Holstein-Schauenburg, died childless in 1640. See Marwedel 1976, name index.

41. On R. (Yudah) Leyb Hildesum, see Duckesz 1915, pp. 45–46. He married Esther, the daughter of Nathan Spanier, in Stadthagen and then moved with his in-laws to Altona. He died in 1663 (see his tombstone inscription, Duckesz 1915, p. 28, no. 55). On his relation to Chaim Hamel, see Family Tree B.

42. On his wife Esther, the daughter of Nathan Spanier, see Duckesz 1915, p. 46; for her tombstone inscription, see Duckesz 1915, p. 28, no. 56. This is the only place where Glikl mentions Esther's first name; later on, she is merely called "the wife of Yudah Leyb Hildesum."

43. This fair (Kieler Umschlag) was an annual market held in January in Kiel (see Landau 1901, p. 66; Feilchenfeld 1913, p. 24, n. 5).

44. Cf. Esther 2:15, which associates the biblical Esther with the woman Glikl is describing.

nobility favored her greatly. They gave their children dowries of three to four hundred reichstaler, yet their sons-in-law were very wealthy men, like the late Reb Elia,[45] a very wealthy man with thirty thousand reichstaler, and Reb Moshe Goldzieher[46] — also a very wealthy man, and so forth. His son Reb Moshe was a very wealthy man too, and honest to his dying day. His son Reb Lipman[47] was not such a wealthy man, yet he earned a good, honest living, as did his other children. I make this point precisely because it is not the large dowries that count most, as could be seen in those days, when people gave their children small dowries yet they prospered.

Let us return to our subject. When my grandfather Reb Nathan of Ellrich, of blessed memory, was served with the edict of expulsion, as mentioned,[48] he went to the house of Reb Leyb Hildesum, son-in-law of Reb Nathan Spanier, bringing great wealth with him. Esther, Reb Leyb's wife, often told me fabulous stories of that wealth: entire crates filled with gold chains and other jewelry, large purses filled with pearls; there was not a richer man for as far as one hundred leagues. Unfortunately, all this did not last long; the plague came, heaven forfend!, and my grandfather and several of his children died. My grandmother, of blessed memory,[49] still had two unmarried daughters. The three were left *naked and lacking everything.*[50] She told me how they were forced to endure poverty, the poor things. They did not even have a bed — they had to sleep on floors of wood or stone. Although she already had a married daughter,[51] this daughter was unable to offer her any help. She also had a married son, Reb Mordechai, who did very well, was very wealthy, but at that time he, his wife, and their child also died of the plague,[52] God preserve us.

45. Elia Ballin served for thirty-six years as the parnas of Glikl's community (see Feilchenfeld 1913, p. 134, n. 27a). He married Zisse, the daughter of Leyb Hildesum, and his daughter Miriam married Glikl's son, Nathan (see Duckesz 1915, pp. 34, 46; Book Four, p. 167, and Family Trees B and C).
46. For details concerning Moshe Goldzieher, including an explanation of his last name meaning "goldsmith," and the date of his death, 1681, see Duckesz 1915, pp. 40–412; Family Tree B.
47. Lipman and his brother Moshe, mentioned earlier, the sons of Leyb Hildesum and his wife Esther (see Family Tree B) are only mentioned here and there are no further details about them.
48. See this Book, p. 65.
49. This refers to grandmother Matte; see following text.
50. Cf. Deut 28:48.
51. Named Gluk (see this Book, p. 68, and Family Tree A).
52. According to tombstone inscriptions in Altona, Mordechai (the son of Nathan of Ellrich) and his wife Chana, the daughter of Yeshaya Hekscher, died of the plague on Thursday and were

Thus was my beloved grandmother left with her two fatherless daughters in great distress, forced to move from house to house *until the indignation should pass.*[53] Once the plague abated somewhat, she wanted to go back to her own home and air out her things but found very little left there. Her most prized possessions were gone. Tenants who had been living in her house had pried up the floorboards, broken into everything, and taken most of her possessions, leaving her and her fatherless daughters, poor things, with very little. What could she do, the poor creature? My grandmother, may she rest in peace, still had several pledges that provided a living for her and her daughters. The two fatherless girls were my aunt Ulk[54] and my mother, Beyle, may she live long. My grandmother managed to scrimp and save until finally she had enough money to marry off the orphan Ulk and betrothe her to the son of the late R. David Hanau,[55] one of the most learned men of his generation, who held the title of *Moreynu*;[56] I believe he was the head of a rabbinical court in Friesland. After that he went to Altona and was appointed head of the rabbinical court there. The bridegroom's name was Reb Elia Cohen,[57] of blessed memory; his father gave him a dowry of five hundred reichstaler. In a short time he amassed great wealth and was highly successful, but unfortunately he died young, not even forty years old. Had God, blessed be He, spared his life, he would have become a great man, for *the Lord lent success to everything he undertook.*[58] If he took a handful of garbage, it turned to gold. But fate overtook him too soon.

During this time, there were also disputes over leadership positions in

---

buried on Friday, November 12, 1638. See Duckesz 1915, p. 22, nn. 13–14; see also Duckesz 1915, pp. 33–34, nn. 13–14 (no. 13 also mentions the death of Glikl's grandfather, whose tombstone did not survive); Grunwald 1904, p. 104, n. 1; Feilchenfeld 1913, p. 26, n. 16.

53. Isa. 26:20.

54. Ulk was the older sister of Beyle, Glikl's mother, and younger than her married sister, Gluk (see Family Tree A). On her marriage, see following text.

55. R. David (ben Menachem HaCohen) Hanau was Altona's first rabbi, and served in this position from 1641 to 1660. See Feilchenfeld 1913, p. 27, n. 19; Wolfsberg-Aviad 1960, p. 50.

56. A rabbinical title; see Pollack 1971, pp. 265–266, n. 66; Abrahams 1969, p. 356, n. 1; Güdemann 1880–1888, III, pp. 43–44.

57. On Elia (ben David Hanau) Cohen (see Duckesz 1903, p. 2), husband of Ulk, the sister of Glikl's mother, and therefore also the brother-in-law of Reb Leyb, Glikl's father, see Family Tree A. For a short time, he was the parnas of Altona.

58. Cf. Gen 39:3.

the community. My father, of blessed memory, was an officer of the community for many years,[59] until the late Elia Cohen started to ponder: he
was a young man growing wealthier by the day; he was learned, of a good
family — his father was our master and teacher R. David Hanau — and this
young man started telling people time and again: "Why shouldn't I too
be a community leader like my brother-in-law Leyb?[60] Am I not as clever
as my brother-in-law Leyb? Am I not as rich as he is? Is my family not as
good as his?" But God, blessed be He, who directs and decides when things
should happen and for what purpose, took him at that time. There were
disputes in the community in his lifetime too;[61] as can be expected, some
supported one party, some another. Unfortunately, this made it a very bad
time for our community. First to die was Fayvlman,[62] one of the community leaders. Then Chaim Fürst died,[63] the most prosperous man among us,
also an officer of the community. Then Avraham Shammes[64] fell sick and
died, saying with his dying breath: "I have been summoned to the heavenly
court as a witness." The late Chaim Fürst had a son called Reb Zalman,[65]
a gabbai; he too died — a prominent man, very learned. I forget the other
heads of households now who died too. In this way God, blessed be He,
put an end to the disputes among the community leaders.[66]

Let us return to my maternal grandmother, Matte,[67] of blessed memory.
After she married off my late aunt Ulk, she was left penniless with the fatherless child my mother, may she live long, a girl of eleven; she moved in
with her late daughter Gluk,[68] who was already married to the late Yakov

59. We have no information concerning the position of Glikl's father as lay leader of the Altona
community.

60. Meaning Glikl's father, Leyb Pinkerle (see this Book, n. 57, and Family Tree A).

61. According to the dates when the following people mentioned died, this would be the year 1653,
which was during the lifetime of the previously mentioned Elia Cohen.

62. Philipp (Fayvlman) Heilbut died on March 10, 1653 (see Simonsen 1905, p. 103).

63. Chaim Fürst died on March 18, 1653 (see Simonsen 1905, p. 103; Duckesz 1915, p. 38 and his
tombstone inscription there, and p. 24, n. 31).

64. His surname (Hebrew shammash), meaning "sexton," or "beadle," refers to his role in the
community, but there is no record of his name on Altona tombstones (see Simonsen 1905, p. 103).

65. Reb Zalman, the son of Chaim Fürst, died on March 20, 1653 (see Simonsen 1905, p. 103).

66. Glikl views the deaths of these community leaders as God's punishment for their deeds. This
belief is echoed in descriptions of other events (see, for example, Book Five, pp. 251–253).

67. Glikl now returns to her subject after her earlier digression (this Book).

68. See this Book, n. 51. "Glikl" is a diminutive of "Gluk."

Ree.[69] This Yakov Ree, while not wealthy, was a good man who gave his children four to five hundred reichstaler in dowries, yet made excellent matches for them; all the sons-in-law were excellent young men,[70] and he associated with good families. Now, after my maternal grandmother had been there for some time — there were perhaps too many visits from her orphan grandchildren,[71] or perhaps some other misunderstanding such as arises between parents and children — the poor woman moved with her orphan daughter to my aunt Ulk's.[72] They earned their own living, that is, my mother, may she live long, was an expert lacemaker in gold and silver; God helped her so that the merchants of Hamburg gave her gold and silver to make into lace, with the late Yakov Ree acting as guarantor the first time. Once the merchants saw that she was honest, delivering what she promised them on time, they trusted her. My mother, may she live long, employed several girls to make lace under my mother's supervision; in this way she was able to provide for herself and her mother and to clothe herself in neat, clean fashion. But the poor women had not much more than that; my mother often had to make do with a piece of bread for the entire day, accepting everything with love, putting her trust in God, blessed be He, who had not forsaken her, and she maintains that trust to this day. How I wish I had her nature! But God does not give everyone the same measure.

Now, my father, of blessed memory, as I mentioned,[73] before marrying my mother, may she live long, was married to another woman, by the name of Reytse, who was apparently an extremely talented person, a most capable woman who ran a large, respected household; she ultimately died[74] without having any children with my father, of blessed memory. This

69. On Yakov Ree, see Duckesz 1915, pp. 49–50, and his tombstone inscription there, p. 30, n. 68. For his daughters and sons-in-law, see next note and Family Tree A.

70. On Yakov Ree's three sons-in law — Fayvesh Cohen, husband of his daughter Reyze; Ber Cohen, husband of Beyle; and Yudah Rothschild, husband of Elkele — see Family Tree A (cf. Duckesz 1915, p. 49). "Young men" may as well mean "yeshiva students."

71. Apparently the orphans of her son Mordechai, who died in the plague (see this Book, p. 66, n. 52).

72. Glikl's grandmother moved with Glikl's mother to Glikl's aunt Ulk, who had married Elia Cohen.

73. See earlier in this Book, p. 64.

74. Reytse, or Reytschen, daughter of Isaac, died on Thursday, August 23, 1640 (see Duckesz 1915, p. 22, no. 18, and pp. 34–35, no. 18; Simonsen 1905, p. 104, end of n. 1). It follows that Glikl's father married her mother shortly after he was widowed, given that he had two daughters with Glikl's mother prior to Glikl's birth in 1645/1646.

woman already had an only daughter. In this way did my father, of blessed memory, gain — along with his first wife — a stepdaughter too, second to none in both beauty and deed. She spoke fluent French, which turned out one time to be most advantageous for my father, of blessed memory. For my father, of blessed memory, had received a pledge from a certain non-Jewish gentleman, valued at five hundred reichstaler. Well, after some time, this gentleman returned with two other gentlemen, seeking to redeem his pledge. My father, of blessed memory, suspecting nothing, goes upstairs to get the pledge. His stepdaughter was standing at the clavichord,[75] playing the instrument so as to render the gentlemen's wait less tedious.

The two gentlemen, who were standing near her, start conferring together: "When the Jew comes back with our pledge, we'll grab it from him without giving him the money and get out of here." They were speaking French, never dreaming that the maiden could understand them. As my father, of blessed memory, comes back with the pledge, she starts singing loudly: *"Beware! Not the pledge! Today — here, tomorrow — gone!"*[76] In her haste, the poor girl couldn't express herself any better. So my father, of blessed memory, says to the gentleman: "Sir, where's the money?" Says the man: "Give me the pledge." Says my father, of blessed memory: "I'm not giving any pledge; first I must have the money." One of the men then turns to the others and says: "Fellows, we've been duped, the whore must know French," and with that they bolted from the house, shouting threats. Next day the gentleman returns alone, pays my father, of blessed memory, the principal with interest, and redeems his pledge, saying: "Useful for you — you invested wisely when you had your daughter learn French,"[77] and with that he went on his way.

Now, my father, of blessed memory, kept his stepdaughter with him at

75. *Klafzimmer* is a musical instrument (clavichord? spinet?) resembling a small upright piano. The word is possibly derived by popular etymology from *clavicymbalum* (see Kaufmann 1896, p. 34, n. 3).

76. The final line from a comic song (in Hebrew) of trickery and conspiracy (see Noy 1968, pp. 39–42; the song is on p. 40). According to Noy, the quotation of the song in Glikl's memoirs is its earliest known occurrence (1968, p. 39). For more details, see Turniansky 2006a, p. 74, n. 180.

77. We do not have precise knowledge about girls in Ashkenaz studying foreign languages during this period (the late 1620s or early 1630s), the date of Glikl's father's first marriage, based on my calculations.

home, treating her always like his own flesh and blood; he even found her an excellent match and married her off—she got Reb Kalman Aurich's son from Aurich[78]—but she died, may she rest in peace, during her first childbirth, and a few days later her corpse was stripped of its shrouds. She appeared in a dream and revealed this.[79] So they dug her up out of her grave and found it to be true. The women quickly set about sewing new shrouds for her. As they were sitting there sewing, the maid came into the room and said, "For God's sake, hurry up with your sewing; can't you see that the dead one is sitting among you?" But the women could see nothing. When they finished, they gave the shrouds to the dead one. So she never came back again in her entire life, and rested in peace.

I have recounted how my father, of blessed memory, married my mother, as well as something of their life together. As soon as my father, of blessed memory, married my mother, may she live long, he brought my grand-mother Matte, may she rest in peace, to eat at his table and live under his roof for the rest of her life. He showed her every possible respect, just as if she were his own mother. My mother now returned the few nightgowns[80] that my poor grandmother had given her, all with my father's knowledge. In short, she was very comfortable, as if she were in her own home. May God, blessed be He, treat us and our children favorably, thanks to those good deeds. She lived under his roof for over seventeen years,[81] in the greatest comfort.

After this, the Jews of Vilnius fled Poland,[82] many of them coming to Hamburg; many suffered from an infectious disease. There was no hospice or other facility where the sick could be tended, so they lay in our attic, at least ten sick people, while my father provided for them. Some of them

78. A town in Lower Saxony.
79. On the theme of the dead appearing in dreams, including for this particular purpose of recounting that they have been stripped of their shrouds, see Bar-Levav 1997, pp. 132–134.
80. The following text makes clear that these nightgowns were part of the dowry that she received from her mother prior to her marriage.
81. If this figure is accurate, then Glikl's parents were married no later than 1640, a short time after her grandmother was widowed when her husband died of the plague in 1638. The grandmother therefore married off her two daughters in less than two years, and Glikl's mother gave birth to her three daughters in the space of five to six years.
82. In 1655 the Muscovite army attacked Vilna, and the Jews fled the city (for details on these events, see Turniansky 2006a, p. 76, n. 196).

recovered; others died. My sister Elkele,[83] may she live long, and I took to our beds with the same disease. My devout grandmother, of blessed memory, visited all the sick, caring for their every need. She insisted on doing this over the protests of my father and mother, climbing upstairs three or four times a day to the patients in the attic. She ended up catching the disease herself and lay sick for ten days until she died *at a ripe old age, with a good name.*[84] She was seventy-four when she died, as alert as a woman of forty. Her confessions and confidences cannot be repeated, nor can I describe the praise and thanks she lavished upon my father, of blessed memory. Every week my father and mother would give her half a reichstaler or two marks to spend on herself as she wished. My father never returned home from a fair without bringing her something. She saved up the money and would give loans against small pledges. When she was on her deathbed, she said to my father: "My son, I am going the way of all flesh.[85] I have lived in your house for so long, and you have treated me as you would treat your own mother. Not only have you given me the very best food and drink and fine clothes — you also gave me money. So what did I do with the money? I saved it up, not using it, lending only a little at a time against small pledges, so that I should now have about two hundred reichstaler in all. Who is more deserving of this money than my dear son-in-law? For it is all from him. But if my dear son-in-law should wish to give it up and pass it on to my two grandchildren, poor things, the orphans of my son Reb Mordechai — I leave it to yourself to decide." Reb Judah and Reb Anshl,[86] and all her children and sons-in-law had to be present on this occasion too. My father, of blessed memory, answered her as follows: "My dear mother and mother-in-law, I beg of you, let me reassure you. May God preserve you with us for a long time yet, so that you will be able to

---

83. Glikl's elder sister; see Family Tree A.

84. On "a ripe old age," cf. Gen 25:8; on a "good name," cf. b.Berakhot 17a.

85. This echoes "I am going the way of all the earth" (1 Kgs 2:2; see also Josh 23:14), which signifies to die or pass away.

86. Perhaps this is Reb Anshl Wimpfen, Glikl's relative (see Book Five, p. 246, n. 191; Feilchenfeld 1913, p. 33, n. 25a, and p. 244, n. 70; Simonsen 1905, p. 105, n. 2). Based on this assumption, his colleague (both most probably in the role of witnesses to the dying's confession) was his father-in-law, Reb Judah Rothschild (see Feilchenfeld 1913, p. 240, n. 66), who was married to Elkele, the daughter of Gluk, Glikl's aunt, mentioned earlier (see also Family Tree A).

give the money to whomever you wish. I willingly waive any claim to it; once God, blessed be He, restores your strength, I will make you a present of another one hundred reichstaler for you to turn to further profit as you see fit." When my grandmother heard my father say these words, she was overcome with joy, the poor woman, and rained blessings upon him and my mother and their children, praising them to everybody. The next day she fell asleep peacefully and was buried with the honor she deserved.[87] May we find favor thanks to her good deeds, we and our children and our children's children.

Let us return to my father, of blessed memory, who married off my sister Hendele,[88] may she rest in peace. I mentioned it briefly, for why should I go on at length. I wrote but briefly how my mother, may she live long, the poor woman, a miserable orphan, trusted in God, blessed be He, and He helped her with such munificent generosity, as the following story shows. Even if one of her children happened to be less successful than another, most of them, thank God, did well and made a good living. So if one trusts implicitly in God, blessed be He, almighty God does not forsake him, blessed be He forevermore.

It is a lovely story,[89] a consolation to sad, anxious hearts, showing that we must never lose hope that God will come to our aid, as happened to a certain pious Jew. Although he endured poverty, suffering, and all manner of troubles, he nevertheless accepted it all with forbearance, never forsaking God, who stood by him and showed him kindness, as you shall read here.

There once was a pious Jew who had two small sons and a pious wife. He had a small sum of money to live on, but was ignorant of business matters and knew only how to study. However, the man was eager to earn a living to provide for his wife and children without needing gifts from anybody. But he was unlucky — the poor man accumulated debts that he

87. The following is inscribed on her tombstone in the Altona cemetery: "Here is buried the modest woman Matte the daughter of Yakov, of blessed memory, the wife of the parnas and leader Nathan Ellrich, of blessed memory, who restored her soul to the Lord on Wednesday [should read Thursday], June 26, 1656 and was buried on June 27" (see *Grabbüchern* of 1874, no. 1089 [3925]; see also this Book, p. 72).

88. In another diminutive form, Glikl's eldest sister is called Hendlche (see this Book, n. 30). The author now returns to her subject after her digression.

89. The formula "a lovely story" (*ayn sheyn mayse*) was a common opening of Yiddish folktales.

FIGURE 11

Gravestone of Grandmother Matte in the Altona Cemetery.
In *David hamekhuneh Daniel beR. Yakov Valzrode Cohen,*
Toldot mishpahat Cohen *(Jerusalem: Hotzaat*
Hamishpahah 1995), p. 117.

could not repay, nor would anyone act as his guarantor. His creditors sued him in a court of law. The judge ruled that since he could not pay, nor did he have a guarantor, he must be thrown in jail. And that is indeed what happened. His pious wife set to weeping and wailing, wondering how she would provide for herself and her two small children, especially now that her husband was in jail, and she, poor thing, had to care for him too. As she wept, an old man came up to her and inquired why she was weeping. The woman, seeing how dignified and imposing the old man was, recounted all her woes to him. Said the old man: "Cease your weeping; God will come to your aid. Since your husband learns Torah, God will not forsake you, for God does not forsake a scholar; if God does not help a man in his youth — He will help him later in life. I know that much suffering is still in store for you; you, your husband, and your children will endure many hardships, but God will turn it all to good, if you will only be patient." He continued to console her, and advised her to find work as a washerwoman, washing people's clothes in exchange for payment: "In this way you will provide for yourself, your husband, and your children — as long as you are not timid about asking people to give you their clothes to wash."

The woman allowed the old man to console her and thanked him warmly, saying she would do as he said. Then the old man went on his way and she saw him no more. The woman went home to prepare something for her husband's evening meal and enjoined him to be patient and persevere with his studies. She would labor night and day to provide for him and her small children. Thereupon the pious man began weeping bitterly, joined by his pious wife, until surely God in heaven must have taken pity on them. The pious, clever woman recovered first, saying: "Dear husband, weeping and wailing will not provide bread for us and our children. I will go see what God has in store for me so that I can earn enough to provide for you and the children." Said the man: "Go then, dear wife, may God help us." The woman went home with her children to sleep. Next day, she rose early, her children still asleep, and went around to the houses in the city asking to take in washing. People felt sorry for her and gave her clothes to wash, so the poor creature became a washerwoman. The city was built on the seashore; every day the woman and her two sons went down to the seashore, where she washed the clothes and then spread them out on the grass to dry.

One day, as she was washing clothes in this fashion, a ship neared the shore. The sailor saw the woman and beheld her beauty. Said the woman: "Sir, why are you staring at me?" Answered the sailor: "My dear lady, I feel very sorry for you. Tell me, how much do they pay you to wash a garment?" Said the woman: "I get two pennies for washing a man's shirt, since I must wash it thoroughly." Said the sailor: "My dear lady, I will gladly give you four pennies if you agree to wash my shirt thoroughly." She replied: "I will wash it gladly." The woman took the shirt and washed it thoroughly, then spread it out on the grass to dry. While the sailor waited for his shirt to dry, he studied the washerwoman. The woman took the dry shirt and folded it neatly. As the sailor could not bring his vessel right up to the shore, it came to a stop at arm's length from shore. He tossed her the four pennies wrapped in paper, and she caught them. Said the sailor: "Kindly hand me my shirt." The woman brought the shirt and held it out to him on the ship. The sailor seized her hand and pulled her onto the ship, then sailed quickly away. The woman cried out loudly on the ship, while her two small children cried out on shore, all to no avail, for she was already far out at sea, and her cries could no longer be heard.

When the two children could no longer see or hear their mother, they hastened to their father in the jail, weeping bitterly, and recounted what had befallen their mother. When their father heard this, he wept aloud, wailing: "God, O God, why have you forsaken me[90] in my plight? Now I have no one left in this world to provide for me here in jail." Amid this keening and wailing, he fell asleep. He dreamed he was in a vast desert, surrounded by wild animals waiting to tear his flesh and devour him. The man shuddered in fear, turning hither and thither in his distress until he spotted a large herd of cattle and sheep. When the wild animals saw the herd, they left the man alone and pursued the herd instead. The man fled to a castle by the sea where there were many ships. In the castle he was seated on a throne, and he and the sailors were very pleased. When he awoke, he pondered this dream, saying to himself: "The dream proves that my misery will pass; God will come to my rescue and will bring me joy once again through sailors, since a sailor was the cause of my misery."

90. Cf. the Yiddish traditional translation (*taytsh*) of Ps 22:2.

It so happened that the king died, and his son was crowned king. The new king waived all taxes in the city for three years, to find favor with the people, and he also set all the prisoners free. Among them were the good scholar and his two sons. The man wandered around the marketplace, not knowing how he would earn a penny to buy bread for his children. Then he lifted his eyes and saw[91] a ship about to set sail for the East Indies.[92] Said the man to his two children: "Come, since your mother was abducted by a sailor, let us too board a ship; perhaps we will find your mother; perhaps God will enable us to find each other again." The man approached the captain, requesting passage on the ship for himself and his two children, for he was too poor to afford to buy even a piece of bread. The man recounted his tale to the captain, who took pity on him and let him and the two children board the ship, providing them generously with food and drink. When they reached the open sea, God caused a heavy storm that wrecked the ship, and all those aboard were drowned. Only the wise man[93] and his two children and the captain who had given them food and drink survived; they each seized a plank from the wreckage and clung on tightly. The two children clung to a single plank until the sea flung them to foreign lands. The wise man was flung to a great desert inhabited by savages. The princess of the savages spotted him as she herded sheep and cattle in the desert. She was stark naked, with only her hair and a girdle of fig leaves to cover her nakedness. She approached the man in a friendly manner so that he might take her for his wife. He too was friendly, for a great fear was upon him, and he let her know that he wished to marry her. The savages, seeing this, cheered; young and old alike came running from the mountain caves where they lived. They pounced on him, eager to drink his blood and eat his flesh. Their king was with them too. The wise man was frightened nearly to death, but the king's daughter, seeing this, hinted to him that he need not be afraid. She implored her father to spare the man's life, since

91. Cf. the Yiddish *taytsh* for Gen 22:4, 13; 19:28; 24:63.
92. The East Indies (Ostindien) is a common toponym in Old Yiddish folktales, but the West Indies (Westindien) is more popular.
93. Up to this point, the protagonist ("the pious Jew") is referred to as "the *talmid ḥakham*" (the "wise man," "sage"); this is later on sporadically replaced by "the ruler" (*Fürst*, meaning "prince" or "duke"), which becomes the only title in the last part of the story, except for two mentions of "prince."

she wished to marry him. The king did as she wished, sparing the man's life. The wise man was obliged to lie with her at night, and they lived as man and wife. Although inwardly he thought often of his pious, beautiful wife who was taken from him under such distressing circumstances, he could change nothing, so he accepted it all with forbearance, maintaining his conviction that God, blessed be He, would come to his aid and reunite him with his dear wife and children.

After they had been living together for some time, she conceived and bore a savage boy. Every day the man would tend the sheep in the desert. Then he had been with them for two years, forced to eat the flesh of wild asses and other wild animals. He lay with his savage wife in the mountain caves. The man and his wife both were covered in hair, so that he resembled a savage. One day he was standing on a hill in the desert, not far from the sea, thinking of all the trials he had endured in his life, how he had lost his pious, clever wife and his children — and, worst of all, how he would be forced to live out his days amid stupid wild creatures who would eventually tire of him one day, devour his flesh, and break his bones; he would not be buried among Jews as a good Jew should. "The best thing for me to do is to leap off this hill and drown myself in the sea, like my two drowned children," for he did not know that the waves had carried them ashore. In this way he would rejoin them and rejoice with them in the world to come. The man confessed his sins before God, weeping hot bitter tears. When he had concluded his confession, he ran to the sea intending to drown himself. Suddenly he heard a voice calling his name: "Desperate man, why lose hope and destroy your soul? Return to the hill you were standing on; dig there until you find a chest filled with coins and precious stones, a great treasure. Drag the chest to the seashore and stand there for a while, until a ship comes along on its way to Antioch.[94] Call out to the crew to take you with them; they will rescue you with your treasure chest. In this way you will become a king and do very well; this will mark the end of your troubles and the beginning of your happiness."

As soon as the wise man heard this, he returned to the hill and began digging, as the voice had instructed him. When he found the chest of gold

---

94. The ancient capital of the Greek kingdom is a toponym in Yiddish folktales.

and precious stones, he dragged it down to the seashore. He raised his eyes and beheld a ship at sea with human figures on board. In a loud voice he called out to them to take him with them, since he was a human being just like them. Hearing his voice, his human speech, they sailed up to him. After he had recounted his tale, they promptly took him and his chest on board the ship.

The savage woman, his wife, heard his voice from the ship and recognized it. She ran toward the ship with the savage child in her arms, calling out to her husband to take her with him. But he mocked her: "What have I to do with savages? I already have a better wife than you." He kept on talking to her like this. The woman, hearing that he would return to her no more, was seized by a fierce anger; she caught up the child by his feet and tore him in two, flinging one half onto the ship and furiously devouring the other half,[95] and then she fled. The wise man sailed away on the ship. They reached an island and went ashore. He opened the treasure chest and found it full of gold and precious stones of immeasurable value. He paid the captain gladly and ordered that the chest be delivered to the inn. At night he lay thoughtfully on his straw pallet: "If I could buy the island from the king, I'd build a castle and a city; that way I'd have a regular income with no fear of my money being stolen." Early the next morning he went to the king and purchased the island, a few miles in length, from him and built a castle and an entire city there. The island's inhabitants welcomed him as their ruler. He recalled his wife and children, lost under such distressing circumstances. He had a sudden thought: "Since it was a sailor who took my wife from me, and all sailors must appear before me at my castle, I will order that no ship be allowed to depart until the captain has informed me of its arrival. If he fails to do so he will lose his ship and all his cargo." And so it was: all the captains informed him of their arrival and came to dine with him.

Time passed, but he could find out nothing about his wife and children.

---

95. This is a popular motif in folktales (see Idelson-Shein 2010). For the particulars of this motif, see Davis 1995, pp. 39–40, and pp. 244–245, nn. 139–141; Davis 2001, pp. 41–44. Davis believes that Glikl learned of this motif from a source in a foreign language and interwove it into this story on her own initiative. I disagree with this hypothesis; see this Book, nn. 100–101. See also Turniansky 2001, pp. 77–79.

One day, during Passover, the wise man was contentedly eating his midday meal when his servant came in to say that a wealthy, energetic captain was there, requesting that he not be detained long. Said the wise man: "Today is a festival; I cannot inquire of him what cargo he is carrying. He must wait until the festival is over.[96] Let him come dine with me." The captain came in and was invited to sit. The captain begged to be allowed to set sail, to no avail. He was obliged to remain and dine with the ruler. The wise man inquired where he was from and if he had a wife and children. The captain told him where he was from, adding that he had two wives: one stayed at home with their three children. "She is the homemaker. The other wife is extremely delicate and unfit for housework, but she is very clever. That's why I always take her with me to supervise the ship: she collects the money, enters the transactions, and supervises all my affairs. And I have never lain with her." Asked the wise man: "My dear captain, please tell me why you have never lain with her?" Answered the captain: "This woman used to have a husband, a very wise man who taught her a riddle. This is what she says: 'Anyone who solves this riddle is as wise as my husband, so I will let him lie with me. Otherwise — I would rather kill myself or be killed before letting anyone lie with me, for it is not right for a lowly man to ride the king's horse.'" Said the wise man: "My dear captain, I entreat you, tell me the riddle." Said the captain:[97] "The woman claims that a wingless bird flies from the sky to the ground and perches on a pretty little tree, making it sway from side to side. The bird, which cannot be seen, gives the tree strength, so that it bursts into glorious bloom. It draws in all the strength it can, then, all of a sudden, it withers and dies. The bird, flying up into the air, starts warbling and singing: 'Oh, poor tree! Who has taken away your strength? You enjoyed it so much, but it will never return. I was the source of your strength. What good is it now that you are all withered?' Your Majesty, that is her riddle; I cannot solve it."

The wise man was shocked to hear this, for he knew it was his own riddle, and the woman must be his wife. The captain, seeing the wise man taken aback, said to him: "Dear sir, why are you so startled?" He replied:

96. Being an observant Jew, he could not discuss business matters during the festival.
97. In the original (see Turniansky 2006a, pp. 96, 98, 100, 102, 104), the following riddles and their solutions (in this Book) are rhymed.

"I am amazed by the wise, wonderful riddle. I would like to hear it from the woman herself, in case perchance you have left something out or added something. If she tells the same riddle, I will give it my consideration — perhaps I can solve it." The wise man sent a servant straightaway to fetch the woman. The servant sped off and said to her: "Prepare to come with me to our ruler, to eat and drink with him and your husband."

When the good woman heard this, she felt a pang of fear, for she knew not why she was being summoned, and feared she was going from the frying pan into the fire. But what could the good woman do? She was obliged to go where she was taken. So she dressed and adorned herself as befitting one about to enter the king's presence. The woman came to the castle and was announced; the king commanded that she be brought to him. She was led inside and seated at the table next to the captain. The wise man greeted her and scanned her face somewhat doubtfully, for he did not recognize her. She did not recognize him either, as many years had passed since their parting, and they were changed in both appearance and dress.

The wise man remained silent as they ate and drank, but he was not happy, and sat there sunk in profound thought. Said the captain to the wise man: "Sir, why are you so glum, sunk in troubled thoughts? If it displeases you that we are prolonging the meal unduly, let us finish, say our thanks, and be on our way." Said the wise man: "No, you are my esteemed guests. It is just that I am pondering the riddle. I am eager to hear it from the woman herself." The captain asked his wife to tell the ruler the riddle, and she recounted it as earlier. Said he: "Where did you hear this riddle?" She replied: "Sir, I had a pious husband, a great Jewish rabbi, who would tell me tales and old riddles of this kind. The answer to this riddle is known to no man." Answered the wise man: "If someone were to give you the answer, would you acknowledge the truth?" She replied: "Dear sir, no man in the world can solve the riddle correctly except for my first husband." Answered the wise man: "I can solve the riddle. The bird that flies from the sky to the ground is the human soul. The small tree it perches on is the human body that is like a beautiful flourishing tree with many branches — this is youth, likened to a beautiful garden of pleasure. The bird making the tree sway from side to side is the soul, which animates and sets in motion all our limbs. But no one can see the bird, for the soul is hidden away within the body. The tree which first gathers strength, then withers, means that man is never content with what he has, but constantly wants to possess everything he sees. This often causes him to lose what he has, for injustice devours justice. Suddenly man dies and leaves everything behind. The bird then flies into the air; this is the soul keening over the body, saying: 'As long as you were alive, you were not content with what you had. You could not rest nor sleep until I gave you wealth. Now you are withering, leaving everything behind. What good is your death to me or to you? If only you had used your wealth to do good deeds, we would have been better off.' This then is the right answer to the riddle. If you wish to acknowledge the truth, I am willing to take you back."

The woman, studying the wise man carefully, now recognized him as her husband. She sprang up, embraced him, and wept profusely. They rejoiced and held a banquet. The captain fell to his knees in terror and begged for his life. Said the wise man: "Since you have not lain with my wife, I will spare your life. But since you took what was not yours, I will take it away from you." He confiscated all the captain's goods, then let him go. The couple remained devout and enjoyed great happiness and wealth. They recounted to each other what had befallen them, expressing great sorrow on account of the children drowned at sea, so they believed.

One day it was so exceedingly hot that it was impossible to sleep at night. The ships' crews all came out to chat and pass the time. Among them were the two sons, who did not know that their father and mother were there too. Said the two youths: "Let us tell riddles to pass the time." All were pleased; it was agreed that the first man to solve a riddle correctly would receive ten gulden. If the riddle could not be solved, the man who had posed it would receive ten gulden. The others said: "Let the two brothers pose their riddles first, for they are cleverer than we are." The brothers began as follows: "We saw a most beautiful girl, but her eyes are blind. Her figure is delicate and soft, but it does not exist. She rises early every morning, but does not show herself all day long. At night she returns, dressed in finery, but her jewels have never been created and do not exist in the world at all. Through closed eyes she can be seen; when eyes open — she vanishes. This then is the riddle for you to solve."

All wondered at the riddle, saying that it was too difficult to solve. There was an old merchant among them who insisted upon solving the riddle. The brothers rejected his answer as false. They argued until dawn without agreeing as to who should receive the ten gulden. Said the captain: "Heed my words: let us go to the ruler in the castle for him to judge which of you is right." Agreeing, they went to see the ruler, who asked: "What good tidings do you bring at this early hour?" They told him what had happened, and repeated the clever riddle and the old merchant's answer.

When the ruler heard the riddle he was seized by panic. He studied the youths, recognizing them, for they had not grown much. He said to them: "How did you know that the old merchant's answer to the riddle was wrong?" They replied: "Dear sir, our father was a most learned man, and he is the one who devised this riddle and provided its answer. No one can solve it except for us and our father." Said the ruler: "If I solved it, would I therefore be your father?" They replied: "Any man who gives the correct answer to the riddle is most certainly our father, for he told the riddle to no one save us, his children, and we were silent until now." Said the ruler: "Hear my solution to the riddle; perhaps I speak the truth." Said the king: "As I understand it, the beautiful girl is the youthful time in the lives of young men. They think only of beautiful girls all day long. As a result, they dream of a beautiful girl at night. But her eyes are unseeing, for she appears in a dream, in darkest night, when eyes are useless, and even when one's eyes are open one can see nothing at night. That's why the beautiful girl can see nothing. In the morning she disappears; for when one wakes in the morning, the dream is gone and is left outside all day, till night. Then the girl comes back, wearing jewels that were never created and do not exist in the world at all. This is how it must be understood: since this was seen only in a dream, the jewels were never created and do not exist. This then is the answer. If you acknowledge the truth, I will take you back as my sons."

The brothers were thunderstruck by this answer; they exchanged looks, realizing that this was indeed their father. They began weeping with joy, so overcome with amazement that they could not speak. Their father and mother sprang from their chairs and embraced the boys, and all wept so loudly that they were heard far away. It became known that these were the ruler's sons. After a long while the boys recovered and began telling all that had befallen them till now. Everyone rejoiced; the king held a banquet for all his court, and all rejoiced together with them. He was a prince, and his children were princes. He commanded his children to be devout and worship God wholeheartedly so that God would always come to their aid.[98] "When God wishes a man ill, his friends all fall silent; they give him neither advice nor help; they turn away and say: 'This man is unlucky' and leave him all alone; he has not one friend in a thousand. But when God wishes a man good, his enemies all fall silent, though their number be twofold." At seeing and hearing all this, many members of the ships' crews converted, and a nice Jewish community was established there.

From this we learn that we should be patient, accept that everything is for the best, and console the poor even if we have nothing to give them. In this way God will remember us and protect us from harm.[99] He will deliver us from our long, hard exile and will bring us to the Holy Land. Then joy will replace our sorrow. I, the author,[100] wish for God's compassion, blessed be He; may He grant us our request. This is my hope. If we act righteously, God will do as we ask. But right now we are not sufficiently repentant; our sins are numerous. Therefore, we must wait for the time God has set.

I found this story written in a book by a distinguished man, Prager by name.[101]

Let us return to our purpose and go on writing about my father, of blessed memory; even twenty pages would not be too many. He strove

98. In the original (see Turniansky 2006a, p. 104), the following sentences (up to "At seeing and hearing...") are in rhyme.

99. Here, too, this and the following sentences up to the end of the paragraph are in rhyme in the original (see Turniansky 2006a, p. 106), following very closely, in form and content, the customary ending of numerous Old Yiddish printed books.

100. The use of the masculine form of the noun "author," together with the rhymed sections, the archaic language of the *taytsh* (the traditional translation of the Bible into Yiddish) throughout the story, its typical style (so different from Glikl's writing), and many other details are clear evidence that Glikl copied it directly from a Yiddish book. See n. 95, and next note.

101. Since the book or booklet where Glikl found the story has not been found, we cannot identify the author (for several possibilities, see Turniansky 2006a, p. 107, n. 276). The story under discussion is a comprehensive and very complex version of a tale about a man who never swore an oath (see Aarne and Thompson 1987, no. 938, Placidas). Another complex version found its way into the *Midrash Aseret Hadibrot* and from there to the Yiddish *Mayse-bukh* (see Yassif 1987). On the diffusion of the motifs in Glikl's version, see Davis 1995, pp. 38–41, and pp. 244–247, nn. 136–142. On her belief that this version is the product of Glikl's own interweaving of motifs, see Davis 2001, pp. 41–45. I, however, am positive that Glikl copied here a previously printed story in its entirety (see my comments earlier and following; see also Turniansky 2001, pp. 77–79).

to make respectable matches for his children and did more than he was able toward this end, making the best possible matches for that time, as I mentioned in my Book One.[102] For a long time he served as parnas of his community, and during his service everything worked out very well; the community's situation was good, *every man sitting under his vine and under his fig tree.*[103] The community did not owe a penny, although I recall from my youth that they had serious disputes, such as are common unfortunately in our own times in every community where evil people plot. That is precisely what happened to my father and his colleagues when he served as parnas of the community, and evil people opposed them and would have brought disaster upon the community. Two of them even obtained writs from the king appointing them to the position of parnas, that is, by royal appointment.[104] They all died and came before God in heaven to give an account of themselves; I will not write their names — it is sufficiently well known in our community who they were. However, *the Lord frustrates the plans of the wicked*[105] and *God stands in the divine assembly.*[106] So the parnasim and leaders put an end to the whole matter, with God's help; they went to Copenhagen,[107] to His Majesty the King, with a full report. His Majesty the King was a devout man, a lover of justice, so thank God everything worked out, and God, blessed be He, put down the wicked ones.[108] Arranging the matter did not even cost much money since they were exceedingly careful with the funds of individuals and of the community and did not accrue debts. If they needed several hundred reichstaler, the community leader would lay out the amount and be fully reimbursed afterward so as not to lay a burden on the community. My God, when I give this matter due thought, I see that life in those days was so much happier than it is today, although people did not possess even half of what people have

102. Glikl mentions her father for the first time only in Book Two. Her mistake might have been due to a previous different division of her work into "books" (see also n. 113).

103. Cf. 1 Kgs 5:5 and more.

104. In 1664 several Jews attempted to take over the Altona community with the assistance of King Friedrich III (see Marwedel 1976, pp. 142–150).

105. Cf. Ps 33:10; Job 10:3, 21:16.

106. Cf. Ps 82:1.

107. Where the King of Denmark, who ruled Altona, resided (see this Book, n. 9).

108. Cf. Ps 147:6 (in Yiddish translation).

nowadays — may they enjoy it and prosper. May it be increased by God and not diminished. *In their days and in our days, You will deliver Judah and Israel and we shall be redeemed.*[109]

After this, when I was not yet twelve years old, my father, of blessed memory, betrothed me; I was betrothed for about two years. My wedding took place in Hamel. My father and mother traveled with me to the wedding. Our party comprised about twenty people. At that time it was not yet customary to travel by post chaise, so we had to hire carts from the villagers for our trip to Hannover; in Hannover, we immediately wrote to Hamel telling them to dispatch carriages to Hannover. My mother, may she live long, was convinced that coaches could be obtained in Hamel just like in Hamburg. She thought that my father-in-law should at the very least send one coach for the bridal party. But on the third day, three or four peasants' carts arrived, with horses that should themselves have been loaded onto the carts.

My mother, may she live long, was somewhat annoyed but could do nothing about it. So we seated ourselves in the peasant carts, praying to the God of Israel, and made it to Hamel. In the evening there was a festive meal. What good people, my father-in-law, of blessed memory, and my mother-in-law — you do not find many people like Reb Yosef Hamel, of blessed memory! My father-in-law toasted my mother, may she live long, with a large goblet of wine. My mother was still somewhat annoyed that they had not sent a coach for us. My father-in-law, a shrewd, likable man, a jokester, knew she was annoyed; he said to my mother: "Listen, my dear, please do not be annoyed — Hamel is not Hamburg. We have no coaches here, we are simple country folk. I will tell you what happened to me when I was a bridegroom traveling to my own wedding. My father, Shmuel Stuckert, was parnas of all of Hessen.[110] I was betrothed to Freydchen, Nathan Spanier's daughter.[111] For my dowry I received two thousand reichstaler, and my father, of blessed memory, promised me fifteen hundred reichstaler. That was a large dowry in those days. When my wedding day

109. Cf. Jer 23:6; see also the "Prayer for the Welfare of the Government," Maḥzor Rosh Hashanah 2014, p. 142.
110. See Feilchenfeld 1913, p. 36, n. 2.
111. See this Book, p. 65, n. 38.

was close, my father, of blessed memory, hired an emissary named Fish.[112] My father slung my dowry over this man's shoulder for him to carry to Stadthagen, where my father-in-law, Nathan Spanier, lived. I set out with the emissary Fish for Stadthagen. At that time, Reb Leyb—I mentioned him in my first book[113]—was also living in Stadthagen; he too was a son-in-law of my father-in-law's,[114] of blessed memory. As I approached Stadthagen, it was announced that the bridegroom was not far off. The late Reb Leyb and his companions rode out to meet the bridegroom. That same Reb Leyb was from Hildesheim, from a family that lived in great elegance. As he approaches the bridegroom, he sees that he and the emissary Fish are on foot. Reb Leyb rides back to give the bride the news: 'Freydchen's bridegroom is coming, riding a fish.' Now that I am able to ride good horses, I must ask you not to take it to heart." In this manner all her annoyance dissipated amid friendly laughter, and the wedding was held with much rejoicing.

After my wedding, my father and mother returned home. I was a child of less than fourteen, and I had to stay alone, without my father and mother, in a foreign land, among strangers. But all this was not hard for me, since I enjoyed the generosity of my pious father-in-law, of blessed memory, and my late mother-in-law. They were distinguished people, most decent, and they maintained me extremely well, better than I deserved.

How can I describe at length how righteous and kind my in-laws, of blessed memory, were, what an upright man he was, like *an angel of God*.[115] Everyone knows what Hamel is, compared to Hamburg; I was a young girl, used to being indulged in every way since childhood by parents, friends, and relatives. To come from a city like Hamburg to a place where there were only two Jewish households! Hamel itself is a miserable place of no interest; but all this was not important to me because I was so fond of my father-in-law, of blessed memory—when he would rise at three in the morning and put on his synagogue jacket and murmur outside my bedroom door

112. Fish is the nickname for Ephraim, based on Gen 48:16.
113. This Leyb (Hildesum) is mentioned for the first time in Book Two (see p. 65). For the possible reason for Glikl's mistake, see earlier in this Book, and n. 102.
114. Leyb Hildesum married a daughter of Nathan Spanier (see this Book, p. 65, n. 42), Esther, the sister of Freydchen who married Yosef Hamel, and who is telling the story here (see Family Tree B).
115. Cf. 1 Sam 29:9.

—I forgot Hamburg entirely. What a holy man he was! May his memory be a blessing, may we all find favor with God thanks to his good deeds; may he intercede on our behalf so that God may not inflict any further hardships upon us and we do not endure further shame or commit any transgression.

This is all clearly evident in his outstanding, respectable children. His eldest son, Reb Moshe, a fine young man, was about to be married. So he traveled to the wedding with our master and teacher R. Moshe—a distinguished man, and with a servant called "Shot-at Yakov,"[116] and he took his dowry with him. When they reached Bremervörde, they were attacked by robbers who stole the money and fatally wounded the three of them. They were brought to town, and physicians and barber-surgeons[117] were summoned urgently. The physicians thought that the bridegroom and our master and teacher R. Moshe would live but that the life of the servant Shot-at Yakov was in danger. But two days later the two of them died, while Yakov survived—this is how he got the name "Shot-at Yakov." It is not hard to imagine the grief and sorrow of the unfortunate parents; although they made every effort on every level to seek revenge,[118] it was all to no avail; there was no revenge. May God, blessed be He, avenge their deaths.

I knew the second son,[119] *brimming over with Torah learning like a pomegranate split open.*[120] My father-in-law, of blessed memory, sent him to Poland[121] as a young man, where he studied and acquired an excellent reputation; he was betrothed there in Poznan, a good match with the daughter of Reb Chaim Boaz of Poznan.[122] After his wedding, he applied himself even more diligently to his studies and became more and more learned until he became a very prominent man in the community of Poznan. But

---

116. The reason for this sobriquet is told later on.

117. In Glikl's times, "barber-surgeons" (unlike physicians) engaged in anything from shaving and cutting hair to tooth-pulling, blood-letting, and amputating limbs; see Kossoy and Ohry 1992.

118. Meaning attempts to catch the Gentile murderer and bring him to justice (see *Pinkas Va'ad Arba Aratzot* 1945, p. 547).

119. On "Our master and teacher R. Avraham," see the text that follows.

120. This phrase combines two expressions (see Song 4:3, 6:7; Rashi on Song 4:3; b.Berakhot 57a).

121. On Poland as center of Torah study appealing to students from Germany, especially in the seventeenth century, see Shmeruk 1961; see also Kaufmann 1896, p. 62, n. 2. Three of Yosef Hamel's six sons studied in Poland (see following text).

122. See Avron 1967, p. 139, n. 19. Avraham married Chaim Boaz's daughter Sulke.

a few years later, during the war of Chmielnicki[123] when there were fierce massacres throughout Poland in all the communities, he came to my father-in-law, *naked, bare, lacking everything*,[124] with his wife and one daughter.[125] The daughter was born by sheer miracle, for he and his wife had been married for seventeen years without any children. Then his mother-in-law fell ill and lay dying. She sent for her daughter, wife of my brother-in-law, our master and teacher R. Avraham, and told her: "My dear daughter, I am in God's hands, about to die. If I am granted the chance to appear before God, blessed be He, I will pray for you to have children." Saying this, she died, a distinguished, devout woman. After her death, my sister-in-law Sulke, wife of R. Avraham, conceived and gave birth to a baby girl, naming her Sara after her mother. Seven years later she gave birth to a boy, called Shmuel.[126] There is much that I could write about this R. Avraham. My father-in-law, of blessed memory, set him up in Hannover. He had a very good situation there, but he was tempted to move to Hamel, which proved to be his downfall and his children's too. People made him promises and entered into partnership with him — but did not keep their word, may God forgive them. My brother-in-law, our master and teacher R. Avraham, was a great scholar, an extremely learned man who spoke very little, but when he did open his mouth — his very breath was pure wisdom; it was worth listening to him carefully when he spoke. I might mention him again.[127]

Then my father-in-law had a daughter, Yente. He betrothed her as a young girl to the son of Reb Sussman Gans, who lived in Minden an der Weser. This same Sussman Gans had gained the reputation of a wealthy man with one hundred thousand. One day, when my father-in-law and Reb Sussman Gans were drinking together, they arranged the marriage while drunk. The next day, when Sussman Gans sobered, he regretted the

123. This refers to Bogdan Chmielnicki and the massacres of 1648–1649 (see Perles 1865, p. 58, n. 87).

124. Cf. Ezek 16:7, 22, 37; and Deut 28:48.

125. In fact, Abraham Hamel did not leave Poznan due to the massacres of 1648–1649, but around 1660 (see Halpern 1968, p. 211, n. 63) due to his excommunication for having avoided fulfilling his communal obligations (see *Pinkas Va'ad Arba Aratzot* 1945, pp. 93–94).

126. Later on, Shmuel married his cousin Chana, the daughter of Glikl and Chaim Hamel (see Book Four, p. 181, n. 196; and Family Trees B and C).

127. See Book Three, pp. 106, 109–110; Book Four, n. 196.

match. But my father-in-law, of blessed memory, was an honorable man;[128] what is done cannot be undone, and so the matter stood. Since the bride and bridegroom were still very young, Reb Sussman Gans sent his son Zalman[129] to study in Poland. A short time later, Reb Sussman Gans died without any relatives to supervise his estate. His wealth vanished. Reb Sussman Gans's widow married another man, Reb Fayvesh.[130]

After a few years, the bridegroom returned from Poland. Instead of the many thousands that my in-laws thought he had, he barely had a few hundred. My father-in-law, of blessed memory, wanted to break off the engagement because of this, but my mother-in-law, may she live long, would not hear of it, not wishing to disgrace the orphan. So they were married and lived in Minden for several years. Reb Fayvesh's wife married off the one son she'd had with Reb Fayvesh. When they came to the *Spinnholz*,[131] there were expensive utensils on the table, and great wealth was in evidence. That same Zalman Gans, my father-in-law's son-in-law, saw this wealth and perhaps recognized many utensils as having belonged to his father, Sussman Gans, while he himself had inherited very little of his father's wealth. And so he entered the study and took a small chest containing documents that he believed he was entitled to. But why should I go on at length? Twenty reams of paper would not suffice if I wanted to write about all that ensued. The next day, Reb Fayvesh, noticing that his chest of documents was missing, immediately suspected his stepson.[132] They

128. Apparently, due to his character and status, Yosef Hamel was able to prevent Sussman Gans from canceling the betrothal (see also Feilchenfeld 1913, p. 41, n. 9).

129. I have no more information about Sussman Gans and his son Zalman (see following text) than what is recounted here.

130. See Kaufmann 1896, p. 64, n. 2. The manuscript of his notes on the events discussed herein is at the Bodleian Library in Oxford (Ms. Mich 109; see also Neubauer 1886–1906, no. 908). Kaufmann published these notes under the title "Aufzeichnungen des Phöbus Gans aus Minden" in an appendix to his book on Glikl (see Kaufmann 1896, pp. 334–394; Feilchenfeld 1913, p. 43, n. 10).

131. A party held for the soon-to-be-married couple on Friday evening; see Pollack 1971, pp. 32–34; Güdemann 1880–1888, III, pp. 119–120; Kaufmann 1896, p. 64, n. 3; Feilchenfeld 1913, p. 42, n. 9; Abrahams 1969, p. 144, n. 1.

132. In his own notes (see this Book, n. 130), Reb Fayvesh states that he found it difficult to ascertain "who did this evil deed." He went to the parnas and, in accordance with Jewish law, declared his loss in the synagogue, and went to great lengths to search for it in many places and among many people, before he suspected his stepson.

began quarreling, and my father-in-law, of blessed memory, found himself embroiled in the dispute.[133] It ended up costing my father-in-law and Reb Fayvesh more than two thousand reichstaler each[134] in litigation over many years in the Gentile courts. They hounded each other relentlessly. Once Reb Fayvesh caused my father-in-law, of blessed memory, to be arrested,[135] and my father-in-law often caused Reb Fayvesh to be arrested. It continued like this until neither of them had any money left. My father-in-law, however, came out of it better off. Finally people intervened and summoned rabbis and rabbinical judges from the community of Frankfurt to put an end to the matter. They came and spent a long time dealing with the affair, but nothing was arranged; all they did was charge a great deal of money. One of the rabbinical judges was from the town of Gelnhausen, and with the money he brought with him he built himself a nice room and had a goose[136] painted on it; next to the goose stood three or four rabbis dressed in clerical garb, each one of them plucking a feather from the goose.

Afterward my father-in-law, of blessed memory, took his son-in-law Zalman Gans and daughter Yente from Minden and settled them in Hannover; he obtained right of residence there for them and for one child. Hannover was a very important city, so Reb Zalman Gans was happy there and became wealthy. But his happiness was short-lived—he died in his prime. My sister-in-law Yente remained a widow for several years, unwilling to remarry since she was a young, energetic woman. My brother-in-law, the wealthy and honorable Reb Lipman,[137] was lucky that Reb Zalman

133. Reb Fayvesh described the dispute in detail along with the lengthy litigation process (see this Book, n. 130). The event took place in the early 1650s, before Glikl was married and heard her husband's family's side of the story, which was quite different from the other side.

134. The amount (twenty thousand) stipulated in the manuscript must be wrong (see Kaufmann 1896, p. 64; Feilchenfeld 1913, p. 43).

135. In his notes (see this Book, n. 130), Reb Fayvesh says that he never caused the arrest of Zalman Gans or of his father-in-law. He claimed that "all that I did against Gans was in order to save what was mine," and that he never sued Yosef Hamel and never demanded to imprison him or to impound his possessions (see Kaufmann 1896, p. 370).

136. Since "Gans," Reb Fayvesh's surname, means "goose."

137. Lipman Cohen, better known as Leffmann Behrentds/Behrens (1634–1714), was an outstanding court Jew (see *Encyclopedia Judaica* 1972, vol. 4, col. 396; Feilchenfeld 1913, p. 44, n. 12; for more detail, see Stern 1950, pp. 64–72). He lived in Hannover, married Yente, the daughter of Yosef Hamel (the widow of Zalman Gans), and thus became Glikl's brother-in-law (see Family Tree B).

Gans died before he came along.[138] When he married my sister-in-law
Yente, he was not yet the man he is today. But God who is great, who *raises
up and casts down*,[139] has all the power. The privilege to live in Hannover
cost my father-in-law a great deal of money and effort. Once he arranged it,
he thought that this right would remain for his children and his children's
children forever. But who was this good man toiling for? For strangers,[140]
as is written, *leaving their wealth to others*.[141] What can I say? All is as God
wishes in His kindness. That is enough.

The third child[142] of my father-in-law was our master and teacher
R. Shmuel; he too studied in Poland and married a woman from a distinguished family, daughter of an esteemed rabbi; her father was our master
and teacher R. Sholem, head of the rabbinical court in Lemberg.[143] In short,
he was in Poland too; he came here during the war[144] bringing nothing
with him either. My father-in-law, of blessed memory, provided for him,
his wife, and their children for a while. After that he was appointed head of
the rabbinical court in Hildesheim.[145] Why should I write of this at length?
I could never describe what a devout, holy man he was. He knew precisely
when his moment of death was to be; all Hildesheim knows the story.

Then came his fourth child, our master and teacher R. Itsik, of blessed
memory; I did not know him. He lived in the community of Frankfurt.
What a pure soul, what a scholar — this can be judged by those who knew
him. *None did arise like him*.[146] He too was only fifty years old when he
died, having enjoyed prosperity and honor, and with *a good name*.[147] He

138. According to the belief that the deceased make room for the living (see Feilchenfeld 1913, p. 56,
n. 2; and cf. Book Three, n. 5).

139. Cf. 1 Sam 2:6.

140. Glikl's intention is unclear since her sister-in-law Yente had six children with her first husband
and two more with her second husband (see Family Tree B), with whom she lived in Hannover.

141. Ps 49:11.

142. It is, in fact, the fourth, but Glikl does not count the first son, Moshe, who was killed while he
was a youth (see this Book, p. 88), and she continues counting this way until the end of her narrative
about her father-in-law's children.

143. Most probably one of two heads of the rabbinical court in Lemberg called Sholem (see Buber
1895, p. 203).

144. Alludes to Chmielnicki massacres, 1648–1649; see Halpern 1968, p. 211, n. 63.

145. For more details, see Feilchenfeld 1913, p. 45, n. 14.

146. Cf. "nor did any like him arise after him" (2 Kgs 23:25).

147. Cf. b.Berakhot 17a; and see this Book, n. 84.

studied Torah night and day, fulfilling the obligation to *recite it day and night.*[148]

The fifth child was his late daughter Esther,[149] may she rest in peace. It is impossible to put down here what an outstanding, modest woman she was, how much she suffered without showing anger. She bore everything with forbearance, until *her soul departed in purity.*[150] I would like to write at length of this modest woman, her deeds, and her patience, but *my silence is better than my speech.*[151] It suffices that everyone knows what a distinguished woman she was.

His sixth child was Reb Leyb Bonn, a distinguished man. Though not a great scholar, he was well-read, an honest man. For a long time he was parnas of the province of Köln. He lived in Bonn and died very young, *in prosperity and honor.* His seventh child was his late daughter Chana—she can indeed be compared to Hannah[152]—a most upright, devout person. Sadly, she too died young, leaving no fortune. The eighth child was your dear devoted father, of blessed memory. I will not dwell on him here—you will find it in the proper place.[153]

My dear children, I write this for you in case your dear children or grandchildren come to you one of these days, knowing nothing of their family. For this reason I have set this down for you here in brief, so that you might know what kind of people you come from.

After my wedding my husband and I lived for a year in Hamel, where we accomplished very little, since Hamel was not a place of commerce. We did business with the villagers and pawnbroking. My husband, of blessed memory, was not content with that; from the very beginning of our marriage he meant to move to Hamburg, as is written: *"A man is led where he wants to go."*[154] God, great and kind, led us well; if only we still had

---

148. Cf. Josh 1:8.

149. Esther married Leyb Hannover and lived in Hannover (see Kauffman 1896, p. 67, n. 2). Glikl mentions her only once more (see Book Three, p. 108, n. 52). Glikl's following insinuations about Esther's life and death remain unclear.

150. Cf. b.Sanhedrin 68b; and see Rashi's commentary.

151. Cf. b.Yevamot 65a; b.Gittin 46b.

152. An allusion to the biblical Hannah (1 Sam 1:2).

153. This apparently refers to the description that follows.

154. Cf. b.Makkot 10b.

the *crown on our head!*[155] But *the Lord has given, and the Lord has taken away;*[156] what cannot be undone must be endured.

A year after we were married, my husband, of blessed memory, refused to stay in Hamel any longer, although my in-laws would have been very glad for us to stay in Hamel and offered us their house just as it stood, with all its furnishings. But my husband refused. With their permission, we moved here to Hamburg. We were both still inexperienced children, knowing very little or nothing about business dealings in Hamburg; but God who is great and compassionate led my husband away from *his father's house and from his country*[157] and stood by him throughout, faithfully assisting him. *God be blessed for all the kindnesses He has shown us.*

As soon as we reached Hamburg, my father, of blessed memory, wrote out two years' room and board[158] for us, and we lived with him. Now, my husband, as an outsider knowing nothing of the place, looked around, taking stock. The jewelry trade at that time was not as brisk as it is today; married people and engaged youths among the Gentiles wore very little jewelry or none at all. It was the fashion to wear only gold chains; when one wanted to give a present, it too would be of gold. Although there was not as much profit in it as in precious stones, my husband's first deal was in gold trading. He would go from house to house buying up gold, then sell it back to the goldsmiths or to the traders; there was a good profit in it. Although my husband worked hard all day long, running around to close business deals, he never missed his daily study session. For a long time he'd fast on Torah-reading days,[159] until he began taking long trips and was afflicted with pain; he had been very sickly as a child, needing much medical attention. Still, he never spared himself and worked very hard to provide a good living for his wife and children; he was such a devoted father, there are very few men like him. A lot could be written about his exceptional love for his wife and children. He was a remarkably good-tempered man,

155. Allusion to "The crown has fallen from our head" (Lam 5:15), which serves as an expression of woe for the death of the head of the family, here Glikl's husband.
156. Job 1:21.
157. Cf. Gen 12:1.
158. Lit. *kest*, the room and board expenses of the young couple in the early years of their marriage paid for by their parents (see Timm 1999, pp. 46–48).
159. Mondays and Thursdays.

and he never sought any official position. On the contrary, he shunned
the possibility entirely, and scoffed at the kind of people who made such
efforts to gain these positions. In short, he was the perfect embodiment of
a devout Jew, as were his father and brothers. I know very few men, even
great rabbis, who prayed with such conviction as he did, as I know well. If
someone claiming he had a great bargain wished to speak to him while he
was praying in his room, neither I nor anyone in the household dared go
tell him. In this way in fact he incurred the loss of many hundreds. But he
did not account it of any importance, and served God so devotedly, praying
with such conviction, that God repaid him twofold, as is written "*Trust in
the Lord, and the Lord will be your trust.*"[160] How modest and patient was
the dear man, of blessed memory—he was one of a kind. He often suffered
at the hands of those who were close to him as well as those who were not,
accepting it all stoically. In such cases I succumbed to human weakness and
lost my temper; he would laugh at me, saying: "You are naïve—I trust in
God and care little for what people say." May we find favor in this world
and the world to come, thanks to his good deeds.

When we came to Hamburg, I conceived immediately, just when my
mother did, may she live long. At the appointed hour, God graciously
granted me a little girl. I was young, and although it was hard for me, un-
accustomed as I was to such matters, I was very happy that God above had
given me a beautiful, healthy daughter. My dear loyal, devout mother was
also about to give birth and was very pleased that I gave birth first; that way
she could take care of me for a little while longer, as I was still such a young
girl. Eight days later my mother too gave birth to a little girl. There was no
cause for jealousy or recrimination between us.[161] The two of us lay side by
side in the same room. We had no rest, due to all the people who hastened
to see the wonder: a mother and daughter giving birth together, lying in
the same room.

I must recount a most amusing thing that happened to us, to stave off
tedium and lengthen the book a little. It was winter when my mother, may
she live long, and I were lying side by side in the birthing bed, and the heated
room was small. My father, of blessed memory, had a large family and the

160. Cf. Jer 17:7.
161. Probably because neither of them gave birth to a boy.

room grew very crowded, although parents and children accept each other lovingly. I left the birthing bed eight days before my mother. To make the heated room a little less crowded, I went upstairs to sleep in my own bedroom, but since I was still very young, my mother would not allow me to take my baby with me to my room. So I left the baby in my mother's room, where she had the maid with her. My mother told me not to worry at all about the baby: when she cried, the maid would bring her upstairs to me to nurse, then bring her back and put her in her crib, and I agreed to this. I slept in this fashion for several nights; toward midnight the maid would bring me the baby to nurse. One night, I woke up at about three o'clock and said to my husband, of blessed memory: "Why hasn't the maid brought the baby yet?" My husband, of blessed memory, said that the baby was probably still sleeping, but I could not rest, and I ran downstairs to check on my baby. I went to the crib—she was not there. I was frantic, but I did not want to make noise, so as not to startle my mother and wake her. I shook the maid; I wanted to rouse her quietly, but she was sound asleep. I was forced to yell loudly till finally I managed to wake her up. "Where's my baby?" I asked her, but she was talking incomprehensibly in her sleep. With all the commotion my mother woke up too and said to the maid: "For God's sake, where is Gliklchen's baby?" But the maid was so drowsy that she could not answer. I said to my mother: "Mother, maybe my baby is in your bed?" She said: "No, I have my own baby here," clutching the baby tightly as if someone was trying to wrest the baby away from her. It occurred to me that I had seen her baby sleeping peacefully in her crib when I glanced in as I went by. So I said: "Mother, give me my baby—your baby is lying in her crib." She still refused to believe me until I brought her a candle and handed over her baby for her to examine carefully. So I gave my mother her baby and took mine. The entire house woke up in an uproar. But afterward confusion turned to laughter, and people said: "We were just about to summon King Solomon."[162]

During the first year we lived with my parents, even though we had two years' living expenses.[163] But since it was very crowded in my father's house, my husband did not want to stay there any longer, nor would he take a penny from my parents for the second year's living expenses. So we rented

162. To judge which of the two women was the mother of the baby (1 Kgs 3).
163. See this Book, n. 158.

a nice house, paying fifty reichstaler rent for the year, and hoping for good luck we moved into our own house with the servants. God Almighty has provided for us generously there, to this day. Had God not inflicted this blow on us, taking away so soon the crown on my head,[164] I know there would be no happier, more agreeable couple in the whole world. But we must bear everything patiently and pray to God to be compassionate and gracious in afflicting us, for His divine kindness is very great.

We lived in a home of our own; as young people we practiced some economy, yet we did everything properly, as it should be, and ran a well-respected household. Our first servant was Avraham Kantor of Hildesheim; at first we employed him to look after the children. A few years later he left us to engage in some commerce on his own. Then he married a widow from here. She was married to him for a short time until she died; he remarried, a young girl from Amsterdam, and they lived in Hamburg. We gave him an advance and sent him to Copenhagen. In short, today he is a man of means with ten thousand reichstaler and more, so they say.

When my daughter Tsipor was two years old I gave birth again, to my Nathan, may he live long. How happy my husband was![165] Impossible to describe the lavish circumcision ceremony my husband, of blessed memory, gave. May God, blessed be He, grant me many such occasions with all my children. Sadly, I no longer have any consolation or help, except for the kindnesses I hope to receive from my children, so I pray to mighty God to add His own graciousness and compassion.

With this I conclude my second book. I ask all who read this to think well of my foolishness. As I said, it stems from hardship and affliction. And so, with the help of God, who gives me strength to bear all my afflictions — praised be He, *who gives strength to the weary*[166] — I begin my third book, with the help of God above.

END OF BOOK TWO

---

164. See this Book, n. 155.
165. Because a male child was born.
166. Cf. Isa 40:29, and among the preliminary morning blessings (see Siddur 2016, p. 28).

BOOK THREE

Who can, who should, write or recount everything that happens to us in our lifetime, we mortal sinners, and all the amazing events that befall us? When I was about twenty-five years old, my husband, of blessed memory, was very preoccupied with his business affairs; although still young, I did my part by his side. I do not write this to praise myself — my husband, of blessed memory, did not take advice from anyone but did whatever the two of us decided together.

At that time there was a young man in Hannover, Mordechai, may God avenge his death, who worked for my brother-in-law Reb Lipman.[1] This young man came to Hamburg and stayed with us. In brief, we took a liking to the young man and engaged him to travel for us on business wherever we decided to send him. The young man was from Poland and spoke fluent Polish. So we sent him to Danzig,[2] where we had heard there were plenty of ounce pearls[3] for sale; most of the jewelry trade in those days was in ounce pearls. We provided him with a letter of credit for several hundred reichstaler and sent him off to Danzig after instructing him a little about buying pearls. Had we given more thought at the time to buying jewelry in Danzig than to selling it, we would have made a lot more, but everyone was so caught up in trading in ounce pearls that they gave no thought to any other kind of business. This same Mordechai, may God avenge his death, then set out for Danzig where he began buying pearls and sending them here;[4] his buying went very well, with a good profit.

1. Reb Lipman was the second husband of Yente, the sister of Glikl's husband, who lived in Hannover (see Book Two, p. 91, n. 137).
2. A port city in Poland bordering with Germany; two fairs were held there annually — on August 4 and November 11 (see *Pinkas Va'ad Arba Aratsot* 1945, p. 543).
3. Small pearls of various sizes sold by weight and not by piece, thus designated according to their weight in ounces (see Verdenhalven 1968, p. 50). Merchants subsequently sorted and resold them according to size, and this was quite profitable (see Feilchenfeld 1913, p. 55, n. 1).
4. "Here" refers to Hamburg, where Glikl lived at the time of these events.

This same Mordechai, may God avenge his death, being of marriageable age, did not wish to remain in Danzig any longer; he wanted to marry, so he came here and was immediately betrothed to the daughter of the late Lang Nathan,[5] and he set an engagement period of only six months. My husband, of blessed memory, wanted Mordechai to go to Danzig again in the meantime, before his wedding, but unfortunately it was ordained in heaven that he did not want to go to Danzig, saying: "My wedding day is in less than six months. It takes time to travel there and back, and I want to go to Germany to buy wine." Said my husband, of blessed memory: "What are you talking about, buying wine? I want nothing to do with your wine dealings." Said Mordechai, may God avenge his death: "If you don't want anything to do with it, I will buy it on my own, with my own money." My husband, of blessed memory, did not like this and tried to persuade him both by cajoling and by reproaching, but sadly to no avail; Mordechai was so set on the ill-fated journey that no one could dissuade him. My husband, of blessed memory, dispatched Mordechai's future father-in-law to speak to him and try to dissuade him from making the ill-fated journey, all to no avail. He was so obstinate that no one could make him change his mind. Apparently this good man was meant to make room for someone else,[6] for if God had kept him alive, perhaps Reb Yudah and Issachar Katz[7] would not have made their fortunes, as will be told presently.

As I wrote, Mordechai, may God avenge his death, refused to be dissuaded, nor did my husband, of blessed memory, want to enter into partnership with him in the wine business. He therefore went at his own expense, taking with him about six hundred reichstaler. When he reached Hannover, he gave his money to my brother-in-law Reb Lipman for him to transfer it to where he meant to buy the wine. Now, to leave Hannover he had to get to Hildesheim; but he, may God avenge his death, was an extremely tight-fisted man, and he refused to pay the expense of traveling by post chaise.[8] More precisely, God, blessed be He, did not wish this. So,

5. "Long" or "Tall" Nathan was probably called so due to his height. In the course of time, the adjective became a surname.

6. See Book Two, n. 138.

7. Both, Yudah Berlin (or Berliner) and Issachar Katz (Cohen) worked for Chaim Hamel when they were young and afterward became very wealthy.

8. On this form of transportation during Glikl's time, see Book Two, p. 86.

Hannover being only three miles from Hildesheim, he walked; he walked to Hildesheim alone. As he approached Hildesheim, being no further away than the distance permitted to walk on the Sabbath,[9] he encountered a villager, a poacher, who says: "Jew, give me money for a drink or I'll shoot you." Mordechai, may God avenge his death, mocked him, because the road from Hannover to Hildesheim is as safe as that from Hamburg to Altona. The poacher repeated: "You dirty Jew, what are you thinking so much for? Say yes or no." In the end the poacher drew his weapon and shot Mordechai right in the head, may God avenge his death, and he fell dead on the spot.

This road is never quiet for even a quarter of an hour, yet bad luck would have it that there were no passersby just then. That was the end destined for this good, decent, trustworthy young man, at an early age. Instead of being proud on his wedding day, he was made to crawl into the dark earth in such horrible circumstances. Oh God, when I think of it now, my hair stands on end; he was truly a good, honest, God-fearing young man. Had God spared his life, he would have achieved great things, and we would have done well too. God knows how my husband, of blessed memory, and I mourned and grieved over him, as will be told presently. After he lay there for a while in his own young blood, people started coming from Hildesheim and found him in that terrible condition, recognizing him instantly, as he was well known throughout the whole country. They thereupon interceded on his behalf and had him buried without delay. Words cannot describe the sorrow and grief throughout the whole country. But what good was all that? His young life was over. People from Hannover and Hildesheim wrote us about it right away, since they knew that he, may God avenge his death, was in partnership with us, and they supposed that he must have been carrying a lot of our money on him. But he had only several reichstaler for travel expenses. When we received those letters, I was pregnant with my daughter Matte,[10] of blessed memory; it can easily be imagined how shocked we were, my husband, of blessed memory, and I, and how we grieved, as I said,

---

9. A Jew is permitted to walk up to two thousand cubits from his place of residence on the Sabbath (see Lewinsky 1975, p. 801).

10. Matte was Glikl's third child (see Family Tree C). The addition of the formula "of blessed memory" reflects the point in time at which Glikl is writing and not, of course, the period she is describing.

for he was a thoroughly honest, upright man with whom we could have done a lot of business. But what is done cannot be undone; especially where death is concerned, we must leave everything to God above. Despite the extensive investigation held in Hannover and Hildesheim with the purpose of revenging the murder,[11] it proved futile because the murderer, may his name be blotted out, escaped and was seen no more. May God avenge Mordechai's death and the death of all the other holy, pious martyrs.

Thus we were left with no one we could employ to do business for us, but after a short while the distinguished Reb Yudah Berliner[12] and Reb Yakov Obernkirchen arrived here. This same Reb Yakov, a matchmaker, had proposed a match between the said Reb Yudah and the daughter of Pinchas Harburg; but this was not ordained by God, blessed be He. On whose account was it canceled — I do not know. This same Reb Yudah spent some time in my house since he was related by marriage to my husband, of blessed memory. Reb Yudah and my brother-in-law Reb Lipman were second cousins.[13] After he had been with us for some weeks, we found him most agreeable in every way. He was very knowledgeable[14] and astute in business too, very sharp. My husband, of blessed memory, says to me: "Gliklchen,[15] what do you think of our employing this young man and sending him to Danzig? He seems a clever young man." So I say to my husband, of blessed memory: "The same thought crossed my mind several times, because we need someone again." So we spoke to him, and he agreed immediately; before eight days had gone by, he was on his way to Danzig. What he had[16] was *all that he owned*:[17] amber worth twenty or

---

11. See Book Two, n. 118.

12. On Reb Yudah Berliner, see this Book, nn. 7, 18, and the index of names. The title *katzin* (rendered here as "distinguished" and very wealthy lay leader of the community) befits his status at the time of writing (see this Book, n. 154), not during the period described here.

13. Reb Yudah's father, Eliezer Lipman, and Reb Lipman's mother, Leah, were brother and sister. Reb Lipman Cohen was Glikl's brother-in-law since he was married to Yente, the sister of Glikl's husband (see Family Tree B; Kaufmann 1806, p. 79, n. 1).

14. In religious matters (see Kaufmann 1896, p. 79, n. 2).

15. Term of endearment and diminutive form of Glikl (which is itself the diminutive of Gluk (see Landau 1901, pp. 39–40).

16. This refers to the possessions he had when he came to Hamburg.

17. Cf. Gen 25:5, 24:36, 25:5, 36:6, and many more.

thirty reichstaler, which he left with my husband, of blessed memory, to sell or keep for him. You see, my dear children, when faithful God wishes to help someone, He can turn a little into a lot; this little capital that was nothing at all brought Reb Yudah his great wealth, and he became the prominent man he is today.[18] Reb Yudah stayed in Danzig for some time, doing good business there, that is, he was buying ounce pearls but did not make much effort to seek out more deals, for at that time credit was not as easily obtainable in Hamburg as it is now, and we were still young, without much money. Nevertheless, we provided him with letters of credit, and from time to time we also sent him bills of exchange, so he was not lacking for funds. He stayed there for about two years, then returned here. My husband, of blessed memory, calculated his earnings and gave him eight or nine hundred reichstaler, his share of the profits. With that money he went to Hannover to hang about and look for a match.

In the meantime, I gave birth to my late daughter Matte.[19] She was a beautiful child, as shall be recounted presently. At that time people were starting to talk about Shabtai Tzvi,[20] but *woe unto us, for we have sinned*[21] and have not lived to see the fulfillment of what we heard of and clung to in our thoughts. When I recall how young and old alike all over the world began repenting of their sins, as is well known, it cannot be described. Ah God, Lord of the universe, we were hoping that You, compassionate God, would have mercy on Israel, Your wretched people, and redeem us. We hoped for this fervently, as a woman on the birthstool, in great labor and anguish, expects that after all her pain and suffering she will rejoice in her child. But after all her pain and suffering, nothing came but wind.[22]

The same thing, my great God and king, happened to us. We heard the

18. At the time that this was written, Reb Yudah (Jost Liebmann) was already one of the wealthiest and most prominent court Jews; he supplied jewels to the first King of Prussia as well as to his father before him (see this Book, p. 134, n. 154).

19. See this Book, p. 101, n. 10.

20. Glikl is talking about the end of 1665, when the first letters of the Sabbatean movement reached Hamburg on November 30, 1665 (see this Book, n. 26). For a comprehensive discussion of the report by Glikl on Shabtai Tzvi, and that of others, see Carlebach 2001, pp. 238–253.

21. Lam 5:16.

22. This is apparently a delicate way of saying that the woman did not give birth but only let out gas (see following text for further references to this idiom).

tidings, and all your beloved servants and children strove to engage in repentance, prayer, and charity all over the world, and your beloved people of Israel sat on the birthstool, yet after all that arduous repentance, prayer, and charity during the two or three years[23] they sat on the birthstool — nothing came but wind. Not only were we denied the sight of the child we had made such efforts for, going so far with our belief that we were completely convinced — alas, because of our many sins[24] we were left just as we were. Yet, my God and master, Your people Israel do not despair; they await Your mercy daily that You may redeem them. *Even though he may tarry, still I await him every day.*[25] When this becomes Your holy wish, You will surely remember Your people Israel.

What joy every time we received letters[26] — indescribable. Most of the letters were for the Sephardim,[27] who would bring them to their synagogue to read aloud. The Ashkenazim too, young and old alike, went to the Sephardi synagogue.[28] Every time the young Portuguese men would don their best clothes with a wide sash of green silk[29] — the costume of Shabtai Tzvi. In this way they all went to their synagogue *with timbrel and dance*[30]

23. This period of time goes far beyond Shabtai Tzvi's conversion to Islam: the first news regarding him as the messiah was received in November 1665 (see this Book, n. 26), and his conversion took place on September 5, 1666 (see Scholem 1973, p. 673); thus, less than a year had passed between these two events. Glikl's report of this time period apparently reflects what she remembers of peoples' expectations of redemption during that period (and see this Book, p. 105, n. 37).

24. Not always is the formula "because of our many sins" used in its literal meaning. Quite often it means "alas," "woe is me / us," "unfortunately," "regretfully," and the like.

25. From Maimonides's "Thirteen Principles," see Siddur 2016, p. 24.

26. On the letters concerning Shabtai Tzvi that arrived in Hamburg between the end of November 1665 (see this Book, n. 20) and February 1666, see Scholem 1973, pp. 569–574.

27. On this and on what happened to the Sephardi community in the wake of the news of Shabtai Tzvi, see Studemund-Halévy 2000, pp. 202–212; see also Scholem 1973, pp. 569, 573. On the Sephardim, see Book Two, p. 62, n. 20.

28. The fact that Ashkenazim would go to the Sephardim's synagogue, known as the Portuguese Synagogue, was considered an unusual occurrence since both communities usually kept themselves separate from one another (see Richarz 2001, p. 19). This is confirmed by Glikl's scant references to the Sephardim in her memoirs and the nature of her contact with this community (see here and also Book Two, n. 20; Book Four, pp. 158–159, 192, n. 54; and Book Five, p. 198, n. 5).

29. On the green sash worn by Shabtai Tzvi, see Scholem 1973, p. 674, n. 238; a green coat that he wore is also mentioned (p. 241). Scholem neglects to mention that green is the symbolic color of Islam and Mohammed's descendants, and that Jews were prohibited from wearing it. Shabtai Tzvi must have made use of this color as an act of defiance against Islam.

30. Cf. Exod 15:20; Judg 11:34.

as during *the rejoicing of Beit Ha-Shoʾeva*[31] and read the letters aloud. Some of them, poor things, sold everything they owned,[32] home and all, in daily hope of redemption. My late father-in-law was then living in Hamel; he now left his *house and all its good things*[33] and moved to the community of Hildesheim.[34] He sent to us in Hamburg two large barrels containing an assortment of linens with foodstuffs such as peas, beans, dried meat,[35] and other groceries like prunes, anything that would keep, for this good man, of blessed memory, thought people would simply depart and make the journey from Hamburg[36] to the Holy Land. Those barrels stood in my house for over a year. Finally, fearing that the meat and other perishables would spoil, they wrote telling us to open the barrels and take out the food-stuffs so that the linens would not be ruined. The barrels stood like this for three years and more,[37] for he believed he would be needing them for his journey. But this was not yet the desire of God Almighty. We know well what God most high promised us, and had we been righteous, upright, and not so wicked, I know for certain that God, blessed be He, would have mercy on us, if only we had observed *love your fellow as yourself.*[38] But God have mercy, look how we do observe it! The envy, the groundless hatred among us! This cannot bring us anything good. Yet, my revered God and master, the fulfillment of Your promises to us shall come, with majestic glory and graciousness. And though it may tarry ever so long due to our sins, it shall certainly come, at Your appointed hour. We hope for this and pray that You, great God, will let us rejoice in perfect redemption one day.

31. About the celebration of *Beit Ha-Shoʾeva* (the place of water drawing), the sages said: "Anyone who has never seen the rejoicing at the place of [water] drawing, has never seen rejoicing in all his days" (m.Sukkot 5:1).

32. See Kaufmann 1896, p. 82, n. 1. On reports of Jews from various places selling all that they owned in the expectation that redemption would shortly arrive, see Scholem 1973, pp. 475, 477, 532, 553–554, 558–559, and more. Glikl's account regarding her father-in-law's preparations for his departure to the land of Israel is mentioned in Scholem 1973, p. 588.

33. Cf. "and houses full of all good things" (Deut 6:11).

34. For a different reason for his move to Hildesheim, see Book Four, p. 153, n. 35.

35. Meat that was dried by smoking or by being hung outdoors to preserve it.

36. Probably because Hamburg was a port town.

37. On the expectations, see Scholem 1973, p. 587, n. 319; p. 756, n. 188; pp. 788–789; see also this Book, n. 23.

38. Cf. Lev 19:18.

Let me then conclude this matter for the time being and begin again.[39] When I gave birth to my daughter Matte, rumors started spreading in Hamburg that there was, God preserve us!, a plague in town, heaven forfend![40] The plague worsened and three or four Jewish homes were contaminated, due to our many sins, and all the inhabitants died one by one until the houses stood practically empty. It was a time of great distress; the dead were treated very poorly,[41] God preserve us. Most of the households moved from Hamburg to Altona, with pledges worth several thousand reichstaler; the pledges ranged in worth from ten to thirty reichstaler, and even one hundred reichstaler, because a pawnshop has to give loans against pledges worth eight schillings just as against those worth twenty reichstaler. The plague — heaven forfend! — spread to the entire city, God preserve us, and the residents gave us no peace. Although we knew they were infected, we had to allow them to redeem their pledges; had we moved to Altona, they would have followed us there too. So we decided to go to Hamel with our small children, since my father-in-law, of blessed memory, was living there at the time.[42] One day after Yom Kippur we straightaway left Hamburg, reaching Hannover one day before the Festival of Sukkot.[43] We stayed with my brother-in-law, our master and teacher R. Avraham, who was still living in Hannover then.[44] Since the festival was about to begin, they did not want to let us continue on our journey. So we spent Sukkot in Hannover. With me were my daughter Tsipor, four years old, and my son Nathan, two years old, may they live long, and my daughter Matte, of blessed memory, who was about eight weeks old. My brother-in-law Reb Leyb Han-

39. Here Glikl returns to the birth of her daughter, Matte, which was previously mentioned (see this Book, p. 103) and served as the point of departure for the account of Shabtai Tzvi.

40. This expression is used to ward off the evil previously mentioned. According to Feilchenfeld, the plague commenced in July 1664 (see Feilchenfeld 1913, p. 63, n. 8), but this date does not accord with the chronology in the narrative: Glikl's daughter Matte was eight weeks old when the family fled from Hamburg due to the plague (see following text). According to Glikl, Matte was born before Shabtai Tzvi became a topic of discussion, that is, at the end of 1665 (on chronological issues, see Marwedel 2001b).

41. On the problems of burying the dead during a plague, see Turniansky 1988, pp. 194–195.

42. Hence, the plague occurred before her father-in-law moved to Hildesheim (see this Book, n. 34).

43. This means that they traveled for three days. See map for the route from Hamburg to Hamel, which passes through Hannover.

44. Later on, R. Avraham, the brother of Glikl's husband, moved to Hamel (see Book Two, p. 89).

nover[45] invited us to spend the first days of Sukkot with him; there was a synagogue in Reb Leyb's house. On the holiday, my husband, of blessed memory, was in the synagogue, while I was downstairs in the heated room, about to dress my daughter Tsipor.

I must write of a small misfortune that we had when my husband, of blessed memory, was still alive, and of other troublesome cares that often cannot be expressed in words, especially now, alas. Who can I complain to now, who can I tell this to? We have *no one to rely upon but our Father in Heaven*[46] to help us and the rest of Israel and *He gives us joy for as long as He has afflicted us.*[47] It is true that even during my husband's lifetime we had worries here and there because of *the pain of bringing up children;*[48] some of these can be told, others should not or cannot be told. But my beloved companion could console me for all my troubles, and when all my cares were upon me, his comforting words eased all my woes. But who will console me now? Who will listen to the anguished thoughts of a sad heart, as my dear beloved husband said even on his deathbed, less than half an hour before his pure soul expired. My pious mother fell across his bed weeping, saying: "My dear son-in-law, don't you want to tell me something or give me some instructions?" He replied: "Mother dear, I don't know what to say or what instructions to give, just that you console my poor Gliklchen." After that he wished to say no more, as will be told later, in the proper place.[49] So who will console me? To whom can I pour out my bitter distress, where can I turn? Right now I am simply drowning in troubles and black thoughts, woe is me! Indeed, several bad things happened to us, as recounted next. This too was a real misfortune, which kind God promptly removed, in His gracious compassion.

Let me begin once more from where I left off. While I was dressing my daughter Tsipor, may she live long, the girl twisted in my arms at my touch. I say: "Dearest Tsipor, what's bothering you?" The girl says: "Mother dear-

45. Leyb Hannover was the husband of Esther, the sister of Glikl's husband (see Book Two, p. 83, n. 149).
46. Cf. m.Sotah 9:15 (beraita). See also Book One, n. 64.
47. Cf. Ps 90:15.
48. Cf. b.Shabbat 89b; b.Eruvin 100b.
49. For the description of the situation, see Book Five, p. 199.

est, I have a terrible pain under my arm." So I look to see what she had there, and I see a suppurating sore under her arm.[50] My maid was with me there. When my husband, of blessed memory, had a similar small sore, a barber-surgeon[51] in Hannover dressed it with a small bandage. So I tell the maid: "Go to Chaim — he's upstairs in the synagogue — and ask him which barber-surgeon he went to and where he lives. Take the girl there for him to bandage her arm."

I was not thinking of anything bad. The maid enters the synagogue and asks my husband, of blessed memory, where the barber-surgeon lived, and he tells her. In order to get to the men's section, you have to pass through the women's section. The maid was just walking out when my late sisters-in-law Yente, Sulke, and Esther,[52] who were sitting in the synagogue, ask her: "What were you doing in the men's section?" The maid replies innocently, she too not thinking of anything bad: "Our little girl has a sore under her arm, so I asked my employer which barber-surgeon treated him for his sore. I'll take the child there." The women were immediately terrified, being big cowards about such matters anyway, given that we had come from Hamburg under such a threat.[53] Well, they leaned their heads together and discussed it. Now, in the synagogue there was also an old Polish woman, a guest.[54] She overhears the story and sees how frightened my sisters-in-law are, so she says: "Don't be frightened, nothing will happen. I've been dealing with this kind of business for over twenty years. If you like, I'll go downstairs to examine the little girl. I'll tell you right away if it's dangerous, God forbid, and what you have to do." "Yes, for God's sake, go examine her well so that we do not endanger ourselves, God forbid!" they said.

I knew nothing of all this. The old Polish woman comes downstairs, say-

50. This was a characteristic symptom of the plague.
51. On barber-surgeons, see Book Two, p. 88, n. 117.
52. Yente was the sister of Glikl's husband, the widow of Zalman Gans, and the wife of Lipman Cohen; Sulke was the wife of R. Avraham, the brother of Glikl's husband; and Esther — the sister of Glikl's husband and the wife of Leyb Hannover (see Family Tree B).
53. Referring to their fear of the plague, which caused Glikl's family to leave Hamburg (see this Book, p. 106 and elsewhere), and clearly the child's sore increased this fear.
54. This Jewish woman, as well as the Polish man mentioned later on (this Book, p. 110, n. 61) were two of the many "itinerant mendicants" from Poland who visited Ashkenazi communities during this period (see Halpern 1968, p. 409, explanation 2).

ing, "Where is the little girl?" "Why?" I say. She says: "I am a healer.[55] I'll give the girl something that will make her feel better immediately." Fearing nothing, I lead the girl to her; she examines the little girl then dashes away from her back upstairs to the women, causing panic among them, and tells the women: "Run away, all of you who can flee, for you have, alas, the genuine plague in the house. The little girl has the genuine pestilence, heaven forfend!"

Well, easy to imagine the commotion and screaming among the women, especially such big cowards. Men and women all left the synagogue at a run, right in the middle of the most important prayers on the holy festival day, mercy upon us. Hastily they thrust the maid and the little girl out the door; no one wanted them in the house, and they would not let them inside. It's easy to understand how we felt. I kept crying and screaming, begging, in God's name: "My friends, think twice of what you are doing. My daughter has nothing wrong with her. You can see for yourselves that my daughter is healthy and well, thank God. The girl had a head cold with runny nose, poor thing. Before leaving Hamburg I applied some ointment, and it went from her head to the sore. When you catch something like this,[56] God forbid, you get ten different symptoms.[57] Just look, my child is running around in the street eating a roll." But all to no avail. "If this gets out," they said, "and His Excellency the Duke hears that there is such a thing in his city,[58] God forbid, what a catastrophe it will be!" The old woman stood before me and said right to my face that she was prepared to put her head on the block if it turned out that the child had nothing whatsoever wrong with her. What were we to do? I pleaded: "For pity's sake, let me stay with the child. Wherever my child goes, I go too. Let me go to her!" But they refused this too. In short, my brothers-in-law, our master and teacher R. Avraham Segal, Reb Lipman, and Reb Leyb immediately sat down to consult with their wives to see what could be done: where to hide the maid and the girl; how to keep it from the authorities. We would all be

---

55. A woman who cares for sick people using traditional medicine.
56. Glikl avoids mentioning the term "plague."
57. For the ten symptoms of the plague, see Katz 1707, 129b.
58. Hannover was the *Residenzstadt* of the duke (Herzog), who was from the young dynasty of the house of Braunschweig-Lüneburg (see Feilchenfeld 1913, p. 67, n. 11a).

in grave danger, God help us, if the duke found out. It was decided to dress the maid and the girl in old tattered rags and send them to a village less than the Sabbath limit's distance from Hannover—the village was called Hainholz[59]—there they would go to the home of one of the villagers, saying that the Jews of Hannover would not invite them to spend the festival days with them, on the grounds that there were already too many beggars in Hannover, and would not let them enter the city. They wished therefore to spend the holy days in the village, staying with them and compensating them for their trouble. "We're sure that they will send us food and drink[60] from Hannover; they would not leave us without food and make us suffer hunger on the holy days."

There was an old man from Poland[61] staying in Hannover. We hired this man to go with the old Polish woman and accompany the maid and the little girl for a few days until we knew how things stood. However, the two of them refused to budge before being paid thirty reichstaler in cash for putting themselves at such risk. So my brothers-in-law our master and teacher R. Avraham Segal, Reb Lipman, and Reb Leyb sat down to discuss with the Hannover community's teacher, who was also a scholar,[62] whether it was permitted to desecrate the festival by giving them money on the holy day. Finally they agreed among themselves to pay them, saying it was a time of peril and lives were at stake.[63] So—we were to send our dear little girl away on the holy festival day and pretend we believed there was something wrong with her, God forbid. I will let any good father or mother judge for themselves how we felt. My husband, of blessed memory, stood in a corner, *weeping and pleading*, while I stood in the other.[64] Surely it was thanks to my devout husband's good deeds that God heeded him, as is written *"and the Lord responded to his plea."*[65] I do not believe that our father Abraham

---

59. Today a suburb of Hannover (see Landau 1901, p. 66 and map).

60. Most certainly due to kashrut (Jewish dietary laws) considerations.

61. A Jewish "itinerant mendicant," as the Polish woman mentioned earlier (see this Book, n. 54).

62. Since this refers to a scholarly discussion on the Jewish law, the scholar was included.

63. According to the rule in Jewish law that "saving a life takes precedence over the Sabbath."

64. Cf. Rashi's commentary on Gen 25:21: "This man stands in a corner and prays and this woman stands in a corner and prays." (see also the following note and Feilchenfeld 1913, p. 69, n. 14); "weeping and pleading," cf. Hos 12:5.

65. Cf. Gen 25:21.

felt any more pain at the binding of Isaac than we did at that moment; for our father Abraham acted on divine command, out of love for God, blessed be He, therefore he bore his misery cheerfully. But as for us, this blow came when we were among strangers[66] and weighed down our hearts. But what can you do? We must bear it all, *just as one says a blessing for a good hap, so should he say one for an evil hap.*[67] I dressed my maid in clothes turned inside-out and bundled up a few things for the child, tying the bundle on the maid as if she were a beggar-woman. I dressed the poor girl in old tattered rags too; they walked along in this way, my good maid and my beloved little girl with the old man and old woman to the village.

It's easy to imagine the nature of the priestly blessing[68] we said upon parting from the girl, and how we shed hundreds of tears at leaving her. Although the girl was as cheerful and gay as any child who understands nothing, poor thing, we all — all of us in Hannover — were *weeping and pleading,*[69] and we spent the holy day in sadness.

And so they went to the village and were welcomed at their lodgings in the home of one of the villagers, since they had money, and money always helps. The villager asked them: "Isn't today your festival day? Why then aren't you staying with the Jews?" Their answer was that there were already many beggars in Hannover, so they had been denied entry to the city; yet they were sure that the Jews of Hannover would send them food during the holy days.

We returned together to the synagogue, but the services were already over. Reb Yudah Berliner was in Hannover at that time, still a bachelor,[70] and had been doing some business with us. There was also someone called Reb Michl[71] there, a young man from Poland who taught the children.[72]

66. That is, outside of Hamburg, their hometown.

67. Cf. b.Berakhot 48b, 54a; m.Berakhot 9:5.

68. When parting from friends and relatives, Ashkenazi Jews used to recite the priestly blessing (Num 6:24–27). This is the source of the saying *"birkas kohanim nachsagen."* See Sadan 1975, vol. 2, pp. 9–11; Feilchenfeld 1913, p. 70, n. 15; Tendlau 1860, p. 361.

69. See this Book, n. 64.

70. As mentioned earlier in this Book, Reb Yudah was then in Hannover looking for a match.

71. "Michl" or "Mechl" is the "secular" version of the Hebrew name Yechiel. The combination "Yechiel-Michl" was prevalent among Polish Jews (see following text).

72. Teachers of young children (*melamdim*) from Poland in Hamburg and throughout Germany were a widespread phenomenon in Ashkenaz at that time; see Book Five, pp. 223–224.

He later married a woman from Hildesheim, where he lives now, a well-respected, wealthy man, and a leader of the Hildesheim community. This same Reb Michl was also a part-time servant, as is the custom in Ashkenaz, where young men such as he are employed to teach the children. When we left the synagogue, Reb Leyb sent for us to come to the meal, for, as I mentioned, he had invited us to stay in his house on the eve of the festival; but it is not hard to imagine how we felt. My husband, of blessed memory, said: "Before we eat anything, I must bring some food to my little girl and to the others — it is a festival day, after all." They said: "Yes, obviously, you're right, none of us will eat a thing until some food is brought to those outside," for it was very close to Hannover, the same distance as from Altona to Hamburg. So some food was collected; everybody contributed something. But who would take it to them? Everyone was reluctant. Said Reb Yudah: "I'll take it to them." "I'll go with him," said Reb Michl; my husband, of blessed memory, accompanied them too, because he loved the little girl so dearly. But the people of Hannover did not trust my husband, thinking: "If he goes with them, he won't be able to help going near the child." So my brother-in-law Reb Lipman was obliged to accompany them too.

So they all went together to bring the food. The maid with the girl and their escort[73] were so hungry that they had gone to take a walk in the fields, poor things. When the poor girl saw my husband, of blessed memory, she was filled with joy and wanted to run to her father, as any child would. Reb Lipman, my brother-in-law, shouted out to them to hold the girl, that the old man should come get the food. They had to restrain my husband too, as with a rope, to keep him from approaching the dear child. Now both he and the little girl were wailing, because my husband, of blessed memory, could see that she was safe and sound, thank God, but he was not permitted to go to her. They therefore placed the food and drink on the grass, and the maid and her escort went to get it. Then my husband, of blessed memory, left with his companions. It went on like this until Shmini Atzeret.[74] The old man and old woman had bandages and ointment for

73. Meaning the old Polish man and woman who accompanied the child and the servant (see earlier).
74. Shmini Atzeret ("the assembly of the eighth day") directly follows the festival of Sukkot, which is celebrated for seven days.

dressing the sore, and it healed nicely. Indeed, the child was healthy and well, gamboling around the field like a young ram. We said to the Hannoverians: "What was the point of your nonsense? You see that our little girl is healthy and well, thank God, and presents no danger whatsoever, thank God. Let the poor child come back here." Once again they held a consultation but decided not to allow the little girl and her escorts to return to Hannover before Simḥat Torah.[75] What could we do? We had to accept this as well. On Simḥat Torah, then, Reb Michl went to fetch the girl and her escorts and bring them back to Hannover. Anyone could see our joy, mine and my husband's, of blessed memory, and that of all those present, until all could not help weeping with joy. *The eye weeps and the heart rejoices.*[76] They all wanted to gobble her up[77] — never was there such a beautiful, gracious child. For a long time the girl was called nothing but "the Maiden of Hainholz." And so, my dear children, this unfortunate incident ended well, in joy and happiness; we cannot praise and thank God Almighty enough for this, for showing me, his unworthy servant, such gracious compassion. Were I to write ten books, still I could not describe everything. For in everything that great, gracious God causes to happen to me I see and feel His great compassion.

I will not recount all the various sicknesses, God preserve us, that I often had to endure with my dear children, until many times I wished I could sacrifice half of what I have for my children to be restored to health. But the one righteous God aided me in His mercy, truly in the blink of an eye, with such compassion that I knew not where the suffering had gone. God the righteous removed our burdensome affliction of so many years, the cause of such anxiety, all at once, and restored our child safe and sound; for this we will forever and ever give thanks to God above. May almighty God continue thus. See what our faithful God does: when we feel utterly helpless and disconsolate, He comes to our aid, just when we least expect it. And since we do not merit this, it must surely be due to the mercy of the heavenly Father. For I, a sinner, consider myself unworthy of

75. Simḥat Torah ("rejoicing in the Torah"), celebrated the day after Shmini Atzeret (see previous note).

76. For possible sources of this expression, see Turniansky 2006a, p. 232, n. 128.

77. Idiomatic expression used to highlight the amazement that the girl arouses in those who see her.

the compassion of our faithful God, who gives me life and provides for me so that I may live in dignity, to this day, in addition to the thousands of other kindnesses that He, almighty God, has so generously done for me. Were I to kneel down every single day and pray to merciful God, it would be nothing at all compared with what He has done for us mortal sinners. While things do not always go according to our wishes, and we, as human beings, are sometimes disappointed by our children or by strangers, I suppose these must be debts we incur on account of our deeds. For we sin every day, every hour, every moment, failing to serve God above as we should. Yet He continues to show us kindness, blessed be He, for which we are eternally grateful to Him. All I ask of our great Maker is the patience to accept whatever befalls us miserable mortal sinners with love, and to give thanks and praise to almighty God for everything, since everything comes from Him; the Lord has given, and the Lord has taken away, blessed be the name of the Lord forevermore.[78]

Here is a nice story[79] showing what happened to an empress who accepted all her afflictions with forbearance, and the outcome. Emperor Charlemagne was a powerful emperor, as is written in all the books in *taytsh*.[80] It so happened that he was without a wife at the time. He and his counsellors therefore considered it favorable that he should become betrothed to Empress Irene of the Eastern lands, who had no husband and reigned all alone over the entire Empire of the East.[81] And so Emperor Charlemagne sent a delegation of dignitaries to Empress Irene to seek her hand in marriage, hoping that the Empires of Germany and of the East would in this way become conjoined in love, friendship, and harmony. So Charlemagne's envoys were dispatched to Constantinople to ask the empress in his name if she would be his empress and have a treaty of lasting peace between the two kingdoms. Empress Irene was not altogether indif-

---

78. Cf. Job 1:21 in Yiddish translation.

79. The oldest source of the following story on the Byzantine Empress Irene of Constantinople (752–803) is the *Chronographia* (or *Chronicles*) of Teophanes (758–818); see http://www.roman -emperors.org/irene.htm. On Glikl's version, see this Book, n. 83.

80. The term *taytsh* (from *deutsch*) was used by Glikl and her contemporaries to designate their Jewish language (Yiddish) as well as German, the language of their environment. The same applies to the term *loshn Ashkenaz* (the language of Ashkenaz).

81. Irene was regent from 797 to 802. On her character in the tale, see this Book, n. 83.

ferent and said she would return the appropriate response in the course of the coming days.

The emperor's envoys were delighted with this reply and waited expectantly for her to accept the offer so that they could bring their emperor such a valuable prize. They wished to hold festivities in Constantinople; in return, the entire city would gleefully turn out to welcome them. And so they awaited the empress's final reply. But, my God, what a change came over the pious empress in so short a time; instead of concluding the matter of the marriage as expected, the envoys were obliged to witness a most saddening occurrence with their own eyes, when Empress Irene was removed from the throne in their very presence and summarily deposed. For a nobleman of Constantinople's patricians, by the name of Nikephoros or Nikephor, having declared himself emperor and gained much support, now got all the kingdom's servants on his side and hastily had himself crowned emperor.

Right after the coronation, he approached Empress Irene in person with placating words, speaking to her from his treacherous heart in a conciliatory manner as he began justifying himself at inordinate length, saying that everything that had been done, had been done against his will; he himself would have liked nothing better than to remain in his former lowly position and serve her forevermore, as befitting a loyal servant. But since the most prominent gentlemen in the kingdom, along with the ordinary folk, all wished to relieve her of the heavy burden of ruling the realm so that she could take her ease, they had decided together to charge him — although he considered himself totally unworthy — with the heavy duties of kingship. However, in the end — in order to avert catastrophe and all kinds of unpleasantness — he too had given his consent and was obliged to accept the elevated position offered to him. He hoped this would not cause her chagrin and that she would neither hide nor withhold from him secrets of state and of the imperial treasury. Furthermore, if he had been anxious even beforehand to ensure that no harm befall her, all the more so now, for the duration of his reign, so that she might enjoy extraordinary favors.

Empress Irene replied with great emotion: "Dear Nikephor, God above, who rules all human kingdoms and bestows the kingdom upon whomever

He chooses—He crowns and deposes kings at will—seated first myself, his unworthy servant, on the throne, though I did nothing to deserve this high position, and in His kindness He has kept me in that position until now. Whereas now, due to my many sins and wicked deeds, He has snatched kingdom and government away from me. For this I must ever praise Him, and, like a righteous lady, say along with patient Job: "the Lord has given, and the Lord has taken away, blessed be the name of the Lord."[82] But if you have attained this position of power by honest means, it is now your responsibility, and when the time comes you will be called upon to account for it before God. As for myself—I have had several similar experiences. I did not lack the means to abort your plot and deal with you as I have dealt with many others before you who plotted similarly against me. Yet, due to my soft heart, I was the cause of this change, and I helped bring about what I now behold, which cannot be undone. Therefore, I request of you most cordially: have mercy on me and allow me to live out the rest of my days in peace, in the palace that I built." Nikephoros promised to fulfil her wish and show her every honor, as long as she swore by her life to reveal to him all the treasures of the empire and hand them over to him without withholding even the slightest one. However, after she swore it and handed over the imperial treasury, he commanded in the presence of Charlemagne's emissaries that she be exiled to the isle of Lesbos. She died there of sorrow the very next year.[83] So you see, all this happened to such an exalted empress, who accepted it all with forbearance. From this we learn that every person must suffer patiently, accepting everything God inflicts upon him with forbearance, as I have already written.

82. In this translation of Job 1:21, the name used to denote God reflects the German translation; see Luther's version: "Der HERR hats gegeben, der HERR hats genomen, Der name des HERRN sey gelobt," which accords with the fact that a non-Jewish lady is speaking.

83. Glikl's account, which portrays Empress Irene as a noble and righteous figure, is quite different from Empress Irene's image in popular stories in general, and Jewish stories in particular, where she is described as a cruel, bloodthirsty, and power-hungry woman (see, for example, Winston 1954, pp. 352–356; Graboïs 1967, pp. 22–58). This negative portrait of Empress Irene appears in all the sources cited by Davis 1995, p. 26, and on pp. 236–237, nn. 83–85, with the exception of the Greek source mentioned earlier in this Book, n. 79, which is the only parallel version to Glikl's account. Nevertheless, not only is there no known German translation of this source, but also it was not used in medieval times as a source for accounts of Charlemagne (on this and the probability that Glikl read stories in German, see Turniansky 2001, pp. 76–84; on possible ways that this story reached Glikl, see Turniansky 1993, pp. 175–176; Turniansky 1994c, p. 63; Turniansky 2004, pp.146–147).

I will now return to my Maiden of Hainholz.[84] We celebrated a wonderful Simḥat Torah, rejoicing that God had delivered us from our trouble,
may He deliver us and all of Israel from all our troubles in the future, amen.
We remained in Hannover until the beginning of the month of Ḥeshvan.
Then we traveled with the small children and the maid to Hamel, intending to stay in Hamel until the situation in Hamburg improved. But we had
not a moment's peace, since we were involved in a big business deal. We
had a man called Green Moshe[85] in Poland; we received letters from him
saying that he had a total of over six hundred lot[86] of ounce pearls. He
brought these to Hamburg and wrote to my husband, of blessed memory,
to tell him the quantity of pearls he was carrying, saying that my husband
should come to Hamburg right away. But my husband, of blessed memory,
did not go to Hamburg right away but stayed in Hamel about another two
weeks since the situation in Hamburg was very bad. My in-laws refused to
allow my husband to go to Hamburg — they would not even let us receive
a letter from there.[87] If we did get a letter, we had to fumigate it two or
three times,[88] then, as soon as we had read it, we had to throw it into the
Leine River.[89]

Once we were sitting together chatting, when suddenly Green Moshe
comes into the room. It was a cold winter and he wore a hood drawn over
his head. We recognized him immediately and motioned for him to leave,
since no one else had seen him in the room. If my in-laws knew that we had
a visitor from Hamburg, they would have thrown us out along with him.
Indeed, we were in real danger from the authorities — anyone harboring a
person from Hamburg[90] in his home risked his very life. All were subjected

84. To what she started to tell earlier in this Book, pp. 107–113.
85. I have no information regarding this man, known as (the) Green Moshe, nor do I know the reason for his adjective. Ada Rappaport-Albert suggests that it may have been associated with Shabtai
Tzvi's color (see this Book, n. 29), pointing to Moshe's being one of his followers.
86. Measure of weight: 15.5–16.5 grams (see Verdenhalven 1968, p. 33).
87. According to the belief that even a letter sent from a place infected with the plague (in this case,
Hamburg) could infect those who received it. This is the reason that the authorities, by law, confiscated letters (like those letters sent in 1588 from plague-infected Cracow to Prague and confiscated
there; see Weinryb 1928).
88. Fumigation was considered a method of sterilization.
89. The Leine River is located near Hannover (see map), and Glikl mistakenly confused it with
the Weser River, located near Hamel, where these events occurred (Feilchenfeld 1913, p. 73, n. 18).
90. Because of the plague there; see this Book, p. 106.

to scrupulous searches at the city gates and in the squares. So we asked Green Moshe: "How did you get into the city?" He answered: "I told them I was a clerk for the judge of Hachem (a village not far from Hamel)."[91] What could we do? He was there already, with all the pearls. We could not very well hide him somewhere without my in-laws' knowledge. We were forced to tell them; though they did not like it, there was nothing to be done about it.

Green Moshe would not let my husband alone, demanding that he travel with him to sell the pearls so that he, Moshe, could set out again to buy new merchandise. Well, what was my husband, of blessed memory, supposed to do? He had already invested a lot of money, and, on top of that, this was not merchandise you want to leave lying around for a long time, since it does not yield a big profit and if left lying around — the interest swallows up the profits. So he decided to go with Green Moshe to Hamburg to handle the sale of the pearls and to assess the situation there so that I and the children could return to my little nest, as I was already very tired. We lacked for nothing, it is true, but I was accustomed to Hamburg, where our business was.

When my husband, of blessed memory, reached Hamburg, he immediately took his pearls, worth certainly six thousand reichstaler banco,[92] to traders going to Muscovy[93] and showed them his stones. He went to at least six traders, but they all made him low offers yielding only a small profit. That was in the month of Shvat.[94] My husband, of blessed memory, did not know what to do. He had to pay the bills of exchange required for trading in pearls.[95] But all the Muscovite ships sail for Hamburg in the month of Av, making the month of Tammuz the best time to sell. Since they had all

91. This may refer to Hochheim (see Kaufmann 1896, p. 99, n. 2); however, there is no such place near Hamel. Other suggestions are Hayen (Feilchenfeld 1913, p. 73, n. 19), Hajen or Hagen (Landau 1901, p. 66), or Lachem (as Levinsky, cited by Landau, proposed; see Landau 1901, p. 66).
92. Italian term for an international unit of calculation for trade in the seventeenth and eighteenth centuries that evaluates the worth of the money in the bank independent of the rate of exchange (see Robert 1989).
93. The Russian empire at that time (on its trade with European countries, see Munck 1990, pp. 128–132; on its trade with Hamburg, see the general comment in Feilchenfeld 1913, p. 75, n. 20).
94. In the Gregorian calendar, Shvat occurs on January–February; Av (see following text) on June–July; and Tammuz (see following text) on July–August.
95. Either in general or in order to pay for the pearls that he already possessed.

made him low offers, my husband, of blessed memory, decided to pawn the pearls. He got six thousand reichstaler for them until the beginning of the month of Tammuz, thinking he would get better prices afterward. He was sorely mistaken, however, since letters came from Muscovy saying there was a great war on.[96] This made the traders feel less inclined to buy pearls. What could he do? He was forced to sell, getting four hundred reichstaler less than he had been offered before, and, on top of that, he had to pay six months' interest too.[97] It follows that the first trader is always the best —this should be taken into account; also, a trader must be able to say no just as quickly as yes.

In Hamburg, my husband, of blessed memory, inquired what the situation was like. Everyone told him that things were calm now, as indeed they were. Seeing this, he sent me one Yakov, may he rest in peace, a most trustworthy man except for one fault: he was extremely fond of drink, simply could not resist temptation. Well, my good Yakov reached Hannover, stayed there, and wrote that I should come with my children, as the post chaise to Hamburg departed from Hannover.[98] I then wrote at once to young Avraham Kantor in Hildesheim,[99] who used to work for us, to come immediately to Hamel and accompany me to Hamburg. We went to Hannover, where we met our "Shot-at Yakov."[100] He immediately went to summon the clerk, his sworn drinking companion, arranged our trip with him on Friday, and we spent the Sabbath in Hannover. The weather was terrible, and I had three small children with me. All Sabbath long my brother-in-law Reb Lipman and sister-in-law Yente talked to "Shot-at Yakov," entreating him to take good care of us and to make sure not to get drunk as usual. He promised Reb Lipman and Yente that he would not get drunk, would drink only in moderation, whereupon they shook hands on it. But you will soon hear how he kept that promise.

On Sunday morning I left Hannover with the children, may God protect

96. Because Glikl is apparently writing about the second half of the 1660s, this may refer to the Russo-Polish war prior to the Treaty of Andrusovo in 1667 (see Munck 1990, p. 206).

97. That is, for the period from the month of Shvat to the beginning of Tammuz, as detailed earlier.

98. Glikl is making her way back by the same route she came: Hamel-Hannover-Hamburg (see this Book).

99. On his service in Glikl's household and business, see Book Two, p. 97.

100. On "Shot-at Yakov," see Book Two, p. 88, where it is told how he acquired this nickname.

them, along with the servants and my able escort Yakov. We were accompanied, as travelers always are, by the mail clerk himself, Yakov's drinking companion, as I said. Yakov helped us into the carriages and arranged our belongings, then he and the clerk started walking alongside the carriages. I expected them to walk in this fashion until we left the city gates, then to join us in the carriages. As soon as we left the city gates, I told Yakov and the clerk to join us in the open carriage so that we should not lose time and make it to our inn at a reasonable hour. Said Yakov: "Just go on, in the name of God; the clerk and I will go through the village; he wants to have a word with someone there. We'll walk just as fast as you ride, and we'll soon catch up with you." However, I did not know the secret: the village lies close to Hannover; it is called Langenhagen, it is an entire mile long, and its wheat beer, called Breihahn,[101] is unsurpassed in all the land. And so my good escort Yakov and the mail clerk sat down in Langenhagen for a good day's drinking, and a good part of the night too, as will be told presently, while I knew nothing of this. As we rode on, I kept looking back for my Yakov, but — no Yakov.

We rode on until we came to a crossing, two leagues from Hannover, where one has to pay a toll.[102] The coachman driving the post chaise said: "There's a toll to pay here." I paid the toll and told the coachman to drive on so that we could reach the inn on time, since the weather was such that you would not turn even a dog out of doors.[103] It was around Purim time.[104] It was raining, a fine rain mixed with snow that froze as soon as it touched us. The poor children were suffering terribly; again I urged the coachman to drive on, as he could see for himself what the weather was like, and we were outside, exposed to the elements. But the coachman said: "I am not allowed to drive on until the mail clerk comes. He bid me wait there for

101. On Breihahn, the name of the beer Glikl mentions, see Feilchenfeld 1913, p. 78, n. 23; and Abrahams 1962, p. 56, n. 1.

102. The customs station at the border between Calenberg and Lüneberg-Celle (see Feilchenfeld 1913, p. 78, n. 24).

103. Cf. "Es ist Wetter drauss, man jagt nicht gern einen alten Hund hinaus" (Wander 1987, V, p. 216, no. *186; there he also cites the Yiddish version, "An aveyre a hunt aroystsutraybn" (see Stutchkoff 1950, p. 155).

104. That is, during the European winter. Glikl had already been almost five months away from home, having left the day after Yom Kippur because of the plague (see this Book, p. 106).

him and Yakov." What could I do? We sat there like that for another two hours until the toll-collector came, took pity on us, and allowed us to descend from the open carriage and go into his heated office so that the poor children could warm up.

Well, we spent another hour in there. I finally said to the toll-collector: "Please, sir, make the coachman drive on so that I can reach the inn by nightfall with my small children; you can see what the weather is like—we can make no progress even by day, so how will we get anywhere in pitch blackness? If—God forbid—the carriage were to overturn in the night, we risk breaking our necks." Whereupon the toll-collector orders the coachman to drive on without further delay. Said the coachman: "Sir, if I drive on, Petersen the clerk will break my neck and I won't get a penny of my fee." But the toll-collector was a good, decent man, and he made the coachman drive on with us, saying: "When those two drunken clowns show up, they can hire horses and ride on after you, as you're spending the night at the inn." What could the coachman do? He was thereupon obliged to drive on with us.

Well, we drove on in the awful weather, but we made it to the inn. There we found a well-heated room, and we were made welcome. Although the room was crammed with coachmen and other passersby, terribly crowded, people were kind and took pity on the poor children who hadn't a dry stitch[105] on them, poor things. I hung up their clothes to dry while the children recovered, poor things. We had good food with us[106] and the inn had excellent wheat beer. In this way we restored our spirits after the arduous ride, with good food and drink, staying up until the late hours of the night on the assumption that the two drinking mates would show up eventually. But they never came. I asked for a straw pallet and stretched out with my children. I could not fall asleep, but I thanked God that I was able to give my children some rest.

Sunk in thought, I lay sleepless until about midnight, when a shout was heard in the room. It was the mail clerk, drunk, running into the room brandishing a dagger and threatening to kill the coachman for driving away on his own. The coachman was trying to justify himself as best he could.

---

105. Cf. "Er hat keinen trocken Faden am Leibe" (Wander 1987, I, p. 914, no. 30).
106. They most probably took food with them due to kashrut concerns.

The innkeeper came in too, and finally they got the clerk to quiet down. I sat there miserably in a corner, silent as a little mouse, since the man was crazy drunk; I was terribly anxious because Yakov was nowhere to be seen. After a while the clerk sat down to eat, and I saw he had calmed down somewhat. I went up to him, saying: "Sir, Mr. Petersen, where did you leave my Yakov?" "Where could I have left him? He couldn't travel any further; he stopped by a fence near a pond. Maybe he's drowned by now." This really scared me. I did not know what to do; he was a Jew, a human being, and I was all alone. I asked the innkeeper to send me two villagers who could try to find him and bring him here. The two villagers rode off on horseback and found my good Yakov as good as dead, half an hour's distance from the village, faint with travel and drunkenness. His good coat, the small amount of money he had — all gone. So the villagers sat him on a horse and brought him to the inn. Despite being furious with him, I thanked God upon seeing him again. It cost me more than seven reichstaler. I gave him something to eat. So my fine servant who was supposed to be taking care of me and my children — I wound up taking care of him instead.

At daybreak the drivers brought the carriages for us to continue on our way. The children, the servants, and I all settled down in the carriages. I told my Yakov to sit down too and stop behaving like that. He said: "No, I'm just going inside for a minute to make sure nothing was left behind." I believed him, but my good Yakov and the clerk sat down again in the inn and started swilling all over again. I sent the drivers in to tell them to come out immediately, that we had been sitting in the open carriages in nasty weather for a long time. The drivers started shouting: "What's going on here, their horses had to stand for so long in the terrible weather that they were collapsing." But all this was to no avail: the clerk was in fact the boss, and the drivers were obliged to wait for him. So once again we sat waiting for two hours, and we did not get underway until the two of them, thoroughly drunk, finally took their seats in the carriages. Well, what more can I write? We went through the exact same business all over again at all the other inns, but God, blessed be He, helped us reach Harburg safely, just a league's distance from Hamburg, where my father and my husband, of blessed memory, were waiting, and they came out to greet us. It is easy to picture how glad we all were to see each other. From there we took the river ferry together to Hamburg,[107] thanking God, blessed be He, that all our relatives were well and that only a few Jewish homes had been contaminated in my absence. The commotion[108] had not died down entirely, things were still troublesome at times, but all was well with the Jews and remained so, thank God; may God continue to protect us and all of Israel and deliver us from all our troubles.

Once again we were in our beloved Hamburg; we had been away from Hamburg for half a year, and, believe me, we calculated that the losses from the pearls and the interest cost us more than twelve hundred reichstaler. Still, we thanked and praised God above for delivering us from trouble, along with our entire family. Money is of little importance: *Give me the persons, and take the possessions for yourself;*[109] God, blessed be He, has always provided for us all over again. After this, those who had moved from Hamburg to Altona because of the plague began returning to the city one by one, resuming their business dealings, as hardly any business had been conducted during the plague since it was impossible to get from one place to another.

A short while afterward, my husband, of blessed memory, went to the Leipzig fair,[110] where he was taken very ill. Leipzig was extremely dangerous at that time — if a Jew died there, God forbid, it cost him everything he had.[111] Reb Yudah was also in Leipzig just then[112] and was very kind to my husband, of blessed memory, and looked after him. When my husband was feeling a little better, Reb Yudah spoke to him as a good friend, asking

---

107. On the Elbe River.
108. Here again, as earlier in this Book, p. 109, n. 56, Glikl avoids mentioning the term "plague."
109. Cf. Gen 14:21.
110. On the Leipzig fair and its Jewish visitors, see Freudenthal 1928, pp. 7–22; and pp. 7–8, n. 1, on the visits of Chaim Hamel's family in general. On the visit of Chaim himself, see under the name Hain (Heine) Goldschmidt, Freudenthal 1928, p. 125. Based on the events prior to Glikl's discussion of this visit (Shabtai Tzvi, the plague in Hamburg), she might be referring to the fair in 1668 (see Freudenthal 1928), but it is more likely that the visit took place at a later date (see this Book, n. 114).
111. Concerning this information, which is not mentioned by Freudenthal 1928, see Feilchenfeld 1913, p. 84, n. 1; and Book Four, p. 182.
112. On Yudah Berliner's visits to the Leipzig fair, see Freudenthal 1928, p. 39, under the name Jost Liebmann. There is no record there of a visit in 1668 (cf. this Book, n. 111). The first record of a joint visit by Yudah Berliner and Chaim Hamel is in 1675. According to Freudenthal 1902, p. 28, this visit by Chaim Hamel, which took place in 1675, was terminated before the end of the fair due to his illness, which did indeed happen (see following text).

my husband, of blessed memory, what he was thinking of, making such difficult trips, for he was not a healthy man; in short, my husband, of blessed memory, should enter into partnership with him. He himself was a young man, able to travel all over the world and make plenty of money for them both to live on very nicely. My husband, of blessed memory, replied: "I can't give you an answer here in Leipzig. I am still not quite well. I can't stay in Leipzig any longer, for fear that my health will deteriorate further, God forbid. I'll hire a carriage to take me home.[113] Since it's payment week[114] and there isn't much to do at the fair anyway, you can ride with me for free. When we get to my house, God willing, we can discuss the matter; my Gliklchen will be there to give her valuable opinion." For the dear man, of blessed memory, did nothing without my knowledge.

Reb Yudah was already married by then. My husband, of blessed memory, had persuaded his devout brother, our master and teacher R. Shmuel, of blessed memory, to marry off his daughter[115] to Reb Yudah, and R. Shmuel gave five hundred reichstaler as dowry. So the two of them came here together from Leipzig. My husband, of blessed memory, was not yet restored to full health, though he did not have to stay in bed. Thanks to divine providence, he was feeling much better, due mainly to God's help. It took over eight days, and during the entire time Reb Yudah gave my ears not a moment's peace, urging me to convince my husband to form a partnership with him: what was I thinking? I was not doing my duty in permitting my husband to travel all over like that. If something had happened to him in Leipzig, God forbid, he would have lost both his health and his capital.

It is true that I did not like those journeys at all, since they were often dangerous, like the time my husband was taken ill in Leipzig; even before that, my husband came home once in the middle of the fair, and I knew nothing about it. I'm looking out the door and I see my husband approaching. It is easy to understand how startled I was, and there were other similar occurrences. Who can describe it all in writing? Once my husband, of

113. Meaning a private carriage that would not have any other passengers.
114. This apparently refers to the week at the end of the fair, during which deals were closed and payments made.
115. Malka, the daughter of R. Shmuel, who was the brother of Chaim Hamel (see Book Two, p. 92), was Reb Yudah's first wife (see Kaufmann 1896, p. 108, n. 4; Feilchenfeld 1913, p. 85, n. 2), and hence Glikl was the aunt of Malka and became the aunt of Reb Yudah (see Family Tree B).

blessed memory, went to the Leipzig winter fair; that is, the New Year's fair.[116] He was traveling with some other Jews bound for here, but they did not arrive on the day they should have, by my calculations. Then the woman who brings the mail brings me some letters from Frankfurt, saying: "They had some bad news at the Imperial Post Office, may God have mercy — two carriages with Jews and gentiles who were about to cross the Elbe to Zollenspieker[117] sank because the ice was so heavy that it shattered the ferryboat." My God, I nearly died of fright. I started screaming and wailing, as you can imagine. Just then Green Moshe came into the room — I have already mentioned him[118] — and at finding me in such a state, he asks me what happened. I tell him and say: "I beg you, for God's sake, take a horse right away and ride to Zollenspieker to find out what happened." Although Green Moshe and others tried to reassure me, I could not calm down. So Green Moshe rode away on horseback. I hastened to a man with horses for hire; he promptly dispatched his servant on horseback via a different route. As soon as I return home, distraught, I see my husband in the heated room, warming himself and drying out his wet clothes. The weather was awful, and everything the mail carrier had recounted was one big lie.

I write this because the trips were an ongoing source of worry and alarm, and I certainly would have preferred arranging it so that my husband, of blessed memory, could stay at home. For this reason I was not indifferent concerning our partnership with Reb Yudah. Reb Yudah then discussed it with us again, making us his best offer. I told Reb Yudah: "Everything you say sounds fine, but you can see for yourself that we have a large household and a load of responsibilities. We need more than one thousand reichstaler a year for our household expenses, in addition to interest payments for the business and other expenses; I don't see where it will come from." Reb Yudah replied: "Is that what's worrying you? I will make a note of it: if you do not make a profit of at least one thousand reichstaler banco[119] a year, you have the option of dissolving the partnership." These and other such

116. Neujahrsmesse — the fair that took place in Leipzig during the winter, close to the Gregorian New Year's day. It was therefore known as "the cold Leipzig fair."

117. Zollenspieker: a toll house located on the banks of the Elbe River (see Feilchenfeld 1913, p. 86, n. 4; Landau 1901, p. 66).

118. See this Book, n. 85.

119. See this Book, n. 92.

promises he made, too many to write down. I discussed it with my husband, of blessed memory, telling him of my conversation with Reb Yudah and of his ambitious plans. Said my husband, of blessed memory: "My dear child, talking is all very well. I have a great many expenses to meet, and I don't see how I can do that through partnership with Reb Yudah." So I said to my husband, of blessed memory: "We can try it for a year. When I get a chance I will draft a short agreement and show it to you to see how you like it."

That night I sat by myself to draft an agreement. All this time, Reb Yudah kept urging us to agree, telling us not to worry; we should just turn all the business dealings over to him; he had all kinds of methods and knew enough about business for us to do very well. I said: "How can we do that—turn all our business dealings over to you?" Said Reb Yudah: "I know well that you own jewelry worth many thousands, and you will not give that up. Let us agree that you may sell or exchange that jewelry as you please." That was the first clause. Second, the partnership would last ten years, with accounting done every year. If there was not an annual profit of at least two thousand reichstaler for the duration of the partnership, my husband, of blessed memory, had the option of getting out of the partnership—without this, we would not enter into any partnership. In the event the partnership was dissolved, everything was to be sold so that each party could get his share. Third, my husband, of blessed memory, would go to Amsterdam with Reb Yudah two or three times to teach him all about buying, while Reb Yudah would have all the merchandise at hand to sell. Fourth, my husband, of blessed memory, would invest five or six thousand reichstaler in the business, while Reb Yudah would invest two thousand reichstaler; he would have the right to sell or exchange all of my husband's merchandise: jewelry and other goods, as he saw fit. A formal agreement along these lines was duly drawn up, and it was strictly observed in all respects. Reb Yudah then returned to Hildesheim,[120] saying that first he'd pick up the money he was committed to invest, then, in two or three weeks, they would travel together to Amsterdam.

In preparation for the trip, my husband, of blessed memory, transferred his money to Amsterdam. The only thing missing was for Reb Yudah to

120. Where he resided since his marriage to Malka (see this Book, p. 124, n. 115).

arrive with his money — sure enough, he showed up at the appointed time, with a bill of exchange for five hundred reichstaler. We said to him: "Reb Yudah, what is this? There should be two thousand here!" He replied: "I left some gold with my wife in Hildesheim to sell and transfer the balance to me here." We were reassured.

And so, in the name of the God of Israel, they arrived in Amsterdam together, well pleased. My husband, of blessed memory, started buying up small quantities as was customary at the time. Every time the mail came, my husband, of blessed memory, would ask: "Did you get your bill of exchange yet?" In short, every time the mail came, Reb Yudah would say: "I'm just about to get it," "Here it comes now" — but there was never anything — he received nothing at all. What was my husband, of blessed memory, supposed to do? Reb Yudah spoke to him soothingly and told him stories. My husband, of blessed memory, invested his money, in addition to Reb Yudah's five hundred reichstaler, buying merchandise in Amsterdam, since in Amsterdam you can invest on the spot. My husband, of blessed memory, then returned home; Reb Yudah went to Hildesheim, taking with him everything my husband had bought. He traveled back and forth, selling and trading as he saw fit. When my husband, of blessed memory, returned home, he talked to me a little, complaining about the partnership with Reb Yudah — saying that I had pushed him into it, that if Reb Yudah did not comply with the agreement from the very start, what would come next? What would be the end of all this? It was enough to make you burst, doing business like this.

I tried to reassure him to the best of my ability, saying what was quite true: "Reb Yudah is a young man. How much of a dowry did he get? Five hundred reichstaler, and he had eight or nine hundred when he stopped working for us;[121] that was only two years ago, so there was no way he could have raised two thousand reichstaler. Think of it: Reb Yudah has nothing, he is sent off on trips as before, and we entrust him with thousands as we have done. It's all in his hands. If God, blessed be He, wants to give someone good luck, He can do it for a little bit just the same as for a lot." What could he do? Whether he liked it or not, we were already involved, obliged to see it through.

---

121. As was related earlier in this Book, pp. 102–103.

Some time passed in this way. Reb Yudah made some profit, as he wrote to us from time to time, but *a handful cannot satisfy a lion.*[122] In short, why should I write at length? The year was almost over and both of us were dissatisfied. We realized that there was not enough profit to maintain even one household, let alone two. Finally, after one year's partnership, my husband, of blessed memory, went to Hildesheim and went over the accounts that showed that neither of them could make a living this way. So my husband, of blessed memory, spoke to Reb Yudah as to a brother: "You realize that neither of us can make a living from this partnership. According to the agreement, the partnership is to yield an annual profit of at least two thousand reichstaler, and, as you surely know, the profit is even less than one thousand reichstaler." Reb Yudah too realized that they could not both make a living this way. They therefore amicably and in good faith absolved each other of the partnership. My husband, of blessed memory, wrote out writs of dissolution,[123] one for himself and one for Reb Yudah, which they both signed as required.

There remained several thousand in rings and other jewelry, all of which my husband had deposited with Reb Yudah for him to sell and pay the proceeds over to my husband, of blessed memory. The date of payment was set, but the date came and went without any payment. We duly wrote explicitly to Reb Yudah that he knew quite well what he had committed himself to in writing. Payment was overdue and he must transfer the funds to Hamburg forthwith. Reb Yudah duly wrote back that he had not yet sold everything but would nonetheless make every effort to transfer a bill of exchange to us as soon as possible. It went on like this for over a year without our managing to get anything out of Reb Yudah. Once again my husband, of blessed memory, went to Hildesheim, with the intention of obtaining his money from Reb Yudah, but he got something quite different. After Reb Yudah put my husband off repeatedly with excuses for a few days, it turns out that Reb Yudah told my husband, of blessed memory: "I'm not paying you even a penny of the money, and I wish I had kept twice as much of your money, because our partnership was supposed to last for ten years according to

122. Cf. b.Berakhot 3b, b.Sanhedrin 16a.
123. An agreement that ends the contract for both parties.

the agreement,[124] but it lasted only one year. I'm suing you for thousands, and everything you own — all of it — is mine. Everything you own won't be enough to pay me."

My husband got terribly scared: "Reb Yudah, what are you talking about? Is this the thanks I get for all I've done for you? You came to me *naked and bare*,[125] with nothing at all, then after a short time with me, you left with nine hundred reichstaler in cash. I entrusted you with many thousands; I showed you all the places I knew where something could be done, and above all — I considered you a trustworthy, honest man. I intervened on your behalf for my brother, our master and teacher R. Shmuel Segal, to give you his daughter in marriage.[126] And after all that, it was you who breached the agreement: instead of the two thousand reichstaler you were supposed to invest, you invested only five hundred. In addition, our agreement says that 'if the partnership does not yield an annual profit of two thousand reichstaler — the partnership is to be dissolved.' Now, you know very well that we barely made a profit of one thousand reichstaler, while the agreement states explicitly that if there is not a profit of the said amount, I have the option of withdrawing. In the end, it was not worthwhile for either of us; that's why we absolved each other amicably and in good faith, as in our writ of dissolution. What more do you want? I entreat you, do not give people the opportunity to gossip, *for we are kinsmen*,[127] we can still do business together, with God's help," and so forth. But all this was useless with my good Reb Yudah;[128] he remained adamant. What was my husband, of blessed memory, to do? After much discussion and argument, people intervened, and the two of them shook hands on it, agreeing that each of them would engage an arbitrator[129] to appear before the head of the

124. According to second clause of the agreement; see this Book, p. 126.

125. As in Ezek 16:7 and elsewhere.

126. See this Book, n. 115.

127. Cf. Gen 13:8.

128. Perhaps ironically said (cf. the use of "good" for "The Shot-at Yakov" earlier in this Book, pp. 119, 120). Nevertheless, subsequently Glikl treats Reb Yudah with forgiveness, admiration, and respect (see this Book, pp. 133, 134).

129. According to the judicial principle "Monetary cases [are judged] by three [judges]. One [litigant] selects one and the other selects one" (see, for example, m.Sanhedrin 3a; b.Bava Metzi'a 20a).

rabbinical court in Hildesheim; a date four months later was set accordingly. My husband, of blessed memory, was forced to agree to all this, for *he cannot contend with what is stronger than he*[130] — and it is well known that no one is more obdurate than a man *who controls everything.*[131]

And so my husband, of blessed memory, returned home with the outcome just related, and told me all about it. We were truly chagrined, for we knew that we had dealt honestly with this man and treated him exceedingly well, God will surely reward us for it. My husband, of blessed memory, was slightly aggrieved with me because this partnership was of my doing. But God knows that I acted in the best of faith, thinking that my husband, of blessed memory, would not have to embark on such long journeys anymore. I did not expect such an outcome, and I never imagined that Reb Yudah would behave thus, for I took him for a trustworthy man. Whether it happened because Reb Yudah suspected my husband, of blessed memory, of doing business or something connected to the partnership without his knowledge, I do not know. Or perhaps it was a certain business deal, to be mentioned,[132] that sparked the whole thing, as will soon be made clear.

Well, what can you do? What is done cannot be undone. Reb Yudah still had a large sum of money belonging to us. This was not at all to our liking. I asked my husband, of blessed memory, why he had arranged for the trial to be held in Hildesheim — it should be held in a neutral place[133] — to which he answered irritably: "Had you been there, you surely would have arranged it better. That man has his hands on what is mine, so I have to do what he wants instead of what I want."[134] In short, our argument too came to an end. We could do nothing but be patient and put everything in the hands of the good Lord. He who delivered us from so many troubles and so many bad business deals will help us out of this too. We were young and had just started doing well for ourselves, business was very good — we simply could not resign ourselves to the risk of incurring such losses (see

130. Cf. Eccl 6:10.
131. From the Rosh Hashanah and Yom Kippur liturgical poem recited during the mussaf service (see Maḥzor Rosh Hashanah 2014, p. 581; see also Feilchenfeld 1913, p. 94, n. 10).
132. See the deals mentioned in the following text.
133. Not in Hildesheim, where Reb Yudah resided at that time.
134. The plaintiff cannot force the defendant to be tried in a location that he doesn't want (see b.Sanhedrin 31b).

previous page).[135] When my husband, of blessed memory, received the writ dissolving the partnership from Reb Yudah — my husband, of blessed memory, had returned from Hildesheim — there was a Frenchman here with all kinds of merchandise. My husband, of blessed memory, bartered with him, making good deals. But that's the way it is among Jews, when someone makes a profit of one hundred reichstaler, people turn it into thousands. There were indeed rumors that my husband, of blessed memory, had made a profit of many thousands. This was right after the partnership was dissolved, and the rumors must have reached Reb Yudah. Perhaps he believed them, or made himself believe that my husband, of blessed memory, had knowledge of this deal while still in partnership with him. All the more so, since people were saying that the deal yielded a profit of many thousands. Whether Reb Yudah was dishonest in this, whether he regretted parting company with my husband, of blessed memory, or whether he did not want to give up such a sum of money — God only knows. We had not sensed any dishonesty or fraudulence in him, except for his nagging us so persistently about this matter and his not being too happy about parting with what he had. *Man sees only what is visible, but the Lord sees into the heart.*[136] Possibly he convinced himself that he was in the right and stuck to that view. *A man cannot see [anything] to his own disadvantage.*[137] For us it was especially painful and difficult since we knew our own truth: that we had dealt with this man honestly and in good faith; we were so good to him — only for him to repay us this way.

Well, *whatever the All-Merciful does is for good.*[138] The fair at Frankfurt-am-Main was approaching, which my husband, of blessed memory, had to attend, as he attended all the fairs. He stayed with his brother, our master and teacher R. Itsik,[139] of blessed memory. He recounted to his brother everything that had passed between himself and Reb Yudah and asked him to recommend an honest, learned man, since he had to present himself in Hildesheim on a certain day, and each party had to engage his

---

135. This is Glikl's note, and is written in Hebrew.
136. Cf. 1 Sam 16:7.
137. Cf. b.Shabbat 119a; b.Ketubbot 105b.
138. Cf. b.Berakhot 60b.
139. See Book Two, p. 92.

own arbitrator in this matter of breach of contract. My brother-in-law, our master and teacher the pious R. Itsik, of blessed memory, said at once to my husband: "You will lose all you have if you appear in court in his community." "What should I have done?" said my husband. "I was not able to arrange it any better." My husband, of blessed memory, then proceeded to set out his claims and rights in detail to my brother-in-law, R. Itsik, of blessed memory, to which the latter replied: "Yes, my brother, you are right in everything, and you would win and be awarded all the money had the judges not been biased, and if the trial were being held in a neutral place." To which my husband replied: "That cannot be changed anymore, let it be as the good Lord decrees. I have to get out of this; just recommend the right person." After some reflection, my brother-in-law, of blessed memory, said: "There is a trustworthy young man here called Reb Asher; he is a rabbinical judge in our community. He is quite good but I already told you what I think." So my husband, of blessed memory, went to him and showed him all his contracts and writs. Reb Asher said to my husband, of blessed memory: "Don't worry, you are in the right; I'll go with you." This they did when the fair was over. During the fair, my husband, of blessed memory, spoke to his brother and asked him if he could recommend an honest young man to assist him in the business. In short, he recommended Issachar Cohen[140] — who was, alas, a real Herod[141] to my entire family; more about him at the proper time and place.[142]

The fair ended. My husband, of blessed memory, and his arbitrator went to the trial in Hildesheim. In short, why should I dwell on this at length, I could write a hundred pages on the subject, about everything that happened there. Our arbitrator had no chance of success given that he stood alone opposite two men of the other party. Reb Asher would not be pressured into agreeing to an unfair decision knowing that if he failed to reach a compromise with them, he would be put in jail, at least that's what they

---

140. See this Book, nn. 7, 142; Book Four, p. 170, n. 149.

141. Regarding extremely rare mention of Herod as an evil figure in Ashkenazi literature (where Amalek, Pharaoh, Haman, and Titus are often mentioned), see Davis 1995, p. 248, n. 152; and *Encyopedia Judaica* 1972, vol. 8, col. 384.

142. Where it suits Glikl's chronological order. Nevertheless, in her description of Issachar Cohen, Glikl does not tell the complete story of his evil deeds as she promises here and in Book Four, p. 170, n. 149 (cf. Feilchenfeld 1913, p. 97, n. 12a).

threatened. And so my good Reb Asher left Hildesheim secretly, leaving behind a lengthy responsum[143] justifying my husband's claims. All to no avail. In short, the head of the rabbinical court of Hildesheim[144] and a parnas of the community[145] — I will not name either of them, they are all in the world to come — supported Reb Yudah body and soul, and sought to impose on my husband, of blessed memory, a compromise he found unacceptable. My husband, of blessed memory, did not therefore wish to agree to this, and the matter might have reached complicated proceedings in a Gentile court of law. But at the time, my father-in-law, of blessed memory, was living in Hildesheim; I will recount in due course how he came to be living there.[146] My father-in-law was actually in tears as he pleaded with my husband: "Dear son, surely you understand what is happening here, I beseech you, for God's sake, don't get into deeper trouble, be patient and make the best compromise you can. God, blessed be He, will repay you" — and that is what in fact happened, as will be told in due course.[147] What was my husband, of blessed memory, to do? Reb Yudah was hanging on to what belonged to us, and it was hard to get him to part with it; so my husband was forced to settle. It is easy to imagine what kind of settlement ensued. But it is well known that we did not possess so much as twice the amount that all this cost us. I do not blame Reb Yudah so much as those who assisted him, *for a man cannot see [anything] to his own disadvantage.*[148]

In short, all that is over now. We forgave them all — Reb Yudah and those who assisted him, nor do we bear any grudge against Reb Yudah, who must have believed that he was in the right and that we owed him

143. A written legal opinion based on Jewish law.

144. R. Shmuel (the brother of Chaim Hamel and the father-in-law of Yudah Berliner; see earlier in this Book) did not serve as the head of the rabbinical court in Hildesheim during the trial in question. If he had, he would have had to disqualify himself since he was a relative of the litigants (see next note).

145. During this event R. Shmuel (see previous note) was still a parnas. In this capacity, he apparently tried to operate against his brother and in favor of his son-in-law. It is perhaps for this reason that Glikl does not mention here the late parnas's name (R. Shmuel died in 1687) nor does she mention the reason for the emotional intervention of her father in-law, Reb Yosef Hamel, who apparently tried to prevent a dispute between his two sons, Chaim and Shmuel (see following text; and also Feilchenfeld 1913, p. 98, n. 14).

146. See Book Four. In fact, Glikl already mentioned this, earlier in this book.

147. See following text, after n. 149 ("But the good Lord").

148. See this Book, n. 140.

money, otherwise he would not perhaps have acted as he did. It's true that my husband, of blessed memory, took all this very hard, but who could have helped him? *He who prays over what has already happened, this prayer is in vain.*[149] But the good Lord recognized our probity and sent us — before four weeks had passed — such a business deal that we recuperated all our losses. Later on, my husband, of blessed memory, had a relationship of trust and friendship with Reb Yudah, as I will recount with regard to the great honor Reb Yudah and his wife accorded me when I was in Berlin.[150] He did business with my children all the time too, so we have no real complaint against him. If only the business partnership had been successful and shown a good profit, I think there would not have been any unpleasantness between us. It seems that this was Issachar's fate — that we had to part ways with Reb Yudah, then Issachar began to flourish, as will be told.[151]

Even though this matter[152] is trivial, as is this whole book of mine, it was written nonetheless, to stave off my pointless melancholy thoughts when sorrowful brooding distressed me so. It also goes to show how human affairs change over time. *God, blessed be He, makes ladders, lifting one up, causing another to descend.*[153] Reb Yudah came to us with nothing at all, and God, blessed be He, helped him so much that I believe even one hundred thousand reichstaler banco would not suffice to buy him out now;[154] he enjoys such business and esteem from His Excellency the Kurfürst[155] that I believe that if he continues to prosper in this way and if God, blessed be He, does not object, he will die when his time comes as the richest man in all Ashkenaz. This incident also shows how we helped many others succeed, God willing, and all those who had business dealings with us became as rich as kings, though most of them showed us no gratitude for it, as is the

149. Cf. m.Berakhot 9:3. Similar to "No use crying over spilt milk."

150. See Book Five, p. 209, n. 46.

151. On Issachar Katz (Cohen) see this Book, pp. 100, 132; and "what will be told" in Book Four, p. 170.

152. The business with Reb Yudah.

153. Cf. Gen Rab. 68:4.

154. Reb Yudah Berliner (1640–1702) came to be one of the most prominent court Jews (see "Jost Liebmann," in *Encyclopaedia Judaica* 1972, vol. 11, cols. 225–226; Lowenthal 1978, p. 282, n. 3).

155. Refers to the Great Elector Friedrich Wilhelm III of Brandenburg, who became Friedrich I, King of Prussia.

way of the world. Quite the contrary, some of those to whom we rendered good repaid us or our children with evil. Almighty God is right: we mortal sinners cannot say — we do not even know — what is good or bad for us; we often think, when encountering some misfortune, that it is certainly bad for our interests. But it is possible that the very thing we think is against us is actually in our favor. Had righteous, honest Mordechai survived, may God avenge his death, perhaps others would have remained unharmed, and he too would certainly have become a great man.[156]

After this we employed Green Moshe. We did not have such extensive business dealings with him, still, as I mentioned, we did good business with him in ounce pearls. He would travel great distances, leaving his wife and children here for us to provide for, without our knowing whether our profits would exceed the expenses. Regarding this it is said: *Send your bread forth upon the waters; for after many days you will find it.*[157] In short, we did not really make big profits from this, yet we parted amicably and would have continued together for a long while yet, had he not moved from Hamburg to Schottland, near Danzig.[158] He settled down there and did very well.

Avraham Kantor of Copenhagen, whom I have already mentioned,[159] was a servant in our house, well behaved and honest. After that we sent him to Copenhagen several more times, where he got rich, having settled there with his wife and children. After that we had no further partnership with him. They say that today he is worth fifteen thousand reichstaler, doing well in business and giving his children thousands in dowries. I could write a lot about what we did for him, but who would acknowledge it? We human beings are ungrateful creatures.

My cousin Mordechai Cohen,[160] a young man at the time, and Leyb

156. On Mordechai, see opening of this Book. Glikl is apparently somewhat changing her previous opinion concerning the purpose of Mordechai's death.

157. Eccl 11:1.

158. Schottland: a suburb of Danzig outside of the municipal boundary of the city. See Kaufmann 1896, p. 122, n. 5; Feilchenfeld 1913, p. 102, n. 18.

159. See Book Two, p. 97: Glikl here mistakenly switches Hildesheim, where Avraham Kantor came from, with Copenhagen, where he resided when she wrote the narrative (and see more in the following text).

160. He was the son of her aunt Ulk, her mother's sister, and Elia Cohen (see Family Tree A; Feilchenfeld 1913, p. 102, n. 19).

Besheri[161] entered into partnership with my husband, of blessed memory, and he sent them to England after providing them with letters of credit and cash. But war prevented them from reaching England, so they never made the trip.[162] Despite their not reaching England, they nonetheless invested a goodly sum in Amsterdam, at good interest. Subsequently, my cousin Mordechai Cohen traveled to Holland[163] and Brabant,[164] realizing excellent profits, that trip being the start of all his business and wealth. I have already mentioned the esteemed Reb Yudah who, with God's help, became an important man through us.

My brother-in-law Reb Elia Segal[165] was young and inexperienced, ignorant in business matters. My husband, of blessed memory, immediately gave him an extended line of credit, then sent him to Amsterdam with credit of twenty thousand reichstaler. Many householders who are now pillars of the community thanked God when we gave them a line of credit. I could mention many more names, but all this is of no use to me. Where now is the kindness that you, decent and honest Reb Chaim Hamel, of blessed memory, showed the entire world, willingly helping everyone, rendering kindnesses to everyone, sometimes with a profit, sometimes — at a loss; at times even when he knew for sure that he would not see any profit at all, he acted nonetheless out of genuine kindness. And now your dear, decent children, though they may suffer occasional misfortune, are so honest that they would rather die than cause harm to others. But those we helped so much have all forgotten it, though they could have helped my children — so young, who sadly lost their righteous father so early on, and now they are *like sheep that have no shepherd*.[166] They could have assisted;

161. Glikl mentions him only once more (Book Five, p. 217). Feilchenfeld's suggestion (see Feilchenfeld 1913, p. 102, n. 19a) that his surname is Pexeira as in Texeira and that he is a Sephardi Jew should be rejected, for this would involve appending a Sephardi surname to an Ashkenazi given name.

162. Probably the war between France, led by Louis XIV, and Holland in 1667–1668, during which England, allied with France, threatened the Dutch coastline and caused difficulties for marine transport (see Feilchenfeld 1913, p. 102, n. 20).

163. On the trade of German Jews with Holland during this period, see Israel 1989, pp. 174, 176.

164. Flemish Brabant, a province of Flanders, Belgium (see map).

165. Elia Segal (Ries) was the husband of Matte, Glikl's sister (see Family Tree A; see also Kaufmann 1896, p. 123, n. 3; on the relations between the two families, see Book Four, nn. 174–176.

166. Cf. Num. 27:17; 1 Kgs. 22:17.

actually, it was quite the other way around, may God have mercy: I wish they had neither helped nor hindered us. As a matter of fact, they caused my children losses of thousands, and because of them the money belonging to my son Reb Mordechai[167] was dispensed among the common people. The head of the council and all members of the tribunal agreed that the deal was legitimate and that there was no need to return some of the merchandise to the merchants, since he had bought it in honest good faith. Still, they would not leave him in peace. On the eve of Yom Kippur he was forced to get rid of his goods and reach a settlement with the merchants; unfortunately, this was the main cause of his ruin.[168]

Our mood at that time — may the good Lord take it into account, it will serve as penance for our sins. It was for the sake of heaven that my son was thus persecuted.[169] *May God reward them according to their deeds.*[170] I cannot blame the man I have in mind, as I do not know his thoughts, *man sees only what is visible . . .*[171] But this I do know: my children were young and needed some credit as is customary in business; they sought to sell off several bills of exchange for this purpose; the merchants took the bills of exchange from them and told them to come back when the Bourse[172] closed. I think that same merchant consulted a certain Jew he trusted, and when my children returned to the merchant after the Bourse closed to get their money against those valid bills of exchange which had valid bank endorsements, the merchant returned their bills of exchange to them, and this was why they often did not know how to help themselves. I beseech you, great and only God, from the bottom of my heart, forgive me in case I may have acted wrongly toward the man I am referring to; it is quite possible that everything he did was for heaven.[173] Therefore, we

---

167. Glikl's sixth child (see Family Tree C; see also Feilchenfeld 1913, p. 104, n. 22).

168. On this affair Glikl conceals more than she reveals. Only later on, in Book Four, p. 153, does she tell of the birth and rearing of her son Mordechai. Then and subsequently, in all her mentions of this son, there isn't even a hint of the events mentioned here.

169. Here Glikl may wish to infer that the pressure put upon her son to pay, although he was legally exempt, was meant to maintain good relations with the non-Jewish traders, and to prevent the Jews from acquiring a bad reputation (Feilchenfeld 1913, p. 104, n. 23).

170. Cf. Ps 62:13.

171. Cf. 1 Sam 16:7.

172. This refers to the Hamburg Bourse.

173. See this Book, n. 169.

must put everything in the hands of almighty God, not forgetting that this world of vanity is fleeting.

Indeed, mighty God, You know how I spend my time in grief and sorrow. I was a woman held in great esteem by my devoted husband throughout our long life together; I was the apple of his eye. But upon his death everything vanished: my wealth, my honor, for which I will weep all my life, despite being aware of my weakness — I am committing a grave sin by wasting my time in such sorrow and mourning. It would be better to kneel down every day and praise mighty God, to thank and praise Him for His great kindness to me, unworthy as I am. To this day I sit at my own table, I eat as much as I like, I lie down in my own bed at night, and I still have some money left to live on, for as long as it shall please mighty God. I have my beloved children, even if now and then the affairs of this or that one do not work out as well as one would have liked; still, we live and praise our Maker. So many people in this world are more honest, righteous, and devout than I am, yet have much less, not enough *food* even *for one meal*.[174] I know such people personally; I know they are exceptionally righteous. How can I thank and praise my Maker enough for all the kindnesses He does for us though we are unworthy, as I have written.[175] If only we sinful human beings acknowledged our Maker's great kindness in creating us from a lump of clay and letting us know His great, holy, awesome name so that we can worship our Maker with all our hearts. For, my dear children, look what a sinful person does in order to find favor with a king who is mere *flesh and blood, here today and tomorrow in the grave*;[176] no one knows how long that flesh and blood king who dispenses favors will live, or how long the person receiving the favors will live. And what are those favors bestowed by a king of flesh and blood? The king can make a person important or cause him to receive much money. But all this is only for a while, not for eternity. Even if everything remains in a person's possession till the day he dies — still it is all completely worthless; bitter death obliterates everything; all one's wealth and honor are of no use at all, for *there is no authority*

---

174. Cf. m.Shabbat 16:2; b.Shabbat 117b, 118a, and elsewhere.
175. Glikl expanded upon this theme earlier, especially in Book One.
176. Cf.: ". . . when standing before an earthly king who is here today and tomorrow in the grave" (b.Berakhot 33a).

over the day of death.[177] People know all this quite well, yet still they believe they must loyally serve kings of flesh and blood to attain the temporary. All the more so, then, must we consider day and night how to best serve God, blessed be He, most high of kings, who is eternal, the source of all the favors we receive from kings of flesh and blood. God, blessed be He, is the one who gives the kings everything and puts it into their hearts to dispense favor, according to His holy will, for *the mind of the king is in the Lord's hand.*[178] The gifts from a king of flesh and blood are nothing compared to what God, blessed be He, gives the faithful — namely, eternity — infinite, immeasurable, perpetual.

And so, my beloved children, take comfort and bear your grief with a long-suffering spirit. Serve almighty God with all your hearts when times are bad, God forbid, just as when times are good. Even if we believe that what mighty God inflicts upon us is so burdensome that it is nearly un-bearable, we must realize that mighty God does not inflict upon his ser-vants more than we can bear. Happy is the man who accepts whatever God causes to happen to him or his children in good spirit and with equanimity. Therefore I too ask of my Maker only that He give me patience. Everything that happens to us in this world that is not to our liking comes about in return for our deeds, so we must bear that too with patience, *just as we say a blessing for a good hap, so should we say one for an evil hap.*[179] A loyal slave of a king of flesh and blood risks body and soul for his master though his master can reward him only with wealth and valuables for this fleeting time — we do not know how long it will last, as I said. By contrast, our reward from our God lasts forevermore; just as He is eternal, so is His great compassion.

Let us then put everything in God's hands, as I return to where I left off.[180] My late daughter Matte was then three years old. You never saw such a clever, adorable girl. We were not the only ones who loved her dearly — anyone who saw or heard the cute little girl adored her. But the good

177. Cf. Eccl 8:8.
178. Cf. Prov 21:1.
179. Cf. b.Berakhot 48b, 54a; m.Berakhot 9:5.
180. Is Glikl referring to the end of the episode with her son Mordechai earlier in this Book, or to another matter?

Lord loved her even more, and when she turned three, the child's arms
and legs suddenly swelled up. Although many doctors came to the house
and gave her medicine of all kinds, it was the good Lord's wish to take her
back to Him; after four weeks of great suffering and terrible pain, the Lord
took away his share and left us our share[181] to our great sorrow and grief,
and my husband, of blessed memory, and I were both so grief-stricken that
it cannot be described. I am very much afraid that I have greatly sinned in
this against God above, without thinking of the story of R. Yochanan, to
be told presently.[182] May God have mercy, given that there are even worse
punishments in the world, as I came to learn at first hand.[183]

My husband, of blessed memory, and I were so grief-stricken that we
both suffered from serious illnesses for a long time. We brought this on
ourselves through our grief. I was pregnant at the time, about to give birth
to my daughter Chana,[184] may she live long, and due to my consuming grief
over my dear dead child whose death I could not accept, I was seriously ill
throughout the period after the birth.[185] The doctors doubted I would re-
cover and wanted to take desperate measures.[186] But while they were planning these and explaining things to my family, without having the slightest
idea that I knew anything about it, I told my husband, of blessed memory,
and my mother, may she live long, that I would not take that medicine;
this they reported to the doctors. Although the doctors did their utmost
to convince me to take the medicine, all their talk was to no avail; I told
them they could say whatever they liked — I was not taking anything more.
If faithful God wants to help me, He will, without any medicine; if it is
ordained by almighty God, what good are all the medicines in the world?
In short, I asked my husband, of blessed memory, to dismiss all the doctors
and pay their fee, which he did. God, blessed be He, gave me strength, and
five weeks after the birth I went to synagogue, albeit with great difficulty;

181. Cf. "There are three partners in man, the Holy One blessed be He, his father and his mother.
When his time to depart from the world approaches, the Holy One, blessed be He, takes away His
share and leaves the shares of his father and mother with them" (b.Niddah 31a).
182. See this Book, pp. 141–142.
183. Glikl is apparently referring to her husband's death.
184. Glikl's fourth child (see Family Tree C).
185. During this period, women used to remain in bed.
186. Measures that endanger the life of the patient in order to save him or her.

nevertheless I thanked and praised God. I felt a little bit better each day, until finally I sent my nurses away, the wet-nurse, all of them, and with the help of God above I started supervising the household on my own. Ultimately I was forced to forget my beloved little girl, as God decreed, *you are put out of mind like the dead*[187] as we learn from the following story about the deeds of extremely righteous men.[188]

This is why it is always necessary to forbear and show restraint in times of sorrow. When, God forbid, a person incurs some misfortune, whether it concerns his children or health or money—even if that person considers himself most devout, thinking to himself: Oh, dear God, why do You send me such misfortune? I truly do not know how I have sinned so awfully —one should not behave in this fashion. Instead, *whatever the disaster that may come*,[189] a person should accept it all with love, justifying God's judgment and saying: *blessed are You, true judge*.[190] Everything mighty God does is just. We should know this: Everything God does to us is all for our good. *Who can say "What are You doing?"*[191] This everyone must know: all that God does for man is for his own good. Who knows if it is not often better for us to undergo pain and suffering, loss of children, relatives, money, God forbid, and such things, than to enjoy only good, with no misfortune? God, blessed be He, is merciful, otherwise who could face judgment in the world to come?

Why should I go on at length? As I have often mentioned, our sages have written of everything, for example: the late R. Yochanan, a great sage of the Mishnah,[192] lost nine of his children during his lifetime, leaving him with only one son in his old age, a boy of three.[193] One day, the servants

---

187. Cf. Ps 31:13; see also Rashi's commentary on Gen 37:35, which presents a situation similar to Glikl's.

188. Here Glikl refers, in fact, to two stories: that of R. Yochanan and that of King David (see this Book, pp. 141–142, 143–144).

189. Cf. m.Ta'anit 3:8; b.Ta'anit 18a, 22b.

190. The formula recited in the *Tsiduk HaDin* prayer at Jewish funerals. Cf. m.Berakhot 9:2.

191. Cf. Job 9:12; Eccl 8:4. This phrase appears in the prayer just mentioned. Glikl's subsequent description continues to be influenced by this prayer.

192. Glikl calls Reb Yochanan Tanna while in fact he belonged to the Amoraim and not to the Tannaim (see also this Book, n. 195).

193. In the sources of this story (see this Book, n. 194), the child's age is not mentioned; however, Matte, Glikl's daughter, was three years old when she died (see this Book, pp. 140–141).

were washing the clothes and a cauldron of water was set on the fire until it began to boil and seethed. Near the cauldron was a bench for setting down the washing, and the little boy was set down there without anyone giving him a second thought. The boy wanted to look into the cauldron, as children will, and stood up on the bench. But since the bench was uneven it toppled over along with the child, who fell into the cauldron of boiling water. The boy screamed in anguish. All took fright and ran as one to the cauldron. The boy's father, rushing to pull him out, was left holding a single finger of the little hand, for he was already cooked. R. Yochanan banged his head against the wall and ran to the study-house, shouting to his students: "Grieve over my bad luck; this is the little bone of my tenth son, my sacrifice to God." From then on he wore the little bone around his neck as a memento. Whenever a scholar came to visit him who had not been there before, he would show him the little bone for his own pleasure, as though he were showing him his son.[194] And so, my dear children, if this is what happened to the illustrious, devout R. Yochanan — what might happen to someone else? For this same R. Yochanan[195] was a great scholar, he studied Torah, Mishnah, and Talmud, understood the Work of the Chariot and the Work of Creation, knew too how to invoke angels and demons, and was a great kabbalist; he understood what the stars in the heavens mean, and the trembling of a leaf on a tree. Despite all this, disaster befell him; he accepted it with love, remaining a devout Jew to the end of his days.

And so, my beloved children, I know of course that people usually bemoan financial loss as well as the loss of children, but what good is all our sorrowing and lamenting? If only there was a drop of good in it, but it is all to no avail. We ruin our bodies and ravage our souls as well. Such grief suppresses the body, so with a sorrowful body we cannot serve God above

---

194. Only one phrase of this story appears in the Talmud: "This is the [little] bone of my tenth son," and it is attributed to the Amora R. Yochanan bar Nafcha (see b.Berakhot 5b; b.Bava Batra 115a). For details on the evolution of the story, see Turniansky 2006a, p. 239, n. 529; see also Riemer 2008. 195. In the following paragraph, Glikl mistakenly connects the story of the Amora R. Yochanan bar Nafcha (see previous note) to the description of the personality of the Tanna R. Yochanan ben Zakkai in b.Sukkot 28a, b.Bava Batra 131a, and other sources. The differences between these sources and Glikl's version with its *taytsh* translation language and style strongly suggest a mediating Yiddish version.

as we should, for the holy Divine Spirit cannot dwell in a sorrowful body. Just as in ancient times, when the prophets wanted to invoke the Divine Spirit, they would bring different kinds of musicians and have music played to make the body happy, as is recounted several times in our books.[196]

I, your mother, was bereaved in my husband's lifetime by the death of a child of about three who was like no other child, as I have already written, and I was not wise enough to recall the late devout King David whose first-born, the son he had with Bathsheba, suffered from an illness. During the bouts of illness, King David observed mourning, fasted, gave to charity, and prayed, but God, blessed be He, took the child. When the boy died, all the king's servants fell silent and kept it a secret, saying: "The king observed mourning when the boy was ill and there was still some hope that he would live—what will the king do now, once he finds out that the boy is dead and there is no longer any hope?" So no one would say a thing. But devout King David inferred from their silence that the boy was dead. He asked the servants if the boy was dead, but no one replied. Thus he realized that his beloved son was indeed dead. He then rose from where he was sitting in the ashes,[197] requested some water, and bid his servants to bring him food and drink, then he ate and drank. This amazed the servants. Finally one of them was bold enough to ask: "Your Highness, when the boy was still alive you observed deep mourning, you neither ate nor drank; day and night you remained sitting in the ashes, but as soon as you heard that your son was dead, you justified the Divine judgment, as one should, and you said: *Blessed are You, true judge, the Lord has given, and the Lord has taken away; blessed be the name of the Lord forever and ever.*[198] Then immediately you rose and asked for food and water, as though the boy were still alive." The king told them: "I will tell you, my loyal servants. While the boy was ill and still had a soul, I did everything possible. I wailed, screamed, I repented, prayed, gave to charity,[199] thinking perhaps God, blessed be He, would show mercy and heal him. But when all this was to no avail, and

196. Cf. b.Shabbat 30b, and its connection to 2 Kgs 3:15. For more details, see Turniansky 2006a, p. 241, n. 538.

197. According to the biblical mourning custom (see also Job 2:8; Jon 3:6).

198. A combination of Ps 119:137, m.Berakhot 9:2, and Job 1:21.

199. See Book One, n. 20.

God, blessed be He, has taken back his pledge, what good is wailing and weeping? My son will never come back to us; we shall go to him."[200]

You see, then, how the late devout King David behaved. We must learn from this and leave everything in God's hands. We have sinned greatly;[201] afterward, as long as I still had my husband, of blessed memory, every time we foolishly believed that we were suffering all kinds of misfortunes, I, a sinner, despaired easily, because of my bad character, and I thought — when we suffered a loss or damage, in money or anything else — that we had reached the very bottom. Despite it all, mighty God delivered us in His compassionate kindness, as in the matter of Reb Moshe Helmstedt who I will start telling about in my fourth book.[202] With this I conclude my third book.

God, eternal and mighty, will surely be compassionate and lead us out of Exile, to serve Him as we should, and all nations will recognize that we are Your beloved people and You — mighty God, You are our father. Be compassionate with us, as a father is with his children. You are our Lord; we are Your servants. Hence, we will not cease to pray to our merciful God until He shows mercy to His servants. I, a maidservant of mighty God, beseech You, as a servant-girl beseeches her mistress, for our hearts are dependent upon You alone.[203]

END OF MY THIRD BOOK

AND WITH GOD'S HELP WE WILL BEGIN OUR

FOURTH BOOK.

---

200. For the story that ends here, cf. 2 Sam 12:15–23, which ends with the statement "I shall go to him, but he will never come back to me."

201. Since they were overwhelmed with sorrow over their daughter's death and refused to be comforted.

202. See Book Four, p. 165.

203. This passage echoes High Holiday prayers (for the detailed sources, see Turniansky 2006a, p. 244, n. 553). In the paragraph under discussion, Glikl highlights her plea as a woman in three places: she states that "we are Your [male and female] servants" while the original text only mentions [male] servants; she describes herself as "a maidservant of mighty God" similarly to Hannah in 1 Sam 1:11, in which the word "maidservant" is reiterated three times; and in the simile "as a servant-girl beseeches her mistress," which echoes the verse "as the eyes of a slave-girl follow the hand of her mistress, so our eyes are towards the Lord our God" (Ps 123:2).

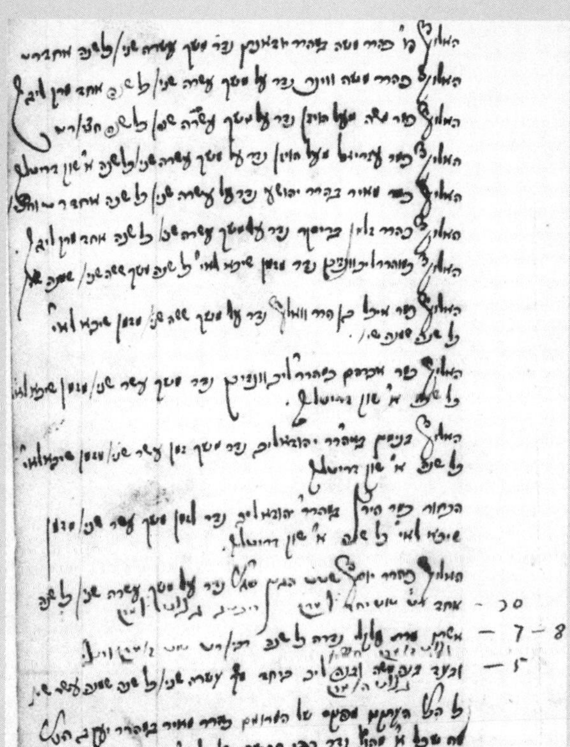

FIGURE 12

Glikl's handwriting, at the
bottom of the community ledger.
Central Archive of the History of the Jewish People, Jerusalem.

BOOK FOUR

My daughter Chana[1] grew to be a most intelligent girl; perhaps I will return to this later.[2] At that time, a ship from the East Indies carrying a large quantity of raw diamonds fell into the hands of the King of Denmark.[3] The ship lay at anchor at Glückstadt, and every one of the sailors had some diamonds. Jews therefore went to Glückstadt to buy — there was a good profit in it. There were two Jews who knew that a certain burgher in Norway had a large share of these diamonds. Together they hatched a nefarious plot to get at the house where the diamonds were kept, may God forgive us — I believe it was a baker's house, for diamonds were very cheap. This wicked, unholy gang came to Norway and began inquiring where the burgher with the diamonds lived; they came to his house, made his acquaintance, and managed to find out where he kept his treasure — then they came and stole it all. This was after the burgher lodged them in his house. Early in the morning they left the house and hired a small boat, thinking that their affairs had gone very well indeed. But this was not the wish of almighty God; when the burgher woke up in the morning, he inquired after his two guests. The porter said that they had left the house early in the morning. This raised the burgher's suspicions, for one who keeps such a treasure is constantly worrying about it. So he carefully checked the box where he kept his hoard, but found nothing there. Immediately he suspected that his two guests had done it. Without delay, he ran to the seaport and asked the sailors if they had seen two Jews sailing away. They told him: "Yes, such-and-such a sailor took them from here an hour ago." Hastily he hired a boat and four oarsmen, and they set out in pursuit of the fugitives, until soon they beheld the boat bearing the thieves. Upon perceiving that

1. Glikl's fourth child (see Family Tree C and her first mention in Book Three, p. 140).
2. Does Glikl mean here Chana's vision of her dying grandfather (see this Book, p. 184)?
3. Christian V, who reigned from 1670 to 1699.

they were being pursued, the thieves flung the entire hoard overboard. In short, the burgher caught them. Over their loud protests they were made to sail back with the burgher: "Consider well what you are doing. We are honest men. You won't find anything of yours among our things; you are shaming us. We will find a way to pay you back" (they had thrown the treasure overboard into the sea to better deny the charges against them). But our Ten Commandments tell us: *You shall not steal.*[4] So God, blessed be He, did not help them, and they were brought right back to the place they had departed from. They were stripped naked and searched carefully, but they denied everything. But it did them no good whatsoever. They were severely tortured until finally they admitted their guilt; they had thrown the treasure overboard when they saw they were being pursued, so that when searched — nothing would be found on them and they could deny all. But, as I said, this was not God's will, and both men were sentenced to be hanged. One thief immediately converted to the Christian faith,[5] but the other had always been honest, with honest parents, from Wandsbeck.[6] He did not want to convert; he sanctified God's name for all to see.[7] I knew him and his parents well; his whole life he had always behaved as an honest, decent man. It seems his comrade, who had always been a scoundrel, led him astray. This, then, was the end meant for him; no doubt his soul went to Heaven, for he *acquired eternity in a single hour.*[8] Out of respect for his family I cannot give his name, but the whole story is well known in Hamburg. God, blessed be He, has certainly had His name sanctified, for the man gave his life for God though he could have saved his own life like

4. Exod 20:13.

5. Similar accounts of criminals and thieves who were sentenced to death and whose choice either to convert or to remain steadfast in their faith determined whether they were saved or sent to death, thus sanctifying God, are documented in various forms. Such stories were mostly documented in the Yiddish genre of "historical" songs (see Turniansky 1989, pp. 42–52), among them songs praising the accused Jew who remains steadfast in his faith, as Glikl does later (see, for example, Turniansky 1989, p. 44, n. 1; Shmeruk 1985, pp. 57–69).

6. One of the three AHW communities: Altona, Hamburg, and Wandsbeck (see Marwedel 1982). This is Glikl's sole mention of this community, which had close administrative and geographic ties to Hamburg and Altona.

7. That is, he gave up his life publicly as a martyr for the sake of the God and the Torah of Israel (see this Book, n. 5).

8. Cf. b.Avodah Zarah 10b and elsewhere.

his comrade. But he observed *"and with all your soul,"*[9] so his death quite certainly was *a penance for all his sins.*[10]

Every person should learn a lesson from this, not to give in to our baser nature for the sake of contemptible money. It is not enough for a person to believe he will serve God with his entire soul and lay down his life in sanctification of God's name when required to do so. That is all very well, indeed it is appropriate for every Jew to believe it and act accordingly, as R. Akiva said: *When shall I have the opportunity of fulfilling this? Now that I have the opportunity shall I not fulfill it?*[11] However, right afterward it says *and with all your might* — this refers to money,[12] for we must serve God with money too. This should not be taken to mean that it suffices to be very charitable with one's money. While this too is a means of serving God, and is to His liking, in my humble opinion, the meaning is surely this: Just as one is prepared to lay down one's life for God, blessed be He, so too one must use one's money to serve God.

Some people *value their money over their life.*[13] The following is the correct way to serve God: *with all your soul and with all your might*[14] — by disregarding contemptible money. When God gives a person wealth, that person should invest it well by discharging his duties, as I wrote earlier.[15] And if our baser nature seeks to tempt him and he goes after money that does not belong to him, this can cause much trouble, so much so that lives are actually in danger — man endangers life and limb for the sake of money. We see this every day, alas. Our sages were right, then, in saying that some people prefer contemptible money to their own body[16] — for these people, even the soul depends on despicable money. Woe is the man to whom God gives wealth and duties,[17] who knows not how to discharge

9. Deut 6:5; and cf. b.Berakhot 61b and elsewhere.
10. Cf. m.Sanhedrin 6:2; b.Sanhedrin 43b. This phrase is used frequently in medieval Hebrew and in the Responsa literature.
11. Cf. the story told about Rabbi Akiva (b.Ber. 61b).
12. See Deut 6:5; m.Berakhot 9:5, "and with all thy might, that is, with all thy wealth."
13. Cf. b.Berakhot 61b, in a discussion of the same verse discussed here.
14. Cf. Deut 6:5.
15. See early in Book One, p. 51.
16. Glikl's free Yiddish translation of the statement quoted earlier, n. 13.
17. That is, God appoints him as a steward charged with properly managing the money entrusted to his care (also see early in Book One, p. 51).

them. His miserable, obstinate heart and his despicable baser nature prevent him from investing his money during his lifetime at high interest — in fact, inestimable;[18] he prefers to leave his children a large inheritance after his death instead of taking part of it for himself, as is written: *A man is his own relative.*[19]

An even greater folly arises when people who do not even have any children nevertheless pursue money hotly, clenching their fists against the poor and needy. Although they know quite well that they possess a fortune that will provide for them to the end of their days, they are anxious and do not willingly part with their money, never having enough, as is written: *Nobody dies with half of his desire gratified.*[20] Of such as these, the late King Solomon said in Ecclesiastes: *The man who is alone, with no companion, who has neither son nor brother; yet he amasses wealth without limit:*[21] This refers to people who do or do not have children and who possess a large fortune. And what does it say about poor, penniless creatures, or about people who used to be rich and come from a rich family — should we forgive them when they happen to do something for the sake of money? God forbid that we even think of it. For the destitute, the needy, the impoverished — all these must remember not to miss out on the reward coming to them in the world to come because of their sins in this world. For a destitute man is likely to think to himself: "I will steal the rich man's money; he has so much while I have nothing, and am I not a human being just like the rich man, I have to live too. God created us both."

The same goes for the impoverished man, poor creature, who is likely to think: "I once had a fortune, but I lost it; I will make it my business to acquire another fortune — by honest or dishonest means." May God take pity on such people and lead them from the crooked path back to the straight one, so that they choose the eternal over the transitory and accept

18. That is, it is impossible to measure or evaluate its worth. This possibly means that the interest is of no value in this world, in contrast to charity and good deeds, the fruits of which a man eats in this world, while the principal remains for him in the world to come, as noted by Rabinovitz 1929, p. 59.
19. Cf. b.Yevamot 25b; b.Sanhedrin 9b; and elsewhere.
20. Cf. Eccl Rab 1:32.
21. Eccl 4:8.

everything with love, as I have written.[22] Remember: *God, blessed be He, brings one down and lifts up another.*[23]

Thus, everyone must exercise care, merchants especially must make an effort not to devote themselves to their business affairs night and day; and even if they do know how to study, their business causes them to forget our holy Torah, as is written: *Many designs are in a man's mind, But it is the Lord's plan that is accomplished.*[24] *Heh-yod-aleph* stands for Hillel, Joseph, and Elazar.[25]

I heard the following explanation[26] of the three letters *heh-yod-aleph*: sometime in the future, God, blessed be He, will pass judgment on all poor people and ask them why they did not study Torah in this world. Should the poor man reply: "Master of the Universe, You know very well that I was a poor man and had to work hard to provide for myself and my wife and children." To this God answers: "Were you poorer than Hillel, of whom it is written: Anyone wishing to enter the study-house to study had to pay the shammash a coin every day. One Friday, good Hillel wanted very much to go to the study-house but had no coin to pay the shammash. So he climbed up to the window and hung on to hear the Halakhah lesson. Snow fell on good Hillel, poor thing, covering him entirely. It was nearly Sabbath, and the people within the study-house could not understand why it was so dark. When they looked out at the street they saw that good Hillel, poor thing, was completely covered in snow, frozen through and through. The shammash was instructed to light a fire right away and lay Hillel down beside it in the hope of reviving him. Said the shammash: "It is the Sabbath already." Said our sages: "Ai, Hillel is certainly worth the desecration of the Sabbath." They succeeded in reviving him. This is why the court on high finds the poor guilty if they have not studied Torah or have not done good deeds, for

22. In various places early in Book One.

23. Cf. Ps 75:8.

24. Prov 19:21. The apostrophes in the three-letter Hebrew word meaning "that is" indicate that each letter of the word will now be explicated.

25. Here and once more later on, Glikl writes mistakenly "Eliezer."

26. For the basis of the story that begins here about Hillel, Joseph, and Elazar ben Ḥarsom, see b.Yoma 35b. See notes that follow for possible additional sources of other details in the version brought by Glikl.

Hillel was so poor that he did not even have a coin to pay the shammash, yet despite all, he did not neglect the study of Torah. All the more so, for Hillel was such a great scholar that, had he sought to turn his learning to profit in this world by simply agreeing to accept gifts, his house would have filled up with gold and silver, for he was one of our greatest sages of the Mishnah. Nevertheless, he yearned for nothing but studying Torah, accepting his poverty with love, trusting implicitly in God. Thus Hillel condemns the poor.

Next to be brought are the wicked who luxuriated in the voluptuousness of this world and kept *company with harlots*[27] and decked themselves out for them, and committed all manner of sin. These too are brought to judgment to be questioned why they engaged in so much wrongdoing and kept *company with harlots*. So the man says: "Master of the Universe, I was a handsome man, easily led into temptation, and women desired me until I had no choice but to satisfy them." Then they say to him: "Were you more handsome than Joseph the virtuous, and was your temptation greater than Joseph's in the house with his master's wife? Morning and night she sent over his white garments,[28] a gold comb for his hair,[29] and other jewelry, not to mention the great temptation and things she offered him. Despite all this, good Joseph the virtuous did not yield and overcame temptation, not wanting to defile himself, as is written: *He did not yield to her request to lie beside her, to be with her.*[30] This should be understood in the following way: he did not want to lie with her in this world so as not to be with her in the world to come; because of this the poor man found himself in prison under such distressing circumstances. Were it not for God's abounding compassion, he could have lost his life too. Despite all this, he disregarded everything so that temptation should not overcome him. For this reason, Joseph the virtuous condemns the wicked.[31] Why should I write

27. See Prov 29:3, "but he who keeps company with harlots will lose his wealth." The expression is applied to Joseph in b.Sotah 36b and elsewhere.

28. Cf. "The garments she put on for him in the morning, she did not wear in the evening" (b.Yoma 35b).

29. Cf. "She said to him: Your hair is so very beautiful. Here is the gold comb that is in the house; take it and comb your hair" (see *Sefer Hayashar* 1986, p. 200).

30. Gen 39:10; cf. b.Yoma 35b, which does not quote the verse word for word.

31. For a comparison between Glikl's version and the original story about Joseph (b.Yoma 35b), see Turniansky 1993, pp. 164–166; Turniansky 1994c, pp. 51–54; Turniansky 2004, pp. 133–135; Turniansky 1996, p. 195.

about it at length? Our sages have already written all about it in books of morals.

Next, the rich are summoned, sleek and fat, who spent all their time consuming good food and drink, without a thought for God and His commandments. They too, in turn, are asked why they failed to study Torah and observe the commandments. If they reply that they had no time for it because of their wealth and far-flung business dealings, they are asked: "Was your wealth greater than that of Elazar son of Ḥarsom, who owned so very many cities on land and sea and many ships sailing the seas, yet nothing could deter him from the study of Torah. For this reason, good Elazar condemns the rich. We see that our excuses will be of very little use to us in the world to come, so best *be wholehearted with the Lord your God.*[32]

Let us begin again. I gave birth to my son Reb Mordechai Segal,[33] may his mature years be as pleasant and happy as his childhood. But what good does my wishing do? God above has already decided how everything will turn out.

I have already written in Book Three of our expectations of redemption and of how my father-in-law, of blessed memory, sent two barrels to us in the belief he would be traveling with them to Eretz Israel with the ingathering of the exiles.[34] But when he saw that nothing came of it, he and my mother-in-law, may she live long, moved from Hamel to Hildesheim,[35] where there was a nice community only five leagues from Hamel. They lived there for a while. My husband, of blessed memory, loved and honored his parents very much, so he suggested: "My Gliklchen, let's go to Hildesheim to visit my parents; you haven't seen them for over twelve years."[36] I agreed willingly. We took the servants and three children,[37] and set out for Hildesheim. I

---

32. Deut 18:13.

33. The author's fifth child (see Family Tree C).

34. See Book Three, p. 105.

35. According to Glikl (Book Three, p. 105, n. 34), it was actually the expectation of the imminent redemption, not the disappointment when it did not occur, that motivated the couple to move from Hamel to Hildesheim.

36. Apparently since she stayed with her husband and children in their house in Hamel during the plague in Hamburg (see Book Three, p. 117).

37. Up to this point, Glikl has mentioned five births: those of Tsipor, Nathan, Matte (who died at the age of three, before Chana was born; see Book Three, p. 140), Chana, and Mordechai. Except for Mordechai the baby (see following text), we do not know which children went with the parents. But if they indeed took three children, it is not clear how more than one child was left at home (see this Book, p. 154).

was still nursing my son Reb Mordechai Segal, not yet one year old. The servant working for us at the time was called Shmuel — a very good-looking young man nicknamed "gentle Shmuel," since we had another servant the children called "clumsy Shmuel." We reached Hildesheim; my in-laws were very glad to see us, since my husband, of blessed memory, was their youngest child, and we were doing very well.

We took what we considered to be a substantial gift in Hildesheim and brought it to them. We stayed there for nearly three weeks, enjoying being together. Then we returned home safe and sound. My father-in-law, of blessed memory, presented us with a little vase — worth about twenty reichstaler — but we liked it anyway, as though he had given us one hundred reichstaler. My father-in-law was extremely wealthy, worth over twenty thousand reichstaler, and had already married off all his children; the trip cost us over one hundred and fifty reichstaler. We were so happy with the little vase worth twenty reichstaler that my father-in-law gave us, as if it was worth a hundred. We were genuinely happy, not like children these days, who expect their parents to give them absolutely everything, without first asking if they can afford it or not.

We returned home to find all the children[38] well. My father-in-law, of blessed memory, lived in Hildesheim for a few years; it cost him about ten thousand reichstaler for three or four years. They did not have a large household yet had many expenses, and these good people realized they had no prospects in Hildesheim. So they moved from Hildesheim to Hannover and moved in with my brother-in-law, the distinguished Reb Lipman.[39] They remained there until both of them passed away in Hannover *with a good name, at a ripe old age.*[40] I will tell more about this later.[41]

Our business was doing very well. My oldest daughter, Tsipor, may she live long, was almost twelve years old. Now, Reb Leyb, son of Reb Anshl,[42] was living in Amsterdam and proposed a match with my relative by mar-

38. See previous note.
39. The second husband of Glikl's sister-in-law Yente (see Book Two, p. 91, n. 137).
40. On "with a good name," cf. b.Berakhot 17a; on "a ripe old age," cf. Gen 25:8.
41. Glikl recounts her in-laws' deaths in this Book, pp. 183–186.
42. I do not have information about this matchmaker other than the designation "Hamburger" (see this Book, n. 55).

riage, Kossman,[43] son of the late Elia Cleve.[44] Since my husband, of blessed memory, traveled to Amsterdam regularly twice a year, he left six weeks earlier than planned, writing to the matchmaker that he was making the trip in any case and would see what should be done. There was a war on at the time,[45] making it necessary for Elia Cleve to move with his people to Amsterdam.

As soon as my husband got to Amsterdam, rumors spread that my husband was there to make a match with Elia Cleve. That was on mail day, when people read their letters at the Bourse; many people did not believe it, so that large bets were placed at the Bourse, *one says thus and another says thus*.[46] Many refused to believe the match would actually take place, as Elia Cleve was a most influential man, with a reputation of being very wealthy, worth over one hundred thousand reichstaler, which was quite true, while my husband was still a young man, and we had just started doing well for ourselves; my husband had a houseful of small children to care for, may God preserve them. But whatever God above decides — must be. It must be, even if people are not pleased with it. Forty days before a baby is born, it is proclaimed in heaven: Such-and-such a man will marry such-and-such a woman.[47] And so my husband made the match with Elia Cleve. My husband, of blessed memory, gave my daughter, may she live long, twenty-two hundred reichstaler in Dutch money;[48] the marriage was to take place a year and a half later, in Cleve. In addition, my husband had to give one hundred reichstaler toward wedding expenses.

43. (Moshe) Kossman Gompertz, the son of Elia Cleve (see next note) and the grandson of Mordechai Gumpel (see Book Two, n. 31). He became Glikl's son-in-law by marrying her daughter Tsipor. In the late 1680s and the 1690s, he was an important printer in Amsterdam (see Steinschneider 1852–1860, col. 2972, no. 8688).

44. Elia Gompertz Cleve, son of Mordechai Gumpl Gompertz (see Book Two, n. 31). He founded his wealthy family's banking business and enjoyed the trust of the great Kurfürst of Weddingenburg and his ministers at Cleve, and was parnas and most prominent leader of the Jews of that duchy (see Feilchenfeld 1913, p. 116, n. 4).

45. The war between Louis XIV of France and Holland, which began in 1672 (see Munck 1990, p. 234). The Great Elector of Brandenburg was allied with the Dutch, which put his possessions in Cleve in greater danger of a French attack than Holland itself (see Feilchenfeld 1913, p. 116, n. 5).

46. Cf. 1 Kgs 22:20, here meaning "for and against."

47. Free Yiddish translation of b.Sotah 2a and/or b.Sanhedrin 22a.

48. That is, the worth of twenty-two hundred reichstaler in Dutch currency (florins or ducats).

When the time came for the wedding to take place, we went to Cleve — my husband, of blessed memory, and myself, with the infant,[49] and my daughter Tsipor the bride, may she live long, R. Meir of the kloyz,[50] who is now the head of the rabbinical court at Friedberg, and our servant, "gentle Shmuel,"[51] and a maidservant. The whole entourage finally set out for the wedding. We took the boat from Altona in the company of Mordechai Cohen,[52] Meir Ilius, and Aaron Todelche.[53] I cannot begin to describe what a gay journey it was.

Well, after a gay, delightful journey we arrived safely in Amsterdam, but it was still three weeks before the wedding.[54] We stayed with the previously mentioned Reb Leyb Hamburger,[55] spending over twelve ducats[56] a week without a second thought, since in those three weeks we spent there before the wedding — my husband, of blessed memory, made half the dowry amount.[57]

Two weeks before the wedding, over twenty of us went to Cleve with *timbrel and dancing*,[58] where we were warmly welcomed and much honored. There we entered a house truly fit for a king, outfitted as comfortably as a lord's home. Now, we had not a moment's peace all day long because of the eminent men and women of the nobility who all came around wanting to see the bride. And in truth, my daughter, may she live long, was very beautiful, second to none.

49. Probably Leyb, Glikl's seventh child, born, according to my calculations, at about the time his sister Tsipor was married, when she was thirteen or fourteen.

50. Apparently from the kloyz, a place of study, in Altona. This might be R. Meir, son of R. Wolf Ashkenazi (see Wolfsberg-Aviad, et al., 1960, p. 50). On the institution of the kloyz, see *YIVO Encyclopedia* 2008, pp. 907–909; on the kloyz in Altona, see Reiner 1993, p. 297–298. However, if the kloyz in Altona was indeed founded only in 1690, it is difficult to explain why R. Meir is already referred to as "of the kloyz" at the time of Tsipor's wedding in 1673 or 1674, unless this is based on later knowledge.

51. Regarding this man and his appellation, see this Book, p. 154.

52. Glikl's cousin (see Book Three, p. 135, n. 160).

53. I have no information about these men.

54. It emerges in the following text that this refers to three weeks before they left Amsterdam for Cleve, not three weeks before the wedding.

55. The matchmaker, Reb Leyb Hamburger, son of Reb Anshl, who was mentioned earlier in this Book, p. 154, n. 42.

56. Ducat, a unit of currency (see North 1995, p. 96).

57. One thousand one hundred reichstaler, half of the amount mentioned earlier.

58. Cf. Exod 15:20; Judg 11:34.

Elaborate wedding preparations were in full swing. The prince[59] happened to be in Cleve—at that time the elder son,[60] the crown prince,[61] was still alive—a young nobleman of about thirteen,[62] to judge from his appearance. But not long afterward the elder prince died, whereupon his younger brother succeeded him as crown prince.[63] Prince Moritz[64] was there too, along with other officials and notables. All of them notified us in advance that they wished to attend the wedding ceremony. No doubt my in-law Reb Elia Cleve had prepared in good time for such illustrious guests, so that on the wedding day itself, right after the ceremony under the wedding canopy, he had an excellent light lunch served with all kinds of desserts and expensive imported wines and fruits.

It is not hard to imagine all the commotion; the groom's father Reb Elia, may he rest in peace, and all his relations devoted themselves solely to attending and accommodating the notables as befitting their station, and there was no time even to pass the dowry from one to the other to count it, as is customary.[65] So we just put our dowry in a bag; the groom's father, the late Reb Elia Cleve, did the same with his dowry, and we sealed the bags intending to count the money after the wedding. When the bride and bridegroom were already standing under the wedding canopy, it emerged that in all the commotion—no one had remembered to have a marriage contract drawn up. What to do? All the notables, the young prince too,

---

59. This refers to Prince Friedrich (1657–1713), the second son (see next note) of Friedrich Wilhelm, the Great Elector of Brandenburg.

60. Karl Emil (1655–1674), the elder son (see previous note) of Friedrich Wilhelm.

61. Kurprinz, i.e., first in line to succeed his father as Great Elector of Brandenburg.

62. Based on the estimated age of the prince, who was born in 1657, it can be assumed that the wedding took place around 1670. A later, probably more accurate date emerges based on other information: the bride was born in 1661, when her mother was about sixteen (the details are in various places in Book Two), and was married at about thirteen and a half; she was matched when she was "almost twelve" (see earlier in this Book, p. 154), that is, in fact, "not long before" the death of Karl Emil (see next note).

63. As a result of his elder brother Karl Emil's death in 1674 (see this Book, n. 60), Friedrich inherited his place, and as a result of his father's death in 1688, he became the Great Elector of Brandenburg, Friedrich Wilhelm the Third. In 1701, he was crowned King of Prussia, Friedrich the First (see Kaufman 1896, p. 146, nn. 2–3; Feilchenfeld 1913, pp. 118–119, nn. 8–9).

64. Fürst Moritz von Nassau, who in 1647 became Statthalter of the duchy of Cleve (see Feilchenfeld 1913, p. 119, n. 9).

65. Before the marriage ceremony, each side hands over his dowry to the other so that they can count the money and thus ensure that the amounts agreed upon were in fact transferred.

were standing there trying to get a look. Our master and teacher R. Meir, head of the rabbinical court,[66] said that the bridegroom should name a guarantor[67] and pledge[68] to have a marriage contract for his bride drawn up immediately after the wedding ceremony. The head of the rabbinical court then read out the marriage contract from a book.[69] So much for the wedding ceremony. Then all the illustrious guests were ushered into Reb Elia Cleve's spacious drawing room, paneled in gilded leather, where a large table was set with all kinds of *royal dainties*.[70] The notables were all entertained lavishly.

My son Reb Mordechai was then a child of about five; never had a more beautiful child been seen in the whole world, and we dressed him very neatly and becomingly. The notables practically gobbled him up,[71] especially His Excellency the Prince, who would not let go of his hand. When the distinguished guests had eaten the desserts and fruit and copiously sampled the wines, the table was cleared and removed. Several people in disguise entered the room to perform for us, giving a very entertaining performance. Finally, the troupe did the dance of death,[72] extraordinarily beautiful.

Many prominent Portuguese Jews[73] attended the wedding too, among them one named Moccata,[74] a dealer in jewelry and precious stones, who had a nice little gold watch inlaid with diamonds, worth five hundred

---

66. Meir Raudnitz, who was then Rabbi in Cleve and later in Wesel. He died in Altona in 1724 (see Feilchenfeld 1913, p. 120, n. 11).

67. A guarantor who takes it upon himself to repay the loan if the lender wants to collect it from him (see b.Bava Batra 173b–174a).

68. Lit. "receipt of an acquisition." Confirmation of an agreement between two people according to the traditional practice of transferring an object from one person to another, or by one person holding the corner of the other's garment or kerchief.

69. From such a book as, for example, *Sefer Naḥalat Shiva*, which presents various versions of the marriage contract (see *Naḥalat Shiva* 1992, p. 46, no. 12; and also pp. 89–93, 96–97).

70. Cf. Gen 49:20.

71. From excess wonderment (see also Book Three, n. 76).

72. We know very little about this custom. See Feilchenfeld 1913, p. 121, n. 13; Katz 1993, pp. 195–199; Pollack 1971, p. 38.

73. This apparently refers to Jews from Spain and Portugal, but it is unclear whether they were residents of Cleve or came to the wedding from Amsterdam or Hamburg.

74. Without a first name, we do not know which member of the famous Moccata family is being referred to (see Kellenbenz 1958, p. 192, n. 30).

reichstaler. The bridegroom's father, Reb Elia, wanted to get the watch from Moccata and present it to the prince, but an old friend standing nearby prevented him, saying: "What for? Do you want to give the young prince such an expensive gift? Had it been the elder crown prince it could have been done." But as mentioned, the elder crown prince died and the younger crown prince succeeded him, who is crown prince yet.[75] But the bridegroom's father, Elia, whenever he went to see his old friend who had prevented his presenting a gift to the young prince, would reprimand him angrily. In fact, had Elia given the gift to the young prince, it is likely that the latter would never have forgotten it—these illustrious personages never forget such things. But *He who prays for what has already happened, this prayer is in vain.*[76] The young prince, together with Prince Moritz[77] and all the notables, departed, highly pleased. No Jew had been similarly honored in a hundred years. Thus was the wedding concluded amid joy and gladness.

After the wedding I went to Emmerich to visit my late sister Hendl's[78] grave. What sorrow and heartbreak I suffered—God knows; it is always sad when such a young person, and so beautiful, must chew the black dirt.[79] She was not even twenty-five years old. But what good is all this? We must resign ourselves to God's will, whatever that may be. She left a son and a daughter. The boy was a promising young man who studied diligently, but alas, he died young, unmarried, and was mourned by relatives and strangers alike.

On Sunday after the wedding we set out again for Amsterdam, well pleased, on the reverse journey back home, as is written: *And he went on his journeys.*[80] We reached Amsterdam and stayed there for about another two

75. Prince Friedrich was crown prince from 1688 until he ascended to the throne in 1701 (see this Book, n. 64). Glikl wrote this passage after 1691 (see opening of Book One) and before she married Hertz Levy in 1700 (see Book Six, n. 129).

76. Cf. m.Berakhot 9:3. Similar to "No use crying over spilt milk."

77. See this Book, n. 64.

78. Glikl also refers to her oldest sister as Hendlche and Hendele. On her marriage to a son of Mordechai Gompertz, see Book Two, p. 63, nn. 30, 31.

79. An idiom meaning "to be dead" (cf. Book Seven, n. 3).

80. Gen 13:3 (JPS 1917 [The Holy Scriptures, Tanakh 1917 ed. Philadelphia: Jewish Publication Society]). Based on Rashi's interpretation there: "When he returned from Egypt to the land of Canaan, he would spend the night in those inns where he had spent the night on his way to

weeks for my husband to do some business, then set out from Amsterdam toward Delfzyl.[81] You travel via the Dollart Sea,[82] called that since even the strongest man alive is taken violently ill there unless he is accustomed to the swift currents that make the vessel lurch. So we boarded the ship, leaving the baby and the servants in the cabin on deck — almost as big as a house — while my husband, of blessed memory, and I rented a small room from the captain so that we could be alone. An aperture in the wall which could be opened or shut allowed us to see into the cabin and pass things through. In the small room were two cots where we could lie down. My husband, of blessed memory, said to me: "My Gliklchen, stretch out comfortably on the cot and I'll cover you; take care and don't move a muscle, just lie still — that way the sea won't do you any harm." I had never sailed that route before, though my husband was experienced, having sailed on the Dollart two or three times. I did as my husband said and lay still. The maidservant was caring for my baby in the cabin on deck; the weather was awful, with a counter-wind. The ship swung about till everybody on board was horribly seasick, vomiting — pardon the expression.[83] Nothing in the world is worse than being seasick. The throes of death can be no worse. I did not feel it as long as I remained lying still, but the maidservant was sick too, unable to move, and my poor baby boy was with her. The baby began screaming; maybe he felt sick too. The maidservant could not move at all and just let the poor child scream, but as a mother who feels for her children, I could not bear to listen to him anymore. I had to get up from the cot where I was lying; she handed me the baby through the aperture and I placed him on my breast. But my God, it was torture — I was immediately overcome

---

Egypt." Actually, Glikl and family did not travel home exactly the same way they came. On the way to the wedding, they sailed from Altona to Amsterdam and then traveled overland to Cleve. But on the way home, they traveled overland from Cleve to Amsterdam, then sailed to Delfzyl (see following text), and then traveled overland to Hamburg.

81. Delfzyl (or Delfzijl) is a harbor city in the province of Groningen on the northern coast of the Netherlands.

82. Dollart is the name of a bay in the Wadden Sea between the northern Netherlands and Germany. Glikl's following explanation indicates that she understood the name of the place according to its similarity to the noun "douleur" (in French, "pain" or "trouble"; see also this Book, n. 90; Feilchenfeld 1913, p. 123 n. 16).

83. A polite expression asking forgiveness for the mention of an action or something unpleasant or offensive (here, vomiting). Glikl uses this expression only once more (see this Book, p. 192).

by terror of death. I was sure my end was at hand, so I started saying the confession prayer as well as I could, whatever I knew by heart. My husband, of blessed memory, was lying on his cot, knowing very well that I was not fatally ill; as soon as you plant your feet on the ground again, the seasickness goes away. As I was reciting the confession prayer with all my thoughts bent on God, my husband lay there laughing. Hearing this, I thought: I'm lying here about to die — and my husband is laughing. Though I was really very angry, it was no time for us to quarrel about it — I had not the strength to utter a single word. I had to remain prostrate, a miserable creature, for at least half an hour longer, until we reached shore and disembarked. Our seasickness then disappeared, thank God.

Since it was late at night when we reached Delfzyl, we could not go to an inn or to the home of any Jew. The sky was threatening, we were at a loss — we thought we would have to spend the night in the street, and we had to observe a fast the next day: it was "Remember the Covenant" day.[84] No one had eaten anything all day on the ship; we were all feeling nauseous and fatigued from the sea voyage. We did not want to sleep in the street with nothing to eat or drink. At last my husband went at night to the house of a Jew whose brother was married to the daughter of Chaim Fürst,[85] and asked if we could stay the night so the children would have a roof over their heads. The man replied: "Come in, for God's sake, welcome to my home. I can give you a good bed but I have no food," as it was late and his wife was away from home, in Emden. My husband, glad that we had at least a place to sleep, returned in good spirits to take us back to the house — but my God, there was nothing to eat or drink; everybody was already in bed. What little bread we still had left we gave to the children as I thanked God that I could now get to bed. The bed was very comfortable and did us more good than food and drink. We rose early the next morning for "Remember the Covenant" day,[86] then set out for Emden[87] where we stayed with Reb Avraham of Stadthagen.[88]

---

84. Called so after the refrain to the penitential prayers said on the eve of Rosh Hashanah (see Lewinsky 1975, p. 169). On the fast, see *Minhagot Wermaiza* 1987, p. 134.
85. See Book Two, p. 61, n. 13.
86. For more details on this fast, see Turniansky 2006a, p. 280, n. 192.
87. The trip from Delfzyl to Emden across the inner section of the Dollart seems to have met no difficulties (see Feilchenfeld 1913, p. 127, n. 18).
88. Referred to immediately after this as Avraham Emden. Regarding him, see this Book, n. 89.

He and my husband were close relatives; Reb Avraham Emden's father, Reb
Moshe Kramer of Stadthagen, was my husband's uncle.[89] We spent a very
nice Rosh Hashanah in Emden, completely forgetting our unpleasant experience.[90] This Reb Avraham was a prominent man; not only was he most
hospitable and gracious to us — he also had six "ticket-guests"[91] at his table
who were invited to partake of food and drink just like us. I have to say that
I have never seen any other rich man act like this.

At nightfall, once Rosh Hashanah was over, we all left Emden, intending to reach home by Yom Kippur; we made good time until we reached
Wittmund. At Wittmund we hired a boat going to Hamburg. A day's sailing from Wittmund is a place called Wangerooge,[92] where ships anchor to
pay the toll and replenish supplies. As soon as we reached Wangerooge, the
official said: "Where are you bound for?" "Hamburg," said my husband.
"Beware," said the official, "you cannot go to Hamburg — the sea is full of
pirate ships that seize whatever they can." It was getting close to Yom Kippur
and we had paid the captain ten reichstaler for the hire of his boat. We had
no choice but to chalk up the loss and return to Wittmund to spend Yom
Kippur there. We stayed with Braynele, another cousin of my husband's.[93]
We consulted them about continuing our journey: we could not travel by
sea because of the pirates; on land there were troops everywhere.[94] So we
consulted the people of Wittmund. The widow Braynele was the daughter
of the late Reb Leyb Altona of Hamburg, a most devout, wise woman, and,
most important, also a very close relative of my husband's, with whom we
had always remained close and good friends. She did all she could to help
us continue on our journey. Eventually it was decided that we would travel

---

89. They were therefore first cousins: Avraham Emden's father, Moshe Kramer, and Chaim Hamel's
father, Yosef Hamel, were brothers (see Family Tree B).

90. Lit. "our douleur," refers to the travails of sailing the Dollart (see this Book, n. 82).

91. Yiddish: *pletn-gest*, poor visitors or itinerant mendicants who were invited to meals through the
use of vouchers or tickets that directed them to hosts from the community (see Pollack 1971, p. 163,
and his many references on p. 322, n. 33; *Takanot Medinat Mehrin* 1952, p. 164, n. 3; Abrahams 1962,
p. 82, n. 1). "Plet" is from the French "billet."

92. The easternmost of the islands of East Prussia.

93. Braynele (less common diminutive of Brayne than the parallel Brayndele) was the daughter of
Reb Leyb Hildesheim (Altona) and his wife Esther, the sister of Freydchen, Chaim Hamel's mother
(see Family Tree B).

94. This refers to the war between Holland and France (see this Book, n. 45; and see following text).

home by land after Yom Kippur, and that my husband, of blessed memory, would go to Aurich to obtain a travel pass from General Buditz, since General Buditz had served under kings and dukes and everybody liked him; a travel pass issued by him would ensure us safe passage. In addition, Meir Aurich would see to it that General Buditz would assign a trustworthy officer to escort us on our journey. My husband, of blessed memory, ended up traveling to Aurich on the eve of Yom Kippur. He returned just as we were about to start the meal,[95] having arranged everything to his satisfaction. With him was a reliable corporal who would escort us to Hamburg.

After Yom Kippur we had to hire a carriage to Oldenburg — what we paid could practically have bought the horses and carriage too, since no one wanted to make the risky trip. The drivers were all apprehensive about their horses. My husband too was anxious and much perturbed, as can be imagined. I was obliged to take off my good traveling dress and don old rags.[96] Reb Meir, who was with us, as I mentioned,[97] told my husband: "My dear Reb Chaim, why are you so worried? And why are you making your wife dress so hideously?" My husband answered: "God knows I'm not worried about myself or the money I'm carrying — it's the womenfolk I'm worried about, my wife and the maidservant." Said Reb Meir: "No need to worry; seriously, Reb Chaim, you are wrong about your wife — you should not have made her dress so hideously, nobody would have harmed her anyway." My husband, of blessed memory, was very angry at Reb Meir's joking and took it very much to heart.

We left Wittmund after midnight, accompanied by Brayne and all of Wittmund for a good part of the way, with their best wishes for a good journey. We reached Oldenburg safely. Why should I write of what we went through at Bremervörde[98] and the other places. Our trustworthy corporal and our good travel pass enabled us to get there, with God's help. When we got to Oldenburg the whole city was swarming with soldiers; once again we had a difficult time. The drivers of the carriage we had brought with

---

95. That is, the short distance between Wittmund and Aurich allowed him to travel on the eve of Yom Kippur and return before the pre-fast meal.
96. So as not to draw attention on the journey.
97. R. Meir of the kloyz (see this Book, p. 156, n. 50).
98. Bremervörde is forty kilometers from Hamburg on the way there from Oldenburg. For more details, see Turniansky 2006a, p. 285, n. 230.

us from Wittmund would not continue any further for all the money in the world. My husband, of blessed memory, ran around trying to hire a carriage to take us to a certain village two leagues' distance and was finally obliged to pay a fortune. We left Oldenburg that evening and reached the village safely toward evening, and stayed the night, intending to hire another carriage there to continue on our way. That night we were sitting by the fire; the innkeeper and other locals were there too, smoking. We got to talking about different places and about this and that. One of the villagers happened to say something about the Duke of Hannover: "My master[99] too sent twelve thousand men to Holland."[100] On hearing this, my husband grew greatly relieved at finding himself in a Hannoverian state,[101] since the Lüneburg dukes[102] keep their land entirely free of any injustice —a soldier is not allowed to harass even a chicken.[103] My husband then asked how far Hannover was from that village. "Eight leagues," replied the villager. My husband calculated with the villager's help and found that he could still reach Hannover by Sukkot if he left in the morning. So my husband, of blessed memory, hired a carriage, and we set out that very night. My husband was very pleased at the opportunity to observe "Honor thy father and thy mother" with his wife and children by spending the festival with his parents, after all the anxiety, worry, and troubles we had been through. As we approached Hannover in high spirits, my father-in-law came out to greet us, like an angel, like the prophet Elijah, carrying a cane, his beard white as snow down to his waist, his ruddy cheeks glowing. In short, anyone trying to paint a portrait of a handsome old gentleman could never have painted him better. The pleasure we all took at the sight of him and our enjoyment during the first days of the Sukkot festival[104] cannot be

99. Meaning the Duke of Hannover, in whose territory the speaker lived.

100. The soldiers were sent to Holland because in this war between Holland and France (see this Book, n. 45), Hannover sided with France against Holland and her ally the Duke of Brandenburg (see Feilchenfeld 1913, p. 130, n. 25).

101. The Lüneburg-Celle duchy was named after its capital city, Hannover (and see next note). This conversation reflects the fluidity of the political situation, in which people might not know what authority governs their whereabouts at a given moment.

102. That is, the Dukes of Hannover, who were then from the Lüneburg-Celle line.

103. Apparently an idiomatic expression, though I could not find it in other sources.

104. That is, the first two days of Sukkot (the fifteenth and sixteenth of Tishrei), which are full holidays outside of Israel (and see following text).

described. Still, as soon as the festival was over we set out for Hamburg. Although my in-laws very much wanted us to spend the rest of the festival with them, our circumstances prevented us from doing so, and we parted from them with reasonable explanations. We left in good spirits — but I never saw either one of them again. May God, when He takes me from this sinful world, let me sit by their side in heaven.

We would gladly have let the corporal go on his way and paid him well, but he begged us to take him along to Hamburg; he had heard so much of the city but had never been there. Since he had really behaved very well on the road, my husband, of blessed memory, could not refuse him and took him along with us to Hamburg. Reaching Hamburg safely on the eve of the second holiday of the Sukkot festival, we found the whole family in good health, thank God, for which we must give thanks to God above. However, the trip, door to door,[105] cost us more than four hundred reichstaler, though we hardly gave that a thought since we had extensive business dealings, thank God, and *Blessed be the Lord, who has not withheld His steadfast faithfulness* from us.[106] After all our upheavals, we were finally home again.

A man called Reb Moshe lived for a time in Helmstedt, which I believe is about five leagues from Hildesheim.[107] There is a Hochschule there, which makes it an evil place.[108] This same Reb Moshe Helmstedt[109] was served with an expulsion order and was forced to leave Helmstedt. He went to Pommern and managed to obtain residency rights in Stettin,[110] where he was granted extraordinary privileges[111] as well as the Stettin mint. This meant that he and he alone had the right to mint coins in Stettin. The document stated the price they would pay to buy the raw metal for minting

105. Meaning from the time they left home until they returned.

106. Cf. Gen 24:27.

107. According to Feilchenfeld, the distance between Helmstedt and Hildesheim is about ten meilen (see Feilchenfeld 1913, p. 132, n. 26).

108. This refers to the university founded in the city in 1576. The city was considered a bad place for the Jews due to the danger of the students attacking them (see Kaufmann 1896, p. 157, n. 2; Feilchenfeld 1913, p. 132, n. 26).

109. All I know about this man is what is told about him in the following text.

110. Stettin (Szczecin) in Pommern (Pomerania). Until the Treaty of Stockholm in 1720, Stettin belonged, along with all of Vorpommern, to Sweden (see Feilchenfeld 1913, p. 140, n. 32).

111. See Book Two, n. 11.

marks;[112] a commissary was appointed by the authorities to oversee the work. Now, this Reb Moshe Helmstedt had no resources of his own to run such a large enterprise. He therefore wrote to my husband, enclosing his privilege writs, with the proposition that if my husband would supply him with the silver,[113] my husband would receive a share in the mint and in all the jewelry that he bought or sold. Stettin was an extremely important place; Jews had not lived there for perhaps more than a hundred years.[114] But many Jews frequently traveled there seeking good bargains buying pearls and other precious stones, and they did a good business in precious stones. My husband, of blessed memory, calculated that the third-taler coins[115] minted in Stettin would yield a good profit; one hundred thousand such coins could easily be exchanged for new Lüneburg or Brandenburg coins of the same denomination. So my husband, of blessed memory, wrote back saying that if he acted honestly and in good faith, my husband would enter into partnership with him. Before moving to Stettin, Reb Moshe had lived for some years in Berlin,[116] where he still owed a lot of money; this unfortunately we did not know. We knew he was not a wealthy man, but we saw that he had a valid residence permit and extensive privileges — the entire country was wide open for him; he and ten others like him could have attained great wealth and high position. However, we only found out about his debts after we suffered the great loss, as I will recount presently.[117]

My son Nathan Segal[118] was about fifteen at the time, and we sent him to Stettin to keep an eye on things. We started sending Reb Moshe large quantities of silver; he sent it right off to the mint, then sent to us in return

112. Lit. "mark fein." The adjective "fein" here refers to the pure, unadulterated quality of the metal in the coins (see Feilchenfeld's comment, Feilchenfeld 1913, p. 132, n. 27; see also "feines Gold, feines Silber," in Paul 1966, p. 196 [fein]).

113. That is, the metal needed to produce the coins.

114. The Jews were expelled from Stettin in 1492–1493, and only returned there in the seventeenth century (see *Encyclopedia Judaica* 1972, vol. 15, col. 399). Glikl calls the city "a very important place" because of its economic opportunities.

115. Lit. drittels (in German, "Dritteln"), coins worth one-third of a taler (see Feilchenfeld 1913, p. 133).

116. For evidence of Reb Moshe Helmstedt living in Berlin in 1677, see Kaufmann 1896, p. 161, n. 8.

117. See later in this Book.

118. The author's second child.

Stettin third-taler coins, which we were able to sell immediately during a single Bourse session. There was a good profit in it: sometimes two percent, sometimes more or a little less, depending on the third-taler exchange rate at the Bourse. We also received several shipments of pearls, another source of good profit, so we were well satisfied.

Shortly before, about a year earlier, I gave birth to my daughter Esther,[119] may she live long. People started proposing matches for our son Nathan Segal, including one with the orphan[120] of the distinguished parnas and "good man" of the community board Reb Elia Ballin.[121] Another match that was proposed—this one was practically agreed upon—was with the daughter of the distinguished Reb Shmuel Oppenheim,[122] but God delayed it so that it never came about, since the parents on both sides were supposed to deposit the dowries with my pious brother-in-law, our master and teacher R. Itsik Segal[123] in Frankfurt. We always had several thousand in precious stones on deposit with him, and the previously mentioned distinguished Reb Shmuel was also supposed to send his dowry to Frankfurt

which he did. But it was wintertime, a big flood delayed the delivery of the dowry, and it was fourteen days overdue. Meanwhile our matchmakers kept pestering us and wouldn't drop the match with the orphan. My husband, of blessed memory, got to thinking: "I haven't heard anything from my brother R. Itsik in Frankfurt about receiving the money as agreed. The distinguished Reb Shmuel Oppenheimer must have had second thoughts. If we let the match with the orphan slip away too, we'll find ourselves sitting in the filth between two stools."[124] So, hoping for good luck, we decided

---

119. The author's sixth child, and not the fourth as per Feilchenfeld 1913, p. 326). Glikl's son Nathan was about fourteen when his sister Esther was born; according to Feilchenfeld, she would have been four years younger than Nathan.

120. Her name, Miriam, appears in this Book, p. 193; see also Book Five, p. 255.

121. For details about him, see Book Two, n. 45.

122. Shmuel Oppenheim or Oppenheimer (1630–1703) was a court Jew and military supplier, first in Heidelberg (to the Elector Karl Ludwig) and then in Vienna. For his activities on behalf of the Jews, they honored him with the epithet *Judenkaiser* (see about him *Encyclopedia Hebraica* 1988, vol. 2, cols. 85–86; *Encyclopedia Judaica* 1972, vol. 12, cols. 1431–1433, Feilchenfeld 1913, p. 134, n. 28; Lowenthal 1978, p. 286, n. 9; Abrahams 1962, p. 86, n. 1).

123. See Book Two, p. 92.

124. Cf. Wander 1987, IV, p. 940, no. 68*.

to go ahead with the match with that orphan. The mother of the fatherless girl[125] had promised four thousand reichstaler banco[126] in addition to the bride's trousseau,[127] while we gave our son Nathan Segal twenty-four hundred reichstaler banco. The betrothal ceremony took place, with wishes for good luck. Eight days later we get a letter from my brother-in-law R. Itsik, of blessed memory, announcing that the money had arrived and that my husband should send him power of attorney immediately, without further delay. But it was too late. My husband, of blessed memory, wrote to his brother to explain that when the money was two weeks overdue, he had surmised that Reb Shmuel had changed his mind. Since this was a good match, he had not wanted to lose it over a slight uncertainty. He expressed the wish that the esteemed Reb Shmuel too would find a suitable match for his daughter. But my God, what a reply came from my brother-in-law Rabbi Itsik to this letter! How furious that man was in his letter — I cannot describe. But what is done cannot be undone. We were most satisfied with the highly desirable match we made. My relative by marriage Reb Elia[128] was known as a trustworthy man among Jews and non-Jews alike. He was parnas of our community[129] for several years until the day he died, and the four thousand reichstaler banco made a good-sized dowry. Had Providence seen fit to give this couple a happy fate, with success — like the esteemed Reb Shmuel,[130] who grew more successful every day — things would have been fine. But good, compassionate God deals out his gifts and generosity to whomever he chooses to honor, while we ignorant mortals have no right to utter a word; we must thank our kind Maker for everything. As soon as our son Nathan Segal was betrothed, we bid him come home so that he could give his bride a gift, which he did, at a most elegant, festive meal. They started off happily in every respect, thank God.

125. Regarding Zisse, the widow of Elia Ballin and the orphan's mother, see Feilchenfeld 1913, p. 135, n. 28b.

126. See Book Three, n. 92.

127. Clothes, undergarments, utensils, and so on, brought by the bride.

128. Reb Elia Ballin (see this Book, n. 121, and Book Two, n. 45).

129. That is, the Jewish community of Hamburg.

130. Reb Shmuel Oppenheimer, with whose daughter the match did not come about (see previous text).

About two weeks afterward, the bridegroom, my son Nathan, returned to
Stettin.[131]

We continued doing business with Reb Moshe Helmstedt,[132] but he was
deceitful — and deceitful hearts cannot be patient. When they have money,
whether it belongs to them or not — as soon as they get their hands on it
they immediately call it their own, as we — God have mercy — found out.
His first misfortune began when he sought to cheat the commissary or the
cashier of one thousand reichstaler by arguing that the cashier had made a
mistake; and when the latter would not admit to any mistake, claiming that
justice was on his side, Reb Moshe began litigating against the cashier in the
Stettin courts, an extremely costly process. Moreover, he was a pompous,
obese, stuffed, arrogant wicked man. At any given time he had ten to twelve
thousand reichstaler banco of ours on hand, never worrying himself, as an
honest man would, about the money not being his own or having to return
it to whoever had given it to him on credit. Still, no doubt his thoughts did
not go much farther than seeing so much money near at hand. He wanted
to enjoy it while it was there, buying himself a fancy carriage and the best
pair of horses to be had in Stettin, and he kept two or three servants. He
lived like a prince, though the profits were not that high. In any case, as
I already mentioned, he had lived in Berlin before moving to Stettin,[133]
being forced to move away from there because of debts and quarrels. But
the pompous fool, once he got his hands on good Reb Chaim Hamel's
money, could not control himself any longer, perhaps thinking: "I must
show my enemies in Berlin what kind of man I've become" — he took his
light carriage and four horses and took two or three thousand reichstaler in
third-talers with him, and wrote to us implying that he meant to exchange
them for ducats, then send us the ducats from Berlin by post. This was
common practice; as there was a commission of one percent, it made sense
to send ducats. Also, the shipping costs were much cheaper than for third-
talers. All this was fine and good. But when my good Moshe Helmstedt[134]

131. That is, he returned to the place from which he had come for the engagement.
132. See this Book, pp. 165–166.
133. See this Book, p. 166, n. 116.
134. Obviously, this is said ironically, as in, for example, the mention of "my good Yakov" (e.g., see
Book Three, p. 119).

arrived in Berlin, he started rattling his money, for a man can hide neither his character nor his money.[135] His creditors, Jews and non-Jews, heard of this and had my good Reb Moshe arrested.

What more can I say? He could not leave Berlin. It cost him eighteen hundred reichstaler. And there went the money of good Reb Chaim Hamel. Reb Moshe returned to Stettin but never sent any ducats or third-talers to Reb Chaim. At that time he had over twelve thousand reichstaler banco of ours. In the end we were reimbursed for two thousand reichstaler banco — and all this while Reb Moshe was writing to us demanding more money because the mint had been closed down. My son Nathan Segal, though the situation was not to his liking, could not say a word to us about it, since all his letters were opened. In the end he sent us a message via some merchants to say that my husband, of blessed memory, should do nothing but should just come to Stettin.

At that time, Issachar[136] came here from Kurland.[137] I really should have written about the whole Issachar story before, because he had been with us ten years earlier — but I'll wait with it for the time being and tell it separately;[138] it is of no matter whether his story comes sooner or later. In any case, my husband says to Issachar: "You must come to Stettin with me, I have to see what's going on there." On arriving in Stettin, they intended to balance the books with Reb Moshe Helmstedt, but he put them off from one day to the next, giving my husband several bills of exchange for Hamburg and a small quantity of pearls and gold. In short, my husband refused to be put off any longer. Moshe Helmstedt was forced to go over the accounts with him. Five thousand five hundred reichstaler banco were missing, nor could he account for them. Easy to imagine how upset my husband, of blessed memory, was to discover this. Said Reb Moshe to my

135. According to one opinion, this is a version of the proverb "Natur und Liebe lassen sich nicht bergen" (Nature and love cannot be hidden; see Landau 1901, p. 48). For other opinions, see Feilchenfeld 1913, p. 138, n. 29. Prof. Simon Neuberg believes that this is a version of the proverb "Eiter und Geblüt lassen sich nicht bergen" (Pus and blood cannot be hidden).
136. Issachar Cohen (see Book Three, nn. 7, 140).
137. The area of Eastern Latvia and southward (see *Encyclopedia Judaica* 1972, vol. 5, cols. 1003–1006). Issachar might have been sent to Kurland by Chaim Hamel (as per Feilchenfeld 1913, p. 139, n. 30a).
138. Glikl does not keep this promise in her memoir, nor does she keep another promise about this matter (see Book Three, n. 151).

husband, of blessed memory: "Listen, brother, I know very well that you are dissatisfied with the accounts. I cannot blame you for that. I was at fault in investing your money. Don't worry, I'll give you bills of exchange of my own; you'll be paid in full in less than a year and a half. Now come up to my synagogue with me." My husband goes up with him to the synagogue in his house. Then he takes the holy Torah scroll out from the ark, takes it in his arms,[139] and swears by all its holy letters and other things—which I do not want to mention in vain[140]—when the time came to pay off the bills of exchange he would repay my husband in full; he had the means to repay him, but right now his assets were all tied up. Once he paid the money back to my husband, he would make sure he was perfectly satisfied, adding more such talk not even worth putting down on paper. Issachar angrily challenged my husband to go to court, though it was not at all to my husband's liking; my husband was reluctant since he would have to appear before the tribunal of Stettin. That's Sweden—an evil place.[141] So my husband, distressed, departed with his bills of exchange and came to Hamburg bearing the sad news. Though he—peace unto him—did not want to tell me, it was impossible for him to hide something like that from me. I happened to be pregnant with my son Reb Leyb,[142] so I was now bankrupt and pregnant.[143] It is easy to imagine how we felt: just two weeks earlier we had incurred a loss of fifteen hundred reichstaler because of a bankruptcy in Prague, and another thousand with a merchant in Hamburg. My son Nathan was engaged to be married[144] in about six months' time—this cost us more than three thousand reichstaler.

In short, we calculated that our expenses that year totaled eleven thousand reichstaler banco, and we could still be called young, having married

---

139. According to "there is no oath made without one's holding some holy object," and "the object kept must be the holy scrolls" (b.Shabbat 38a).

140. Glikl is obviously referring to the commandment "You shall not swear falsely by the name of the Lord your God" (Exod 20:7).

141. It is possible that Glikl's attitude stems from the general attitude toward Sweden in her milieu (see Book Two, p. 61).

142. The author's seventh child (see Family Tree C).

143. In the Yiddish original, an idiom meaning "pain piled on pain" or "trouble piled on trouble." See Tendlau 1860, p. 195, no. 626, where parallels from the Midrash are also cited to explain the phrase.

144. As is recounted in this Book, pp. 167–168.

off only one child,[145] while we had a house full of children,[146] may God protect them, so that we were struggling to maintain our good reputation.[147] What's more, we had to keep it all a secret. I was quite ill with distress over all this, but in public I blamed my pregnancy even though *a fire was burning inside me*.[148] Thus my husband, of blessed memory, consoled me and I consoled him, as best we could. This was just before the Frankfurt-am-Main fair. My husband was supposed to attend just like he attended all the fairs. He came back from Stettin on Thursday morning, and on Friday he was already supposed to leave for Frankfurt-am-Main. He said goodbye to me in a grim mood. Before he left, I implored Issachar,[149] for God's sake, go with him. My husband, of blessed memory, was so downcast that I did not want to let him travel on his own. But Issachar, who proved his evilness at every turn, did so in this case too, refusing to accompany him unless my husband promised to give him two percent of everything he bought or sold. What could we do? I could not let my husband, of blessed memory, travel on his own. So we had no choice but to do whatever Issachar wanted. My husband entreated me not to think about it[150] anymore, for God's sake, since nothing could be changed, and I had to clasp his hand as promise that I would forget it, and my husband too promised me not to think about it anymore. We had no real faith in the bills of exchange,[151] and in fact we received payment for only one of them out of all the money he owed us. As for all the rest, he denied his signature on them all, which cost us several hundred more in expenses.

My husband, of blessed memory, reached Harburg[152] on Friday and spent the Sabbath there, until the Sabbath was over and the post chaise set

---

145. The daughter Tsipor (on her marriage, see earlier in this book).

146. Before she gave birth to her son Leyb (see this Book, nn. 142, 162), Glikl had given birth to six children: Tsipor, Nathan, Matte, Chana, Mordechai, and Esther. After Matte's death (Book Three, p. 140) and Tsipor's marriage (earlier in this Book), four children were left at home.

147. According to the context, this refers to maintaining a good reputation in order to make good matches for the children.

148. Opening of a lamentation for the Ninth of Av (see *Kinot* 2011, p. 514).

149. Issachar Cohen, who accompanied him on his trip to Stettin (see this Book, p. 170, n. 136).

150. The matter of Moshe Helmstedt recounted earlier.

151. That Moshe Helmstedt gave them (see earlier in this Book).

152. About six miles from Hamburg.

out from Harburg. He wrote me a long consoling letter from there saying that I must calm down despite everything; God, blessed be He, would compensate us for it all somewhere else, as indeed happened. My husband reached the holy community of Frankfurt-am-Main, and it was his best fair ever—he made thousands at that fair; we thanked God above, who never took away his loving compassion and always sent us a cure for any injury.[153] At the time I was convinced that no one in the world could possibly have such real troubles and worries as I did, forgetting that the entire world is full of suffering—everyone finds his own[154]—like the philosopher who was walking down the street one day. He meets a good friend of his and greets him, asks how he's doing. The friend thanks him and replies: "My dear friend, I am not doing well at all. I have more worries and troubles than anyone in the whole world." Says the philosopher: "My good friend, if you like, come up to the roof with me and I will show you all the houses in the entire city, and I will tell you what troubles and tragedies are hidden within each one. If you like, take your troubles and fling them away to where those other troubles are. Choose whichever you like; maybe you will find something to your liking." The two of them go up on the roof. The philosopher shows his friend a calamity in this house, a calamity in that. "Now do as I told you." Said his friend: "Yes, I see that every house conceals much distress and worry, as much as I have, perhaps even more. I'll keep my own troubles."[155] This is our human way of thinking—every person thinks he suffers more than anyone else. This is why it is best to be patient, for when almighty God so wishes—He can remove all troubles.

Then my father, of blessed memory, fell severely ill with the gout, heaven help us, and his body started to swell up; this illness was to cause his death. He lay *on his bed of suffering*[156] for over three months. We were up with him every night, sometimes until midnight, thinking every time that we would wait with him for the end. When the time finally came, and God wanted to take him from the transitory to the eternal, we were sitting there one night —my husband, of blessed memory, myself, and my mother, may she live

153. A variation on the proverb "God sends the cure before the injury" (see Stutchkoff 1950, p. 427).
154. A well-known proverb (see Book One, p. 57, n. 65).
155. For a different version of this story, see Book One, p. 57.
156. Cf. Ps 41:4.

long. It was very late at night, and I was toward the end of my pregnancy.
My mother persuaded us, my husband and myself, to go home. About
an hour after we had gone to bed, someone from my father's house came
knocking at the door for my husband to accompany him immediately to
my father's house. We were used to this, for it happened often. My husband
would not let me go with him and convinced me to stay in bed. If it became
necessary, he would send for me. I allowed him to convince me and went
to bed, and I fell immediately into a deep sleep. As soon as my husband
reached my father's house, that very instant — he died. It was about midnight. My husband would not let them wake me, saying there was time
enough to wake me in two or three hours. But in my deepest sleep, something came and knocked three times at my door; the entire house seemed
about to collapse. I jumped right out of bed, asking who's that knocking,
but *there was no voice, nor any that answered*,[157] no reply. I threw my robe
on and ran over to my father's house, may his memory be a blessing. There
I found what I have already described.[158] It is easy to imagine how I felt and
how we all grieved. But what good is it all? It was decreed that I should lose
my dear father, who lived to a ripe old age and had an excellent reputation.
On the twenty-fourth of Tevet[159] he passed from this world, *leaving us and
all Israel alive*.[160] I was inconsolable for a long time, until God blessed me
after the thirty days of mourning[161] with a baby boy, and his name Leyb
was reborn.[162] Yet it seemed his birth boded ill, since upon entering this

157. Cf. 1 Kgs 18:26, 29.

158. That is, that her father passed away.

159. January–February. The year was 1673, as per Simonsen 1905, p. 99, and not 1670, as per Grunwald 1904, p. 283. For detailed calculations, see Turniansky 2006, p. 308, n. 394.

160. Phrase announcing a person's death, borrowed from b.Berakhot 61b and used mainly in Responsa literature.

161. Lit. *shloyshim*.

162. That is, the name of Glikl's father, Leyb, was reborn by naming the newborn after his late grandfather, as was customary in Ashkenaz. This is the only place in her book that Glikl mentions her
father's name. In the Metz memorial registry, she is listed as "Glik bas (daughter of) Yudah Yosef"
(see *Pinkas Metz* 1829, p. 3a; and Figure 2). The "secular" name "Leyb" (which is Yiddish for "lion")
is frequently appended to the Hebrew "holy" name "Judah," on the basis of Jacob's blessing ("Judah
is a lion's whelp," Gen 49:9). However, Glikl calls her father, as well as her son who bears his name,
just "Leyb," not "Yudah-Leyb" or "Yudah-Yosef," and so does everybody else, except when only his
"holy" name "Yudah" is used during service in the synagogue. Glikl never mentions her father's
surname, Pinkerle, which derives from a name of a place in Moravia (see the index to Frænkel 1999,
I, pp. 171–172; Kaufmann 1896, p. xvi; Feilchenfeld 1913, p. 322). In other sources, the appellation

sorrowful world he did nothing for twenty-four hours but lie there moaning, until the midwife and all the women present thought he would not live. But it was dear God who wanted the child to grow stronger from day to day, and in this way was I consoled by the child who took my father's place, and I rejoiced at having the boy.

My beloved mother was left a widow with three fatherless children.[163] My father left her sixteen hundred reichstaler in accordance with her marriage contract, and about fourteen hundred reichstaler for every child. The fatherless children could have had even more, but they lost over one thousand reichstaler apiece, as I might recount later.[164] My husband, of blessed memory, and my brother-in-law Reb Yosef Segal[165] wanted no part of the inheritance, though each had a writ for half a brother's share[166] in the inheritance — they chose not to realize it, leaving everything to my mother and the fatherless children. A year after my father, of blessed memory, passed away, my husband and his brother-in-law Yosef Segal arranged the betrothal of my brother, Wolf,[167] to the daughter of Reb Yakov Lichtenstadt,[168] a prominent, highly respected man. He was parnas of the region until his death, a very wealthy man. In the end he had a dispute with his stepson Reb Avraham Lichtenstadt[169] and ultimately lost his fortune toward the end of his life. My brother-in-law Yosef Segal accompanied my brother, Reb Wolf, to the betrothal ceremony, then, at the time of the next

"Pinkerle-Stade" is added to his name (see Simonsen 1905, pp. 99–100; index to Frænkel 1999, I, p. 180).

163. Meaning Matte, Wolf, and Rivka, Glikl's younger (and at that time unmarried) siblings (see below and Family Tree A).

164. Glikl does not write about this matter in what follows.

165. The husband of Elkele, Glikl's sister.

166. A writ in which a father promises his daughter a share in the inheritance, specifically, half the share of each of her brothers (for further information, see Yuval 1989, pp. 30–32). From Glikl's wording it is clear that both she and her sister Elkele transferred the writs to their husbands, who in turn gave up their shares in favor of Glikl's younger sisters Matte and Rivka, and her brother Wolf, who were married after the father died (see following text). It is not clear whether the younger sisters also received such a writ. The merchandise that their late father left was sold at an auction to pay for the three dowries.

167. Glikl's younger brother, her parents' only son.

168. The first Primator (head representative) of the Landesjudenschaft, the organization of Bohemian Jews. He died in 1672 (see *Encyclopedia Judaica* 1972, vol. 10, col. 1403).

169. He served as Primator after his father's death in 1672 until 1693 (see *Encyclopedia Judaica* 1972, vol. 10, col. 1403).

Leipzig fair, my husband accompanied him to the wedding ceremony, with Issachar,[170] our servant at the time. My brother-in-law Reb Yosef Segal and my husband, of blessed memory, paid all their expenses, without asking my mother for any reimbursement. When my brother-in-law Reb Yosef Segal came back with the bridegroom[171] from the betrothal ceremony, he recounted how lavish and elegant it all was, for Reb Yakov Lichtenstadt still held his high position then. After that my husband, of blessed memory, accompanied my brother to the wedding ceremony, also a lavish occasion; then my husband returned home while my brother and his wife stayed there[172] for a while.

When Father died, everything he had was invested in jewelry. My husband, with Reb Yosef Segal, my brother-in-law, of blessed memory, went to the trouble of arranging an auction and sold everything so that my mother, may she live long, would be able to marry off the fatherless children when something suitable should come along. In fact, not long afterward, my sister Matte[173] was betrothed in Leipzig to the son of our master and teacher the distinguished R. Modl Dayan.[174] The wedding was held here in Hamburg. It is well known what an important man this Rabbi Modl Dayan was, and his pious wife Pessele[175] — surely there's been no one like her in the whole world since the matriarchs Sarah, Rivka, Rachel, and Leah. Truly no woman could hold a candle to her when it comes to piety and righteousness, especially as she was a woman of valor and ran the business. She provided a most ample living for her husband and his sons, in Vienna as well

170. Mentioned earlier in this Book, p. 170.

171. They returned home, to Hamburg, where both lived.

172. Glikl does not mention where the young couple stayed or where the betrothal and the wedding took place. According to the functions of the bridegroom and his father (see this Book, nn. 168, 169), we may assume it was Prague.

173. See this Book, n. 163.

174. This refers to Modl Ries, a scion of one of the wealthiest families of court Jews in Vienna (see *Encyclopedia Judaica* 1972, vol. 15, col. 406). He was a judge (hence his cognomen *Dayan*) in the rabbinical court of the Viennese Jewish community. After the expulsion from Vienna in 1670, he was among the founders of the Berlin community of Vienna exiles and remained very active there (see Kaufmann 1896, p. 170, n. 1; Feilchenfeld 1913, p. 147, n. 34; Abrahams 1962, p. 92, n. 1).

175. Pessele was the daughter of the Viennese community leader David Yakov Neumark and the sister of R. Shlomo Zalman Mirels, who later became the rabbi of the three AHW communities (for more about him, see Book Five, n. 63). She was also the mother of Elia Ries, husband of Glikl's sister Matte (see Kaufmann 1896, p. 170, nn. 1–3; Feilchenfeld 1913, p. 147, n. 34; Family Tree A).

as in Berlin, where they lived later on,[176] because our master and teacher
R. Modl was bedridden, able to conduct business only in a limited way;
he was a very wise, shrewd man — the whole world spoke about him. He
was well liked by His Highness the Prince Elector of Brandenburg,[177] who
once remarked that if the man's legs had been like his head, he would have
no equal. They both passed away in Berlin, prosperous and well respected.
It was astonishing to read her will; I will write nothing about it. Anyone
wishing to read her will can still find it at her children's; surely they never
threw it away.

The only one left, poor thing, was my youngest sister, Rivka,[178] who
actually made a good match too, getting the son of my late brother-in-law
Reb Leyb Bonn,[179] a very honest man. He was parnas in the region for
many years as well as a man of significant wealth. Reb Leyb, along with
his son, Reb Shmuel Segal, came here to celebrate the wedding;[180] it was
most dignified, with much rejoicing. My mother held such elegant, lavish
weddings that no one could tell that she was a widow, poor thing; it was
all as though my father, of blessed memory, were still alive. Not a single
prominent member of the community failed to attend and honor her with
his presence. After the wedding, my brother in law Reb Leyb returned
home, and within less than six months he went the way of all men.[181] He
died a prosperous and well-respected man, but[182] then my brother-in-law
Reb Shmuel Bonn and my sister[183] moved to Bonn to live in his father's
house, and he prospered there and was exceedingly generous in his good
deeds. He was appointed parnas to take the place of his late father. But a
few years later, during the war between His Highness the King of France,

176. The Ries family, who lived in Vienna until the expulsion of the Jews in 1670, were among the
first of the exiles to settle in Berlin (see this Book, n. 174, and the references there).

177. Kurfurst Friedrich Wilhelm, the Great Elector of Brandenburg, before he was crowned King of
Prussia in 1701 (see this Book, n. 63).

178. This sister was born a week after Glikl gave birth to her oldest daughter (see this Book, p. 93).

179. Leyb Bonn was the brother of Chaim Hamel, Glikl's husband.

180. They traveled from Bonn, the home of the groom's family, to Hamburg, where the bride lived
with her widowed mother.

181. Meaning "he passed away." Cf. "I am going the way of all the earth" (1 Kgs 2:2).

182. The import of this word is made clear only in the following text, in light of the heir's troubles.

183. That is, her sister Rivka (see earlier) and her husband. As a result of her sister's marriage to her
brother-in-law's son, Glikl became the sister-in-law of both father and son.

His Highness the Emperor, and Holland,[184] the French invaded Bonn and captured the city—the house he had inherited from his father, along with the other houses—all was burned and sacked.[185] In this way he lost everything he had, poor creature, so that he could not live there any longer— that is why he came to Hamburg. No need to tell how he prospered again, then once again, alas, lost it all. It does no good to tell of it here. The poor man is truly a most honest, God-fearing person, may God deliver him from his troubles, along with all of Israel. His children too—they were born, raised, and married in prosperous, respectable circumstances; but on some of them, alas, fortune did not smile. May God, kind and compassionate, blessed be He, show mercy on them all once again, despite everything. For it is said: No one can call himself fortunate before his death,[186] as in the following story.

Once upon a time there was a mighty king who kept a philosopher in his court, called Solon.[187] The king held the philosopher in the highest esteem, for he was truly a very wise man. One day King Croesus[188] orders his servants to dress him in his royal robes and summons all his courtiers to come pay him obeisance in their best finery. He also orders that his finest precious stones and his most priceless treasures be taken out and displayed. Next, the king orders that his philosopher be summoned to the king's presence. Solon enters, kneels, and prostrates himself,[189] as is proper. King Croesus says to the philosopher: "My dear Solon, you have observed all our sumptuous treasure and wealth assembled here. Have you ever beheld anyone more fortunate than I?" The philosopher replies: "My gracious king, I have observed well, yet I cannot consider you as fortunate as a certain man

184. This refers to the Nine Years' War (1688–1697), fought by Louis XIV, the King of France, against Kaiser Leopold I, Holland, and the other League of Augsburg countries (see Munck 1990, pp. 375–376, and the note that follows).

185. Bonn, which was then the seat of the Archbishop of Cologne, was conquered by the French in 1689, as a result of which the *Judengasse* was burned (see *Encyclopedia Judaica* 1972, vol. 4, col. 1210; Feilchenfeld 1913, p. 149, n. 36).

186. A partial translation of the Latin proverb "Dicique beatus ante obitum nemo supremaque funera debet" (No one should be called happy before he is dead and buried). Solon tells the proverb to Croesus, King of Lydia, in the story by Herodotus (see Herodotus 1.29–45). One version of the story appears in the following text.

187. An Athenian statesman and poet (app. 638–558 BCE). One of the Seven Wise Men of Greece.

188. The last King of Lydia (563–546 BCE).

189. Cf. m.Yoma 6:2.

from Athens. This man had ten children and educated them all well during his lifetime. He was a wealthy man who married off all his children to well-respected families. He and his children served their country faithfully. Now, not only was this resident of Athens a highly respected man: he also lived to see his children wealthy, prosperous, and highly respected, till he reached a ripe old age. And so he died contented. I consider him more fortunate than Your Highness. While it is true that the king enjoys great wealth, respect, and glory, His Majesty is still young; who knows what his end will be. Another king or prince might declare war on the king and emerge victorious, seize all the king's wealth, and exile the king from his country and his court. He might even take the king's life. Can a man be fortunate whose end is so wretched and miserable, God forbid?" Says King Croesus: "Solon, how dare you value a private individual's happiness over our majesty the king's?" Says Solon: "Your Royal Highness, I do so because that man died happy. No man whose end is unknown should be complacent. It is possible — it is to be hoped — that the king will remain fortunate till his end. However, it is also possible that what I spoke of will come to pass." Thereupon the king, incensed, took up his gold scepter and prodded Solon with it, forbidding him to return to the king's court ever again. So good Solon departed. Several years passed. King Croesus retained his wealth and splendor and forgot all about his good, wise philosopher. A short while afterward, the king found himself embroiled in a border dispute that quickly deteriorated into a bloody war lasting several years. It was Croesus's fate to lose the war, while his adversary — another king — took Croesus prisoner. That king conquered all Croesus's lands and fortified them, then returned with the captive Croesus to his country. His ministers and generals conferred as to the preferred method of the king's execution. It was decided that he be burned at the stake. Preparations for such a major event began, with people coming from near and far to see mighty King Croesus burned at the stake. A huge bonfire was made, with different kinds of balsamic oils and other sweet-smelling fragrances to burn along with King Croesus so that he would go up in a royal conflagration. The other king — the one who had defeated Croesus — stood at the window watching as Croesus was led to the stake. As he was being led in this way, Croesus remembers his wise, loyal philosopher who told him that no man should consider himself fortunate until his death. That is when he started screaming and lamenting: "O Solon, how right you were to say that no man should consider himself fortunate until his end is upon him." The other king, who had ordered the preparation of this hot bath with no water,[190] was watching at the window and heard Croesus lamenting bitterly. So he ordered his attendants to have Croesus brought immediately to him again, and this was indeed done without delay. Croesus fell to his knees before his victorious enemy. The king commanded him to rise—he had something to say: "My Croesus, when you were being led to the horror of your death, what were you shouting and lamenting about so loudly?" So Croesus recounted all that had passed with his philosopher Solon—how he had mocked his words and banished him, then had continued his wrongdoing, "until this moment, when I beheld the horror of death and recalled the words of my wise, loyal philosopher: a man should not consider himself fortunate until he knows his end; then I called out to him with those few words as I faced the horror of death." The victorious king listened to him with kind compassion, thinking to himself: "Croesus too was once a great king, until God delivered him into my hands. Who knows? I am not dead yet—the same fate might be in store for me one day." Thereupon he pardoned Croesus and gave back to him his life and his land, and his courtiers too. So if our actions prove successful, we mortals still should not boast; we must remember that we know not how or what our end will be, as we have just read in this story.[191]

Now, my mother, may she live long, married off all her children, in prosperity, honor, and with every possible comfort. When my father died, may his memory be a blessing, my mother, may she live long, was forty-four years old.[192] She had opportunities for many good matches, and could have remarried and had great wealth again. But the dear good soul never wanted

190. This probably refers to burning at the stake, but I have not found this expression in other sources.

191. There are many differences between Glikl's version and the better-known versions of the story (see Herodotus 1.29–45; Plutarch 1932, pp. 113–115; and the sources cited by Elkoshi 1981, pp. 143–144. A brief version of the story also appears in Arrian 1971, p. 377). Glikl may therefore have been exposed to the story in a collection of stories about Alexander, a hero she was familiar with (see Book One, pp. 54–56; Book Six, pp. 282–284).

192. Glikl was also about forty-four when her husband died. Like Glikl, her mother was long-lived: she died at seventy-five (thirty-one years after her husband), on August 15, 1704 (see Simonsen 1905, p. 99).

that, preferring instead to remain a widow. She used the little she had left over, poor thing, for her own livelihood, to provide for herself and live in a small house of her own, retaining her housekeeper and living a comfortable, secure life. If God punishes a woman and she loses her first husband, God forbid, may the good Lord give her this thought too.[193] How pleasant is this dear woman's life, how many good deeds she does with what little she has, how patient, no matter what God, blessed be He, causes to befall her — so much can be written on this subject. She remained thus in her dignified widowhood. May God, blessed be He, let her continue like this until the coming of our Messiah. We derive such pleasure from this dear woman, her children and grandchildren — just indescribable. May God, blessed be He, keep her healthy to age one hundred.[194]

After this[195] we betrothed my daughter Chana, may she live long, to the son of my brother-in-law our master and teacher R. Avraham Segal of blessed memory.[196] Whether this match was to our liking or not, it was ordained by God, blessed be He, given that it was my mother-in-law's will,[197] may she rest in peace.

The Frankfurt-am-Main fair was approaching; my husband, of blessed memory, went, as did Reb Yochanan, Reb Mendl, and Leyb Goslar.[198] As soon as the fair was over they had to leave Frankfurt for Leipzig.[199] When

193. Here Glikl might be voicing an ideal that was common in her time, which usually was expressed by men rather than by women, that a widow should remain faithful to her first husband's memory by refraining from remarrying (see Grossman 2004, pp. 253–272; Chovav 2009, pp. 261–262). This idea is echoed by the woman in Glikl's earlier story (see Book Two, p. 80, text before n. 97). For enlightening comprehensive research on Glikl as a widow, and on widowhood in Jewish history, see Rapoport-Albert 2015.

194. A blessing for long life, in a variation from the usual "until 120." This blessing is still found, at least in abbreviated form, in Hebrew writings (see Ashkenazi and Jarden 1966, p. 454).

195. Surely after the death of Glikl's father (see this Book, p. 174), and probably after the marriages of her brother and two sisters (see this Book, pp. 175–177).

196. The second of Chaim Hamel's eight siblings (see Book Two, p. 88). His son Shmuel (see Book Two, p. 189, n. 126) married Chana, Glikl's fourth child.

197. The grandmother of the bride and groom, who were cousins (see earlier). The mention of this lone case of a grandmother's intervention in a grandchild's match is particularly striking in view of the author's silence regarding almost anything to do with her own grandchildren.

198. Like Chaim Hamel, the three were certainly residents of Hamburg. One Mendl Speyer is listed among the attendees at Leipzig fairs in 1683–1685 (see Freudenthal 1928, p. 12). On the Goslar family, see Kaufmann 1896, p. 176, n. 2.

199. For the fair there, see the following text.

they got to Fulda, Reb Yochanan fell ill, and he died four or five days later. My husband, Reb Mendele, and Leyb Goslar as well wanted to remain by his side, but the eminent pious Reb Yochanan, may he rest in peace, refused, so they went to Leipzig — his son Reb Aaron, who had accompanied his father to Frankfurt, stayed at his father's bedside, but even before they reached Leipzig they heard the bad news, alas, that Reb Yochanan was dead. It is easy to imagine how frightened they all were.

As soon as they reached Leipzig, Reb Mendele, son of our master and teacher R. Michl Speyer of Frankfurt-am-Main,[200] was taken ill and lay in bed seven or eight days; alas, he died too. Such fright and commotion in Leipzig is easy to imagine. All this grim news reached us in Hamburg. It is not enough that they saw the tragedy with their own eyes — this decent young man, not yet twenty-four years old, passed away in such distressing circumstances — his father-in-law, Reb Moshe, son of Reb Nathan,[201] was also in Leipzig but did not know how to arrange a Jewish burial for him, for things were very bad and dangerous in Leipzig.[202] To be brief, it took a lot of effort, money, and interceding with influential people to get the body out of there. The body was taken to Dessau, the closest community to Leipzig, six leagues away. It cost over one thousand reichstaler; even so, they were thankful to be able to remove the body from Leipzig. In the meantime, my husband, of blessed memory, and Leyb Goslar also fell gravely ill in Leipzig; their very lives were in danger. So in the middle of the fair, Leyb Goslar and my husband, of blessed memory, got themselves taken to Halberstadt; my husband was accompanied by Reb Moshe Schnauthan and Issachar.[203] When they reached Halberstadt, my husband was so ill that they despaired of saving him. Issachar wrote to me consolingly that it was not a life-threatening illness so that I would not be too alarmed. Issachar pestered my husband for so long that he was forced to sign the letter. But you should have seen his signature — you could not make out a single let-

---

200. The patriarch of a well-known banking family. After his marriage, he settled in Frankfurt-am-Main and became leader of the community. He died in 1692 (see *Encyclopedia Judaica* 1972, vol. 15, col. 266).

201. Later on, his daughter married Glikl's son Mordechai (see this Book, p. 194).

202. See Book Three, p. 123, n. 111.

203. I have no information about Reb Moshe Shnauthan. Issachar is apparently Issachar Cohen, who is frequently mentioned in Book Three.

ter. So it is easy to imagine how I and my children felt. I received the letter on the first day of Shavuot. On the eve of the festival, all our householders returned home from Leipzig except for my husband. It is easy to imagine how panic-stricken we were. We had not even received a letter. The minute the householders arrived, even before entering their homes, they all came to console me and reassure me, everything would be all right, saying whatever they could to get me to calm down. But what good could it do? Easy to imagine what our holiday was like.

I could do nothing, as it was a holiday, but on the first day after the festival, I immediately took my son Reb Mordechai Segal, Reb Yakov, son of Reb Chaim Pollack, and Chava.[204] I sent them to Halberstadt; perhaps they would still find my husband alive, while I — may God remember this to my credit — I arranged for fasting and the study of Torah[205] and other things having to do with *repentance, prayer, and charity*,[206] to the best of my ability. God, blessed be He, had mercy on my husband and provided relief until he recovered somewhat and requested that a carriage be hired for him. He was ill, bedridden; Reb Itsik Kirchhain,[207] with whom he was staying in Halberstadt, let him take along a bed to lie on in the carriage, while those helping him traveled in another carriage. Only one person traveled with him in his carriage, to look after him. In this fashion, ill and weak, my husband came home; we all thanked and praised God almighty for returning him *to us and not to the dust*.[208] God, blessed be He, let him live for another six years,[209] and he married off two more children, as will be told presently. But I forgot — I should have written much earlier about the death of my father-in-law, of blessed memory, which took place long before

204. I have no information about these people. The appellation "Pollack" indicates the origins of the man or his family in Poland.

205. In an attempt to save her husband, Glikl paid men to fast in accordance with the accepted repentance customs, and to study Torah, which was believed to have protective powers (see b.Sotah 21a).

206. See Book One, n. 20.

207. I have no information about this man. His appellation indicates that he or someone in his family had origins in the town of Kirchhain in the Hessen region.

208. Cf. the prayer recited for an ill person who recovers: "Blessed be the All-Merciful who has returned you to us and has not given you to the dust" (b.Ber. 54b). I was not able to find a source for Glikl's brief Hebrew version.

209. Since Glikl's husband died in 1689 (see early in Book Five), it stands to reason that his illness in Leipzig occurred in 1683 (however, see next note).

this. When my husband, of blessed memory, returned from his trip, it was three years and more after my father-in-law, of blessed memory, was taken ill and died.[210] A letter reading: *Your father is ill*[211] reached my husband, whereupon he immediately left off everything and went to Hannover by himself to visit his sick father, remaining there for about three weeks. My father-in-law, as a man of eighty whose strength had ebbed away even prior to this, thought he would die right then and there at seeing my husband, of blessed memory, for my husband was his youngest child, and he dearly *loved this child of his old age.*[212] But when my father-in-law realized that his son Reb Chaim had been with him for three weeks already while God showed no sign of taking him, my father-in-law said: "My son, I asked for you because I wanted you to be present at my deathbed. But you have extensive business dealings, and you've already been here for three weeks. You have done your duty. Now I commend myself to God. Go back to your own home, do." My husband refused, wishing to stay by his father's side, but his father ordered him to go, so he was obliged to return home. His other children who were with him at the time also returned to their homes.

Before my husband had reached home, the following happened. Right opposite our bed was a smaller bed for our children. Just then my daughter Chana, a girl of about eleven, may she live long, was sleeping in that bed. I woke early for "Shomrim laboker"[213] and went to the synagogue. The girl, my daughter Chana, comes running down the stairs from the room, scared stiff, poor thing. The whole household clamored around her: "Chana, what's the matter? Why do you look so terrified?" Says the girl: "Oh God, when I woke up I looked to see if mother was still in bed, but I saw an old man with a long beard lying there. I was so scared that I jumped up and ran down the stairs, but when I looked back at the bed the old man raised his head and never took his eyes off me." When I got home from the syna-

210. Glikl's father-in-law, Reb Yosef Hamel, died in 1677 (see this Book, p. 185, n. 214), six years before his son's illness just described, not "three years and more" as Glikl writes.
211. Gen 48:1.
212. Cf. "Now Israel loved Joseph best of all his sons, for he was the child of his old age" (Gen 37:3).
213. The "Watchmen for the Morning" (phrase appears twice in Ps 130:6) prayer included reciting penitential and supplicatory prayers before the morning prayers, and was sometimes also preceded by the reading of Psalms for that day of the week, so that the entire book of Psalms was completed each week (see Chovav 2009, pp. 339, 352–353, 377, 385–384).

gogue, the murmuring and whispering among the servants had not yet died down. I asked them what was going on, but no one would tell me anything. My husband returned home two days later; he had barely been home eight days when he received a letter informing him that his father, *the righteous Reb Yosef, was dead.*[214]

Shall I tell of my husband's weeping and grieving—it is indescribable. Right after the week of mourning, he engaged ten rabbis and designated a room in the house for prayer only; day and night they did nothing there but study, and my husband did not leave the house for an entire year, making sure all that time not to miss a single recitation of the mourner's prayer. Twelve weeks after my father-in-law's death, my brother-in-law our master and teacher R. Itsik[215] was in Wesel to marry off his son Reb Shmuel. So he went to Hannover to pay his respects at his father's grave, and all his brothers came too and wrote to my husband to join them immediately in Hannover. So he rose early and left for Harburg. So many people were traveling with him that he had a quorum for prayers. In short, he never missed a single mourner's prayer[216] all the way to Hannover, though it cost him a lot of money.[217] Upon reaching Hannover, he read the will. Amazing what a pious, wise will it was. People also talked about my father-in-law's passing —in full command of his faculties and so peacefully;[218] all his righteous children passed away in similar fashion. The inheritance he left was divided among them all in accordance with the will. Not one of them uttered a single improper word against another. My husband, of blessed memory, spent only eight days in Hannover, consoling his dear mother as best he could. He entreated his mother—he would have gladly brought her back

214. Using the epithet for the biblical Joseph (*Yosef Hatzadik*), Glikl expresses once again her great admiration for her father-in-law since she'd gotten to know him (see Book Two, p. 92) and later on (see this book). Reb Yosef died on Saturday, January 23, 1677 (see Feilchenfeld 1913, p. 153, n. 42). For the date of his death and the text praising him in the Hannover memorial register, see Kaufmann 1896, p. xxxviii, n. 2.
215. Glikl's husband's brother, the fifth of his eight siblings (see Book Two, p. 131).
216. The quorum of ten men (minyan) needed in order to recite the mourner's prayer (kaddish). Glikl writes this in order to resolve a possible contradiction between her husband's traveling and her writing earlier that he stayed home in order to have a quorum to recite the mourner's prayer.
217. The reason for the expenditure is not clear to me. Was it because he took men with him in order to have a prayer quorum, and so had to pay their expenses?
218. Lit. echoes "dying by the kiss" (b.Mo'ed Qatan 28b), a natural death at the age of eighty.

to Hamburg with him — but the devout woman absolutely refused to be separated from her righteous husband, *in death as in life*.[219] Two years later she too passed away and was buried by my father-in-law's side. She was eighty-two years old. Really, they were such a sweet, blessed couple, like no other. May God show us favor thanks to their merit. Would that we too could have spent our days in this way, reaching a ripe old age. But God above wanted differently.[220]

After this my husband went to Amsterdam, where a match was proposed to him with my son-in-law Moshe Krumbach.[221] My husband made a rash decision regarding this match, as I will recount presently. Right after the betrothal my husband wrote to me about it. The betrothal was held in Cleve, at the home of my relative by marriage Reb Elia Cleve,[222] since he had power of attorney from my relative by marriage, the distinguished Reb Avraham Krumbach.[223] But before I received the letter informing me that my daughter Esther[224] was betrothed, I received letters from every which way warning us against the match, since the young man had many faults. But less than a day later, I received a letter from my husband saying he had arranged the betrothal and was now setting out on his way home. It is easy to imagine how I felt and what kind of happiness this match brought me. I could do nothing until my husband returned home. He returned a week later, expecting a joyous welcome from me and that we'd be happy together over the match; in fact he found the opposite: I greeted him in low spirits, barely able to open my mouth. It was obvious that something was bothering me, but neither of us wanted to disrupt the joy of our reunion.

219. This echoes the verse "Never parted in life or in death" (2 Sam 1:23).

220. Glikl hints here at her husband's death, which precluded the possibility of her aging together with her husband as her in-laws were able to do.

221. Who would later marry Esther, Glikl's daughter (see Book Five, p. 211), and so already here merits the designation "son-in-law." Moshe was the son of Avraham Krumbach of Metz and his wife, Yachet, the daughter of Reb Elia Cleve (see next note).

222. The father-in-law of Tsipor, Glikl's oldest daughter (see this Book, p. 157).

223. Of the Krumbach-Schwabe family. He was the father of the prospective son-in-law Moshe Krumbach (see this Book, n. 212). On Reb Avraham Krumbach and his family, see Kaufmann 1896, pp. xx, 182, n 4; Feilchenfeld 1913, p. 157, n. 47; Davis 1995, index ("Schwabe," "Abraham"). In Glikl's use of the designation "my relative by marriage" (*meḥutan*), she is not anticipating the future (as she did earlier with his son). Rather, she is referring to an existing relationship: Avraham Krumbach was the son-in-law of Reb Elia Cleve, who was the father-in-law of Glikl's daughter, Tsipor.

224. Glikl's fifth child (see Family Tree C).

A few days went by in this fashion, without either of us mentioning the match. Meantime, my husband too received a letter from a close friend of his who also said that he had heard we were about to make this match and warning us to beware — not to make the match, or at least to have a look at the young man first. My husband was upset at this, saying to me: "Alas, Gliklchen, you probably know about it, I can tell that you're upset." So I showed my husband all the letters I had received before his return. My husband was very alarmed and chagrined, since much too much was recounted about this person, and the boy was reputed to possess every possible fault. We were at a loss about what to do — the match was already arranged. So I wrote to the young man's mother, Yachet:[225] I still recall the very words. I began by cordially expressing best wishes for herself and her family, then continued: "Given that we have received many letters from all over informing us that the bridegroom-to-be has many faults, which we would like to believe is false — if indeed it is false, we request that you send the prospective bridegroom to his prospective bride for the betrothal ceremony, as is the custom.[226] And if these people are gossiping scandalmongers telling falsehoods, as we hope, we will accept the prospective bridegroom with joy and pleasure; he will lack neither luxurious gifts nor all manner of honor. But if it turns out to be true, God forbid, I request that you do not send him here, for we will not defraud our daughter in such a terrible way. Should you decide to send him — in any case we are already related by marriage[227] — on the assumption that in such a case we would not mind and agree despite that to uphold what has been done,[228] kindly refrain from doing so. What will we do if it turns out to be true, God forbid? We will be forced to acquiesce to everything, and you will be able to blame anything at all on my daughter" — and so forth.

225. Lit. "my in-law Yachet," wife of Avraham Krumbach and mother of Moshe, the prospective son-in-law.

226. I am not sure whether the custom to send the bridegroom to the bride for the betrothal ceremony is the same as the custom mentioned in Book Five, p. 210).

227. There are at least two reasons for this designation. The recipient of the letter, Yachet, daughter of Reb Elia Cleve, was the sister of Kossman, Glikl's son-in-law (the husband of her daughter Tsipor; see this Book, p. 155, n. 43); and Zisse, Yachet's sister, was married to Yakov Hannover, the son of Yente, who was the sister of Glikl's husband (see Family Tree D).

228. That is, to carry out the match that was already made by going through with the wedding.

It is easy to picture the distinguished in-law Yachet's outrage at receiving this letter. She replied angrily that she had intended to send the prospective bridegroom to his prospective bride immediately — but now, at seeing what we had written, we would have to come to them, or send someone to Metz. Well, much time was frittered away in an aggravating exchange of letters while we could reach no decision, especially as there was a great war on between the kings of France and Germany,[229] and no one could travel anywhere.[230]

In the meantime we held a lavish wedding for my daughter Chana,[231] may she live long. I also forgot to say that we held a joyous wedding for my son Nathan and the orphan, daughter of Reb Elia Ballin,[232] a long while earlier. Also, that my son-in-law Kossman along with my daughter Tsipor, may she live long, attended too;[233] we covered all their expenses and added presents too. Reb Yakov Hannover and his wife, Zisse,[234] came to the wedding too, as well as many people from out of town, for it was an extremely refined wedding; all told, we spent over ten thousand reichstaler banco that year. God be praised who takes and gives;[235] faithful God always compensated us generously for whatever we lost. If God, blessed be He, had only left me *the crown on my head*,[236] there would be no happier couple in the world. But due to my sins and to all the troubles that God, great and compassionate, has seen fit to visit upon us, He took my husband to all eternity and its pleasures, leaving us in this tiresome, transitory world. We must pray to God that our end may be as He wishes and sees fit; whenever almighty God prescribes it, He will take us to Him to heaven, amen.

After my husband returned from Hannover, where his father's bequest was divided, as you have heard[237] — this was about twelve weeks after his

---

229. On this war, see this Book, p. 178, n. 184. Kaiser Leopold I was the ruler of Germany.

230. Because Metz belonged to the enemy, France.

231. On her engagement, see this Book, p. 181.

232. Glikl recounted the match earlier in this Book, pp. 167–168.

233. They came to the wedding in Hamburg from their home in Amsterdam.

234. This is (Moshe) Yakov Cohen (the son of Chaim Hamel's sister Yente and her husband, Lipman Cohen) and his wife Zisse, the daughter of Elia Cleve (see this Book, n. 227; Feilchenfeld 1913, p. 160, n. 49).

235. A reversal of the order of the verbs in the verse (Job 1:21), to accord with the story.

236. See Book Two, n. 155.

237. The trip to Hannover and the division of the bequest were recounted earlier in this Book, p. 185. The switch from writing to hearing could be due either to the author's mood when she wrote this, or to her having told the story orally to her children on another occasion.

death, and I was pregnant with my son Reb Yosef Segal.[238] Throughout the pregnancy my husband hoped fervently for a boy who would bear my husband's father's name again,[239] as indeed happened, thanks be to God. Here I wish to set down a lesson for my children, one that is actually true: when young pregnant women spot different fruits or any other kind of food, whatever it may be, and they entertain even the slightest desire for it—let them not ignore this—they should eat of it and not follow their foolish heads. Ah, it will do no harm. It might actually be a matter of life and death for them, and the baby in the womb might very well—God forbid—be in danger too, as I found out for myself.

My whole life I had scoffed at hearing that women's cravings could be harmful. I simply refused to believe it. On the contrary, when I was pregnant I'd often see succulent fruit at the market and examine it, but if the fruit seemed too dear I did not buy it, and I suffered no harm. But *times are not all equal*:[240] When I was pregnant with my son Reb Yosef, I found out that things were otherwise. It so happened—when I was in the ninth month of my pregnancy with my son Reb Yosef—that my mother, may she live long, had to take care of something at a lawyer's in the Pferdemarkt.[241] My mother asked me to accompany her. Although it was far from my house, and late afternoon, at the beginning of the month of Kislev,[242] I could not refuse her, since I was still full of energy. So I went with my mother into town. At the lawyer's we saw that a woman living opposite was selling medlars. I've always loved medlars. I told my mother: "Mother, don't forget that I want to buy some medlars on the way back." We took care of what we had come for at the lawyer's, but when we finished it was very late, nearly nighttime, so we went on home, both of us having forgotten the medlars. As soon as I got home, I remembered the medlars and berated myself for forgetting to buy them. I did not give the matter too much thought, however, no more than one does when wishing for something to eat that is not available. In the evening I went to bed feeling

238. The author's eighth child (see Family Tree C).

239. According to the custom in Ashkenaz to name a boy after his late grandfather (cf. this Book, nn. 162, 243).

240. Cf. m.Tamid 1:2; b. Tamid 26a.

241. "The Horse Market," name of a square in Hamburg (cf. Feilchenfeld 1913, p. 161, n. 49a).

242. That is, it was late afternoon in the winter, perhaps close to dark.

fine, in a good mood, but after midnight the labor pains began and I had
to send for the midwife. I gave birth to a baby boy. My husband, of blessed
memory, was told the good news right away; he was overjoyed, as now he
had his father's name again, the righteous Josef, of blessed memory.[243] But I
saw the women who were present at the birth putting their heads together,
whispering. I could not let it go; I asked what they were talking about. Finally they told me that the baby's head and body were completely covered
with brown blotches. They had to bring a candle close to my bed for me to
see for myself. Not only was the baby covered with blotches — he was just
lying there like a heap of rags, moving neither hand nor foot, as though his
soul was about to depart, God forbid. He wouldn't nurse or even open his
mouth. My husband, of blessed memory, saw it too, and we were desperate.
This was on Wednesday night — the following Thursday was supposed to
be the day of his circumcision, but there didn't seem any chance of that
since the baby was growing weaker day by day. The Sabbath arrived, and
on Friday night we held the welcoming for a baby boy,[244] though there was
no sign of improvement in the baby's condition. On Saturday night, as my
husband was making Havdalah,[245] my mother was with me. I said to my
mother: "Dearest mother, please, tell my Sabbath maidservant[246] to come
to me, I want to send her on an errand." My mother asked where I wanted
to send her. I said to my mother, may she live long: "I've been thinking
what could have caused those blotches and the weakness, and I've been
wondering if I was at fault when I wanted medlars and couldn't get them,
since I ended up giving birth that same night. I want to send the woman
out to get a few schillings worth of medlars. I want to smear some of the

243. The newborn was to be named Yosef, after his grandfather who had passed away not long before
(on the grandfather's death, see this Book, n. 210; on the father's hope, see pp. 184–185, p. 189, n. 239).
244. Lit. *zokhor* or *zokher* (male), referring to a *sholem zokher* party, so called based on the saying
"As soon as a male comes into the world peace comes into the world" (b.Niddah 31b). A meal at the
newborn's house on the Sabbath eve before the circumcision, in the new son's honor. The accepted
terminology in Glikl's time was *zokher* (e.g., see *Yosef Ometz* 1965, par. 134, 591, 1024). On the custom, see Pollack 1971, pp. 20, 102–103, 106, 277–278, nn. 60–61 (although Glikl mistakenly calls the
meal *Shabbes Zokher*, which is the Sabbath before Purim).
245. The blessing recited over a cup of wine at the conclusion of the Sabbath or a holiday.
246. Lit. *Shabbes-frau*, a non-Jewish woman whose role was similar to that of a *Shabbes-goy* (note
that Glikl never uses the terms "goy," "goye," or "goyim" in her writing; she uses literal terms such
as "uncircumcised," "not members of the children of Israel," or "non-Jews," all rendered in this
translation as "non-Jews.")

fruit on the baby's mouth; maybe God will have mercy and there will be an improvement." My mother was angry at me, saying: "You always have this kind of nonsense in your head; the weather looks as if earth and sky were about to melt together,[247] the woman won't go out in this weather — in any case, all this is pure nonsense." I said: "Dearest mother, please do me a favor and send the woman; I'll pay her whatever she wants, as long as I get those medlars. If I don't get them I won't have a moment's peace." So we sent for the woman and told her to go get some medlars. The woman hurried off — it was a long way, and the kind of weather that night you wouldn't turn even a dog out of doors.[248] It seemed to me a long time before the woman returned, as whenever you want something very badly — every minute seems like an hour. The woman finally returned with the medlars.

Of course medlars are not the proper food for a newborn baby, because of the sourish taste. I instructed the nurse to loosen the baby's swaddling clothes and sit down with him near the stove and smear some medlar pulp on his mouth. Although everybody laughed at me for this nonsense, I remained obstinate until it was done. The minute the nurse smeared the medlar pulp on the baby's mouth, he opened his little mouth greedily as though wanting to swallow the whole thing at once, and then he was sucking and swallowing the pulp of an entire medlar, when just a moment ago he wouldn't open his mouth even for a drop of milk or for the sugar-water you give babies. The nurse then handed the baby to me in my bed to see if he would nurse. The minute he was at the breast he started suckling like a three-month-old. By the time of the circumcision ceremony, all the blotches had disappeared from his face and body except for one spot on his side, the size of a broad lentil. The baby was healthy and well for the circumcision, a beautiful baby boy, circumcised at the prescribed time, thanks be to God. The circumcision ceremony was lavish, the likes of which had not been seen in Hamburg for a long time. And even though we had just suffered a loss of one thousand mark banco because Isaac Vas[249] had gone

247. Apparently an idiom referring to very stormy weather, though I could not find it in other sources.

248. See Book Three, p. 120, n. 103.

249. This is apparently Isaac Vas de Miranda (see Feilchenfeld 1913, p. 165, n. 55), a Sephardi living in Hamburg who died in 1727 (see Studemund-Halévy 2000, p. 837; and cf. Kellenbenz 2000, p. 476). This is the only time Glikl mentions a business relationship with a Sephardi Jew.

bankrupt, on this day my husband did not give that a thought, so joyful was he at the birth of his son. And so, my children, you see that women's cravings are not sheer nonsense, and they should not always be mocked.

After that[250] I became pregnant again, a difficult pregnancy — in my seventh month I had some kind of outlandish fever, heaven forfend! In the mornings I was cold for four whole hours, then hot for four hours, then I sweated, pardon the expression,[251] for four hours, which was even worse than the cold and the heat. It is easy to imagine the torture I endured. I could not eat a thing even though they brought me all kinds of delicacies. One time my husband asks me to take a little walk with him along the *Wall*,[252] not far from the house, seeing that it was a beautiful summer day, for entertainment; maybe it would give me an appetite. And I say: "You know I have no strength to walk." So that dear man says: "The nurse and I will lead you." I gave in and let them lead me like that on the *Wall* and sit me down on the green grass. Meanwhile, my husband, of blessed memory, had arranged in advance for Todros,[253] the cook at Teixeira,[254] to prepare a meal fit for a royal table while we were out walking, and my husband ordered to have us called when it was ready. And that is what in fact happened. My husband thought that I would return home and see how lovely the table was, set with delicacies, and unbeknownst to me the sight would give me an appetite. But oh God, the minute I came home and walked into the room where the food was, I was overcome by nausea, and I pleaded with them to remove either the food or me from the room. I suffered in this way two whole months, with no strength or will; often I thought to myself: Dear God, when the time comes to give birth, I will not have the strength or the will to help myself. But when the time came, faithful God came to my aid with such kindness that I had a practically painless delivery,

250. Lit. "after the time." We may assume that Glikl is referring to the forty days of impurity after the birth of her son Yosef, and meaning that she became pregnant again a short while after this time period.

251. See this Book, p. 160, n. 83.

252. The promenade in Hamburg near the River Elbe was known as *der Wall*.

253. Name derived from "Theodorus" and used by both Ashkenazi and Sephardi Jews.

254. Manuel Teixeira, a member of the richest Sephardi family in Hamburg. The members of the family were resident diplomatic and financial ministers for the Swedish crown (see Kellenbenz 1958, p. 473; Studemund-Halévy 2000, pp. 791–795; Braden 2001, p. 169, n. 58, *Encyclopedia Judaica* 1972, vol. 15, cols. 911–912).

as if the baby boy just dropped from me. Maybe it was the awful heat inside me that pushed the dear boy out of me like that. He was born a beautiful baby, but the poor child immediately contracted the same fever I had, God protect us. Although we called upon physicians and every manner of human assistance, nothing did any good, and he suffered thus in this world for fourteen days, then God, blessed be He, took him. He took His part and left us the miserable earthly part lying there before us,[255] leaving me a miserable mother without her child. I was to endure two or three more bouts of the fever, though I had recovered before I left the birthing bed. After that I gave birth to my daughter Hendlchen and, two years later, to my son Zanvl, then to my son Reb Moshe, my daughter Freydchen, and my daughter Miriam.[256] The two youngest girls barely knew their father. Why should I write at length of what took place during this time? I gave birth every two years and worked hard, as one does with such a household full of children, may God protect them. I thought no one had a heavier load or worked harder at raising children than I did. But, fool that I was, I did not know how good I had it with my children sitting around my table *like olive saplings around your table.*[257] What can I do, *I must make mention of my offenses.*[258]

And now, my dearest children, here you have the offspring of your father, Rabbi Reb[259] Chaim Hamel Segal, of blessed memory. *How good and how pleasant*[260] it would have been had God, blessed be He, kept us together; we could have led our children to the marriage canopy. But *what shall I say, what shall I speak?*[261] — my sins caused this. I, a sinner, was not worthy enough for that.[262] All is now in God's hands, as will be told presently.

My son Reb Mordechai grew up to be a very handsome young man and was a fine, bright child. May God reward him for the way he honored his

---

255. See Book Three, p. 140, n. 181.
256. These are Glikl's five youngest children (see Family Tree C).
257. Ps 128:3.
258. Cf. Gen 41:9.
259. Here Glikl refers to her husband as "Rabbi Reb," an honorific used mainly for a person with rabbinic ordination.
260. Ps. 133:1.
261. Cf. Gen. 44:16, JPS 1917 (the following sentence associates with the continuation of the verse).
262. Meaning that she was not worthy of marrying off all her children during her husband's lifetime. When her husband died, eight children were still unmarried (see Book Five, p. 201, n. 18).

father and mother. In short, he was successful in every way; he was with my husband in Leipzig when my husband had the colic; everybody in Leipzig kept saying how wonderful the boy was and what an invaluable help to his father. He bent over him all night long, literally did not sleep a wink, did not eat or drink. It is true that it was his duty to behave this way with his father, but my son was still very young. God, blessed be He, came to their aid, and they returned home together, safe and sound.[263]

My husband, of blessed memory, was not a healthy man; for this reason he hastened to marry off his children, may they live long, and took precautions against the day that has, alas, befallen us.[264] My son Reb Mordechai Segal became betrothed to the daughter of the distinguished community leader and "good man" Reb Moshe son of Reb Nathan.[265] My husband, of blessed memory, gave him a dowry of two thousand reichstaler in Danish kroner,[266] and Reb Moshe son of Reb Nathan gave his daughter three thousand reichstaler in Danish kroner. We held the wedding jointly, each side paying expenses; it cost over three hundred reichstaler. We gave them two years' living expenses,[267] and he and his wife stayed with us. But less than six months later, alas, my husband's time came, for God, blessed be He, took my righteous husband, of blessed memory, from me, the crown on my head. In the year 5449[268] God's fury was visited upon us and took away my beloved darling, all my delight,[269] for my husband, of blessed memory, died, alas, and left me a widow with eight children, and the four married children[270] still needed their devoted father very much too.

Now then, *what shall I say and what shall I speak? God hath found out*

263. When Glikl recounts her husband's illness in Leipzig (see this Book, p. 182), she does not mention her son Mordechai's presence and his part in the events, nor does she call the illness by name. Thus she may now be telling about another similar event.

264. That is, the day of his death.

265. See this Book, p. 182, n. 201.

266. Apparently the reichstaler was used as a calculation unit and the amount was paid in Danish kroner (see Friis and Glamann 1958, vol. I, p. 3).

267. See Book Two, p. 94, n. 158.

268. 1689. For the full date (January 16), see Book Five, p. 201, n. 20.

269. In the original, the sentence includes several phrases from the Hebrew sources: "the crown of my head" (see Book Two, n. 151); "God's fury" (a common phrase in the Bible); "took away all my pleasure" (perhaps an echo of Ezek 24:16).

270. That is, her eight unmarried children, and the four married ones: Tsipor, Nathan, Chana, and Mordechai.

our iniquity,[271] that I lost such a dear husband and my children such a well-respected, virtuous and devout father, leaving us as sheep without a shepherd.[272] I had always thought it would be a blessing if God took me first, as I had always been sickly in my husband's lifetime. And whenever I was ailing, the dear man expressed a wish to go before me; he always said: "What will I do with the dear children," for he loved them fiercely. But it is quite obvious that God took him from this world first due to his piety, for he passed away a prosperous, well-respected man who saw nothing bad ahead. He had much wealth, and the children he did marry off enjoyed prosperity and dignity; he himself was a prominent man with an excellent reputation. And when he departed this world in prosperity and dignity, he provided for his children to succeed honestly. It may be said that he died contented, as Solon said in the story,[273] leaving me in distress, alas, and further distress *renewed every morning,*[274] as I will tell in detail in orderly fashion in my fifth book, alas, a book of lamentations[275] and a book of bitter keening. While my husband, of blessed memory, left me sufficient money and assets, all that was nothing compared to the awful bereavement. Let us now conclude the fourth book. God *give us joy for as long as You have afflicted us, for the years we have suffered misfortune.*[276] And now, O God, the one God, have mercy on my orphans, amen and amen.

END OF BOOK FOUR

271. Cf. Gen. 44:16 (JPS 1917); and see this Book, n. 261.
272. Cf. "like sheep that have no shepherd" (Num. 27:17; I Kgs. 22:17).
273. See this Book, pp. 178–180.
274. Cf. "They are renewed every morning" (Lam 3:23).
275. Lit. "a book of Eichah." In this mention Glikl is comparing her Book Five with the biblical Book of Lamentations.
276. Cf. Ps 90:15.

B O O K   F I V E

It is with deepest sorrow that I now begin the fifth book, my beloved children, in which I will recount from start to finish how your dear father was taken ill and died. On 19 Tevet 5449,[1] toward evening, my husband, of blessed memory, your dear father, went into town — a certain merchant had summoned him to close a deal. As he approached the merchant's house there was a sharp stone and he tripped over it and fell, alas, and suffered such an injury, alas, that we are all still lamenting it. He came home miserable. Since I was at my mother's, I was sent for. When I came home, my husband was standing by the fire, groaning. Frightened, I asked him what was wrong, and he replied: "I fell. I fear this is going to cause me a lot of trouble." He could not move at all, alas, and I had to empty his pockets for him, because whenever he went into town his pockets were always full of jewelry. Alas, we did not realize what his injury was, for he had had a hernia for many years, and now when he fell he fell right on the hernia and his bowels slid into each other, God help us.

Now, we always kept a bed in the heated room, but he refused to use it, so we were obliged to take him upstairs to the bedroom. It was so cold, as if earth and sky were about to freeze together.[2] We sat by him all night long doing whatever we could for him, but we could not bear it any longer, and lying in the cold was also very bad for him. He himself finally realized that this was not good for him and we took him downstairs. It was already after midnight when we did this for him, but he showed no improvement. I clearly perceived my fatal blow; I knew it could not end well. So I begged him for God's sake to let me send for a physician and call in some people to come to him, but he said: "I'd rather die than let people know about this." I stood before him weeping and shouting: "What are you talking about? Why shouldn't people know? It's not as if it's because of some sin or

1. January 11, 1689.
2. Cf. Book Four, p. 191, n. 247.

shameful deed." But all my talk was to no avail once he got the ridiculous idea into his head that it could be harmful to the children since people would say that it ran in the family, and he loved his children so very much. So we spent the whole night with him in his agony, applying all sorts of remedies, but it was obvious that the situation was only getting worse, alas. At daybreak I said to him: "Thank God it's morning. Now I'm sending for a physician and a hernia surgeon." He refused, telling me to send for Avraham Lopez[3] — a certain Sephardi who was both a barber-surgeon[4] and a physician. I sent for the man at once. When he saw the bruise, God help us, he said: "Don't worry, I'll dress it and he'll feel better right away. I've treated hundreds such cases and I healed them." This was on Wednesday morning. So Avraham Lopez applied some of his dressings, being of the opinion that this would be beneficial. But, God have mercy, at midday Lopez said: "It's obvious that my treatment is not doing him any good. I'll go fetch a hernia surgeon, a top specialist." The hernia surgeon came and spent all day applying all kinds of poultices with the intention of softening the bruise, but alas, it just grew worse as time went by. On Thursday I sent for another hernia surgeon and two more physicians. One of them was Doctor Fonseca,[5] who told me, after I had spoken with him and explained all the circumstances: "Yes, what can I say? We have here a short process,[6] unfortunately, because the intestines have all slid into each other so he can't move his bowels," and what should have come out below he was vomiting up above, God help us. Nothing he was given did any good, yet still he would not allow anyone else to be with him and commanded us not to reveal a thing. But I comprehended my tragedy and foresaw my terrible misery. Thursday too passed thus, day and night, with similar harrowing afflictions. On Friday Lopez brings in a physician who was from Berlin and had been personal physician to the crown prince for many years; he

3. See Feilchenfeld 1913, p. 173, n. 1; and cf. Studemund-Halévy 2000, pp. 581–582.
4. See Book Two, p. 88, n. 117.
5. Without his given name, it is impossible to ascertain which surgeon of this family is being referred to. Feilchenfeld's suggestion that it is Dr. Joshua Fonseca is reasonable (see Feilchenfeld 1913, p. 174, n. 2; see also the Fonseca family's gravestone inscriptions in Studemund-Halévy 2000, pp. 426–440; also see Kellenbenz 1958, p. 56, n. 118).
6. It is not entirely clear to me whether this refers to the events that had already occurred, to the state of the intestines, or to the expected future.

too gives him something to swallow and applies poultices, but heaven help us, nothing did any good.

It was only on the Sabbath that my brother-in-law Reb Yosef Segal[7] found out — my husband and he were estranged at the time — he came to the house and requested permission to enter the sickroom anyway. So I went in to my husband, of blessed memory, and said: "My brother-in-law Reb Yosef Segal is outside asking to see you," and he said: "Let him in." As soon as my brother-in-law came into the room, he realized what my husband's situation was and dashed his head against the wall, yanking fistfuls of his own hair, then he started wailing bitterly: "Woe is me, to lose such a brother-in-law," and he fell across the bed begging his forgiveness, weeping bitterly. My husband, of blessed memory, replied sincerely: "Dear brother-in-law, I forgive you and everybody else. I too beg your forgiveness." Then my brother-in-law Reb Yosef Segal soothed him, telling him to be patient, God, blessed be He, would provide a cure, to which my husband replied that he accepted all God's doing, blessed be He. To me he did not reveal even the half of his sickness, alas, and my son Reb Leyb, of blessed memory,[8] was still young at the time, about seventeen years old. He was not to leave his father's bedside, and when I would leave the room my husband would draw him close and speak to him, instructing him in moral behavior. The boy was sobbing bitterly, but the minute my husband sensed that I had come back into the room, he'd tell my son Reb Leyb: "Hush, for God's sake, Mother is coming, she shouldn't see you crying." But what good did it do? He lay there in the throes of death and yet was anxious not to sadden me. On the morning of the Sabbath, after the meal, my mother, may she live long, came to see him and embraced and kissed him tearfully, saying: "My son, do you want to leave us like this? Don't you have any instructions for me?"[9] He replied: "My dear mother-in-law, you know I've loved you like my own mother. I have no instructions to give you, only that you console my Gliklchen." Those were the last words the departed said to my mother. Then more physicians and surgeons came but alas, all to no avail. On Saturday evening no one was with him but myself and Avraham Lopez, for the departed wanted no one else with him.

7. Husband of Glikl's sister Elkele (see Family Tree A).
8. Glikl recounts her son Leyb's death at the appropriate place chronologically (see Book Six, p. 285, n. 178).
9. Reb Chaim is being asked to state his last wishes (see also this Book, p. 200, n. 13).

At midnight Avraham Lopez sent for the hernia surgeon, as the injury seemed to him ripe for surgery. As soon as the surgeon went in, they realized what was the matter. The surgeon left, saying that unfortunately there was no possible remedy. Then I said to my husband: "Dearest, may I touch you?" (for I was forbidden to him at that time).[10] He replied: "God forbid, my child, you'll soon be going to the ritual bath"[11] (but alas, he did not live to see that day). So I remained standing by his side a while longer, talking to Avraham Lopez, who said that Reb Fayvesh Levy[12] should be summoned; he had experience with the sick. When the latter arrived—at the time I had a very reliable tutor living in the house, and I had him come downstairs too—it was about two in the morning. As soon as Reb Fayvesh arrived, he goes over to my husband and says: "Reb Chaim, wouldn't you like to tell us your last wishes?"[13] He replies: "I don't know what to say. My wife, she knows everything. She should continue just as she was doing before," and tells Reb Fayvesh to hand him the book by R. Yeshaya;[14] after studying from it for about half an hour, he handed it back. He then started telling Reb Fayvesh and our tutor: "Don't you know what the situation is? Let my wife and children leave the room, it's time. Now I will let all the saddened hearts know of the parting." At that, Reb Fayvesh actually pushed us out of the room by main force. Reb Fayvesh still wanted to stay and talk to him some more about this and that, but he did not want to answer even a single word, talking to himself the whole time, and only his pure lips could be seen moving.[15] This went on for about half an hour. Reb Fayvesh said to

---

10. Glikl explains to the reader the reason for her question to her dying husband: she was menstruating and therefore not permitted to touch him.

11. Refers to immersion in the ritual bath, or *mikveh*, when menstruation is over and an additional time period has passed, after which a husband and wife are permitted to touch.

12. From the following text, it is clear that he served as a confessor for the dying (on this role, see Bar-Levav 1997, pp. 46–47).

13. As earlier in this Book, p. 199, n. 9, Reb Chaim is being asked to state his last wishes regarding the arrangements after his death for his property, children, business, and so on. In his refusal to do so, he also refrained from appointing guardians, as Glikl mentions later on (p. 203, n. 32).

14. This refers to the book of kabbalistic ethics *Shnei Luḥot Habrit* by R. Yeshaya ben Avraham Halevy ish Horowitz, published twice before Chaim Hamel's death in 1689. On sections of the book appropriate for reading aloud or silently on this occasion, see Bar-Levav 1997, p. 68 and n. 192, as well as pp. 206–208; Bar-Levav 2002, especially pp. 78–79.

15. Cf. "Now Hannah was praying in her heart; only her lips moved, but her voice could not be heard" (1 Sam 1:13).

Avraham Lopez: "Avraham, put your ear to Reb Chaim's mouth; perhaps you'll be able to hear what he's saying." So Avraham Lopez put his ear to my husband's mouth, and after bending over him silently for some time trying to make out what my husband, of blessed memory, was saying, he heard him say *Hear, O Israel! The Lord is our God, the Lord alone.*[16] With that he expired, *his pure soul departed.*[17] Thus he passed away, pure and holy, his end attesting what kind of man he was.

And now, my beloved children, what more can I write of our bitter grief, to lose such a husband! Such great honor I enjoyed with him, and now I was left a widow with eight fatherless children[18] including my daughter Esther, may she live long, who was already betrothed. Ah, am I to keen and lament? May God have mercy on us and be a father to my orphans, for You who alone art God, You are the father of orphans.[19] Now I will choke back my weeping and lamenting somewhat, as I fear that I will be grieving over my beloved for the rest of my life. He was buried on Sunday, 24 Tevet 5449,[20] *with a good name.*[21] Such distress and consternation throughout the community cannot be put in writing, for the tragedy was so sudden, alas. So, with my children around me, I sat for the woeful week of mourning, thinking what a woeful situation it was, what a sight: I, a desolate widow, here with my twelve fatherless orphans, may they live long —separated from him. We assembled a regular quorum for prayer right away, and I arranged for men to study regularly at my house, night and day, that entire year, and other things,[22] may God remember them in my favor. My children recited the mourner's prayer diligently. Not a single man or woman failed to pay a condolence visit every day. Nor were we lacking in

16. Deut 6:4, the opening of the first paragraph of the *Shema* prayer. This is also the sentence a person says to sanctify God when being sent to death, when in danger of death, in a sudden fright, and so on. It is considered especially meritorious to die as one is pronouncing the last word of the sentence, as did Chaim Hamel. See, for example, the story about Rabbi Akiva (b.Ber. 61b), as well as Bar-Levav 1997, pp. 353–354.

17. Cf. "and in pronouncing this word his soul departed' (b.Sanhedrin 68a); Rashi to b.Makkot 19b.

18. Here, Glikl counts only her unmarried children (see also Book Four, p. 193, n. 262) and therefore mentions her unmarried daughter Esther's situation.

19. Yiddish translation of Ps 68:6.

20. January 16, 1689. For the inscription on his grave stating that he died and was buried on the same day, see Turniansky 2006a, p. 370, n. 43.

21. Cf. b.Berakhot 17a.

22. Such as prayer and charity, to elevate the soul of the deceased.

tears. You can imagine how we got through the week of mourning. I was *fed tears as daily bread, made to drink great measures of tears,*[23] *who can be likened to you or match you, Maiden of Zion?*[24] *I have been cast down from heaven to earth,* alas.[25] My children, my brothers and sisters and other relatives, all consoled me as well as they could, but one by one they all went home with their loved ones, while I and my orphans were left grief-stricken. That beloved man was mine for thirty years, and I enjoyed all the good a decent woman could or should wish for; he even ensured that after his death I'd be provided for, to continue living in respectable style. But what good was that? God's decree cannot be changed. And so, dearest children of mine, our devoted friend died as a righteous man. He lay ill for only four days, his mind clear until he drew his dying breath. I could write a lot about the things he said to me during that short time. *May my own end and fate be like his,* may my sons and daughters, they should live long, find favor before God thanks to his good deeds. *Gone is his soul, gone too all my dignity and wealth and glory;*[26] he was fortunate to depart this sinful world a prosperous man, much respected; *he suffered no heartbreak or calamity*[27] on account of his sons and daughters, *as is written:* "*because of evil the righteous was taken away.*"[28] But he abandoned me and my unmarried and married children *to sorrow, pain and grief, sorrow and grief increased every day, disaster overtook disaster as my friends and relations stood far off. But what can I and my lamenting do? It was all due to my sins, For these do I weep, My eyes flow with tears,* I will not forget him *to the end of my days,* for he is *engraved on my heart.*[29]

23. Cf. Ps 80:6.

24. Cf. Lam 2:13.

25. Cf. Lam 2:1.

26. In this segment Glikl interweaves phrases, or echoes thereof, from the Hebrew sources in their original language. See, for example, "May my own end and faith be like his," cf. Num 23:10; "May my sons and daughters find favor before God thanks to his good deeds," cf. *Tanḥuma Vayera* 21, and elsewhere; "All my dignity and wealth departed too" echoes Lam 1:6. For more details, see Turniansky 2006a, p. 373, n. 56.

27. This phrase echoes commentaries on Is 57:1–2, which is cited later in the sentence: "He shall not see the evil" (Rashi) and "In order that he should not see the evil." (Radak).

28. Is 57:1. See Rashi's commentary: "The righteous person died due to the evil that was to come in the future."

29. Here too (as earlier in this Book; see n. 26) Glikl interweaves phrases from, or echoes of, Hebrew sources. See, for example, "disaster overtook disaster," cf. Jer 4:20; "as my friends and kinsmen stood

My dear mother and my brothers and sisters consoled me, as mentioned, but alas, these condolences only made my grief worse by the day; such condolences only poured oil on the flames, which rose higher and higher, and my anguish and heartbreak only grew worse. The condolences and encouragement lasted two or three weeks; after that no one knew me anymore. In fact, those we had greatly assisted repaid us with nothing but evil;[30] that's the way of the world. At least that's how it seemed to me in the mood I was in, the brooding of a pitiful widow who abruptly loses such royalty — how can one forget that? — at the time it seems to us, wrongly perhaps, that no one is doing the right thing by us. May God forgive me for it.

You see, my beloved children, on the day that my beloved one still lay dead before me, my pain was not as awful as it became afterward. My pain increased daily, daily I dwelt on the enormity of my pain and my calamity, my catastrophe worsened day by day. But what could I do? Beneficent, mighty God — by virtue of His abounding compassion and His individual providence for us, forlorn, abandoned human beings — it was He who, by the greatness of His compassion and kindness, led me to forbearance, and thus was I able, with God's help, to look after my little orphans, may they live long, to the extent that a weak woman weighted down, alas, with such suffering and cares can do so. After the thirty days of mourning, no brother or sister of mine came to see us, *no kinsman or relative*[31] to ask how are you or how are you managing. If we happened to meet before the thirty days of mourning were up, they uttered only trivialities that did very little to help me or my orphans. My husband, of blessed memory, had not wanted to appoint guardians for them, as mentioned earlier in his exchange with Reb Fayvesh.[32] After the month of mourning, I went over my accounts carefully and found that we owed twenty thousand reichstaler — I already knew that and was not worried about it since I knew quite well that I had the means to pay it all, thank God, and that the same amount would still be left over for my orphaned children and myself to manage on. Still, it's a

---

far off," cf. Ps 38:12; "for these things do I weep, my eyes flow with tears," cf. Lam 1:16; "engraved on my heart," cf. b.Megillah 15b.

30. The Yiddish wording echoes the Hebrew "Why did you repay good with evil?" (Gen 44:4).

31. Lit. "redeemer" (see Lev 25:25–26 and elsewhere).

32. See this Book, p. 200, n. 13.

hard thing for a pitiful widow to owe such an enormous sum when I didn't even have one hundred reichstaler in cash in the house. My sons Nathan and Reb Mordechai Segal came to my aid like loyal children, but they were still young. So I calculated everything up until I had my balance, and considered holding a public auction, which indeed was done.

My dear children, you have read now how your dear righteous father, of blessed memory, your shepherd, your friend, departed this sinful world. You see, my dear children, each one of you must think now of himself, for you have no one, no friend you can trust. And even if you did have many friends you could turn to for help in time of need, God forbid, still you can never trust a friend, for as long as we do not need friends — everybody wants to be our friend, but when we do need a friend, what happens is illustrated in the following story brought here to pass the time.

There once was a king[33] who sent his son to study all manner of knowledge in a far-off land, where the son remained for thirteen years. Then the king wrote to his son that it was time for him to return home. Accordingly, the son returned home to his father. The king sent out crowds of people to greet his son, and they welcomed him joyfully, with honor. The king held a lavish banquet for his son and all rejoiced. After the banquet the king says: "My dear son, did you also have many friends in the city where you studied?" Answers his son: "My lord, king, and father, the entire city was my friend." Said the king: "My son, how did they all come to be your friends?" Then did the son reply: "I held banquets every day, and all of them were my good drinking companions — I always offered them fine wine. In this way they all became my good friends."

Upon hearing his son's words, the king sighed and shook his head. Said the king: "I thought you were studying all manner of knowledge, but I have not yet heard a single wise word from you if you consider your drinking companions true friends. This is wrong, because drinking companions are drunks; they cannot be trusted. As long as there is drinking, there will be no better friends on earth, as if all were born of the same mother. But when there is nothing left to drink, they disappear, wiping their mouths,

33. For the quasi-biblical style of the story in the Yiddish original, and its use of *taytsh* (the translation of the Bible into Yiddish), see Turniansky 2006a, pp. 376–386 and notes. For the origins of the story, see this Book, p. 207, n. 35.

thinking: 'If you invite me — I'll come again, if not — it's my gain.'[34] And if
you don't invite them anymore, or if they find better drinking companions
than yourself, they will think nothing of your drink or your food and will
forget all about your friendship." Replied the son: "My lord my father, do
tell me who is a friend I can count on." Said the king: "Consider no man
your friend until you have put him to the test." The son answered the king:
"And how shall I test him and ascertain his thoughts and intentions so
that I can be sure of his friendship?" Said the king to his son: "Take a calf
and slaughter it in secret, let no one know of it. Put the calf in a sack, sling
it over your shoulder, and go out with it at night. Take it to the home of
your steward and your valet and your secretary; call to each one of them to
come out to meet you in the night and say: 'Oh, what I've been through! I
was drinking all day till now, and I got so drunk that I lost my temper with
my father's chamberlain for bad-mouthing me; when I could not stand to
listen to him any longer I did not hesitate: I drew my sword and stabbed
him to death. Now I'm afraid my father will find out about it; he has a
violent temper, he is liable in his quick rage to take revenge on me. So I put
the corpse in a sack, as you can see, and I'm asking you to help me bury it
now, at night.' In this way you will immediately know what kind of friend
he is to you."

The son did as instructed and carried the carcass at night to the home of
his steward and knocked at the door. The courtier looked out the window
and asked: "Who knocks at my door so late at night?" The king's son replied: "It is your master, the king's son." The steward ran hastily to open the
door, saying: "Ai, what is my lord doing here so late at night?" The king's
son recounted everything and said: "Since you are my loyal steward, please
help me bury the corpse before daybreak." When the steward heard this,
he said: "Keep away from me with such things!" The king's son pleaded
with the steward to help him bury the corpse, but the courtier replied furiously: "I will have nothing to do with drunks and murderers; if you wish
to dismiss me as your steward, there are other masters," and he slammed
the door in the prince's face, leaving him standing there outside. The king's
son went on to the home of his valet, who answered likewise. From there

---

34. The form and content of these sentences clearly indicate that this is a proverb. However, I was
unable to locate its source.

he went on to the home of his secretary and recounted everything to him as well, requesting his help in burying the corpse. The secretary replied: "It is true that I must serve you as long as you are my master, but it is not my job to be a gravedigger; I would gladly do as you ask, but I fear your father and his quick temper — he's liable to kill you and me both. Bury him yourself in the nearby burial ground while I stand guard to warn you if anyone approaches." This they did, and he buried the calf that was in the sack in the burial ground, then each man returned home. The next day, when the three of them met, the steward recounted the misadventure that had befallen the king's son: how the king's son had asked his help in burying the murdered man and how he had to refuse. Said the valet and the secretary: "He came to us too, and we didn't want anything to do with it either, so he buried it himself in the burial ground." The three of them conferred about informing the king of the matter, for they must not hide it from him: "Will not the king think well of us, kill his wayward, wicked son, and regard us as loyal servants?" So agreeing, they reported it to the king. Spake the king: "By my crown, if my son did such a thing, it will cost him his life." Thereupon the king sent for his son and took him to task for all this. But the son would not admit anything. They said to him: "You did indeed put him in the sack and you buried him in the burial ground." Upon hearing this, the king said: "I am sending a servant to there right away; go with him and show him the grave." They did so and brought the sack, sealed with the seal of the king's son, back to the king. Said the king to his son: "What do you say to this?" Said the son: "My lord and dear father, I consecrated a calf for sacrifice, but when I slaughtered it something went wrong and it became unfit for sacrifice. Nor could I just throw it away, since it had been consecrated. That's why I buried it in this sack." Now the king ordered that the sack be opened and emptied of its contents. This done, a dead calf was extricated from the sack. The three servants were shamed, and the king's son ordered that they be thrown in jail, and this was done. The king then sent for his son and said: "You see that a man cannot be considered a friend until he is put to the test." Answered his son: "Indeed, I have now acquired more wisdom than in my thirteen years of study; I have found only half a friend among my servants — my secretary, who stood guard for me. And now, my lord and dear father, please advise me what to do with my servants." Said the king: "I know not what to advise you, unless it be to put all your servants to death so that your secretary — who at least stood guard for you — does not learn treachery from the others." Said the son: "How can I have so many people put to death because of one man?" Said the king: "If one wise man is taken captive along with a thousand fools, and this wise man cannot be freed by any other means, I would advise to put all the fools to death for the sake of saving the one wise man. It is therefore best that you have all your treacherous servants executed so that your secretary, who is half a friend, can become a true friend." Thus he did, and the secretary became a true friend. At last the king's son admitted that one could not trust a friend until he has been put to the test.[35] And so, my dear children, we too can trust no friend, God alone, blessed be He, He will stand by us and aid us. And although you have lost your righteous, faithful father, your Father in heaven is eternal — He will not desert you if you serve Him and pray to Him devoutly. And if you should incur some punishment, God forbid, no one is to blame but yourselves and your own wrongdoings.

Well, why should I go on at length? Let us begin again from where I left off. You have seen how your father passed away, holy and pure. I also wrote that I balanced my accounts and went to my brother-in-law Reb Yosef to ask him to accompany me to my house, since I had calculated the balance and it was my intention to hold a public auction, so he should check the price I had set for each item to see if my prices were too low or too high. So my brother-in-law Reb Yosef Segal came with me and I showed him everything, the price I had fixed for each item. After examining everything, he said: "All your prices are too low. If I were to name such a low price for my merchandise I'd soon go bankrupt, God forbid." I told him: "It seems to me better to name a low price and sell for a high price than to name a high price and sell for a low price. I calculated that even if everything sells at my low prices, it will still bring in a sizable amount of capital for my orphans."

35. I found no direct source for this story. Three Yiddish versions have come down to us: one in a sixteenth-century manuscript (see Neubauer 1886–1906, no. 2213); one in the printed *Sefer Lev Tov* 1620, p. 134a; and one in a manuscript dating from the end of the seventeenth century (see Riemer 2008). All of them differ less or more from Glikl's version in many details as well as in language and style, although Glikl was familiar with the mentioned book and recommended it to her children (see Book One, p. 50, n. 40). Also see Turniansky 1993, pp. 172–173; Turniansky 1994c, p. 60; Turniansky 2004, pp. 142–143. For more on other versions of the story, see Davis 1995, pp. 249–250, n. 163.

I proceeded with arrangements for the auction, which was most successful; everything sold well. Despite the six-months' credit extended to the buyers, everything went very well with no losses incurred, thank God. As soon as some money came in, I paid our outstanding debts, paying everything off within a year, then what money was left over I loaned out at interest.

My daughter Esther, may she live long, had been betrothed for a long time, as mentioned, since we had been unable to make up our minds one way or the other.[36] After the month of mourning I wrote to Yachet, the prospective bridegroom's mother, in Metz, describing my distressing situation, that since I was now a widow and my daughter the bride — an orphan, alas, we should not keep each other waiting any longer — the prospective bridegroom should be sent over here to his prospective bride, to see and be seen, as I have mentioned and written.[37] But this reply came: since I had written so much about her son, and people had slandered her son and I believed them, they did not wish to send the prospective bridegroom. If indeed I held that the truth lies with such gossips and scandal-mongers, I was welcome to send a relative to Metz to look the bridegroom over. Anyway, since there was a great war on between the kings of France and Germany,[38] they could not send the bridegroom under such perilous conditions. This aggravating correspondence dragged on like this for over a year, as I will presently recount.[39]

While this was going on, my son Reb Leyb had also grown up to be a handsome young man with several offers for prestigious matches. My brother-in-law Reb Yosef Segal himself told me that he wanted to give him his daughter in marriage — let my son name his terms.[40] But my son Reb Leyb was not interested, preferring the match from Berlin that proved to be a tragedy, alas, for me and for all of us. Still, I blame no one, only our sins. God above decreed it and took my late righteous husband from this sinful world so that he should not live to see his children bring any ill or ca-

36. On the former developments of this episode, see Book Four, pp. 186–188.
37. See Book Four, p. 187, n. 226.
38. See Book Four, p. 178, n. 184.
39. Glikl recounts the fate of this match in the text that follows (pp. 210–211), but not the correspondence, contrary to her indication here that she will.
40. It seems the terms of the dowry and accessories were to be discussed directly, without the intervention of a matchmaker.

lamity, while I, on the other hand — I was left in this vast vale of tears. Well, why should I go on at length. My son Reb Leyb was a young boy, tempted by evil wicked people into many youthful misdeeds and mischief. This is why I thought to myself: If I arrange a match for my son here in Hamburg, there's too much temptation, and me a widow. Any match I made here would be with the daughter of prosperous businessmen who would not really be able to keep an eye on my son. That's when my brother-in-law Reb Elia Segal[41] proposed a match with the daughter of his brother Reb Hirsh of Berlin.[42] This match pleased me at once, alas, since I was thinking: "This man doesn't have many children and conducts most of his business at home, a strict man — he'll surely watch my son carefully." Therefore I betrothed my son to the aforementioned man's daughter, thinking I had done very well indeed.

When the wedding day approached, I went to Berlin with my son the bridegroom, my son Reb Zanvl, my brother-in-law Reb Elia, and Issachar Cohen,[43] and I stayed with R. Binyamin[44] in Berlin. If I were to write of all the honors shown me by my in-law Reb Hirsh and his uncle our master and teacher R. Binyamin[45] as well as by everyone in Berlin, especially the distinguished Reb Yudah[46] and his wife — I could never describe it in full. Although Reb Yudah was at odds with all the Viennese,[47] he nevertheless sent over the most expensive sweetmeats imaginable for the Sabbath and hosted a wonderful meal in my honor. In short, why should I go on at length. I was treated with more honor than I deserved.

41. Reb Elia Segal, husband of Glikl's sister Matte (see Book Three, p. 136, n. 165), was the son of Modl Dayan Ries (see Book Four, p. 176, n. 174).

42. Reb Hirsh was among the first exiles of Vienna to settle in Berlin (see Feilchenfeld 1913, p. 184, n. 15; and see Book Four, p. 176, n. 174).

43. Thus, the people who accompanied the groom were his mother, his younger brother Zanvl, his uncle Reb Elia Ries, and Issachar Cohen, a partner in the family's business dealings.

44. See next note.

45. R. Binyamin Mirels was in 1673 the head of the Viennese Jewish community in Berlin; he died in 1673. He was the uncle of Hirsh Ries, the bride's father (see Kaufmann 1896, p. 212, n. 2; Feilchenfeld 1913, p. 185, n. 16; and Family Tree E). The Mirels and Ries families came to Berlin from Vienna after the expulsion of the Jews from Vienna in 1670.

46. Reb Yudah Berliner (see Book Three, n. 154). Here Glikl recounts what she promised to tell in Book Three, p. 134, n. 150.

47. That is, with the Vienna exiles living in Berlin, including Glikl's in-laws (for additional details, see Feilchenfeld 1913, p. 185, n. 17).

And so the wedding was most elegant, with much rejoicing. A few days later we returned to Hamburg in high spirits. Before leaving Berlin I had a talk with my in-law Reb Hirsh and requested that he keep an eye on my son, since he was a young boy who knew nothing about business, so he should keep an eye on his business dealings, as I had agreed to the match with his family with the intention that my boy find a father in him. My in-law Reb Hirsh replied that I need not worry about my son, I should hope to worry about all my children as little as I need worry about this boy. But Lord my God, how miserably everything turned out, topsy-turvy! Reb Hirsh actually put in the betrothal contract[48] his guarantee that my son would save four hundred reichstaler a year during the three years he would live at his father-in-law's expense. But he kept that just as he kept the rest, as will be told presently.

I now leave my son Reb Leyb in Berlin and return to my daughter Esther, may she live long. As mentioned, we exchanged many letters without arriving at any outcome. Finally we decided that since the bridegroom's father could not or would not come with the bridegroom-to-be to Hamburg, nor did I want to travel to Metz with my daughter the bride-to-be, we'd reach a compromise: the bridegroom, son of my in-law the distinguished leader of the community Reb Avraham Krumbach,[49] would go to Amsterdam, while I did likewise with my daughter the bride, may she live long, where they could see each other; following their mutual consent, we would hold the wedding there. What could I do? I agreed and wrote that I would be in Amsterdam at the appointed time with my daughter the bride-to-be, may she live long. I hastily made the necessary preparations and set out for Amsterdam with my daughter the bride-to-be and my son Nathan Segal. The company was excellent, and we had a pleasant, enjoyable journey. In Amsterdam we stayed with my son-in-law Kossman,[50] may he live long, but the bridegroom had come to Amsterdam several days earlier and was staying with Reb Moshe Emmerich. Toward evening, after afternoon prayers,

48. A document of financial terms between the bride and groom, determined by the parents or their power of attorney.
49. See Book Four, p. 186, n. 223.
50. The husband of Tsipor, Glikl's daughter. The couple lived in Amsterdam, where the husband was involved in the book-printing business (see Book Four, p. 155, n. 43).

my future son-in-law came over to where we were staying. I was glad and we talked; I found him pleasing in every respect and saw no sign of all the faults people had told us about. We spent two or three hours together; I thanked and praised God in my heart, well satisfied.

In Amsterdam my son Nathan Segal and I traded in precious stones every day. When we had been in Amsterdam eight days, I got a letter from Miriam who was married to my late in-law Elia Cleve,[51] requesting that we do her the honor of paying her a visit at Cleve with the bride- and bridegroom-to-be, since after all they had been the matchmakers and had had a lot of aggravation. Now she wanted a little satisfaction in spite of everything, by our paying her a visit. Although our business affairs made it inconvenient for us to leave, I could not refuse her, so we all went to Cleve. It is true that we both shed tears of joy at seeing each other, as we were seeing each other for the first time in our bleak widowhood,[52] but after the initial sadness it all ended happily, and we enjoyed each other's company immensely. My daughter Tsipor, may she live long, was there with us too. Miriam wanted us to hold the wedding in Amersfoort,[53] but it was not convenient for me, as we had to be back in Amsterdam. We spent five most enjoyable days in Cleve. Then our bride and bridegroom returned with us to Amsterdam. As soon as we reached Amsterdam the wedding was readied, and instead of the few dozen guests we were expecting, over four hundred turned up. In short, we had the most refined wedding, such as had never before been seen in Amsterdam for a hundred years, and it cost us over four hundred reichstaler too. After the wedding I remained in Amsterdam a few weeks longer to handle our business affairs. Then we began preparations for the return journey. I asked my son-in-law Moshe[54] to come with me to Hamburg—I would pay their expenses[55]—but he did not want to. We traveled from Amsterdam to Hamburg in comfort, finding our children and all our close friends in good health.

51. Miriam was the mother of Kossman, husband of Tsipor, Glikl's daughter, and also the grandmother of the prospective groom Moshe, son of Avraham Krumbach (see Family Tree D).
52. Reb Elia Cleve died in 1689, as did Chaim Hamel (see Feilchenfeld 1913, p. 187, n. 18).
53. A small Dutch city near Utrecht (see Feilchenfeld 1913, p. 188, n. 18a).
54. Who had just married Glikl's daughter Esther.
55. It seems Glikl is here suggesting that the newlyweds come to live with her in Hamburg, where she will give them *kest* (room and board for a certain period of time).

Every mail delivery brought me letters from my son Reb Leyb, may he rest in peace:[56] he was running his business well; everybody was praising him as an honest merchant. He traveled to Leipzig to buy fabrics and had a big store in Berlin. My other children did business with him. I wrote to his father-in-law Reb Hirsh several times to ask if he was keeping a close eye on him, since he was a young boy who had never seen how business was conducted, having spent all his time in ḥeder and the study-house. Every time, my in-law, his father-in-law Reb Hirsh, wrote in reply that I was not to worry about the boy. I had to content myself with that, and I believed that everything was going well with my son Reb Leyb.

I still had my unmarried daughter Hendele, may she rest in peace,[57] second to none in beauty and deed. Reb Yozl the matchmaker proposed another disastrous match from Berlin,[58] that is, that's where the widow of Reb Baruch of Berlin[59] lived. This same Reb Baruch had been an important, wealthy man who died leaving two sons and two daughters. Well, the matchmaker proposed a match for my late daughter with this orphan — the eldest of the orphans — saying he was still a young boy, good at his studies, with five thousand reichstaler in cash and half a house — this too worth fifteen hundred reichstaler, in addition to silver ritual objects and some other things. He would get room and board[60] at his mother's for two years, as she still handled all the business affairs. I told the matchmaker that I was not rejecting his offer; I would think it over and let him know. I asked my brother-in-law Reb Yosef Segal and others, close friends, and all of them advised me to accept the match, though they all said: "Why, your son Reb Leyb lives in Berlin; he'll write and let you know everything." So I wrote to my son Reb Leyb Segal telling him to write and let me know the whole truth. He wrote advising me to accept the match since the orphan had five thousand reichstaler as well as some other things, as the matchmaker had said. So I sent my son Leyb power of attorney, and he

56. On Leyb's death, see Book Six, p. 285, n. 178).

57. Glikl's tenth child. The use of the formulaic phrase for a deceased person reflects the time of writing (on Hendele's death, see this Book, p. 221).

58. This refers to the match of her son Leyb (see this Book, p. 208).

59. Baruch (Benedictus) Veit, son of Menaḥem Mann Rausnitz of Vienna, was for a time the leader of the community of Viennese Jews in Berlin, and died in 1689 (see Feilchenfeld 1913, p. 189, n. 19).

60. See Book Two, p. 94, n. 158.

finalized the betrothal in Berlin. To my chagrin, the wedding date was set for another year and a half. I thought all had been arranged satisfactorily, and that since I already had one son in Berlin who was doing well, I'd marry my daughter off there too; that way they could enjoy each other's company. Alas, things turned out completely differently, since, as will be recalled, my son Reb Leyb was still very young and knew nothing about doing business. His father-in-law, instead of looking after him personally, let him wander like *sheep without a shepherd.*[61] My son began conducting a lot of business, as mentioned; he had a big store in Berlin selling all types of fabrics. His father-in-law, Reb Hirsh, married off his son Reb Modl to the daughter of my brother-in-law Reb Yosef Segal.[62] This Reb Modl too was still very young and not very well brought up. Reb Hirsh took the entire dowry of four thousand reichstaler and invested it in my son Reb Leyb Segal's business. My son took Reb Modl on to sit in the store, where he was supposed to help keep an eye on things. But God have mercy if he kept an eye on anything! The servants stole everything, alas. On top of that, other wicked people — there are plenty of these in Berlin as everywhere else — came to him pretending to be doing business with him and stole the very whites out of his eyes. He lent many thousands to Poles, unfortunately — all was lost. My children and I knew nothing of this — we thought he was doing a lot of business and turning a good profit; that's why we extended so much credit to him. At the time, I also had a factory for Hamburg hosiery that I had established on my own at the cost of many thousands. Then my luckless son wrote to me to send him over one thousand reichstalers' worth of hosiery, which I did. When I was at the Braunschweig fair, merchants there from Amsterdam had bills of exchange drawn on the name of my son Reb Leyb Segal, for about eight hundred reichstaler. My son Reb Leyb, of blessed memory, wrote to me in Braunschweig for me to honor his bills of exchange and pay the amount, and he would transfer the money to me in Hamburg. And so, since I have always stood by my children, I decided not to let him be humiliated by having his bills of exchange rejected, so I paid the entire amount as a point of honor. Upon my return home from the

---

61. Cf. "like sheep that have no shepherd" (Num 27:17; 1 Kgs 22:17).
62. Modl, the son of Hirsh Ries, married the daughter of Elkele (Glikl's sister) and Reb Yosef Segal, whose cousin Leyb, Glikl's son, did not want to marry (see this Book, p. 208, and Family Tree E).

Braunschweig fair I was sure I'd find a bill of exchange from my son Reb
Leyb, but there was nothing. Although I wrote to him about it, my son always wrote back with excuses that were not at all to my liking. What could
I do? I had no choice but to content myself with that. Two weeks later, a
good friend came to me, saying: "I cannot keep this from you — I must tell
you that I do not like your son Leyb's business dealings one bit; he's heavily
in debt — he owes his brother-in-law Reb Modl four thousand reichstaler.
Reb Modl is supposed to be keeping an eye on things at the store, but he's
just a boy, he's not capable of it. He's a greedy glutton, so anyone at all can
do as he likes in the store. Your son Reb Leyb is good-hearted and decent
to a fault; he lets anyone at all take control. On top of that, the Berliners
are sucking him dry with the interest rates, then he has the two wolves
over him: one is Reb Wolf, the son of the head of the rabbinical court in
Hamburg, our master and teacher R. Zalman Mirels;[63] the second Wolf
is R. Binyamin's brother-in-law.[64] The latter Reb Wolf comes to the store
every single day and takes what your son sees — and what he does not see.
He also has business dealings with Poles, and I happen to know that he lost
more than four thousand reichstaler in a short time doing business with
them," and more such stories until I nearly dropped dead. I fainted dead
away then and there. The friend who told me all this, seeing how upset I
was, tried to reassure me, saying that I should not get so upset, and if we
took care of it right away we could still save him. I told my sons Nathan
and Reb Mordechai Segal about it — whereupon they too got very upset
— saying that he owed each of them several thousand too. Almighty God,
You know how I felt faced with business dealings of this kind. My son Reb
Leyb owed me more than three thousand reichstaler. Still, I would not have
given the matter a thought had not my two virtuous children mentioned
been also so heavily involved with him. Well, what could we do, pitiful

63. Reb Wolf, the son-in-law of Reb Baruch Rausnitz (see this Book, p. 212, n. 59), was a printer
who lived in Berlin and died there in 1716. His father, R. (Shlomo) Zalman Mirels (b. 1624), was
— together with his brother R. Binyamin Mirels (see this Book, n. 45) — among the founders of the
community of Vienna exiles in Berlin and one of its first leaders. Between 1680 and his death in 1706,
he was head of the rabbinical court of the Altona-Hamburg-Wandsbek community; see Feilchenfeld
1913, p. 192, n. 20; Wolfsberg-Aviad, et al., pp. 51–52. R. Zalman was also the uncle of the father-in
law of Leyb, Glikl's son, as well as being the uncle of Elia Ries, husband of Matte, Glikl's sister.
64. R. Binyamin Mirels (see previous note).

creatures that we are? We could not tell a soul. We decided that I would go with my son Reb Mordechai Segal to the Leipzig fair to see how things stood. Well, easy enough to imagine how we passed the time.

So we traveled to Leipzig,[65] my son Reb Mordechai and myself. My son Reb Leyb Segal was already there when we arrived, as he'd spend some time there at every fair and had a lot of merchandise there. So I had a talk with him: "People are gossiping about you, saying this and that. Remember God and your upright, righteous father, lest you disgrace yourself and us all." He replied: "You need not worry about me at all. Less than four weeks ago, my father-in-law Reb Hirsh had a visit from his brother-in-law Reb Wolf of Prague,[66] who had to go over my accounts with me, and he too saw that my situation is pretty good, thank God." So I said: "Show me your balance sheet," to which he replied: "I don't have it. Do me a favor and come home to Berlin with me; I'll show all of you everything and you'll all be satisfied." To be on the safe side, I told him: "Don't buy any more merchandise for the time being," but then Reb Isaac and Reb Shimon son of Reb Mann of Hamburg[67] went behind my back and sold him fabrics worth more than fourteen hundred reichstaler on credit. When I found out about this, I went to them and asked them to cancel the sale for God's sake, since my son would have to get out of the fabrics business or be utterly ruined. But all this did me no good whatsoever—they made my son buy the fabrics anyway.

After the Leipzig fair I went to Berlin with my sons R. Mordechai Segal and Reb Leyb and his father-in-law, Reb Hirsh, along with all the Berliners. On my first night in Berlin, in my son's house, nothing happened; I was tired from the journey. But we had a talk, and my son said: "I don't need anything, I just have too much invested in stock." So I told him: "You owe me more than three thousand reichstaler. I'm willing to take fabrics at your cost price in lieu of payment." My son Reb Leyb Segal replies: "Mother dear, if you do that I'll be rid of all my troubles, and no one will lose

65. According to Freudenthal, Glikl traveled to the Leipzig fair several times during the 1690s together with her son Reb Mordechai (Marcy), the first time being in 1690 (see Freudenthal 1928, p. 125).

66. I have no information about him, but he is not one of the two "wolves" mentioned earlier.

67. I have no information about either of these men.

anything on my account." So the next day I went with my son to his store where there were indeed large quantities of fabrics. He then gave me three thousand reichstalers' worth of fabrics at his cost price. You can imagine the expression on my face, but I did not give all this a thought; I wanted only to help my child. We proceeded to pack up the fabrics for me to ship to Hamburg. Now, the two bundles of fabrics that my son Reb Leyb had bought from Reb Isaac and Reb Shimon in Leipzig were still there in the store, unopened. So I said to my son: "Send these two bundles back to those people;[68] I'll make sure they take the goods back even if I have to pay for it out of my own pocket. I got my own share back now—how will my sons Nathan and Reb Mordechai Segal get theirs?" My son Reb Leyb took up a few Polish bills of exchange he had received, worth more than twelve thousand reichstaler, and handed them to my son Reb Mordechai: "Here, this is to pay you with."[69] We all went home together—we had spent the whole day in his store. I did not find dinner appetizing, as can be imagined. Early next morning my son Reb Leyb Segal comes into my bedroom and tells me that his father-in-law, Reb Hirsh, had spoken to him; he would not allow the fabrics to leave Berlin because my son Reb Leyb owed his son Reb Modl four thousand reichstaler. If I paid him that amount, I could ship the fabrics anywhere I wanted. My son Reb Leyb told me this with tears in his eyes. What a deathly fright he gave me! I could not get out of bed, and for the duration of my stay in that ill-fated Berlin I could not rise from my bed. I sent for my son's father-in-law, Reb Hirsh, and said: "What are you doing to me, do you intend to slaughter me along with my children?" But why should I write at length, even ten books would not suffice. I was obliged to give Reb Hirsh a bill of exchange for two thousand five hundred reichstaler payable in two weeks' time in Hamburg. While this was going on, Reb Hirsh said: "I do not expect anyone to lose by this, since your son still has the same quantity of fabrics in his store. And he still has fabrics in Frankfurt an-der-Oder worth about two thousand reichstaler as well as many bills of exchange and writs that your son Reb Mordechai Segal has in his possession and can be used to pay all of you." Well, what could we do? We had to resign ourselves to it all, so I signed the bill of exchange

68. That is, to the previously mentioned Reb Isaac and Reb Shimon.
69. The author is quoting her son.

and shipped my fabrics to Hamburg, as mentioned. I went with Reb Hirsh to the store and showed him the two bundles of fabrics for Reb Isaac and Reb Shimon for him to ship them off immediately to these people, despite everything, to release my son from his debt. The bills of exchange and writs that were in the possession of my son Reb Mordechai Segal we handed over to my son's father-in-law, Reb Hirsh—they proved of very little use to us. Reb Hirsh shook hands with my son Reb Mordechai on his promise to send to us in Hamburg without delay that which had been paid for. There remained about two thousand reichstaler my son Reb Leyb still owed Leyb Besheri and Leyb Goslar.[70] He sent me a bill of exchange for that amount with which to pay them. Now, while I could have held on to that bill as our own payment, I thought that if I did so my son Reb Leyb would be utterly ruined, so I gave them the bill of exchange.[71] We traveled home in a morose, embittered mood. I felt only half alive. My dear virtuous son Reb Mordechai tried to distract me, but God knows he was hit harder than I was, poor thing, as it turned out.[72]

The Frankfurt an-der-Oder fair was coming up soon, with all our hopes pinned on recouping there, please God. But instead, his father-in-law came unexpectedly to his store and confiscated everything he owned. Not only did he take all his stock, all his bills of exchange—he also took the two bundles of fabrics, leaving him and us without a penny. Another thing: my son owed a certain merchant a thousand reichstaler against which my son was supposed to give him a bill of exchange for Hamburg, but when all this became known, the merchant would not leave him alone; he wanted to have him thrown in jail in Berlin. What could my son do? His father-in-law would have let him rot in jail before helping him out with so much as a hundred reichstaler, let alone a thousand. My son then said to the merchant: "You can see for yourself that there is nothing to be had here. I'll go to Hamburg with you; my mother and brothers won't let me down. You can have me thrown in jail in Hamburg just as well." Whereupon my son Reb Leyb promptly writes to me: "I'll be at your place on Friday. I can't write why. I'll tell you all about it in person." I received the letter

70. On Leyb Besheri, see Book Three, p. 136, n. 161. On Leyb Goslar, see Book Four, p. 181, n. 198.
71. To the previously mentioned Leyb Besheri and Leyb Goslar.
72. Glikl does not resume discussion of this incident.

a day before his arrival. Easy to imagine how I felt. I could not picture anything good, knowing quite well that his father-in-law had taken everything away from him and that he owed money in Hamburg that he could not pay back. But I quickly pulled myself together. On Friday morning a messenger came: My son Reb Leyb was at the merchant's house; I or one of his brothers must go to him. I was scared out of my wits, could not take a single step. My son Reb Mordechai Segal went to him and brought me the bitter, awful news.[73] I consulted with my brothers-in-law Reb Yosef Segal and Reb Elia Segal,[74] because if this went on and other creditors found out about it, my son would be utterly ruined. In the end it was decided that we would take one thousand reichstaler from the estate[75] and rescue him from the merchant's clutches; he would remain in the merchant's house until evening, then he would stay with me until Sunday, after which, early Sunday morning, I'd send him to Hamel with my brother-in-law Reb Shmuel Bonn[76] — he would stay with my son-in-law Reb Shmuel[77] in Hamel for a while until we could decide what to do with him. And so it was, once again costing me a great deal of money. My son Reb Leyb stayed in Hamel, but to get to Hamel he had to pass through Hannover. While my in-law the distinguished Reb Yakov Hannover[78] had every sympathy for him and felt very sorry for him, this led to no outcome or assistance. True, they wrote to me from Hannover to console and encourage me. I replied whatever was necessary, thanking them for their condolences, which however would achieve nothing; they must intervene and help my son get back on his feet again. He's a young man, God may yet help him. But this is the reply I got from my in-law the esteemed Reb Yakov Hannover: he was willing to assist

---

73. Apparently, this refers to the information about the merchant (see following text).

74. Reb Yosef was the husband of Glikl's sister Elkele, and Reb Elia was the husband of her sister Matte. Both lived in Hamburg.

75. That is, the inheritance left by the late Reb Chaim Hamel.

76. Son of Reb Leyb Hamel (Glikl's husband's brother), who was married to Rivka, Glikl's younger sister (see Book Four, p. 177, n. 183).

77. Son of R. Avraham Hamel (Glikl's husband's brother), who was married to her daughter Chana.

78. Yakov (Cohen) Hannover was the son of Chaim Hamel's sister Yente and her second husband Reb Lipman Cohen (Leffmann Behrens); see Kaufmann 1896, nn. 1, 6; Feilchenfeld 1913, p. 199, n. 26. Glikl calls him "my in-law" because his wife Zisse was the daughter of Reb Elia Cleve, whose son Kossman was married to Glikl's daughter Tsipor.

him with five hundred reichstaler, on condition that my sons Nathan and Reb Mordechai Segal affirmed in writing that they would act as guarantors for the money. Thus we learn, as we learned from the story, that no one may be considered a friend until he has been put to the test. I had been certain that Reb Yakov, being a close relative of my children's, and out of respect for the memory of my husband, of blessed memory, would do much more, pay out thousands for the sake of his uncle's[79] honor. However, he behaved as I have described.

My son Reb Leyb Segal remained in Hamel for six months. Then the crown prince of Brandenburg[80] came to Hannover; I heard about this right away and wrote to my brother-in-law Reb Lipman in Hannover[81] to try to obtain from His Highness the crown prince a laissez-passer for my son so that he could return to Berlin and try to collect on some debts. That way he could satisfy his creditors, for Jews and non-Jews alike held him in high esteem and knew very well that he had lost everything he owned because of wicked scoundrels, may their name be blotted out, and knew too that he was too good-hearted and trusting, alas. He still had a few small outstanding debts owed him there, and he could collect something on them; he thought too that God, blessed be He, would have mercy and would help him get settled again. But heaven was apparently furious with us. My son Reb Leyb returned to Berlin, started dilly-dallying again, doing a little trading, closed up one hole and opened another, as such people tend to do, hoping all the while he'd get by.

As mentioned, I had betrothed my dear pious daughter in Berlin, when I still believed that my son was doing exceedingly well there. But then, when things turned out so dismally, I abhorred Berlin. On top of that, my son Reb Leyb told me that the future bridegroom did not have the amount specified in the documents. Although my son could have attested to this earlier, he was then already preoccupied with his own troubles, and his in-laws were giving him money to help him out, alas, to his ruin.[82] That is why

79. Chaim Hamel (see previous note).

80. See Book Four, p. 157, n. 63; p. 177, n. 177.

81. Reb Lipman Cohen, the distinguished court Jew (see Book Two, p. 91, n. 137).

82. This apparently refers to the parents of his sister's intended bridegroom lending money to Leyb, Glikl's son, thus hastening his getting deeper into debt, and even causing him to hide the truth about his prospective brother-in-law from his mother.

he was obliged to write to me whatever they wanted. I related this to my family and others, now that the date of the dismal wedding was approaching. Whereupon they wrote from Berlin that the future bridegroom had no more than three thousand five hundred reichstaler and half his house.[83] At this, I no longer wanted to go through with the match, because they had not fulfilled the betrothal conditions. The correspondence and warnings continued for over a year, until — let our laments go to God over this — I was literally dragged into it by my hair; I was finally forced to decide to go to Berlin with my daughter and hold the wedding there. My late daughter's dowry remained here in Hamburg, loaned out at interest; the bridegroom's dowry was also loaned out at interest in the care of my trustees in Berlin. Nevertheless I traveled with little joy to the dismal wedding on account of my son Reb Leyb Segal, knowing I would find aggravation there; besides — the match was not at all to my liking, and in fact unfortunately *its ending attests to its beginning*,[84] as will be seen presently.

Thereupon I traveled with my late daughter to Berlin for the wedding, and we stayed with my son Reb Leyb. Although this was painful for me since my son was giving me very little cause for contentment, in spite of everything I restrained myself, without taking things to heart, not wanting to put a damper on my daughter's happiness. Should I write about my son's predicament — God have mercy. What's the use of writing at length? Poor boy, he certainly did his part, ran all over the place, but — as I have recounted. My heart was literally bursting, yet I did not want to display any sadness. So the wedding took place, a joyous, refined affair. The distinguished Reb Yudah Berlin[85] and his wife and their entire family honored us with their presence at the wedding, which astonished all the guests since they never attended Viennese weddings.[86] They also gave the bride a respectable wedding gift, and after the wedding they invited us with the bride and bridegroom to a lavish reception in our honor. When all this was over, we prepared for the trip home, albeit in glum spirits, since I could see the dismal situation my son Reb Leyb Segal was in, alas. In spite of this,

83. And not the promised five thousand (see earlier in this Book, p. 212).
84. Cf. b.Nedarim 48a.
85. See this Book, p. 209, n. 46.
86. On the reason for this, see this Book, p. 209, n. 47.

I built up my hopes that He would have mercy, that God, blessed be He, would help him get back on his feet again. We proceeded to set out for Hamburg, leaving my dear pious daughter in Berlin; alas, I was never to see her again. Perhaps our sorrowful hearts forebode this, for I cannot describe our mutual grief, my dear pious daughter's and my own. It was exactly as if it were inscribed right before us that we would never see each other again in this sinful, dismal world. Thus we parted forevermore.

I returned to Hamburg. Every mail delivery brought me happy letters from my daughter. Although she suffered sorrow and heartbreak on account of my son Reb Leyb, being a pious, perceptive daughter she did not want to cause me sorrow by mentioning it, bearing the heavy burden of all this great sadness and grief on her own, it seems, in her dear virtuous heart. Every day brought new developments, they were *renewed every morning*.[87] First, my son Reb Leyb could no longer remain in Berlin; he was forced to flee Berlin once again and came to Altona under the protection of the President.[88] What sorrow, heartbreak, and distress I suffered on account of this and on account of his creditors! May it atone for our sins. This business cost me a great deal of money every single day. My son fell dangerously ill; every day I sent two physicians, besides attendants and whatever else he needed, from Hamburg to Altona, all of which once again cost me a great deal of money. Finally he recovered somewhat. Next, my modest daughter Hendele fell ill in Berlin, an illness for which alas she paid with her young life, bringing searing grief to me and all who knew her. Ah, my God, what an unbearable punishment it was! Such a dear decent young person, like a linden she was, with all the good qualities and traits as no doubt our matriarchs possessed.[89] She was mourned by all Berlin, especially her mother-in-law, who loved her dearly — indescribable. But what good is all this to a mother's grieving heart like mine? It happened seventeen weeks after her wedding.

I will not dwell on this, will not reopen my old wounds. After the week

87. Lam 3:23.
88. Altona was then governed by a President appointed by the Danish government. Leyb was staying there by his grace while he was forbidden from entering Hamburg because he could not pay his debts to his creditors there (see Feilchenfeld 1913, p. 203, n. 30; and following text in this Book).
89. This refers, of course, to the four matriarchs, Sarah, Rebecca, Rachel, and Leah.

of mourning, my son Reb Leyb Segal requested that I come to him.[90] The moment I walked into his house — *the oak of weeping*![91] He wept, I wept. My son Reb Leyb comforted me as well as he could. Then he said to me: "Mother dear, what will become of me in this dismal situation? I'm a young man, loafing around like an idler; my modest sister, alas, died childless, may she rest in peace; and her husband is required to return her dowry,[92] which now belongs to my brothers.[93] If my brothers could take pity on me just this once and use that money to help me settle with my creditors, I could come back to Hamburg; I think that with God's help I'll be able to make a living again."

My sorrowful heart was filled to bursting. I could not reply for the misery and bitter tears. I said: "How cruel of you! You know how much your virtuous brothers lost on your account until they really can bear it no longer, and now that they are about to get this paltry fistful of money through no action of their own,[94] you want to rip even that out of their sad bitter hearts?" For an hour we wept and wailed pathetically, he and I both, unable to utter another word to each other; silently I wrapped myself in my shawl and went home to Hamburg, weeping and wailing bitterly, telling none of my children about this. But my son the late Reb Leyb did not let up, writing to my children, imploring them so desperately that they — soft-hearted as they are anyway — promised to help him in this, as was indeed soon arranged. He reached a compromise with his creditors and thus came back to me in Hamburg. Hearing of this, his father-in-law, Reb Hirsh Berliner, sent his daughter, Reb Leyb's wife, with one of their children to me in Hamburg too, giving his daughter two reichstaler a week for expenses. Well, what could I do? I was forced to resign myself to everything.

At that time I was doing a brisk business in the fabric trade, selling five or six hundred reichstalers' worth of goods a month. In addition, I attended the Braunschweig fair twice a year, making several thousand at every fair, which would have enabled me to cover the losses I incurred on account of

90. To Altona, where he had found refuge.
91. From Gen 35:8, and meaning "much weeping."
92. According to the regulation that if a wife dies childless within a year or two of marriage, the husband must return the dowry to her parents (see Yuval 1995, pp. 200–201, and n. 36).
93. This seems to be an internal family arrangement, rather than a requirement of Jewish law.
94. Because they would receive the money as a result of their sister's death.

my son Reb Leyb if only I had some peace. My fabric business was doing very well indeed: I imported merchandise from Holland and purchased a large quantity of merchandise in Hamburg too, and I sold it. I had my own fabric store. I did not coddle myself—winter and summer I traveled and in the city I was constantly on the go. In addition, I dealt in ounce pearls which I'd buy from the Jews, then I'd sort them and resell them wherever I knew there was a demand. I had an extended line of credit. If I wanted to make twenty thousand reichstaler banco during a single Bourse session, I could do it. *Yet all this means nothing to me.*[95] There before me was my son Reb Leyb Segal, a decent young man, studious, a virtuous man—that he should be ruined in this way! One day I said to him: "Look, I see no way out for you, unfortunately. I have extensive business dealings. It's starting to be a little too hard for me to manage. If you help me with my business, I'll pay you two percent of everything I sell." Was there ever a happier man than my son Reb Leyb? He accepted joyfully and was extremely industrious and could have done very well too, had his own good-heartedness not ruined him. Through my customers he became well known among the merchants, who extended lines of credit to him; he practically managed everything I owned.

My son Reb Yosef Segal[96] was a youngster of fourteen at the time, a fine lad, a good student. I would gladly have sent him away to study but I did not know where. It so happened that Itsik Pollack employed a tutor for the children, an honest young man, a real scholar from Lissa.[97] Hearing that I wished to send my son away to study, he came over to have a talk with me: he had heard that I wished to send my son Reb Yosef away to study, therefore I should let him, the tutor, accompany the boy. He was not asking so much as a penny for expenses or teaching fees until after two years, when he would present the boy and demonstrate his perfect mastery of the reading of Halakhah and Tosafot.[98] I checked his background, and everybody advised me to accept. Thereupon I signed an agreement with

95. Esther 5:13.
96. Glikl's eighth child (see Family Tree C).
97. Lissa, Polish: Leszno, a city in western Poland (see *Encyclopedia Judaica* 1972, vol. 11, cols. 52–53).
98. The legalistic questions in the Talmud together with their medieval commentaries. On the methods of teaching these topics, see Güdemann 1880–1888, III, p. 62.

him and sent my son off with his teacher to Lissa, in the name of the God of Israel. His letters from Lissa informed me of his safe arrival there, and every week without fail I got letters from him telling how satisfied he was with his teacher and that he was studying diligently. I hoped for nothing more. About a fortnight later, my son Reb Yosef writes to me requesting that I send money to his teacher after all, for expenses and teaching fees for a six-month period,[99] although I was not obliged to do so; Lissa was extremely expensive at the moment, and his teacher was surely wondering where his money would come from, which was somewhat of an encumbrance to their studies. If he were only free of this worry, they could study more assiduously. He had other students from Hamburg who all sent him money, so I should not hold back either, after all.

Since it made no real difference to me to pay sooner rather than later, I transferred fees for six months. So everything was fine, and I heard from travelers that they were studying diligently. But when the six months were nearly up, I get a letter from my son Reb Yosef Segal on Friday afternoon, just as we were about to go to the synagogue, reading as follows:

"Dear Mother: As you know, I have been a loyal son to you my whole life, never doing anything against your wishes. Therefore you will surely not remove your motherly love from me now, nor would you ever let them hand me over to non-Jews. For, dear mother, you should be informed that the community of Lissa owes a great deal of money to Polish noblemen[100] but they can pay them neither principal nor interest. And since the community officials do not know how to solve the problem, they intend to deliver the children of the Ashkenazim[101] to these noblemen as security; the Ashkenazim will be obliged to pay a ransom to get their children back. The community officials revealed this in great secrecy to teachers of the Ashkenazi children, and a young man, a good friend of mine, revealed the secret to me. This is why I did not write of it to you myself but asked this young man to do so, since my teacher keeps a very close eye on me, much

99. On the "semesters" in the traditional schools of Jewish learning, see Yuval 1989, p. 135, n. 8.
100. Polish noblemen and estate owners levied taxes on the Jews, and their word was law. On the debts of the Lissa community during this period, see Feilchenfeld 1913, p. 208, n. 36).
101. Here used to refer to German Jews only. On young Jewish men from Germany who went to study in Poland, see Book Two, p. 88, n. 121.

too close, and reads all my letters. So, dear mother, do turn to almighty God and write to Tokele's son-in-law[102] to give me fifty or sixty reichstaler so that I might settle with my teacher for him to send me home in great secrecy, to save me from their clutches. I entreat you, in the name of God, don't neglect this, because if we are too late and I fall into their hands, God forbid — this is Poland, after all — I will be lost; if it becomes a question of money at that point, it will cost ten times more than it does now. And so, dearest mother, do not forsake your son for such a paltry sum and do not let me be delivered into their hands, God forbid, because it is hard to obtain a release afterward."

When I had read the letter I was overcome by faintness. I sent for my son Reb Mordechai Segal and handed him the letter. It gave him a terrible fright too; this was on the Sabbath. After nightfall[103] we decided that my son Reb Mordechai would set out immediately for Lissa to bring my son Reb Yosef back home with him. So my son Reb Mordechai went to Berlin and continued from there to Frankfurt an-der-Oder, but just as he's about to leave the Frankfurt an-der-Oder city gates, my son Reb Yosef comes riding up to the Frankfurt an-der-Oder gate in a kind of small Polish cart. My son Reb Mordechai Segal spots him and calls out to my son Reb Yosef Segal to climb down from the cart, and the two of them start talking about how he happened to pop up there so unexpectedly, and what kind of letter was this supposed to be that he had written to our mother, may she live long. My son Reb Yosef Segal looks over the letter and says: "What kind of letter is this? I don't know anything about this letter. My teacher must have written it, may his name be blotted out, in order to get a lot of money out of me. Actually, he already got a lot more money out of me than is his due. He took all my belongings away from me, cut the silver buttons off my coat, and pawned it all. When I asked him to return my things, he accused me of spending it all to satisfy my greedy sweet tooth and said I had pawned it all for myself. When I realized that nothing good would come

102. Tokele (diminutive of Tokl) is the name of the mother-in-law, and not that of the father-in-law; it is here used for identifying the son-in-law, most probably a student living with his wife's family. On surnames deriving from the given names of wives and mothers-in-law (including the previously mentioned "Mirels" and "Orgels"), see Timm 1999, especially p. 46. See also Kaufmann 1896, p. 232, n. 3.

103. Due to the holiness of the Sabbath, nothing could be done about the matter until nightfall.

of this, I turned to Tokele's son-in-law for help, who was obliged to reach a compromise with him — he gave him thirty reichstaler, took me away from him, and sent me here. Thanks be to God that I got away from that scoundrel, since he taught me nothing anyway." My son Reb Mordechai Segal was overjoyed at encountering him there, and together they returned immediately to Hamburg by coach. I was overjoyed and promptly engaged a respectable tutor for him.

At about the same time,[104] a tremendous event took place in Hamburg. A certain householder by the name of Avraham Metz lived in Altona, may God avenge his death; he was married to my cousin Sara, daughter of the late Elia Cohen.[105] Before coming to Hamburg he had lived in Herford, and he was married to the daughter of Leyb Herford. Two years after the wedding, his wife died. He then came to Hamburg and married Sara. He was worth about three thousand reichstaler or more, but he was a stranger in Hamburg, unfamiliar with local ways and business practices; he lost money until within just a few years he lost practically all he owned. He lived in Altona and was a moneychanger. One day[106] his wife comes to town asking at the homes of all her friends if her husband had spent the night there by any chance. After all her investigations, she still could not find out where he had spent the night. The woman became anguished. Some say he ran away from her after she quarreled with him. This went on for three years, I believe, while people said whatever they liked, many speaking ill of this martyr,[107] may God avenge his death, things I will not repeat in writing. But our human weakness is such that we often speak of

104. This phrase intends to chronologically connect the incident of Glikl's son Yosef, which must have occurred in 1689 after his father's death, and the incident recounted next, which occurred in 1684, five years before. As in other instances, Glikl does not follow the chronological order of events (see Marwedel 2001b, pp. 123–133).

105. He married Ulk, the sister of Glikl's mother (see Family Tree A; and Feilchenfeld 1913, p. 210, n. 38).

106. According to another account of the event described in the following text, the episode started on the day after Simḥat Torah, October 1, 1684 (see the memoir of Shmuel Zanvl Hekscher in Kaufmann 1896, p. 397; see also Feilchenfeld 1899b, p. 373).

107. The term kadosh, followed by "may God avenge his death," is commonly used to designate a Jew who "sanctified God's name," clung to his faith and died for it. The use of this term regarding victims of murder or disaster (such as fire or plague) was already common in the early modern period. On the broadening of the usage, see Fram and Kasper-Marienberg 2015.

things we have not actually seen, alas. In this manner Sara was left stranded, a grass widow,[108] poor thing, for more than three years, with her poor fatherless children, forced to let people gossip about her husband, may God avenge his death, and pass judgment on him as they pleased.

After this there was a certain householder in the community of Hamburg,[109] a very decent man — though not wealthy he provided an honest living for himself, his wife, and their four sons — he was a moneychanger. Now, the custom is for moneychangers, poor things, to scurry around all day long in search of their livelihood, then toward evening, at the hour of afternoon prayers, they return home and go to the synagogue. Each of them belongs to a study group where he goes to study,[110] and afterward each goes home. It was getting late one night, and this man's wife is expecting her husband home from his study group so that they could eat their meal together. But all her waiting was in vain. The poor thing went round to all her friends looking for him but found no sign of him. Alas, the man was given up as lost. In the morning the news spread everywhere. One said he had been seen here, another said something else. At noon people met at the Bourse and talked about it, whereupon Reb Zanvl son of Reb Meir Hekscher[111] said: "A certain maidservant came to my house yesterday; she had some gold, wanting to know if I had six or seven hundred reichstaler, and if so I should go with her because there was a foreigner at her house with many objects of gold and precious stones to sell. Since I had no money, I didn't

108. Lit. "a living widow," used in the Middle Ages to refer to a Jewish woman whose husband left her without a divorce. Cf. "in living widowhood" (2 Sam 20:3; Rashi ad loc.).

109. In contrast to the moneychanger from Altona who disappeared previously. The Hebrew memoir of Shmuel Zanvl Hekscher (see this Book, n. 110) who recounts the same incident, contains details that Glikl does not mention, such as the name of the missing householder — Aaron ben Moshe — and the date of the event — Wednesday, July 16, 1687 (see Feilchenfeld 1913, p. 212, n. 40).

110. This refers to a group of people who gathered at set times to study a particular book (Mishnah, Talmudic lore, works of Jewish law), as was then customary in the communities of Western and Eastern Europe.

111. A founder of the Altona-Hamburg-Wandsbek community (see Wolfsberg-Aviad 1960, p. 78). He was witness to the incident recounted here and described it in Hebrew on the last, blank pages of the *Zemaḥ David*, a book he owned (Kaufmann published his memoirs as an appendix to his edition of Glikl's book; see Kaufmann 1896, pp. 394–400). He is the author of the bilingual Hebrew-Yiddish "historical" song "A Bitter Eulogy, Wailing, and Lamentation on the Great Fire of the Community of Altona," which was published, *sine loco et anno*, near to the time of the fire in 1712.

go with her." Now, there was another man there by the name of Lipman,[112] who asked what the maidservant looked like and what she had been wearing. Said Reb Zanvl: "She was dressed in such-and-such fashion." Said this Lipman: "I know that maidservant and I also know who she works for. I don't particularly trust the gentleman she works for." Talking in this manner they left the Bourse and went home. This same Lipman goes home and tells his wife: "Would you believe what I have to tell you? The maidservant who works for the son of the innkeeper at the Seamen's Company was at Reb Zanvl Hekscher's wanting him to go with her on condition that he had six or seven hundred reichstaler. I fear that the missing man went with her and was killed." At that, his wife smacks her head and says: "Now I remember! That maidservant was here too and wanted me or you to go with her. You know very well the kind of evil man and murderer that innkeeper is. That important, virtuous man must have been killed in his house." The wife goes on — she was a clever one: "We will have no rest or peace until we find out!" Her husband says: "You're crazy, even if it's true, what can we do? This is Hamburg; we must not breathe a word of it."[113] Things went on like that for a few days. They succeeded in getting the city council to proclaim, to the accompaniment of drums: "Anyone knowing anything of the Jew, alive or dead, who comes forward to report it will receive a prize of one hundred ducats, and his name will never be disclosed." But no one came forward to report anything at all. The matter had nearly been forgotten, as is the way of the world: even a weightier matter of much greater importance, if nothing further is done about it — is doomed to oblivion. The grass widow and her orphans however still grieved.

One Sabbath morning, in the summer, Lipman's wife was unable to sleep, like the King of Spain who asked his Jewish scholar: "What is the meaning of '*See, the guardian of Israel neither slumbers nor sleeps*'?"[114] The scholar explained it literally: "The guardian of Israel does not slumber and does not sleep." Says the king: "No, that is not what it means. I believe the

---

112. In Hekscher's memoir he is identified as "Lipman son of Reb Yakov Shammes" (see Kaufmann 1896, p. 397). Elsewhere he is known as "Lipman Osterode" (Kaufmann 1896, p. 399).
113. Reb Lipman feared that publicizing his wife's suspicions would put the Jews in danger. On the status of the Jews in Hamburg at that time, see Feilchenfeld 1913, p. 214, n. 43.
114. Ps 121:4. The scholar's following explanation is given in Yiddish.

meaning is: 'God the guardian permits us neither slumber nor sleep.' If I had been sleeping as usual this night just when a blood libel against you was being organized, you'd all be lost; but God who is your guardian made it impossible for me to sleep, and I was made to see them flinging a boy into the house of a certain Jew. Had I not seen that, the Jews would all have perished."[115] Similarly, Lipman's wife could not sleep either; every morning she'd stand at the window; she lived on Alter Steinweg,[116] a thoroughfare that everyone entering or leaving Altona must use. It was Friday evening, the poor woman could not sleep at all, and she was driving everyone in the house crazy. Her husband rebuked her: What kind of life is this? She'd end up making herself completely crazy. But she said nothing would do any good; she would not calm down until vengeance was served since she knew for certain, her heart was telling her just one thing: that man[117] had to be the murderer. At daybreak she stood at the window again, looking down at the street. She spotted the man walking along with his wife, and alongside them a servant bearing a large chest. Seeing this, the woman begins screaming: "Oh God, stand by me! I hope now I start getting what I wanted!" She snatches up her overskirt and shawl, and dashes downstairs. Her husband jumps out of bed and runs after her to stop her from getting away, all to no avail; she ran after the man as he walked to Altona along the Elbe[118] until he set the chest down at the river's edge.

Rivka—that's the woman's name—had gotten this one thing into her head: the man had the corpse in that chest. She began running up to people in Altona begging them to help her for God's sake; she knew for certain that she had found the murderer. But people refused, saying that while it's possible to start something right away, who knows how it will end. But she went on screaming for them to just come with her to the President.[119] So two householders went with her to the President and recounted

---

115. For another version of the story that ends here, see *Shevet Yehuda* 1947, pp. 62–63 (Ibn Virga's book appeared in Yiddish translation in Cracow 1591 and Amsterdam 1648). A version of this story was included in the *Mayse-bukh*, Basel 1602 (see Gaster 1981, story no. 185, pp. 400–401). See also Feilchenfeld 1913, p. 215, n. 45.

116. "Old Stoneway," name of a street in Hamburg.

117. The innkeeper's son; see earlier in this Book, p. 228.

118. Hamburg is located along the banks of the Elbe River.

119. See this Book, p. 221, n. 88.

everything. The President too told them: "You are starting something, but if you cannot prove it I will seize all your property." But Rivka would not be put off, saying she would stake her property and her life on it: "I beseech Your Excellency the President, for God's sake, please send someone over there and order the murderer brought here along with all the things in his possession." Whereupon the President sent guards and soldiers to the Elbe to apprehend them. They had just boarded a boat for Harburg, only an hour away from Altona; had they reached Harburg they would have gone scot-free since Harburg belongs to a different province.[120] The guards made it in the nick of time, however, and brought the murderer and his wife to the President, along with the chest. The President ordered the chest opened, but nothing was found inside except for personal belongings of the murderer and his wife. It is easy to picture the fear and anxiety that seized the poor Jews. The murderer was interrogated with all the various methods but would not confess. Quite the contrary—he kept making threats until a great terror fell upon all the Jews. The murderer was from a big, well-known family in Hamburg. Everyone took flight except for this same Rivka, who maintained: "I beseech you, good people, don't give up. You'll see, God will help us yet." In her great anxiety she started running from Altona to the city. As soon as she reached the field separating Hamburg from Altona, she encountered the maidservant who worked for the murderer. Rivka knew her well—she was the same one who had approached Jews wanting them to accompany her to the murderer's house if they had six or seven hundred reichstaler. So Rivka says to the maidservant: "It's lucky for you and for your master and his wife that you ran into me. Your master and his wife have both been arrested in Altona because of the murder they committed, and they have confessed everything. It remains only for you to confess too. Once that's done, the boat is waiting to take you and your master and his wife away from here, because all we Jews want is to know for sure that Avraham[121] is dead so that his wife can

120. Harburg was part of the duchy of Hannover, while Altona was part of the duchy of Holstein, ruled by the King of Denmark.
121. Glikl errs here; Avraham Metz was the name of the Jew who disappeared first (see this Book, p. 226), but here the subject is Aaron ben Moshe (see p. 227, n. 109), who went missing three years later. This error recurs thrice in the following sentences.

remarry.[122] We don't want anything else of you," as she went on and on telling the maidservant stories. This Rivka is a very clever woman; her words made an impression upon the maidservant, who started pouring it all out in detail: how she met Avraham, may God avenge his death, at the Bourse after having first approached Rivka's husband, Lipman, and other Jews as well, but of all of them only poor Avraham fell victim to tragedy, as he had the great misfortune to have on him a large purse containing money. She showed him a small gold chain, adding that in her master's house was an officer with a quantity of gold and diamonds for sale. "So poor Avraham went with me. When he walked into our house, the chopping block was ready for him there. My master took him down to his room, and together we killed him and buried him under our threshold." Now the maidservant says: "Rivka, I'm telling you all this in confidence, surely you won't bring tragedy upon me." Says Rivka to the maidservant: "Are you stupid? Don't you know my loyal heart? I'm doing all this for your master and his wife, so that they can leave Altona immediately, free. As soon as you come and tell it all to our people, everything will be fine." The maidservant thereupon goes with Rivka to the President's house. The President starts interrogating the maidservant, and even though she starts stammering, sorry now for having revealed anything at all, it all came out, especially when she revealed where the corpse was buried. Well, she told the President everything just as she had told Rivka. Next, the President interrogated the murderer and his wife separately. They both denied everything, saying: "Everything our maidservant told you, she made it all up, just like a whore." Once again we were in trouble. The President said: "I cannot help you anymore. If I have the murderer tortured based on his maidservant's testimony and he bears up under torture and refuses to confess, where will this game lead? You must handle it yourselves, stand on your rights in Hamburg. Get permission from the authorities immediately, without delay, to search for the dead man in the murderer's house. Once you find the corpse in accordance with the maidservant's confession, let me handle it from there." The community officials hurried off and by dint of appealing to the authorities received permission to lead some twenty soldiers to the place the maidservant had

---

122. Her status under Jewish law would change from that of a grass widow, who cannot remarry, to that of a widow, who can.

specified and dig there; they were given permission, should they find him, to give him a Jewish burial in Altona.[123] At the same time, however, they were told: "Beware, if you do not find the body, you are all lost, you know the rabble here in Hamburg. We won't be able to stop them."

Now we were all in deep trouble, but that same Rivka was all over the place, telling us not to despair, she knew for certain that the corpse would be found, for the maidservant had spoken in order to save her own life and had given specific *signs and portents*.[124] Whereupon they got some ten brave men and a few sailors known to be brave and loyal, along with several guards, and invoking God's name they all went to the murderer's home, not far from the old slaughterhouse, by the jail-keeper's.[125] In the meantime, the hue and cry was raised in the entire city, and all sorts of craftsmen and all the scoundrels, six hundred thousand[126] strong, assembled in front of the murderer's house, unanimous that if the Jews find the corpse — well and good, if not — *not a hoof shall remain*[127] of the Jews, God forbid. But God, blessed be He, did not leave us in our plight for long. As soon as our people entered the house, they opened up the specified place and found what they were looking for. *But the eye weeps, the heart rejoices:*[128] they wept at finding the righteous young man, about twenty-four years old, under such distressing circumstances; on the other hand, they rejoiced that the community was no longer in danger and that they would soon see vengeance done.[129] They summoned all the councilmen and showed them the corpse where it had been found — according to the maidservant's statement. The council wrote it down in a protocol and issued an affidavit. The corpse was then laid in a cart and taken to Altona. There was a huge crowd of sailors and craftsmen, indescribable, maybe one hundred thousand people,[130] yet no one uttered a single derogatory word. It's true enough, this was an evil

---

123. The Hamburg Jews were buried in the Jewish cemetery in Altona.

124. Cf. Deut 26:8, meaning "clear signs" or "unassailable proofs."

125. On the names of these locations, see Feilchenfeld 1913, p. 220, n. 50.

126. The number of Jews in the Exodus from Egypt (see Exod 12:37; b.Avodah Zarah 24a), here used to mean "a very large crowd."

127. Cf. Exod 10:26.

128. For the possible sources of this expression, see Turniansky 2006a, p. 174, n. 196.

129. See Book Two, p. 88, n. 118.

130. Like "six hundred thousand" (this Book, n. 126), this does not refer to an actual number.

crowd; even when things are peaceful they stir up trouble and hatred of Jews, yet this time they all dispersed quietly.

The next day, the distinguished leaders of the community took the affidavit and brought it to the President in Altona, who held both the murderer and justice in his hands. Moreover, at that time the Jews preferred that the case be tried in Altona. Once again the President presented his arguments to the murderer, confronted him and revealed what had happened,[131] and he confessed to everything. The widow got back some of her husband's money that was found, may God avenge his death. The murderer was remanded into custody pending trial.

Until now, Sara, poor thing, was a grass widow, as I've written,[132] unable to find out a thing about her husband, may God avenge his death, having no choice but to suffer all the gossip, as I've written. Then, after all this happened with the dead man, and the whole world knew very well who the murderer was, it was recalled that before coming to live near the old slaughterhouse, he had been living in his father's house at the Seamen's Company, Hamburg's main inn, right near the Bourse. Whenever merchants, Jews and non-Jews alike, have anything to arrange or accounts to settle among themselves, they go there to drink from silver cups, so the murderer, son of the innkeeper, was well known among the Jews. Now, when it became known that the son was the murderer, and given that Sara's husband was a moneychanger — the moneychangers too would sit in the inn, receiving and paying out the monies they changed, indeed it is a most respectable, well-known inn — Sara knew quite well that her husband, may God avenge his death, and the son were well acquainted. So she went and told her friends: "You know that my husband disappeared in the same way a few years ago, and now this has been discovered. My husband too used to frequent that house. I'm sure this murderer killed my husband too. Help me, maybe God will show mercy and it will be discovered that he killed my husband too, of blessed memory." Well, why should I go on at length. The President was approached and presented with this. The President addressed the murderer with kind words as well as harsh ones, threatening him with severe torture to get him to confess to the murder of Avraham

---

131. That is, informed him that the murdered man's body had been found.
132. Wife of Avraham Metz, the Jew who went missing first (see this Book, p. 226, n. 104).

Metz too. For a long time he would not admit it, saying that he knew Avraham Metz well but not in that way. Finally the President spoke to him at great length, and he admitted that when he was still living in his father's house at the Seamen's Company inn, he had killed Avraham Metz too, may God avenge his death; inside a little room that served as a cheese cellar, where there was a deep pit, that's where he flung him, threw some lime over the body, and sealed it up.

As soon as this became known, officials of the community hastened to the Hamburg council requesting permission as before to hold another investigation. In short, we were in danger once again, even worse than before, since if you turn such an important, famous establishment into a place of murderers — the corpse had better be found there! In short, they found him. He was still wearing a red fur vest with a few silver buttons, and his ritual fringes. They disinterred him too and gave him a Jewish burial[133] amid deep mourning in our community, for it was as if both men had been murdered on that very day. Friends of my cousin Sara examined the corpse carefully before allowing it to be buried, after Sara, his wife, had given some identifying marks on his body from which it could be established that she need not remain a grass widow; this was duly established, and she was permitted to remarry.[134] After this the murderer was sentenced to death by being broken on the wheel[135] and his body, bound with iron bands, hanged from a hook, to make an enduring example of him. However, the wife and the maidservant were pardoned and only exiled from the state.[136]

On the day the murderer was sentenced to death, there was a commotion in Hamburg as had not been seen there for a hundred years over any man sentenced to death; the lives of all Jews were in danger due to the great hatred of Jews that had been roused. In short, we were in great danger on

---

133. Avraham Metz was buried on August 18, 1687; see Grunwald 1904, p. 297; Feilchenfeld 1913, p. 224, n. 53; Brocke 2009, p. 215, n. 6235. For more details, see Fram and Kasper-Marienberg 2015, p. 293 and n. 107.

134. The body must be definitively identified in order for the woman to be declared a widow and thus permitted to remarry.

135. Breaking the bones of the sentenced criminal by dropping an iron wheel on his limbs, or stretching them on the wheel.

136. That is, their sentence — which was carried out — was exile from their home and the surrounding area.

the day the murderer was sentenced.[137] But on account of God, blessed be He, who is a mighty shepherd, and shows us, sinful human beings, abounding kindness, every single day bears out what is written *when they are in the land of their enemies, I will not reject them or spurn them* and so on.[138] We experienced this that day, *Blessed be the Lord who has not withheld His steadfast faithfulness from us.*[139] If only we sinful human beings could appreciate the great miracles and wonders God, blessed be He, enacts daily for us, miserable human beings! And so it all ended well without harm to the Jews.[140]

Let us now begin again where I left off.[141] Several matches were proposed to my son Reb Yosef Segal, but of these only one was made in heaven, the one with my relative by marriage Meir Stadthagen,[142] who lives in Copenhagen. We made the match and signed the betrothal contract in Hamburg, setting a wedding date for about a year's time. As the wedding day approached we began making preparations, since the wedding was to take place in Copenhagen. I made all my preparations and was about to set out on the journey with my son Nathan Segal. At that time my son Nathan Segal was doing a lot of business with the distinguished Reb Shmuel[143] and his son Reb Mendele, and he had agreed to act as guarantor for a great many bills of exchange of theirs that were due for payment. My son Nathan still

137. The great danger mentioned by Glikl is attested to by the order issued by the Senate of Hamburg on September 19, 1687, which warned against harming the Jews or their property on the day of the murderer's execution and stated that anyone violating the order would be severely punished (see Feilchenfeld 1913, p. 225, n. 54; and in greater detail, Freimark 1970–1972, pp. 255–258, where the murderer's name [Diedrich Meinecke] and the actual wording of the order appear).

138. Lev 26:44.

139. Cf. Gen 24:27.

140. News about the described events appeared in the Yiddish newspaper *Dinstagishe un Freitagishe Kurantn* (which was published twice weekly in Amsterdam from August 1686 to December 1687) on July 29; August 1; September 12, 19, and 26; and October 10, 1687. The news was based on the local Dutch newspapers, the *Amsterdamse Courant* and the *Oprechte Haerlemse Courant* (see Pach-Oosterbroek 2014, pp. 228–236). The extensive coverage of the events indicates that the murder and execution of the murderer aroused much interest among Jews and non-Jews beyond where they occurred.

141. Before the account on the murders in Hamburg, this Book, n. 104.

142. Meir Stadthagen was the son of Moshe Kramer Stadthagen (see Kaufmann 1896, p. xliv, near n. 2), the oldest brother of Glikl's father-in-law, Yosef Hamel, making him her husband's cousin (see Family Tree B).

143. Reb Shmuel Oppenheim (see Book Four, p. 167, n. 122).

had not received any remittance from these distinguished gentlemen for requisite payment of their bills of exchange, worth about twenty thousand reichstaler. Not only had my son Nathan Segal received no remittance, he never even got a letter from them to explain why they had failed to send the payment. Nathan was supposed to go to Copenhagen with me for the wedding, but due to the reason just mentioned, he could not go. He was obliged to protect his reputation and that of his business associates. It is easy to imagine how sorry and heartbroken we both were. I'd have to travel to the wedding on my own, with my son Reb Yosef. God alone knows my *heart's bitterness*,[144] how grieved and distressed I was at parting from him[145] not knowing what was happening with the distinguished gentlemen in Vienna.[146] In this way I left Hamburg for Copenhagen with my son the bridegroom, Reb Yosef Segal, and my relative by marriage Moshe son of Meir Stadthagen,[147] and Reb Chaim Cleve's[148] son-in-law, and we reached Copenhagen safely. I was sure that immediately upon arriving in Copenhagen I would find a letter awaiting me from my son Nathan Segal informing me that he had received a letter and the remittance from the distinguished gentlemen in Vienna, and indeed I did receive a letter from my son Nathan —virtuous son that he is— saying that although he had not yet received a letter from Vienna I shouldn't worry about it, I need only rejoice at my son's wedding, may he live long, there was no cause for worry.

Now, while I felt uneasy about this business, I left everything in God's hands, blessed be He, without giving it further thought. We exchanged dowries, and the wedding was to be held the following week. In the meantime *my inmost self must weep*[149] and from one mail delivery to the next I hoped for good news from my son Nathan Segal, which indeed came, a day before the wedding, thank God, informing me that the distinguished Reb Mendele had sent him a substantial remittance of several thousand more than he owed my son Nathan Segal, adding an apology for being away from home, otherwise he would have sent it sooner. Thereupon we held the wed-

144. Cf. "The heart alone knows its bitterness" (Prov 14:10).
145. That is, from her son Nathan.
146. The previously mentioned Reb Shmuel and Reb Mendele.
147. See this Book, p. 235, n. 142.
148. On him, see Feilchenfeld 1913, p. 226, n. 56.
149. Jer 13:17.

ding in joyful good spirits as we thoroughly enjoyed ourselves. After the wedding I was in a great hurry to get back home. I had no traveling companion for the journey other than Moshe son of my in-law Meir,[150] who was not in as great a hurry as myself to take leave of his father and mother. As a result I was forced to remain there for another two weeks after the wedding. Although I received the best treatment and every possible honor, it was not what I wanted; I would have preferred to be in my own home by my children. I badgered the aforementioned Moshe so much that finally he was forced to decide to set out with me on the homeward journey to Hamburg. We got ready to leave and set out for Hamburg, arriving safely, thank God. I asked my son Reb Leyb for a statement of my goods that I had left with him, and he gave me a good statement for each item, which pleased me very much.

Now I still had four orphans left,[151] my son Reb Zanvl, may he rest in peace,[152] and my son Reb Moshe Segal, my daughter Freydchen, and my daughter Miriam, may they live long.[153] Quite a few prominent matches were proposed to me, and I could have resumed a life of wealth and honor, but I thought that would go against my children's best interest, so to my misfortune, as will be understood presently,[154] I rejected them all.

After this my late son Reb Zanvl reached maturity too. I occasionally took him with me to the Braunschweig fair: since he did not want to study, he should learn to be a merchant. My son Reb Moshe Segal was doing well in his studies. So I sent my son Reb Moshe to Frankfurt to study at the kloyz,[155] and I sent my son Reb Zanvl there too, with merchandise. While my late son Reb Zanvl was in Frankfurt, my brother-in-law Reb Yosef Segal[156] gets a

---

150. Who traveled with her to the wedding (see previous text) and was, in fact, the bride's brother. From Glikl's descriptions of her travels throughout her memoir, it becomes clear that she never traveled alone, but always with someone accompanying her, since apparently it was not acceptable for women to travel alone or only with other women.

151. Glikl's four remaining unmarried children out of her twelve children who lost their father.

152. The author's eleventh child. The addition of the formulaic phrase for a deceased person foreshadows his death (see Book Six, p. 273; on his death, see opening of Book Seven, p. 290).

153. The children appear here in order of birth.

154. Glikl hints at what will be told in Book Six. This is evidence of her either planning the work in advance or editing it later.

155. See Reiner 1993, especially p. 299.

156. Husband of her sister Elkele (see Family Tree A).

letter from Reb Moshe Bamberg,[157] his trustworthy friend. This Reb Moshe was writing to my brother-in-law Reb Yosef Segal asking his advice about a match from Hamburg that had been proposed to him for his daughter. My brother-in-law receives this letter on the Sabbath; he sends for me to come to his house, then goes for a walk in the garden with my sister Elkele.[158] No sooner had I walked in than he says to me: "Mazl tov! Your son Zanvl is a bridegroom!" I laughed, saying: "Well, if he's a bridegroom, I should know about it too." He shows me the letter from Reb Moshe Bamberg, who was in Vienna at the time. And the gaon, head of the rabbinical court, our master and teacher R. Shimshon,[159] also writes to my brother-in-law Reb Yosef asking him to write the truth about anything he considered pertinent to the match. I read the letter and tell my brother-in-law Reb Yosef: "I still don't see here that my son Zanvl is a bridegroom." Says my brother-in-law Reb Yosef: "I guarantee you that the letters I will write to Vienna will make your son Zanvl the bridegroom of Reb Moshe Bamberg's daughter."

That same Reb Moshe Bamberg was the brother-in-law of the gaon our master and teacher R. Shimshon of Vienna. So my brother-in-law Reb Yosef immediately sent off letters describing my son Reb Zanvl. The match was duly arranged, by two letters, then R. Shimshon wrote that we should send my son Zanvl to him in Vienna right away, to stay with him until the wedding, to take place in two years' time. What great promises the gaon our master and teacher R. Shimshon promised and wrote, promising that it was *to save life that God sent me*,[160] so that things would be good for him and all his siblings. Subsequently I received several more letters from our master and teacher the distinguished R. Shimshon displaying his friendliness toward me.

My son Zanvl was attending the fair at Frankfurt-am-Main at that time.

157. Reb Moshe Brillin, who lived in Bamberg. He was brother-in-law to R. Shimshon Wertheimer (see Kaufmann 1896, p. 249, n. 2).
158. Wife of R. Yosef Segal.
159. The well-known court Jew Samson Wertheimer, 1658–1724 (see *Encyclopedia Judaica* 1972, vol. 16, cols. 457–459; see also Lowenthal 1978, p. 289–290, n. 17), who lived in Vienna and was married to the sister of the previously mentioned Reb Moshe Bamberg (Glikl notes this herself in the next paragraph). For his many involvements on behalf of the Jews, he was honored with the title *Judenkaiser*, as was his uncle Reb Shmuel Oppenheim, who brought him to Vienna (see Book Four, p. 167, n. 122).
160. Cf. "it was to save life that God sent me ahead of you" (Gen 45:5).

I wrote to him that he was now betrothed to the daughter of Reb Moshe Bamberg; he should go straight from the fair at Frankfurt-am-Main to Vienna and remain there until the wedding. So my son Zanvl left Frankfurt-am-Main for Vienna and arrived there safely. The distinguished head of the rabbinical court, our master and teacher R. Shimshon, welcomed him most courteously and wrote to me that he was well pleased with him, and that he had immediately procured a tutor for him. So my son Zanvl was in Vienna; he was very young and committed youthful pranks, nor did the gaon our master and teacher R. Shimshon watch him too closely. He squandered a lot of money in those two years. To be sure, my son wrote to me about everything and asked to be married as soon as possible since he did not want to remain in Vienna any longer, but his future bride was still very young, a minor,[161] so his engagement lasted nearly three years. After this his father-in-law, Reb Moshe, was in Vienna, and following my frequent letters agreed to hold the wedding at the beginning of the month of Tammuz in Bamberg; my son Zanvl also wrote me that he and his father-in-law, Reb Moshe, were leaving Vienna, and that I should plan to be in Bamberg at the beginning of Tammuz, which I did, as I was attending the Leipzig fair in any case and had planned to go to Bamberg from there. Then I received a letter from the distinguished R. Shimshon saying that due to the great rage against the Jews in Hamburg, I should go from the wedding to Vienna and stay in his house, where he would give me two of his best rooms. And any business I wished to conduct — I had his permission. Toward this end I received from him a valid imperial laissez-passer.[162] I made my preparations accordingly, having no other plan in mind than to leave for Vienna after the wedding. For this purpose I had with me jewelry worth fifty thousand reichstaler that I intended to take to Vienna. However, *many designs are in a man's mind, but it is the Lord's plan that is accomplished.*[163] I set out for Leipzig with my sons Nathan Segal and Reb Moshe Segal, who was still unmarried. We were still in Leipzig when

---

161. That is, she had not yet reached sexual maturity (see b.Yevamot 61b: "One who has emerged from her minority but has not yet attained adolescence").

162. R. Shimshon, who was an influential court Jew with many connections (see this Book, p. 238, n. 159), could easily obtain such a pass.

163. Prov 19:21.

my son Nathan Segal received letters from Hamburg informing him that
due to some business matters he must return home immediately after the
Leipzig fair. Thus was my trip to Vienna canceled, since I did not wish to
go to Vienna without my son Nathan Segal. So I sent all my jewelry back
to Hamburg with him except for some jewelry worth a few thousand that I
kept with me, whereupon I set out from Leipzig to Bamberg accompanied
only by my son Reb Moshe Segal. I suffered terribly on account of the dangerous roads; I — a woman alone, and my son Reb Moshe still very young,
a boy of fifteen. Still, when you have money, you can manage anywhere.
The trip cost a great deal of money.

I reached Bamberg at midnight. In the morning my future in-laws and
the future bride welcomed me. It was my intention to hold the wedding
immediately, at the beginning of the month of Tammuz, but there was a
serious setback since my brother-in-law Reb Yosef Segal had agreed without my knowledge to put down in the marriage conditions the sum of
five thousand reichstaler for my son Reb Zanvl Segal's dowry, though he
only had four thousand reichstaler. I found out about this when I was still
in Hamburg, and wrote immediately to the gaon, head of the rabbinical
court, our master and teacher R. Shimshon, to say he had made a mistake
with the five thousand reichstaler and that my son had no more than four
thousand in German currency, but the distinguished R. Shimshon wrote
back that it was of no consequence, the marriage conditions should stay
as they were, it added prestige, and there would be no argument about it
during the marriage ceremony. But now my in-law the distinguished Reb
Moshe Bamberg was saying something very different: he would abide
strictly by his conditions. This led to major arguments between us that
made it impossible to hold the wedding at the beginning of the month
of Tammuz. Only then did my in-law Reb Moshe write to Vienna. The
gaon, head of the rabbinical court, our master and teacher R. Shimshon
of Vienna, replied with nothing but the truth. In the meantime, before the
letters arrived, my future in-law the distinguished Reb Moshe thought he
could squeeze a little more out of me. But when he saw he could squeeze
nothing more out of me, and then the letters from Vienna arrived saying I
was in the right, the wedding took place in mid-Tammuz, as respectable and
splendid an affair as we Jews can manage. Prominent householders from

all over the country[164] attended the wedding. Among them were the two sons of my in-law Reb Shimshon Baiersdorf,[165] with the matchmaker; in Hamburg I had already received an offer of a match for my son Reb Moshe Segal with the daughter of Reb Shimshon Baiersdorf. As Baiersdorf is only two leagues from Bamberg, I replied to the matchmaker that I had to be in Bamberg anyway for the wedding of my son Reb Zanvl Segal, so I'd bring my son Reb Moshe Segal along, to see and be seen.[166] These two sons — they were already married — spoke to me and told me what dowry their father was intending to give. To that I replied that I had brought along my unmarried son Reb Moshe for that very purpose — to see and be seen. After the wedding we'd take a trip to the holy community of Fürth, two leagues' distance from Baiersdorf;[167] we could reach an agreement there.

Another match in Bamberg was proposed to my son, and one in Fürth. Consequently, I arranged with my in-law Reb Moshe Bamberg for us to take a trip together to Fürth. Now that we've seen the principal[168] in Bamberg — let's see what there is in Fürth and Baiersdorf too. We set out on the pleasant trip, that is, my in-law Reb Moshe and his wife, myself, and my son Reb Moshe Segal. We were in Baiersdorf, where we saw the daughter of my in-law Reb Shimshon.[169] He saw my son too, and we were very close to an agreement, but one thousand marks stood in the way and we could not reach a compromise. So we traveled together to Fürth and stayed the night there. I simply cannot describe the honor shown us there. The most important householders came with their wives to our inn wanting to take us to their homes by main force. In the end we could no longer refuse my cousin Mann son of cousin Mordechai Cohen[170] — all of us must needs go along with him. That evening we were hosted with all the honors; we

164. From the entire area of Bamberg, in Franconia.

165. Reb Samson Solomon Baiersdorf (d. 1712), one of the most prominent court Jews. He and his sons were the Markgraf von Bayreuth's agents (see *Encyclopedia Judaica* 1972, vol. 4, col. 109; Lowenthal 1978, p. 290, nn. 20–21; Stern 1950, pp. 100, 198; see also Kaufmann 1896, p. 252, n. 1; Feilchenfeld 1913, p. 232, n. 58). Glikl explains immediately why she refers to him as "my in-law."

166. Cf. this Book, p. 208.

167. On the distance between Fürth and Baiersdorf, see Feilchenfeld 1913, p. 233, n. 59.

168. A slightly humorous phrase, in that "principal" refers to the bride, while the dowry is the "interest."

169. See this Book, n. 165.

170. See Book Three, p. 135, n. 160.

intended to leave in the morning—which we did—so we did not arrange anything concerning the match in Fürth either and returned to Bamberg. There I immediately began preparations for my return to Hamburg with my son Reb Moshe Segal. It just so happened that the matchmaker who had proposed the match—he lived in Fürth—was in Bamberg the whole time and very much wanted the match from Baiersdorf; nevertheless, I told him my decision: It must be thus and not otherwise. In short, the matchmaker said: "I can see that you are adamant and that you are ready to depart. Please, do me a favor, stay here until two o'clock this afternoon. I have written to them in Baiersdorf telling them everything. I know for a fact that by two o'clock this afternoon we will get a reply that everything is fine, but if no reply comes by two o'clock, I will not delay you any longer." This was acceptable to me, and we proceeded with our preparations for the journey.

My in-law Reb Moshe Bamberg and my son Reb Zanvl wanted to accompany us a few leagues' distance, out of respect. In the meantime, a banquet was prepared, *like Solomon's banquet in his time.*[171] I cannot begin to describe what a decent man is this Reb Moshe, shrewd and clever, showing the utmost respect toward all and sundry. Well, when we had finished eating and drinking it was already three o'clock, and nothing seen nor heard from Baiersdorf. So our entire party settled into a coach, and at about five o'clock we left Bamberg. My in-law the distinguished Reb Moshe Bamberg implored me for us to stay the night at his house, as nightfall was approaching, and be on our way early in the morning, but I absolutely would not hear of it; invoking the name of God, we proceeded on our way. But barely a quarter of an hour after we left the city, the matchmaker comes riding after us, poor thing, asking us to return to Bamberg for God's sake, for the sons of Reb Shimshon Baiersdorf were there, eager to arrange everything satisfactorily. But I did not want to do this, to ride back. So my in-law Reb Moshe says: "Look, up ahead is a nice village with a nice inn. It's nearly nightfall, we won't be riding any further. Let us stay the night at the inn, and if the sons of Reb Shimshon Baiersdorf want to come to us here—let them do so." I was pleased at this; so was the matchmaker, for bringing us thus far, and off he rode back to Bamberg. Before an hour had gone by, there

171. Cf. m.Bava Metzi'a 7:1; b.Bava Metzi'a 49a, 83a, 86b; as well as b.Taanit 29b; b.Eruvin 41a, and so on.

appeared at our inn the head of the rabbinical court our master and teacher
R. Mendl Rothschild of Bamberg,[172] with the two sons of my in-law the
distinguished Reb Shimshon, a certain householder by the name of Leyb
Biber, and his brother Reb Wolf—all of them respectable men and prodigiously wealthy. In short, we did not prolong the discussion and confirmed
the betrothal with wishes for good luck. The two previously mentioned
sons had full power of attorney for their father and signed everything. Thus
we passed that night rejoicing at this auspicious outcome. My in-law Reb
Shimshon was not at his home just then but at Bayreuth with His Excellency the Markgraf of Bayreuth,[173] where he was the most influential man
of all, his court Jew, as everyone knows. His sons accordingly entreated us
to do them a favor and accompany them to Bayreuth out of respect for
their father, which I considered extremely difficult. We had already hired
our coachman till Halberstadt. After discussing it with him, it was agreed
that we would pay him two reichstaler extra to take us to Bayreuth and
from there to Naumberg,[174] where a fair was taking place. Zekele Wiener[175]
was with us too; he persuaded me to do it. My in-law the distinguished
Reb Moshe Bamberg said that if I desired his gracious assistance, he too
would accompany me to Bayreuth. Vainly I tried politely to dissuade him
from this, not wishing him to go to so much trouble on our account, but
we reached an understanding despite everything and our entire party rode
off to Bayreuth. So we arrived, and there we met my in-law the previously
mentioned distinguished Reb Shimshon,[176] who was extremely glad to see
us. As it was the beginning of the month of Av, and *"with the beginning
of Av rejoicings are curtailed,"*[177] we ate only a light supper since there was
nothing in the house.[178] In the morning, however, Reb Shimshon sent out
for several kinds of fine fish and also ordered dairy dishes prepared that

---

172. Mendl Rothschild was rabbi of the state of Bamberg as well as rabbi of Baiersdorf and Bayreuth
(see Kaufmann 1896, p. 255, n. 2; Feilchenfeld 1913, p. 235, n. 61).

173. Markgraf Christian Ernst von Bayreuth (1644–1712).

174. Naumberg an der Saale, in the south of Sachsen-Anhalt.

175. I have no information about this man.

176. He is first mentioned earlier in this Book, p. 241, n. 165.

177. M.Taanit 4:6; b.Taanit 26b, 29a.

178. Apparently they did not keep additional foodstuffs in the house due to the custom of not
eating meat or drinking wine during the "Nine Days" between the beginning of Av and the Ninth
of Av (and see following text).

could be made quickly, as I did not want to delay any longer. My previously mentioned in-law also promised not to detain me after one o'clock. After the meal we took leave of each other, and I, with my son the bridegroom Reb Moshe and Zekele Wiener, settled in the coach and parted from my in-law the distinguished Reb Moshe, truly in tears. Thus were we forced to tear ourselves away for the time being from our joyous reunion, and we returned safely to Hamburg, where we found my children and the whole family in good health, thank God; considering that I had been away from home for twelve weeks, this made me very happy indeed.

After this God, blessed be He, inflicted a strange sickness upon my cousin Beyle,[179] may she rest in peace, wife of our master and teacher R. Ber Cohen. She was unable to pass water, God help us, for four weeks. Although my in-law our master and teacher the distinguished R. Ber Cohen[180] sought out every possible treatment for his wife and consulted all the physicians, it was all to no avail; apparently it had already been decreed by almighty God. For about three weeks she suffered in this unforeseen condition. They did and tried everything, as can be imagined, medications and amulets both. The distinguished R. Ber Cohen was not stingy with his money, whatever it cost, all to no avail. When my cousin Beyle realized that her condition was worsening day by day and all the medicine was of no use, she summoned my brother-in-law Reb Yosef Segal[181] and our master and teacher R. Shmuel Orgels,[182] may they live long, and sent for her husband, R. Ber Cohen; then she addressed him with emotion concerning the orphan Glukchen they had raised in their home. She was about twelve or thirteen years old at the time. Both of them loved the girl so fiercely that no words can describe it. She beseeched her husband to give her some satisfaction before her death

179. She was the daughter of Glikl's aunt Gluk and her husband Yakov Ree (see Book Two, p. 69, nn. 69, 70; and Family Tree A. For more on Beyle, see Feilchenfeld 1913, p. 237, n. 63).

180. Berend Salomon (or Berend Cohen) was a scholar and lay leader in Hamburg (see Duckesz 1908, pp. 20–22) and founded the kloyz there in 1709 (see Feilchenfeld 1913, p. 723, n. 63) or 1707 (see Herzig and Rohde 1991, p. 204, where his portrait appears). Glikl refers to him as "my in-law" because he was married to her cousin Beyle (see previous note).

181. He was Beyle's cousin by his marriage to Elkele, Glikl's sister (see Family Tree A).

182. R. Shmuel, son of Yosef Orgels, author of a commentary on the *Shulḥan Arukh-Oraḥ Ḥayim* (see Steinschneider 1852–1860, p. 2430, no. 7040). He moved from Cracow to Altona and taught Torah widely there until his death in 1700 (see Duckesz 1908, pp. 10–11; Feilchenfeld 1913, p. 238, n. 64).

by giving her his solemn vow that after she died he would marry no other woman except the orphan Glukchen daughter of Reb Fayvesh Cohen, may he live long; our master and teacher R. Ber was the girl's uncle.[183] Tearfully R. Ber gave his solemn vow with a handclasp to the aforementioned Reb Yosef and our master and teacher R. Shmuel, whereupon he performed the confirmation ceremony.[184] As a result, the woman was reassured, saying she could now die willingly, knowing that she had provided well for her Glukchen's future. But, my God, how differently things turn out from what we human beings think! They wrote to the orphan's brother Reb Zelik[185] in Hannover — they had raised him too and had even married him off to the daughter of the distinguished Reb Hertz Hannover[186] — to come see his aunt Beyle who was dangerously ill and was asking to see him before her death (for they loved these two children dearly). In the meantime, the medicines were doing their work; buckets of water poured out of her, which they thought would bring about an improvement. But alas, it had the opposite effect and only hastened her death. When Reb Zelik came he found her seemingly improved, but why should I dwell on this at length? He had not been with her even a single day when God, blessed be He, took her to Him, to the deep sorrow of her husband, all our friends and relations, and the entire community, for she was — may God be gracious to her — a good, wise woman adept at guiding her husband's heart. But what good is all this? All her wealth and property, all the good her husband, our master and teacher the distinguished R. Ber Cohen, did for her, all was futile. He took care to have many people study for her,[187] gave away a lot of money to charity,[188] but apparently her time had come; it had already been decreed

---

183. Fayvesh Cohen was R. Ber Cohen's brother. He married Reyze, daughter of Yakov Ree and sister of Beyle, Ber Cohen's wife (see Simonsen 1905, p. 105). Reyze gave birth to Glukchen (and her brother Zelik/Zeligman; see following text) and then died. Thus, the children were double niece and nephew of Ber Cohen and his wife Beyle (see Family Tree A). Even though their father was alive (the formulaic phrase for the living follows his name), they were raised by their childless aunt and uncle. This may be an instance of the "in loco parentis" practice (see Ozment 1986, pp. 102–109).

184. See Book Four, p. 158, n. 68.

185. Seligmann Behrend, son of the previously mentioned Reb Fayvesh Cohen (see Family Tree A).

186. Son of Leffmann Behrens (see Book Two, p. 91, n. 137; Kaufmann 1896, p. 258, n. 1; Feilchenfeld 1913, p. 239, n. 65).

187. That is, he paid men to study, following the belief that studying Torah has protective and curative power (see b.Sotah 21a).

188. Based on "charity saves from death" (cf. Prov 10:2, 11:4; and b.Shabbat 156b).

during "*Who shall live and who shall die*"[189] on Rosh Hashanah. She died with a good name[190] and was duly buried. Her husband and all her relatives mourned her deeply, as can be imagined, especially my in-law Reb Anshl[191] and his wife, Matte, her niece, and Matte's brother Reuven, who had also been raised in the home of our master and teacher R. Ber Cohen; they were also related[192] to the orphan Glukche: Matte, the late Reb Anshl's wife, and her brother Reuven were Glukchen's cousins.

After the week of mourning they were somewhat consoled, and thought that the home of the distinguished R. Ber Cohen would not be unwelcoming to them[193] now that their cousin Glukchen was to enjoy a prominent position there. Hence, once some time had elapsed after the week of mourning, Glukchen's previously mentioned relatives began to prod the distinguished R. Ber Cohen to announce openly that he intended to marry the orphan Glukchen so that he could shake off the matchmakers and be rid of them; in fact, he had not a moment's peace, given that any man with a daughter would be glad for a match with our master and teacher R. Ber—even if it meant impoverishing himself in the process.[194] R. Ber Cohen put the relatives off time and again, claiming it was still too soon. Ultimately it turned out that he could not marry the orphan since he had raised her in his house from childhood and had treated her like a daughter, hence he could not marry such a girl. Besides, he had no children, and was no youngster; how could he take a wife who would not be able to bear children for a few years yet?[195] If he had to wait a few years until this maiden could bear children—who knows how long a man may live in the

189. From the *Unetaneh Tokef* prayer, recited in the additional prayers for Rosh Hashanah (see Maḥzor Rosh Hashanah 2014, p. 568).

190. On a "good name," cf. b.Berakhot 17a. Beyle died on August 1, 1696; see *Grabbüchern* 1874, n. 882 (634); also see Simonsen 1905, p. 105.

191. Anshl Wimpfen. Glikl calls him "my in-law" because he married Matte (see following text), the daughter of Yudah Rothschild and Elkele, Glikl's cousin (see Family Tree A; and see Feilchenfeld 1913, p. 240, n. 66, and p. 244, n. 70).

192. They were relatives because Elkele (wife of Yudah Rothschild and mother of Matte and Reuven), Reyze (wife of Fayvesh Cohen and mother of Glukchen and her brother Zelik), and Beyle (wife of R. Ber Cohen) were sisters. The three were daughters of Gluk, Glikl's aunt (see Family Tree A).

193. The import of this is somewhat clarified in the story that follows.

194. Perhaps because the bride's side would have to give a large dowry to match the groom's wealth.

195. See "If he has no children he must marry a woman capable of procreation; and if he has children he may marry a woman who is incapable of procreation" (b.Yevamot 61b).

expectation of fulfilling his obligation.[196] This put a scare into all his previously mentioned relatives, who reminded him indignantly that he had
given his dying wife, in the throes of death, his solemn vow and performed
the confirmation ceremony in the presence of witnesses to the effect that
after her death he would take Glukchen as his wife. Said our master and
teacher R. Ber Cohen: "Yes, quite true, but I did it to give my departed wife
satisfaction. Anyway, I was in such a state that I didn't know what to do. I
request that Glukchen absolve me of my solemn vow. I'll give her a large
sum of money for her dowry so that she is able to marry as worthy a man as
myself. As for your fear that you will be unwelcome in my home — if there
is some other maiden in your family who is ripe for marriage, I will take her
as my wife; in any case, I'll do as I said for Glukchen." But, as I said, they
insisted upon his marrying Glukchen. Reb Anshl, his wife, Matte, and her
brother Reuven Rothschild[197] would not hear of any other match except
with Glukchen, fearing perhaps that any other match at all, even with a
woman in their family, would lead to their losing their prestige in the home
of the aforementioned R. Ber. They really did enjoy high prestige with our
master and teacher the distinguished R. Ber Cohen; they had the say *who
shall come in and who shall go out*[198] at his house.

At that time there was my daughter Freydchen,[199] only twelve years
old but quite developed for her age[200] and very pretty, none more so. My
brother Reb Wolf[201] came to me and said: "What are you doing? Why are
you sitting around doing nothing? R. Ber Cohen isn't marrying Glukchen,
why don't I go and propose your daughter to him?" I scoffed derisively at
my brother: "What are you talking about? I should cause harm to the orphan Glukchen?" But my brother assured me, swearing to it, that he knew
for certain that R. Ber was not going to marry Glukchen, and if he did not

196. That is, his obligation to procreate.

197. See this Book, nn. 191, 192. Matte and her brother Reuven were the children of Yudah Rothschild and Elkele, Glikl's cousin (see Family Tree A).

198. Cf. Num 27:21.

199. The older of Glikl's two youngest daughters (see Family Tree C). Freydchen was unmarried and
living in her mother's house.

200. Glikl's intent is doubtless to say that despite her young age, Freydchen had reached sexual
maturity, and could become pregnant and give birth (also see this Book, p. 239, n. 161).

201. Glikl's only brother (she also had four sisters), who was younger than she (see Family Tree A). He
married Idel, daughter of Yakov Lichtenstadt, and died on April 13, 1739 (see Grunwald 1904, p. 101).

marry my daughter — why, he would marry a complete outsider, with the result that we would be unwelcome in his house.

Well, who wouldn't give his enthusiastic consent to a match with our master and teacher R. Ber Cohen, when all the advantages in the world are to be found in him? My brother then went to R. Ber and proposed the match to him, to which he replied that he did not know my daughter and to approach Reb Anshl and his wife and Reb Reuven. If my brother could intervene so that Glukchen could be persuaded to absolve him of his solemn vow to her late aunt Beyle, he would be pleased.[202] However, when my brother approached these relatives they became furious; they say that Matte Rothschild had this to say about it: as far as she was concerned, it would be far better for R. Ber to marry a total stranger than to consent to his marrying my daughter, may she live long. When I heard this, I gave the matter no further thought. Meanwhile, our master and teacher R. Ber spoke to Glukchen asking her to absolve him of his solemn vow; he'd give her a sizeable dowry and find her a distinguished fine young man, but she would not hear of it under any circumstances. Whereupon R. Ber Cohen wrote to rabbis and presented the case, asking them for an annulment of his solemn vow so that he could take a wife. The gaon, head of the rabbinical court of the kloyz in Altona,[203] refused to grant him an annulment, but they say he was granted an annulment by other rabbis. Reb Anshl, although he still very badly wanted R. Ber to marry Glukchen, realized there was no chance whatsoever. It seems that our master and teacher R. Ber Cohen had long since had his eye on the daughter of Tevele Shiff,[204] in fact he married her, and before the year was out she bore him a son. It is easy to imagine how proud our master and teacher R. Ber was at the birth of his son. Reb Anshl had died shortly before, heaven forfend!,[205] a sudden death. He went

---

202. His words make clear that he would be pleased to be freed from his promise to marry Glukchen. However, the question of whether he also meant that as a result he agrees to marry Glikl's daughter is only answered in what follows.

203. R. Tzvi Ashkenazi, the "Ḥakham Tzvi" (*Encyclopedia Judaica* 1972, vol. 3, cols. 733–735); see Feilchenfeld 1913, p. 243, n. 69; Davis 1995, pp. 232–233, n. 65.

204. Her name was Reyzele (see Feilchenfeld 1913, p. 244, n. 10). Tevele is the lay name for David.

205. Glikl uses this specific interjection (*bar-minan*) only when mentioning a plague (e.g., see early in Book Three, p. 106, n. 40) or a sudden death (as Reb Anshl's here or R. Shmuel Orgels's following), a reason for unusual alarm in the community.

to bed hale and hearty, scarcely an hour later his pure soul departed. He was mourned by the entire community as an important, God-fearing man, second to none. After this, while I was at the Leipzig fair[206] — about a year and a half after our master and teacher R. Ber Cohen married — letters arrived at Leipzig saying that R. Ber Cohen's wife was very ill. The next mail delivery brought letters saying she was dead. What a commotion this caused in Leipzig — indescribable. Not long afterward, R. Ber married his late wife's sister. Our master and teacher R. Shmuel Orgels was involved in all these affairs, as our master and teacher R. Ber Cohen thought very highly of him. Some time afterward, this same R. Shmuel, on his way to the synagogue on Friday night, was overcome by faintness, heaven forfend!, and dropped dead. Easy to imagine the alarm in the community. Thus all passed away within a short span of time — Reb Anshl, R. Shmuel Orgels, and R. Ber Cohen's wife,[207] alas. If any injustice was done to my late cousin Beyle by the solemn vow made by R. Ber and witnessed by those previously mentioned, all is known before God, blessed be He, while I and all human beings are too weak to ponder it. All we can do is pray to God, blessed be He, to continue to remove His wrath from us and all of Israel.[208] After this our master and teacher R. Ber Cohen gave Glukchen away in marriage in prosperity and dignity to the son of the distinguished Reb Yudah Berlin,[209] and did much for her siblings too, as is well known to all.

I would not have written all this in my notebook had I not thought it was out of the ordinary and instructive as to how a person's luck is liable to change. For this reason I took the trouble to write down the essence here, for my late modest cousin Beyle believed before her death that she had attained the highest degree of happiness — indeed this was so, going by instinctive human judgment. She was married to our master and teacher

206. Glikl is recorded among the attendees at the Leipzig fair in 1699 as the widow of Hain (Heine) Goldschmidt (see Freudenthal 1928, p. 125). According to the records there, Glikl also attended the fair in 1690, 1692, and 1698.

207. Reb Anshl Wimpfen (see this Book, p. 246, n. 191) died on July 16, 1697; R. Shmuel Orgels (see this Book, p. 144, n. 182) died on February 20, 1700; and Reyzele, daughter of Tevele Shiff, wife of R. Ber Cohen, died on May 15, 1699. See *Grabbüchern* 1874, nn. 944 (5832), 1232 (2886), 886 (635), respectively.

208. For this particular combination of sources, see Turniansky 2006a, p. 474, n. 589.

209. Reb Yudah Berliner (see Book Three, p. 134, n. 154).

R. Ber Cohen, a great scholar, a *Cohen*, from a privileged family, prodigiously wealthy, good-hearted, kind to rich and poor alike. They had a very good life together. Although they had no children of their own, they raised the children of Reb Fayvesh Cohen, Zeligman and his sister Glukchen, who never sensed any difference;[210] they loved these children as if they had been their own flesh and blood. My late cousin Beyle lavished her attention and care exclusively upon these two children. After a great deal of effort on her part, she succeeded through her cleverness — though it was due in greater measure to God's will, blessed be He — in arranging a match between Zeligman and the daughter of the distinguished Reb Hertz Hannover.[211] With my own ears I heard the departed woman say that the boy had cost her over fifteen thousand reichstaler. Such generosity on the part of our master and teacher R. Ber Cohen, to spend such a vast sum on the boy, his nephew, and that of Beyle, the boy's aunt! And they were willing to spend the same amount on Glukchen too. And so, when the young man became a bridegroom and everything was going to her satisfaction, her happiness knew no bounds; she met with esteem and respect unequaled by any other woman in all Ashkenaz. But alas, when the rope is stretched too taut — it snaps.[212] At her peak, in the best period of her life, my late cousin Beyle had to abandon everything she had. On her deathbed she thought, as I wrote, that it would afford her satisfaction for her husband, our master and teacher R. Ber Cohen, to marry Glukchen after her own death, but even this did not happen. So what good did all this good woman's wealth and honor do her? No good at all. *There is no authority over the day of death.*[213] These alone will stand in her favor: her genuine modesty and her many good deeds. Of her entire wealth that is all she is left with. She was about fifty-one years old when she died. Between the two of them they had very little money to begin with[214] — less than nine hundred reichstaler, and God above blessed them abundantly, as is common knowledge. And

---

210. Glikl might mean that the two children felt no difference between the way they were treated and how biological children are treated by their parents.

211. See this Book, p. 245, n. 185.

212. For this German proverb, see Wander 1987, IV, p. 911, nn. 34, 39; and cf. similar Yiddish proverbs in Bernstein 1908, nn. 3728, 3729.

213. Eccl 8:8.

214. That is, the dowries that the two sides brought into their marriage.

God above granted the distinguished R. Ber Cohen great wealth and off-spring,[215] may God, blessed be He, protect him until the coming of the Redeemer and may he continue to flourish, for he has a generous heart, few men are like him.

This is the appropriate place for something I found in the book *Yesh Noḥalin* with glosses by R. Yeshaya,[216] which I had told to me in Yiddish.[217] One evil I have observed under the sun[218] that is extremely difficult for a human being. When God, blessed be He, gives someone riches and property and land, none of this abundance can satisfy him in the world to come. That is, when death approaches and a person is about to die and beholds Death himself, and that person leaves his wealth behind for others or his children—why, at that moment he is fonder of his money than of his miserable soul, not heeding his soul nor granting it what it needs and yearns for, since he is not spreading his wealth around among charities and endowments or making other gifts to the poor and needy: the burden is adjusted to the camel,[219] that is, adjusted to his wealth so that all this charity goes ahead of him to protect him on his way—protect him from the hordes of devils, God save us, and legions of evil malicious demons that inhabit the teeming air between earth and sky; his soul willy-nilly must needs pass among all these hordes and legions of impurity, who attack and harm him and detain him on his way, and inflict all manner of torture and pain, God help us. If, however, he gives to charity—*justice goes before Him*,[220] protecting him on his way and leading him to the place reserved

215. His second wife bore him a son (see this Book, p. 248).

216. Glikl refers here to *Yesh Noḥalin* by Avraham ben Shabtai Halevy ish Horowitz with the glosses by his son Yakov (see Book One, p. 47, n. 26), but erroneously substitutes the commentator's name with that of his much more famous brother, R. Yeshaya, the author of *Shne Luḥot Habrit* (see this Book, p. 200, n. 14).

217. Clearly meaning that someone, holding the Hebrew text before him, translated it orally into Yiddish for Glikl's ears, or dictated his translation to her (for more details, see Turniansky 1993, pp. 161–163; Turniansky 1994c, pp. 49–51; Turniansky 2004, pp. 131–133).

218. Yiddish translation of the verse from Eccl 5:12, which opens the passage Glikl introduces here from *Yesh Noḥalin* 1615, pp. 1b–4b. For more details on the matching of the version brought by Glikl and the original Hebrew text, see Turniansky 2006a, notes to pp. 478–482, and the previous note.

219. Yiddish translation of b.Ketubbot 67a, 104a; for the German version of the proverb, see Wander 1987, II, p. 1121, no. 18).

220. Ps 85:14.

for him, without his suffering torture and pain. Alas, most people give no thought to all this when they see life departing from them. O son of man, you need not be the stupidest of all. Who have you toiled and labored for your whole life? For a world that is not your own, and now, at the very moment when you behold your soul departing, just when you are able to gain the world to come in a single hour,[221] and your reward will be so great if you just give to charity — despite this you do not want to part with your wealth, although you realize you will have to leave it behind to strangers and those who made no effort to acquire it, while you leave empty-handed. Who ever heard of anything so strange? Even if you like to think that you have already given a lot to charity during your lifetime, desist from those thoughts, for a *handful cannot satisfy a lion;*[222] it is certainly not enough for the long, long road you must travel, as we find in the Gemara in Ketubot[223] in the story about the great sage Mar Ukva,[224] may he rest in peace, known to all people for his good deeds during his lifetime, yet on his deathbed he said: "I have such a long road ahead to travel, how meager are the provisions I have for the trip!" Thereupon he promptly gave away half of *all he possessed*[225] to charity, though our sages teach us one should not give away more than one-fifth of one's possessions.[226] This refers to while a person is still alive and well, but at the hour of death one is permitted to give away even everything one owns, for a *man is his own relative,*[227] therefore one thinks to oneself: If Mar Ukva, one of the mightiest cedars of our holy Torah, did so, what then are simple folk to do in our own times?[228] Consequently, every wise, reasonable person should choose a goodly portion for himself and his own soul, for *one's own life comes first.*[229] Really, what good, what improvement, does the miserable soul get by leaving everything to

---

221. Cf. b.Avodah Zarah 10b, and elsewhere.

222. B.Berakhot 3b; b.Sanhedrin 16a, and elsewhere.

223. See b.Ketubbot 67a, which contains the source for the story Glikl cites next from *Yesh Noḥalin* 1615, pp. 3a–b.

224. Glikl calls him "Tanna" (sage of the Mishnah), instead of "Amora" (sage of the Talmud) and appends to his name the formulaic phrase for the deceased.

225. Gen 12:20.

226. Cf. b.Ketubbot 50a, 67b, and elsewhere.

227. Cf. b.Yevamot 25b; b.Sanhedrin 10a, and elsewhere.

228. Cf. *Yesh Noḥalin* 1615, p. 3b.

229. B.Bava Metzi'a 108a.

his children, everything he toiled and labored for, while he himself *whose origin is dust* is flung to *the bottom of the pit*. His *vigor was destroyed.*[230] All this while his heirs continue to occupy his big lovely houses and palaces, wallowing in luxury. They raise their voice in song and praise. While he — he sits solitary in the miserable pit, wailing and groaning. Weeping aloud, he casts his head down in anguish. His heirs feast on delicacies bought with his money, while he himself eats nothing but dirt. Hence, anyone to whom God, blessed be He, has given wisdom and reason will take all this to heart, *for if he is not for himself, who is for him? And if not now, when?*[231] Here the passage ends.[232] Though the great sage writes much more, remonstrations and other things that sweeten like honey,[233] yet I will leave that for the moment, and anyone wishing to know more can read further in the previously mentioned book and in other books. My dear children, for the sake of God, keep a God-fearing heart! Whatever you lack in this world, God, blessed be He, will double and redouble it in the world to come if you serve Him *with all your heart and soul,*[234] as I have already said many times. I will write no more of this.

To return to our subject.[235] After that, I betrothed my daughter Freyd-chen, may she live long, to the son of the distinguished community leader Reb Moshe son of Reb Leyb.[236] In the meantime we had another minor setback that God, blessed be He, in His kindness promptly removed, that is, as mentioned,[237] regarding my son Nathan Segal's business ties with the distinguished Reb Shmuel and his son Reb Mendele. My son Nathan Segal

---

230. Cf. "the bottom of the pit" (Ps 88:7), "whose origin is dust" (Job 4:19; and cf. "his origin is dust," "my vigor was destroyed" [Dan 10:8]).

231. Cf. m.Avot 1:14; and see Glikl's identical wording in *Yesh Noḥalin* 1615, p. 4b.

232. That is, the passage from *Yesh Noḥalin* that someone translated for Glikl into Yiddish (see this Book, p. 251, n. 216).

233. Different from the common Hebrew phrases "sweet like honey" (e.g., see b.Sanhedrin 108b) and "sweeter than honey" (as in Ps 19:11; b.Ketubbot 112a).

234. Deut 11:13, 13:4, and elsewhere.

235. That is, to the description of the engagements and weddings of her four younger children, which was interrupted (see this Book, p. 243, before n. 178).

236. Reb Moshe was a prominent resident of Altona and one of the founders of the Altona kloyz. His son Mordechai married Glikl's daughter Freydchen (on the two of them, see Feilchenfeld 1913, p. 246, n. 72; for more on Mordechai, see Lowenthal 1978, p. 292, n. 27; Davis 1995, pp. 40–41, 42).

237. Here Glikl goes back to the incident with the Viennese gentlemen (see this Book, pp. 235–236) for an expanded recounting and different—somewhat discrepant—details.

had given his guarantee for many bills of exchange of these distinguished gentlemen. A good number of them were due to be cashed, while the due date of some others was still some way off. Now, my son Nathan Segal was accustomed to these gentlemen transferring the funds prior to the due date of the bills of exchange, but the date was nearing and my son Nathan Segal had still received neither letter nor transfer of funds from the distinguished gentlemen. Finally word came that the distinguished Reb Shmuel and his son were in jail.[238] The moment this news reached Hamburg, my son Nathan Segal's credit was completely wiped out; whoever held a bill of exchange payable by my son Nathan Segal, whether drawn on those two distinguished gentlemen or anyone else, rushed to him immediately pressing for payment. Well, what was there to do? Not only did my son Nathan Segal have all those bills of exchange to pay hanging around his neck, in addition to these he also had some more bills of exchange he was obliged to guarantee and ensure that none of them bounced. This was just before the Leipzig fair, which my son Nathan Segal was supposed to attend. So he paid off whatever he could manage, poor man, and went to Leipzig with a heavy heart after pawning all the gold and silver objects and taking leave of me: "Mother dear, I leave you now. God only knows how we will meet again. I still have to pay several thousand. I entreat you to help me as much as you can. I'm certain that those distinguished gentlemen will not desert us." My son Nathan Segal then departed with his party for Leipzig on Sunday. Already on Monday my problems with the bills of exchange due for payment began. I did whatever I could: I pawned everything I owned and sank into debt until I could hold out no longer. On Friday I still had to pay out five hundred reichstaler more, but I was not able to raise even that much. I had good bills of exchange drawn on respectable householders that I tried to sell at the Bourse; I ended up dragging dejectedly all over the Bourse trying to pass the bills of exchange on to brokers. But the brokers returned my bills of exchange to me after closing time, since nobody would so much as glance at bills of exchange. I remained dejected until finally God came to my aid and I paid the five hundred reichstaler. On the Sabbath I decided to go to Leipzig on Sunday. If I found that the distinguished

238. They were imprisoned in Vienna on September 19, 1697, on a false charge (see Kaufmann 1896, p. 268, n. 1; Feilchenfeld 1913, p. 247, n. 73).

gentlemen had transferred funds to Leipzig, I'd go right back home, but if they had not made a transfer I would go from Leipzig to Vienna to my in-law our master and teacher the distinguished R. Shimshon, the head of the rabbinical court,[239] who was our good friend at the time. He would surely help us out. I asked my brother, Reb Wolf,[240] to accompany me. We left Hamburg for Leipzig on Sunday in a hired carriage. When we neared Leipzig, I took a room in a nearby village and sent a messenger to town to summon my children; they reported that the previously mentioned gentlemen had been released from jail and had sent funds in order to repay all their loans honorably. As soon as I heard that, I immediately set out with my brother to return home again, and by Friday, eve of holy Sabbath, in good time,[241] we were back home, thank God. In this way I traveled in six days from Hamburg to Leipzig and from Leipzig back to Hamburg.[242]

Need I describe my children's joy, poor things, especially my daughter-in-law Miriam, Nathan Segal's wife?[243] After all, our parting had been so tragic that we never dreamed we'd meet again so easily. Then comes the Lord's deliverance truly *in the blink of an eye.*[244] Praise and thanks be to God above! Even though the previously mentioned distinguished gentlemen did pay back everything they owed us, they will never, in all their days, ever be able to repay us for the fright, trouble, and worry they gave us. May God have mercy on us in the future as well and provide *our daily bread*[245] in dignity. So this affair too ended well, thank God.

After this I held the wedding of my daughter Freydchen, may she live long, with the son of our master and teacher R. Moshe son of our master and teacher R. Leyb Altona.[246] The wedding, held in Altona, was refined and joyous. Then it was time for the wedding of my son Reb Moshe Segal.[247]

---

239. See this Book, p. 238, n. 159.
240. See this Book, p. 247, n. 201.
241. That is, before the onset of the Sabbath.
242. On today's roads in Germany, the trip back and forth is 764 kilometers.
243. Daughter of Reb Elia Ballin (see Book Four, p. 188, n. 232). In her description of the match, Glikl did not mention the bride's name.
244. See Book One, p. 49, n. 36.
245. Cf. "my daily bread" (Prov 30:8).
246. On Reb Moshe son of Reb Leyb, see this Book, p. 253, n. 236.
247. Glikl's youngest son, born before his sisters Freydchen and Miriam (see this Book, p. 237, n. 153; on his match, see p. 241 in this Book).

I wrote to my in-law R. Shimshon Baiersdorf that I was planning to come to the wedding. But he wrote back saying he could not hold the wedding at the appointed time because God having given him the honor of marrying off his youngest child; this he could not do in his old house but had started building a new one. As soon as the new house was ready he would write to me to come, and we would have a wedding of wealth and dignity. But building the new house was not the only reason; the Markgraf of Bayreuth[248] had a new advisor who chose to oppose my in-law the distinguished R. Shimshon, just like Haman, actually he wanted nothing less than to *exterminate, massacre, and destroy*;[249] in fact he caused him great harm until he knew not where to turn, especially since all he owned was at His Highness the Duke's. This was the main reason for not holding the wedding at the appointed time. However, God above saw all the good that issued forth from his home — especially hospitality toward rich and poor alike, and all the kindnesses he rendered to the Jews throughout the land — he literally ran the entire country. He saw everything he was capable of doing now as well as whatever he would do in the future. Therefore, God, in His abounding kindness and compassion, overturned all of this Haman's evil plans, and changed all the wicked one's evil plans into good, until the evil one was cast down while my in-law was gaining prestige by the day — unbelievable that a Jew could enjoy such favor with His Excellency the country's ruler. May God preserve him until the coming of the Redeemer. Still, an entire year went by before we could hold the wedding. With this I conclude my Book Five.

END OF BOOK FIVE

♠

248. See this Book, p. 243, n. 173.
249. Cf. Esther 3:13, 13:7, 4.

BOOK SIX

I now begin my sixth book, in which I thought I would find all my happiness,[1] and I will recount how I came by the very status I had avoided for fourteen long years,[2] during which time many matches had indeed been proposed to me, the most prestigious in all Ashkenaz. But as long as I thought I could manage to live on the little that my husband left me, may his righteous memory be a blessing, I never even considered changing my status. But[3] if God above weighed my numerous sins and did not let me consider remarrying—when those matches proposed to me would have afforded my children and myself some happiness, and in my wearisome, wretched old age I could have found peace—why then, good, kind God did not wish all that;[4] it is surely due to my sins that He caused me to resolve upon the following match, as will be told presently. Despite all this, I do praise and thank my Maker for showing me more kindness and mercy in my grim punishment than I, an unworthy sinner, deserve and merit. I thank and praise mighty God forevermore for treating me with kindness and mercy and for giving me forbearance in all my troubles. If I am unable to do so by prolonged, frequent fasting or other significant acts of repentance as really I should have done, am obligated to do, it is because I am prevented by my many cares and my sojourn *in a foreign land.*[5] Yet well do I know that such excuses count for very little before God, blessed be He. This is why I write this with trembling hand and hot bitter tears,

1. For this new chapter in Glikl's life, see the fascinating discussion by Shmuel Feiner 2017.
2. Glikl's count is mistaken. Actually, ten years and five months elapsed between her husband's death on January 11, 1689 (see Book Five, p. 197, n. 1), and her marriage to Hertz Levy on June 6, 1700 (see this book, p. 270, n. 84). The error is repeated in this Book, p. 260.
3. Glikl's sentence is difficult to comprehend fully due to the beginning "But" and the convoluted syntax.
4. That is, God did not wish Glikl to benefit from a successful match.
5. Cf. "I have been a stranger in a foreign land" (Ex 2:22, 18:3).

for one should serve God *with all one's soul and all one's might.*[6] Therefore the sinner should not fear for his own body or his money but rather use them to serve God, blessed be He, and excuses are nothing but nonsense. I pray almighty God to treat me with compassion and give me fortitude and strength, let me not harbor any other thoughts than to serve Him so that I might not appear before Him in my filthy garments,[7] as is written *"Repent one day before thy death."*[8] After all, we do not know the day of our death. Therefore, not knowing it, one must repent every day of one's life.[9] This is what I too should have been thinking and doing, given that I could very well have done so, though I do have a poor excuse: I first wanted to make ample provision for all my orphans then afterward go to the Holy Land,[10] which in fact I could have done, especially after the betrothal of my son Reb Moshe Segal. After that, I had only my youngest orphan daughter Miriam, may she live long, to care for. Consequently, I, a sinful woman, should not have married but rather should have first married off my daughter Miriam, then I should have done as a good pious Jewess should: abandon all worldly vanities and, with the little I had left, set out for the Holy Land; there I would have managed to live as a pious Jewess without being burdened down by the troubles and cares of my children and relatives and by worldly vanities, there I would have managed to serve God, blessed be He, *with all my soul and all my might.*[11] But, as I said, due to my sins God led me to think otherwise and did not deem me worthy of this.

Let us now resume where we left off. In the meantime, an entire year went by before I could attend the wedding of my son Reb Moshe Segal.[12] Meanwhile I was plagued by all kinds of misfortunes and troubles — some

6. This combines two verses: "You shall love the Lord your God with all your heart and with all your soul and with all your might" (Deut 6:5) and "to serve the Lord your God with all your heart and soul" (Deut 10:12).

7. Zech 3:3. Rashi's commentary on verse 4 states "the sin is compared to soiled garments."

8. Cf. m.Avot 2:10, and see next note.

9. Cf. the interpretation of "Repent one day before thy death" (see previous note) in b.Shabbat 153a and in Kohelet Rabbah 9:1.

10. On widows moving to the Land of Israel during the sixteenth and seventeenth centuries, see Rapoport-Albert 2015, pp. 502–504; Chayes 2003, p. 234, n. 102; Yaari 1947.

11. See this Book, n. 6.

12. For the reason, see Book Five, pp. 255–256.

on account of my children — costing me a great deal of money even beforehand and now costing me more by the day, no need to write of that. They
are all my beloved children, and I forgive them all — those who cost me
a great deal of money and those who cost me nothing — for my financial
downfall. In spite of this I was still doing a lot of business — since I still
enjoyed an extended line of credit with Jews and non-Jews alike — causing
me immense torture. In summer heat, in winter rain and snow, I traveled to
fairs and stood on my feet in my store at the fairs for days on end all winter
long. Since I was left with only very little of everything I had previously
owned, I endured much deprivation, wanting nothing but a decent living
without becoming a burden to my children, God forbid, or that I should
live *to stand expectantly at another's table,*[13] God forbid. It would pain me
more to stoop to taking charity from my own children, God forbid, than
from strangers, for my children might be led to sin on my account,[14] God
forbid, something that grew worse than death for me day by day. On top
of all this I could no longer bear the strain and running around all over
town on foot. I ignored all this, as I was still conducting a lot of business
and had credit, as I said, but if just once I'd have lost a few rolls of fabric
or defaulted on large debts — I'd have been utterly ruined, God forbid; I'd
have been forced to cheat my creditors, bringing disgrace on myself and
my children and my righteous husband down in the ground. It was then
that I began regretting all those matches I had let pass by that could have
provided the means to enable me to spend my old age in prosperity and
honor, and perhaps even do some good by my children too. But regrets are
all useless. It was too late. God did not wish it, and to my misfortune He
put a different idea in my heart, as will be told presently.

It happened in the year 5459. As mentioned, I wanted to hold the wedding for my son Reb Moshe Segal, but it was not happening. Just then I
receive a letter from my son-in-law Reb Moshe of Metz,[15] may he live long,
dated 15 Sivan 5459,[16] in which he mentioned that Reb Hertz Levy was

13. Cf. b.Betzah 32b.
14. Perhaps by causing them to transgress the commandment to honor one's parents.
15. Moshe, son of Abraham and Yachet Krumbach of Metz, was the husband of Glikl's daughter
Esther (on their match and wedding, see Book Four, pp. 186–189, and Book Five, pp. 210–211).
16. June 2, 1699.

now a widower,[17] and what a respected, learned, wealthy man he was, and
what a household he maintained. In short, he praised the man highly, as
indeed he was, to all appearances. *Man sees only what is visible, the Lord
sees into the heart.*[18] The letter reached me just as I was brooding over my
troubles, especially that I was now a woman of fifty-four,[19] burdened my
whole life by my children and my worries. Had it been so,[20] I could have
still passed my old age peacefully in such a holy community as Metz[21] was
reputed to be at the time, and do my soul good. And I trusted my children
not to recommend the match if it was not right for me. So I wrote back
to my son-in-law: "For fourteen years I've been a widow, the thought of
remarrying never crossing my mind, and although it's common knowledge
that I could have had the most eligible, distinguished men in Ashkenaz, I
never wanted to give my consent. Despite this, seeing that you recommend
him so highly, and if my daughter Esther recommends it too, I accept."
Next, my daughter Esther also wrote, poor thing, telling me everything she
knew about him and what she had seen for herself. We did not go into the
dowry amount in any great detail. I gave my husband literally everything I
had, because he signed a written binding agreement that should I die first,
my heirs would get my money back; should my husband die first, I would
get five hundred reichstaler on top of my dowry[22] (I gave him fifteen hundred reichstaler). My daughter Miriam was a child of eleven[23] at the time,
and my husband gave his binding agreement to give her free room and
board in his house until she should marry. If I had had any more funds,

17. Since Hertz Levy's wife Blimchen died on 14 Iyyar 5495 (May 3, 1699) (see *Pinkas Metz* 1770,
p. 69a; Schwarzfuchs 1971, p. 48, n. 556), the letter was written precisely at the end of the *shloyshim*
(the thirty-day mourning period for the deceased). On a widower marrying after this thirty-day
period, see b.Mo'ed Qatan 23a. This is reflected in the Yiddish proverb used to describe a man who
is as elaborately dressed as a widower seeking a bride: "He looks like a widower after the *shloyshim*"
(see Bernstein 1908, p. 7, no. 5). On Hertz Levy, see this Book, p. 278, n. 138.
18. 1 Sam 16:7.
19. If she was fifty-four when she received the marriage proposal in 1699, she was born in 1645 (see
Book Two, n. 3; and see Marwedel 2001b, pp. 125–126).
20. That is, if only things were as her son-in-law Moshe wrote in his letter. Note that here Glikl is
reticent about the fact that things were not good.
21. On the Jewish community of Metz, see *Encyclopedia Judaica* 1972, vol. 11, cols. 1450–1451.
22. That is, in addition to the amount (stated in the following text) that she gave him as a dowry.
23. Since this was 1700, apparently Miriam was born a short time before her father died in 1689.
(This is additional proof that Glikl was not a widow for fourteen years as she states.)

I would have transferred them to my husband too; I assumed my money could not be kept in a better, safer place than in the hands of this man. Moreover, I was acting for the good of my orphan daughter Miriam: she need not pay anything toward her own expenses, her money is invested in loans at interest, and the man has an excellent reputation for doing business —who knows what else I might be able to do for my children in the way of business. But *many designs are in a man's mind etc., He who is enthroned in heaven laughs.*[24] God, blessed be He, laughed at all my thoughts and plans, woe is me; long beforehand God above had decided upon my ruin and troubles in order to punish me somewhat for my sins, because I put my trust in human beings. I should never have let the thought of remarrying enter my heart—I would never find another Reb Chaim Hamel anyway —instead I should have stayed with my children, accepting the good with the bad with love—whatever God's will—I should have first married off the orphan Miriam then set out for the Holy Land, as I said.[25] But all this is over and done with; what is done cannot be undone. All I can do now is pray to God, blessed be He, that I may see and hear only good things from my children, may they live long. As for myself—I accept everything from God with love, blessed be He and His name. May it please great, just God only to give me forbearance as He has done hitherto, and let it all be atonement for my sins, for I often drink of the doctor's potion that I wrote about in Book One.[26]

The betrothal was duly arranged, but in great secrecy, since I did not want it known for fear that the council departure fees[27] would cost me many hundreds, considering how well known I was in Hamburg. The traders I did business with simply thought I had many thousands of my own.

24. This combines two verses: Prov 19:21 and Ps 2:4. The combination matches the Yiddish proverb "Man thinks and God laughs" ("Der mentsh trakht un got lakht"; see Bernstein 1906, p. 166, no. 32; and a detailed explanation in Furman 1968, p. 248, no. 1007).

25. See this Book, p. 258, and n. 10.

26. See Book One, pp. 47–50.

27. A payment of a share of one's assets to the city council upon moving away. Whether Glikl paid any of the departure payment that she owed to the council is unknown, but it seems she did not pay the departure tax to the Jewish community (sixty marks for herself, and one hundred marks for each of her four children), as registered in December 1699 on the accounts page of the "widow Glikele" in the tax book of the Altona Jewish community (see Marwedel 1983, pp. 79–80; and this Book, p. 145, Figure 12).

Then I went about liquidating my stock and my other things and paying off my debts; I give thanks and praise to God, blessed be He, that when I left Hamburg I owed not a single soul, Jew or non-Jew, so much as a single reichstaler, I give praise and thanks to heaven for rendering unto me this true kindness.

My children (and my siblings and relatives) knew all about the betrothal beforehand: I asked their advice, and although in fact they all advised me to accept, the outcome was awful, as will be recounted presently, *for what I dreaded has come to me.*[28] When I was considering accepting the proposal, I was afraid that if I remained a widow I'd lose everything and be disgraced, God forbid, for I would be forced to cause harm to others, Jews and non-Jews, then I'd be dependent upon my children. But all this did me no good; I had to become dependent upon a husband, alas, to end up with the very same disgrace I was afraid of in the first place. While I can do nothing at all, he is my husband, after all, with whom I had hoped to live in prosperity and honor. On top of this, in my present situation I do not rightly know if in my old age I will even have *a bed to sleep in and a morsel of bread to eat,*[29] so that at this point my fear of being a burden to my children might very well come true. I supposed that by marrying such a successful man with extensive business dealings I would be able to help my children and through him bring them a lot of business. But alas, what happened was exactly the opposite: my son Nathan Segal lost many hundreds that my husband still owes him and would have been practically ruined when none of my husband's bills of exchange were honored, had God not obviously been looking after my son and assisting him. With my orphaned daughter Miriam, I thought I was helping her greatly by enabling her to save her money,[30] poor thing, and I ended up dragging her of all people down with me to ruination, then God, blessed be He, got us out of it, as will be told presently.[31]

And so you see, my dearest children, I weighed everything up carefully, yet everything I thought I was doing for the best actually turned out with

28. Cf. "What I dreaded has come upon me" (Job 3:25).
29. A combination of the common phrases "a morsel of bread" (e.g., Gen 18:5) and "bread to eat" (Gen 28:20).
30. Since Reb Hertz Levy had promised to support her (see earlier in this Book, p. 260).
31. On the fate of Miriam's dowry, see Book Seven, p. 290, n. 9.

the worst possible consequences. It is for this reason that I cannot help but think that my bitter sins are to blame, alas. And so, dearest children of mine, need I go on telling and writing at length? *There is nothing new beneath the sun.*[32] I'm not the only one this happened to, there are many others, worthier and more pious than myself; I am not worthy even of stepping in their footsteps, as you will read in the following story, surely a true story that really happened, may I end up like the pious king.[33] If you yourselves are clever and shrewd, you'll have to admit that it is a true story. Since people like new things,[34] I have copied here in Yiddish this story that comes from the holy tongue[35] to show that even the exceedingly righteous suffer, and God helps them too; may He help us and all of Israel. *Give us joy for as long as You have afflicted us,*[36] amen and amen.

There once was a king in the lands of Araby, a mighty king called Yedidiah.[37] This king had many wives, as was the custom in those days in the East. He had many children with his wives, loved them all dearly and was raising them all as royal princes and princesses. There was one son among them, handsomer than all the rest, and the king loved him best of all his children; for this reason the king also was tolerant of much of this son's mischief and shameful misbehavior, with disastrous results, as you will soon see. The son's name was Abadon. Abadon had a sister, she too a rare beauty, called pretty Danila. The king had another son, Amonis was his name.[38] Amonis fell in love with pretty Danila but could not conquer her,

---

32. Cf. Eccl 1:9.

33. Glikl is swearing that the story about the pious king she is about to tell is the absolute truth.

34. This most likely refers to the new literary fashion of stories such as "A Thousand and One Nights." Note the mentions of Arab and Eastern lands in Glikl's exposition of the following story.

35. Glikl means that she copied (i.e., transferred into her memoir in writing) the story, which had been previously translated from Hebrew into Yiddish (see Turniansky 1993, pp. 168–169; Turniansky 1994c, pp. 55–56; Turniansky 2004, pp. 138–139).

36. Cf. Ps 90:15.

37. This refers to King Solomon (cf. 2 Sam 12:25; and various commentaries: Rashi on 1 Kgs 3:7, the commentary attributed to him in 2 Chron 9:29, and many more). However, it is apparent from the rest of the story that the reference is to King David, not his son Solomon (who is also called by a different name at the end of the story; see this Book, n. 76). Nonetheless, it should be noted that both "David" and "Yedidiah" come from the Hebrew root meaning "beloved."

38. The names of the king's children were transcribed differently by former translators: "Avadon," "Danella," and "Amoris" (Abrahams 1962, p. 153 and following pages), "Emunis" (Pappenheim 1910, p. 264 and following pages; Lowenthal 1978).

nor could he reveal this to a single soul for fear of the king's wrath. Though the king loved Amonis too and held him in high regard, still Amonis dared not speak. As time passed, Amonis was so tormented by his love that he wasted away until one of his companions, a close friend, remarked this and addressed Amonis thus: "My liege and dear friend, I've noticed for a long time now that you are no longer happy and take no pleasure in the company of others. You're always seeking out solitary spots, you've lost a lot of weight, your countenance is quite altered. What then is troubling royal prince Amonis? Clearly he lacks neither riches nor honor. Please, my friend, tell me what's on your mind; it might relieve your suffering, and perhaps I can be of help." To this Amonis replied: My friend, what you say is quite true and perceptive too, yet no one can help me in my suffering; bitter death alone can put an end to my sickness. Nor can I reveal this to a soul except for you, loyal friend, to you I will indeed reveal it before my death, though I know well that you can do nothing to put an end to my torment." Said Amonis: "Heed this, loyal friend, what rare, awful disease and sadness afflict me, such is my sickness and disease: I have sucked up the poisonous beauty of pretty Danila. Such is my sickness and disease. I've tried everything to cure myself of the disease but, God have mercy, the more I try to stay away from pretty Danila, the more lovesick I become. Unless you help me with wise counsel, my friend, I am lost." This only did the friend say: "If you follow my loyal counsel I hope to bring about your immediate recovery. Do as follows: Get into bed and pretend to be ill — actually, you look it — do not allow anyone to come see you except for a few of your most trusted servants who know your secret. Nor should any doctor attend you except for your trusted personal physician. The physician will spread the rumor that you are dangerously ill. The king will surely come see you then and question you about your illness. You, Amonis, must then pretend to be even more ill and weak than you really are, answer the king in a weak voice, say you cannot sleep, you have no appetite, that you've already ordered food prepared for you in different places but 'everything nauseates me,[39] I can't eat a thing. There's just one more thing I can think of, the sole cure that will keep me alive: if it please the king, he will be

---

39. The friend states in first-person direct speech the words Amonis should say to the king.

so kind as to command his daughter Danila to come to my chamber and prepare a meal for me in my sight;[40] God willing it will taste good to me and that way my life will be saved.' I know[41] for certain that the king will not deny you and will send pretty Danila to you. As soon as she enters your room, order everyone out: you want to see if the food tastes better when you are alone. And then you will find a way to take your pleasure, dear Amonis, gently or by force, and whatever then happens cannot be changed. Your mother holds the king's heart in her hands and will find the way to soothe the king's wrath." "Dear friend" — says Amonis — "you've given me such good advice that I feel stronger already. I absolutely must follow your loyal counsel, though I may die for it."

Amonis thereupon went to his room and got into bed as though he were very ill; his trusted personal physician came to see him and made his illness public. No sooner did the king hear of this than he hastened to visit the sick Amonis, inquiring about his illness in friendly fashion, to which Amonis replied weakly as his friend had counseled him and as you have already read.[42] The king promptly gave Amonis his reply: "Take heart, dear son, I will deny you nothing in my entire kingdom. I will send your sister over here right away; I trust you will find her cooking tasty and to your liking so that you regain your health and vigor."[43] Thus saying, the king bid Amonis a warm farewell and promptly sent his daughter to her brother's chamber to prepare tasty dishes so that he might eat something of hers. Pretty Danila, docilely acquiescing to do her father's bidding, went to her brother Amonis's house and requested of the servants whatever she needed to cook a tasty dish. Now, when Amonis perceived that the food was nearly ready, he ordered everyone out of his chamber.[44] Alone with his sister, Amonis said: "Dear sister, bring the food over here to my bed for me to eat from your

40. At this point, it is already abundantly clear that this story is nothing more than an extended, compelling reworking of the story of Amnon, referred to as Amonis, and Tamar, referred to as Danila (cf. 2 Sam 13:1–5). The unnamed friend is Yonadav, son of Shimah (see 2 Sam 13:3).

41. Here, the voice changes from Amonis's first-person words to the king (according to Yonadav's advice) to the continuation of Yonadav's speech to Amonis, using the respectful form of address (plural, in the original).

42. This phrase directed to the reader is not necessarily Glikl's insertion into the text. Directly addressing the reader is common in Old Yiddish literature.

43. Cf. the paragraph up to this point to 2 Sam 13:6.

44. Cf. 2 Sam 13:7–9.

hand,[45] maybe it will taste better." When pretty Danila brought the food over to him he seized her, saying: "Dear sister, you must lie with me,[46] or I will die." Danila was very frightened at this and said: "Dear brother, don't do such a vile thing; instead, ask the king for me; I know for certain that he will not withhold me from you."[47] But all Danila's talk and pleading were to no avail; Amonis pulled her to him and lay with her by force.[48] Now, once Amonis had his way with her, he hated her as passionately as he had loved her before; he thrust her away and ordered her to leave.[49] Bitterly Danila cried: "Is it not enough that you have disgraced me, now you want to thrust me away from you," but Amonis remained impervious to all her lamenting and wailing, and he ordered the servants to throw Danila out of his house. So, wailing and weeping, Danila left the house.[50] Just then she meets her brother Abadon, who perceives her distraught cries and her torn royal robes.[51] Said her brother Abadon: "Sister, you have surely been wronged in your brother's house. Keep silent for now, come with me to my house[52] until I take revenge on your brother." So after telling her brother Abadon everything, Danila was forced to leave the place in shame. Although the king was wrathful at learning of this,[53] the queen, Amonis's mother, got the king, through his great love for her, to pardon Amonis for what he had done. But Abadon the king's son kept this thing in his heart.[54]

Some time afterward, Abadon held a big hunt and invited all the princes of the realm, including his brother Amonis. At nightfall, when the hunt was over, he had a feast prepared. As they were sitting there partaking of the finest food and drink, Abadon gave his servants a sign, and they fell upon Amonis and killed him. At this the princes all took fright, mounted their horses,[55] and rode away; one man went to the king and told him that

45. Cf. 2 Sam 13:10.
46. Cf. 2 Sam 13:10–11.
47. Cf. 2 Sam 13:12–13.
48. Cf. 2 Sam 13:14.
49. Cf. 2 Sam 13:15.
50. Cf. 2 Sam 13:16–18.
51. See 2 Sam 13:19. It is apparent from this that Abadon is Absalom.
52. Cf. 2 Sam 13:20.
53. See 2 Sam 13:21.
54. Cf. 2 Sam 13:22.
55. Cf. 2 Sam 13:23–29.

Abadon had attacked all the king's sons, at which the horror-stricken king grieved bitterly.[56] However, the evil counselor, Amonis's friend, was present there too and told the king: "My king, do not be so horror-stricken, not all the king's sons are dead. I believe only Amonis is dead; no doubt Abadon the king's son took his revenge upon him because of his sister Danila."[57] Even as they were speaking, the king's sons came riding up,[58] but the king was filled with rage at Abadon and ordered Abadon never to show his face before the king again. Abadon, however, unable to bear the thought of living in exile, plotted against the king's life, seeking to ascend the throne, for the king had already declared his other son as his successor. Gradually, with smooth talk, Abadon gathered more and more followers, plotting a great revolt against his father the king, until only very few remained loyal to the king.[59] But Abadon rode to where his father was and conquered the city and was licentious with his father's—the king's —wives.[60] But the king, along with his loyal followers, had left the city in good time, and they were saved.[61] Some servants who had been with the king now went over to Abadon's side and were throwing stones at the king, cursing him roundly.[62] The king's loyal servants then said to him: "If we have to endure these dead dogs humiliating the king, let's attack them even if we get torn to pieces."[63] But the righteous king would not allow it, telling his loyal servants: "If my own son born of my body wants to kill me, why should others not do the same? It is all because of my sins."[64] Eventually the battle grew too fierce for the king, so that he and his men had to retreat to the forests. Despite this, the king reached a fortified city and convinced all his loyal warriors to advance valiantly toward his son Abadon, "For if Abadon comes here to the city we are all lost." The king's troops all agreed readily to the king's plan, and the king prepared to lead his men in an

56. Cf. 2 Sam 13:30–31.
57. Cf. 2 Sam 13:32–33. The story only mentions "the evil counselor, Amonis's friend," without mentioning Yonadav son of Shimah by name (and see similarly this Book, p. 264, n. 39).
58. Cf. 2 Sam 13:36.
59. A drastic abridgment of 2 Sam 15:1–6; and see the end of 2 Sam 12.
60. See 2 Sam 16:22.
61. Cf. 2 Sam 15:14–16.
62. Cf. 2 Sam 16:5–8.
63. Cf. 2 Sam 16:9.
64. Cf. 2 Sam 16:11.

advance,[65] but the king's loyal commanders and generals were not of his opinion and demurred, saying: "The king realizes quite well that the whole war is on the king's account; if Abadon had struck down the king, he wouldn't still be trying to kill anyone else, for then the kingdom would now be his. Let the king therefore hold his position in this city and pray to God for victory over our enemies."[66] Said the king: "Go in peace, God be with you." The king's entire camp and the commanders of thousands then began marching out before the king on their way out of the city.[67] The king gave orders to all the commanders of thousands and the officers, entreating them to show Abadon mercy.[68] The king's troops advanced valiantly against Abadon, putting their faith in God and in their just cause. Although they numbered but half of Abadon's army,[69] God caused tumult in Abadon's camp[70] so that they were all struck down and routed by the king's men; they were struck with terror, for the fear of God and His vengeance confounded Abadon and his camp. Abadon too fled for his life to the desert, but was stabbed to death by the spears of the king's troops.[71]

The battle now subsided, yet no one dared tell the king that his son Abadon was dead. The king asked: "Is Abadon alive?" No one would answer the king, however; everyone avoided the king as though they had lost the war.[72] Seeing this, the king's loyal commanders approached him: "What exactly is the king doing? Ignoring all his men who have so bravely put their lives in danger for the king and his house?[73] It is clear to us that if Abadon alone had lived and all of us been killed, the king wouldn't care a bit.[74] We swear, unless you stand under the gateway arch and speak to the hearts of your people so that they restore you to your kingdom, you will

---

65. This matches 2 Sam 18:2.
66. Cf. 2 Sam 18:3.
67. Cf. 2 Sam 18:4.
68. Cf. 2 Sam 18:5.
69. Apparently based on the mention of ten thousand troops in David's army (2 Sam 18:3), versus the twenty thousand victims in his son's army (2 Sam 18:7).
70. Tumult or confusion, and not "plague" as in 2 Sam 15:7.
71. The story skips the Bible's telling of Absalom's death in 2 Sam 18:9–18, as well as the incident of the messengers that follows.
72. Cf. 2 Sam 19:4.
73. Cf. 2 Sam 19:6.
74. Cf. 2 Sam 19:7.

be in worse trouble than ever before."[75] The king, heeding the words of his commanders, went and stood under the gateway[76] and eloquently appealed to the hearts of every one of the people, then all the king's followers and enemies approached the king, and he pardoned them for everything, all they had done against him, then friend and foe all led him triumphantly back to his realm. The righteous king issued a proclamation throughout the land: "All those who fled fearing the king's punishment shall all return to a gracious welcome, for the king has said: 'Today is like the day I was made king.[77] Therefore I grant general pardon.'" Henceforth the king ruled his kingdom in peace, security, and honor worthy of glory until the end of his days, and it was still during his lifetime that he appointed his son Fried Lieb[78] as his successor and anointed him king.

From this we learn that God's retribution, though it be slow to come, is not absent, and that God deals each his due. Amonis, because of the vile thing he did to his sister, had to be murdered in such demeaning manner in the prime of life by his brother Abadon. The king—having ignored his son Abadon's licentiousness, arrogance, and evildoing, and having failed to punish him due to his great love for his son—was forced to flee from him and endure humiliation, losses, and torments. Were it not for his big heart brimming with contrition so that God gave him special protection, who knows what other scourges might have befallen him or whether he would not have ended up murdered treacherously at his son's hand. Abadon— who committed so many cruelties and murders, who sought to do away with the body and soul of the king his righteous father, who violated the king's concubines—he too was forced to die such a demeaning, horrific death. Everyone must heed this carefully: the Lord of justice deals every-one his due, for everything, as I have often said; we human beings cannot pass judgment on who the Lord punishes and who reaps benefits. God strikes, then heals,[79] His name be eternally blessed.

---

75. Cf. 2 Sam 19:8.

76. Cf. 2 Sam 19:9. From here until the end of the story, the connection with the biblical narrative is tenuous.

77. Cf. 2 Sam 19:23.

78. Meaning "lover of peace" or "beloved of peace" and implying Solomon: The Hebrew name "Shlomo" (Solomon) contains the term *shalom* (peace).

79. Cf. "He injures, but He binds up" (Job 5:18).

Let us resume where we left off,[80] my thinking that by remarrying I and my children could rest secure, but it turned out quite the contrary, as I have told and will yet tell again. The formalities of our understanding[81] were finalized in Metz in the month of Sivan of 5459[82] by my son-in-law Moshe and my in-law Reb Abraham Krumbach and his wife.[83] Well, what can I write about these people? Obviously I don't blame them; they acted entirely for the sake of heaven, believing I'd do very well, as indeed appearances led to believe, though in actual fact something entirely different came of it, alas, as will be told presently. The wedding date was set for Lag ba'Omer 5460.[84] Everything was done quietly for the reason I wrote earlier.[85] Meanwhile I sold off my property so as not to be left with any debts, and I sent the bills of exchange to our master and teacher the distinguished R. Gavriel in Fürth[86] to collect on them and keep the money until we should arrive. In the meantime I was corresponding with my husband, who worded his letters nicely so that I and others who read them found therein only promising, pleasant things; there was no way whatsoever to predict from them, alas, the calamity lurking therein that I was getting myself into and that cannot be changed.

Around Tevet of 5460,[87] just as I was about to set out on the journey with my son R. Moshe to hold his wedding, and from there continue to Metz, God, blessed be He, brought a sickness upon me, may you be spared, that kept me in bed for six weeks, as my husband found out from a certain merchant. Well, the encouraging letters he wrote me and my brother-in-law

80. See this Book, p. 263, before the story.

81. This apparently refers to the formal arrangement of the engagement: signing the betrothal contract, depositing the dowry money of the two sides, and setting the wedding date. All of this was arranged by Glikl's representatives (named in the following text), without her presence.

82. June 1699.

83. Moshe Krumbach, husband of Glikl's daughter Esther, and his parents Abraham and Yachet, who all lived in Metz.

84. That is, Friday, May 7, 1700. Many weddings took place on the holiday of Lag ba'Omer due to the prohibition on holding them during the other days of the Omer, between Passover and Shavuot. However, Glikl's wedding did not take place on the appointed date, but on Thursday, June 6, 1700; see this Book, n. 129. On the reasons for the delay, see following text.

85. See p. 261 in this Book regarding Glikl leaving her city, Hamburg.

86. Gavriel Levy Frankel (on him, see Kaufmann 1896, p. 289; Feilechenfeld 1913, p. 259, n. 6).

87. January 1700.

Reb Yosef,[88] the concern he expressed in commending me to his care — indescribable, but what the intention behind this was — God knows, blessed be He. Whether the intention was the little money I had, I cannot tell. When Heaven had restored me to full health, I traveled in the good company of my son Reb Moshe Segal and my orphan daughter Miriam[89] from Hamburg to Braunschweig, as there was a fair on there.[90] I still had some fabric remnants, and I sold them there. When the fair was over I traveled to Baiersdorf in the good company of my previously mentioned children with the intention of holding the wedding for my son Reb Moshe on the first day of Nissan.[91] We spent Purim in Bamberg. Right after Purim, my late son Zanvl[92] joined me for the trip to Baiersdorf. In Baiersdorf we came to an inn directly opposite the house of my in-law the distinguished Reb Shimshon.[93] Since his new house was not finished yet and there was not enough room in the old house,[94] they came three times a day to pick us up, doing us the honor, to take our meals at my esteemed in-law's, where we were treated royally. *Yet all this means nothing* to me,[95] as I told my in-law and his wife: "It's true that I have no real reason for wanting to leave here as soon as possible, but I do have my own reason why I very much want my son's wedding to be held at the beginning of Nissan. For you know of my understanding[96] which makes it imperative that I be in Metz by Lag ba'Omer (may it come

88. Husband of Elkele, Glikl's sister, who lived in Hamburg. He frequently advised and helped Glikl after she was widowed (see Book Five, pp. 207, 212, 218, 237–238, 240).

89. Actually, neither had a father, but apparently Glikl did not think of him as an orphan due to his imminent marriage (see also Book Five, p. 201, n. 18; p. 237, n. 151).

90. Mentioned in Book Five, p. 213.

91. March 21, 1700.

92. Zanvl was married to the daughter of Reb Moshe Bamberg (see Book Five) and lived in the same city as he. At this time, Zanvl joined his mother on the way to his brother Moshe's wedding. Glikl, referring to him as deceased, foreshadows the story of his death (see opening of Book Seven, p. 289). It is thus reasonable to assume that she wrote this part of her memoir after his death, but it is also possible that she returned to this point and made changes.

93. Glikl calls Reb Shimshon of Baiersdorf "my in-law" because he was father to her son Moshe's future wife.

94. On the delay of the wedding due to the construction of the new house, see Book Five, p. 256.

95. See Esther 5:13. There, too, the context is a lavish meal. See this Book, p. 277, n. 122; and Book Five, p. 233, n. 95.

96. See this Book, p. 270, n. 81. The continuation of the sentence clarifies that Glikl's dowry (and perhaps additional monies) were already held by her groom.

to us for good); the man already has my money," which indeed was the case, as my ill luck would have it. But there was much talk, many suggestions were made. My in-law said I could do whatever I liked, there was no way he could hold the wedding before Shavuot (may it come to us for good). I should go to Metz to get married and take my children along to accompany me; he would give me a hundred ducats for expenses. Well, this I did not want to do. Besides, my pride was injured. I decided therefore to resign myself to what could not be changed, and despite several disagreements between us over various matters regarding the dowry, how to insure it after the wedding, it was all ultimately settled satisfactorily in dignified manner. So I spent ten weeks of my time in Baiersdorf, from Purim till Shavuot of 5460. The wedding took place in Sivan 5460,[97] a most refined affair, with prominent guests arriving from all over the land,[98] and in this way the wedding passed enjoyably, thanks be to God. May God, blessed be He and His great name, grant them good fortune and blessing, may they live a life of prosperity and honor *until the coming of the Redeemer*, may He grant them *legitimate Jewish children who study Torah, may God come to our salvation and send our righteous Messiah in their lifetime and ours*, amen.[99]

  After the wedding I set out for Metz intending to attain there a good, comfortable position for my old age, and do my soul good in such a holy community. But oh, my Lord and Maker, *where to go, where can I flee from Your presence?*[100] Well, in Baiersdorf I hired a man by the name of Kopl, a shammash there, to accompany me on the journey to the holy community of Frankfurt, since in Baiersdorf I had received a letter from my husband informing me that he was sending someone from Metz to Frankfurt to accompany me to Metz. So I set off with my daughter Miriam, may she live long, and Kopl on my journey to Bamberg.[101] My son Reb Moshe

---

97. There are eleven weeks from Purim to Shavuot, and not as the author writes. The year 5460 is 1700, and the wedding took place in May or June.

98. People from various places in the area of Baiersdorf, in the state of Franken.

99. An original combination of phrases from the Hebrew sources, and original phrases similar to them, joined together in a sort of prayer. Glikl's prayer for children who study Torah was answered first of all in her son Moshe, whom she blesses here: he became rabbi of Baiersdorf and the region (see Introduction, n. 4), and copied his mother's memoirs, which survived to our day.

100. Cf. "Where can I escape from Your spirit? Where can I flee from Your presence?" (Ps 139:7).

101. Two reasons for traveling from Baiersdorf to Frankfurt via Lemberg emerge in what follows: to

Segal[102] wanted to accompany me as far as Bamberg, but I would not hear of it since he was still literally in the first week of his marriage. We thus parted sadly with copious tears all around, though I was very glad I had seen to it that my son was respectably married and ensured that he was set up comfortably, thanks be to God; it was really *the eye weeps and the heart rejoices*, nature can't change that. I arrived in Bamberg, staying only one night. In the morning I hired a carriage that I had ordered in advance in Bamberg and set off for the holy community of Frankfurt, unable to prevent my late son Zanvl from riding with me as far as Würzburg, and there we parted from each other forevermore, as will be recounted presently; we ourselves as well as the others sensed in the misery of our hearts that alas, we would never meet again in this world, as will be told in due course.[103] Continuing on my way, I arrived safely at the holy community of Frankfurt on Friday, the twentieth of Sivan, 5460,[104] where I found a certain householder from the holy community of Metz by the name of Leyzer and a letter from my husband; he had sent us some gingerbread and other trifles for the road, his writing very polite so that I never dreamed of the great misfortune in store for me. In the holy community of Frankfurt I was given every honor a woman could possibly get, and this continued for the rest of my journey too as I was shown every possible honor, more than I deserve, especially in the holy community of Fürth—what honor and goodness were lavished on me there! Fürth is only three leagues' distance from Baiersdorf.[105] For this reason, my son Nathan Segal transferred the dowry of my son Reb Moshe Segal and the little money I still had, very

---

return her son Zanvl to his home, and to travel in the coach she had ordered in advance, apparently due to Bamberg's proximity to main roads.

102. The son who had just gotten married in Baiersdorf (and see following text).

103. Glikl's method for keeping her memoirs in chronological order of the events is apparent here. She indeed recounts the death of her son Zanvl in its appropriate place in the chronology (see beginning of Book Seven, p. 289).

104. Glikl is apparently mistaken here, for the twentieth of Sivan 5460 (May 27, 1700) was a Monday, not a Friday. Since she reached Metz on Friday, the twenty-fourth of Sivan (May 31, 1700; see this Book, n. 111), it is reasonable to assume that she reached Frankfurt a week earlier, on Friday the seventeenth of Sivan (May 24, 1700).

105. Fürth is actually south of Baiersdorf and hence not on the way from Bamberg to Würzburg and Frankfurt. Therefore, we may assume that Glikl visited Fürth before she set out on this journey. On her previous visit to Fürth, after the wedding of her son Zanvl in Bamberg and regarding a match for her son Moshe, she was also very impressed with the honor she was accorded there (see Book Five, p. 241).

little indeed, to Fürth into the hands of community leader our master and teacher the distinguished R. Gavriel.[106] Should I write of all the honor I received from him and his entire household — I could never write enough of it. Not only did these decent people go to all that trouble for me in collecting the money against the bills of exchange[107] — in addition they gave part to me and part they sent elsewhere following my instructions, since prior to his wedding I was lending out my son Moshe's money at interest to various people; my in-law Reb Moshe Bamberg did me a kindness by taking one thousand reichstaler from me at interest; the gaon head of the rabbinical court, our master and teacher R. Mendl Rothschild[108] took another thousand reichstaler; and Leyb Biber of Bamberg — another thousand reichstaler. The rest we lent out for him in Baiersdorf. After that I totaled everything up with the distinguished R. Gavriel, wanting to pay him the appropriate commission, but he refused to take so much as a penny, saying "This isn't business money, it's mitzvah money, for good deeds." Although I tried all sorts of reasoning with him, he would not hear of it and did not even include postage expenses in the total. May God, blessed be He, reward him for it.

Let us now return to our journey. Early Monday morning I left Frankfurt with my escort, Leyzer. In the Frankfurt community I had met Reb Liberman of Halberstadt — he was traveling from Halberstadt to Metz to visit his old father, community elder and leader Reb Abraham Speyer[109] — and also Reb Hertz Royfe,[110] in whose company I traveled to Metz. In this way we had a very pleasant trip. Two leagues[111] before Metz, my husband sent his clerk to ride on horseback alongside our carriage until we reached the inn. He had with him all sorts of things to eat and drink, as much as he could load on the horse. This clerk, Lemle Wimpfen, conveyed my

106. Glikl mentioned earlier in this Book (see n. 85) that she transferred the money from the sale of her assets in Hamburg to R. Gavriel. Here she mentions for the first time that she also transferred her son Moshe's dowry to him.

107. Mentioned earlier in this Book, p. 270, n. 86.

108. See Book Five, p. 243, n. 172.

109. See Kaufmann 1896, p. 294, n. 1.

110. Naftali Hertz Wallich; see Kaufmann 1896, p. 294, n. 2.

111. Based on the lengths of time the author mentions later (three hours to the inn and five hours from there to Metz), she is clearly mistaken here about the distance.

husband's compliments. After eating and drinking we traveled on another two or three hours; the messenger Lemle was with us at night but took his leave when we were ready to go to bed — he absolutely had to be in Metz on time, and the place where we were staying was just under five hours' distance from Metz.

Heaven knows it: though everything I saw before me seemed wonderful and fine and apparently rich too, especially given that my husband's letters were altogether courteous and pleasant, still I was not a little despondent. Whether because my poor heart was foreboding how it would all turn out or perhaps because after all I was sad that I was about to go to another husband, it was too late in any case for these reflections. I was thus obliged to overcome and conceal my despondency and sadness of heart.

On Friday, 24 Sivan, 5460,[112] when we were one hour from Metz, again we see the clerk Lemle Wimpfen riding up to us on horseback with another man, alongside a carriage in which a distinguished lady was sitting, the wife of the Metz rabbi,[113] with the distinguished lady the wife of the head of the rabbinical court, our master and teacher R. Aaron,[114] and my distinguished in-law Yachet.[115] They welcomed me most respectfully and courteously, and I was made to join them in their carriage, and in this way we proceeded to Metz. Truly it was a great honor for three such distinguished ladies to come out to greet such a lowly woman as myself. Afterward, however, this honor was quite spoiled for me. Not far from the holy community of Metz, my modest daughter Esther,[116] may she live long, came forth to greet us; she was nearing the end of her pregnancy and had requested to be carried in a litter to welcome her mother. So I descended from the carriage at the home of my son-in-law Moshe, may he live long. He was living at the time in Beyle Krumbach's house. My son-in-law wasn't home, he was in Paris.

112. May 31, 1700 (see this Book, p. 273, n. 104).

113. This apparently refers to the wife of R. Gavriel Eskeles, who was then the rabbi of Metz (see Book Seven, p. 299, n. 60); on the identity of his wife, see Kaufmann 1896, p. 295, n. 1).

114. R. Aaron son of Yosef Israel Worms was born in Metz and served in the rabbinate in Mannheim and in Neuf-Brisach. He then returned to Metz and died there in 1722 (regarding him, see Cahen 1884, pp. 266–267; Kaufmann 1896, p. 295, n. 1; Feilchenfeld 1913, p. 265, n. 12; Ginsburger 1907, p. 489).

115. Wife of Avraham Krumbach and mother of Moshe Krumbach, the husband of Glikl's daughter Esther (see Book Four, p. 187, n. 225).

116. Wife of Moshe Krumbach, who lived in Metz.

These important ladies who had come to welcome me now went home with a polite apology that it was getting close to the Sabbath. I thanked them for the great honor and for all their trouble as well as I knew how, as forthright German etiquette had taught me.[117] My daughter then made me some soup that I might eat, but God above knows my heart was exceedingly heavy; I didn't even know myself what was the matter with me, ascribing it in my mind to the fatigue of travel. An hour later my bridegroom came in with the distinguished parnas of the community Reb Avraham Krumbach;[118] they welcomed me, sat with me for a while, then went on their way. I swear, at first I didn't even know which of them was the bridegroom since I had never seen either of them before in my life — had Reb Avraham not said to me jokingly that I had better not make the mistake of thinking him the bridegroom, to which my reply was silence.

It grew late; it was now already holy Sabbath but I did not go to synagogue. My daughter Esther went to synagogue for, as the whole world said about her — she never missed a synagogue service. What a good reputation she had among all, indescribable, and this was my sole joy and consolation in Metz for as long as God, blessed be He, preserved her health. During services, my stepchildren came over to me and greeted me, but I didn't know who they were, and there was no one there I could ask. So I say to them: "I do not know to what I owe this honor, as I am a stranger here and know nobody." So Hendele[119] says: "Don't you know us? You're supposed to be our mother." So I told them: "If I am to be your mother, you'll be my children too." After a few more words — since people were leaving the synagogue — they went on their way most courteously. My daughter came home from synagogue too. We all sat down at the table. Reb Yeshaya Krumbach was at my daughter's too. When we finished eating, the boy Shlomo — a valet of sorts to my husband — came in with the maidservant bearing two big gold-plated trays, one with the finest, fanciest desserts, the

117. Glikl compares German etiquette, which is direct and candid (mainly in the area of compliments) to the French etiquette customary in Metz, which had been a French city since 1552 (see Feilchenfeld 1913, p. 266, n. 4; Kaufmann 1896, p. 296, n. 1).
118. That is, her intended husband Hertz Levy with her daughter Esther's father-in-law.
119. One of Hertz Levy's five daughters (see Ginsburger 1907, p. 485, n. 2; Davis 1995, index entry "Levy, Hendele/Anne"). He also had two sons (Shlomo and Shmuel, who is mentioned frequently in Glikl's last book). Hendele was married to Reb Yishai Wilstadt.

other with the choicest fruits, imported ones too like lemons, oranges, as
well as finest local fruits, and lying on top was a gold chain with a gold bar
and two large gold-plated goblets filled with wine. This was my "Sabbath
fruit."[120] It was a rare sight. In my dark thoughts I said to myself: May the
end be like the beginning. But oh, dear Lord and Maker, that gold chain
turned literally into shackles and bands of iron. About an hour later, my
bridegroom and my distinguished in-law Yachet[121] came over, stayed for
about half an hour, then, once again, they all went home. Well then, I saw
that everything was done in elegant, lavish style; I really should be a little
happier instead of giving in to my dark, melancholy thoughts, especially
since every single person envied me, declaring openly that I must have done
many good deeds to be so happy and to have the good fortune to get such a
good, accomplished husband and such wealth. *Yet all this means nothing to
me,*[122] my anxious heart was not completely at ease, alas, *its ending attests to
its beginning.*[123] To what should I attribute this? It is due to my sins.

On Sabbath morning my stepdaughter Frumet[124] was sent to call on my
orphan daughter Miriam, who received a small gold chain as her "Sabbath
fruit."[125] Everything was fine, then. In all my son-in-law's[126] letters from
Paris to my daughter, he urged her to be hospitable and make me feel at
home. And the letters were all love and affection, as it should be, but love
only lasted *till when the day blows gently and the shadows flee,*[127] as will all
be told in due course. My son-in-law, may he live long, possibly thought he
had done an excellent deed[128] that would benefit me greatly.

The week went by in this way, and nothing special happened. The following week, on Thursday, the first day of Tammuz, 5460,[129] the wedding

120. Lit. *shabes obs(t)*, a gift given on Sabbath afternoon and named for a custom (see this Book,
p. 279, n. 144).
121. Her future husband Hertz Levy and her daughter Esther's mother-in-law.
122. Esther 5:13; see also this Book, p. 271, n. 95; and Book Five, p. 233, n. 95.
123. Cf. b.Nedarim 48a.
124. Hertz Levy's daughter (see Davis 1995, p. 229, n. 45).
125. Cf. this Book, nn. 120, 144.
126. Moshe Krumbach, husband of Esther, Glikl's daughter.
127. Song 2:17.
128. This refers to the suggestion of the match to Glikl (see early in this Book, pp. 259–260) and
possibly also to helping see it through.
129. June 6, 1700.

took place. In the morning I was led from my daughter's house to the house of a neighbor of my husband's. I sat there until after midday. After midday my husband betrothed me with the betrothal ring, an expensive one, weighing one ounce. Rebbetsn Braynele[130] and the distinguished Yachet[131] were matrons of honor. The wedding ceremony was held in our summer courtyard.[132] After the ceremony I was led to our room,[133] tastefully furnished, next to the study. Food and wedding cake[134] were brought to us there, as is the custom in Ashkenaz.[135] Although I had eaten nothing all day,[136] my heart would not let me eat; my heart was still full, choked from all the weeping. When I had left my daughter Esther's[137] we both wept long and hard, for that's the mood we were in. My husband took me into his study and showed me a large chest containing an assortment of necklaces and rings, but from then to this day he has never given me a single ring or coin of even flimsiest gold or silver, so it's not because of me that he went bankrupt.

I found plenty of servants in my house, both men and women; everywhere I could see or hear there was brimming abundance. His office was filled with gold and silver, all appearances leading to a very different impression than what came to light afterward, alas. He was a long-standing parnas,[138] with him it was literally *by such instruction they shall go out and by such instruction they shall come in*;[139] he was respected and esteemed by all, Jews and non-Jews. On the week following our wedding, the most

130. That is, the wife of the rabbi (whose name is not mentioned).

131. Her daughter Esther's mother-in-law.

132. That is, outdoors, in the open air.

133. That is, a room where the bride and groom symbolically spend some time alone immediately after the wedding ceremony; seclusion is forbidden before a couple is married (see m.Ketubbot 8:1).

134. A warm cake (for details, see Turniansky 2006a, p. 537, n. 267).

135. It is possible that this was the custom in Germany but not in Metz, or that there were differences in the custom between the two places. If so, Glikl is indicating that the cake was baked especially in her honor according to the custom of her place of origin.

136. In accordance with the custom of the bride and groom fasting on the wedding day until after the ceremony.

137. That is, when she left from there to the wedding ceremony.

138. On Hertz (Cerf) Levy, Glikl's second husband, see Davis 1995, index entry "Levy, Hirsch/Cerf."

139. Num 27:21 (and cf. Book Five, p. 247, n. 198).

prominent notables[140] came to welcome me and congratulate me. I could wish for nothing more — except to know French so as to be able to converse with them and reply to each one. But my husband spoke for me.

Some time went by quite enjoyably in this way, as I lacked for nothing. My husband gave me money to defray household expenses. I discovered that the housekeeper was lord and master in the house; she had everything in her control, all the foodstuffs, entire cones of sugar and other things, never asking me what food to prepare or what she should do, which was not to my liking at all; in my household in Hamburg I was not accustomed to letting a servant be lord and master.

This led to many talks with my stepchildren and my sister-in-law Freydl[141] too, but they all told me that the late Blimchen[142] had allowed her to control everything and left everything in her hands, because she never doubted the woman's loyalty. When I came to my house I found there two manservants and two maids, plus a few workmen and messenger-boys. While all this was not to my liking, I was given to understand that it was yet nothing compared to when my husband's first wife was alive. In fact, my stepchildren, those who were already married,[143] would often sigh about it, often hinting to me of the pampering they had had from their late mother. For some of them she actually maintained the entire household. I certainly could not do that; I sent my stepchildren only what food there was around when we had something special. When I bought "Sabbath fruit,"[144] a quarter reichstaler's or one livre's[145] worth, they mocked me, saying that an entire reichstaler and more used to be spent on "Sabbath fruit" every week, and the children would each get a basketful delivered to their homes. For

---

140. This refers to non-Jewish guests (and see Glikl's following statement that she does not speak their language).

141. Hertz Levy's sister (see Ginsburger 1907, p. 482, n. 2).

142. Hertz Levy's first wife (see this Book, p. 260, n. 17).

143. On Glikl's married and unmarried stepchildren in 1700, see Davis 1995, pp. 228–229, n. 45.

144. On the custom of serving fruit in the afternoon in honor of the Sabbath, see *Great Dictionary of the Yiddish Language* 1961, vol. I, p. 393; also see Landau and Wachstein 1911, Hebrew section, p. 291, in whose opinion this first referred to fruit given to children on the Sabbath, and later, by extension, to other gifts.

145. The livre was the currency of France from 1781 to 1794, when it was replaced by the franc. See Feilchenfeld 1913, p. 271, n. 20; cf. North pp. 222–223; Luschin von Ebengreuth 1926, index entry.

a while I resigned myself to this, blessing God, thinking that my having remained in my dejected widowhood had turned out for the best,[146] albeit for me it was all rejoice with trembling,[147] as mentioned.[148]

My husband was a decent man and, according to himself—prosperous too, and I saw the rare gold and silver objects he had, such as I never saw in any other rich man's house in all of Germany. I saw too that the man had extensive business dealings and was scrupulously honest in his business affairs; no one ever had to call twice to collect a debt from him. He always paid promptly, with utmost respect. To all, Jews and non-Jews, he extended credit all over, and large sums of his money were lent out on the street.[149] Moreover, he was a recognized trustee, such a safe choice that anyone with something to keep in a safe place would deposit it with my husband, as my own son-in-law Moshe did when he had to go to Paris a few weeks before my arrival here.[150] He took everything he owned and entrusted it to my husband for safekeeping in his absence, preferring to have it in my husband's keeping than in his own father's. For not only was my husband considered wealthy by everyone, he was also held to be a foremost trustee and an upright man, so I should have harbored fewer doubts as to my wish being now indeed fulfilled.

My husband would groan a great deal at night, and on several occasions I asked him what was wrong, why was he groaning like that. He said nothing was wrong, it was just his nature and habit. I asked the children and my sister-in-law Freydche[151] what it meant, since at first I thought—as everybody said he and his first wife had such a good life together—that he was unable to forget her. But they all assured me they were used to him doing it; he did it when his first wife was alive too. I left it at that though

146. That is, Glikl reasoned at that time that she attained a successful match because she had refused to marry previously (see this Book, pp. 259–260).

147. Cf. Ps 2:11 (JPS 1917).

148. Since there is no punctuation in the original, it is difficult to tell whether this phrase ends the sentence or begins the next one.

149. The Hebrew noun for "street," used when referring to the *Judengasse*, the Jewish quarter of a city (see Pollack 1971, p. 202, n. 5).

150. See this Book, p. 275, between nn. 116 and 117.

151. Same as Freydl (this Book, p. 279, n. 141); here with a different diminutive.

it aggravated me sometimes, not knowing that profound distress[152] lurked beneath his sighing. Sleeping or eating, he was extremely restless.

When I had been here about eight weeks my daughter Esther, may she live long, was blessed with the birth of a baby boy, making me so happy, since my daughter did not have other children;[153] a few beautiful children of hers had died. We all took pleasure in the wonderful boy, heaven protect him. My husband and I were godparents,[154] and my husband as godfather made them a handsome gift: a bowl, gold-plated without and within, weighing three ounces. When my daughter was ready to get up from the birthing bed, he sent her a doubloon[155] as a giving birth present. It was late Elul when my daughter emerged from the birthing bed, healthy and well; at the circumcision ceremony she was on her feet helping with all the preparations. On the third day following the circumcision[156] she was already cooking and had everyone admiring her good cooking and orderliness. Her mother-in-law too, Yachet, may she live long, told me quite a few times: "I have to admit that Esther, may she live long, is a better cook than I am." In fact, when Yachet wanted to cook something good, she'd send for my daughter Esther to come cook for her. And my daughter's good reputation among rich and poor for righteousness, honesty, and every imaginable virtue—I cannot even describe. Sad as she always was over the loss of her many children, still she never let it show overmuch. Her housekeeping was frugal, thrifty, and careful yet everything was in good taste. She always had learned men as well as young students at her table and treated rich and poor alike with courteous respect, so that I had reasons enough to be happy. But God have mercy on our happiness and the fickle luck that marked the start of my despondency in Metz. For on Yom Kippur my sweet grandson

152. Here, Glikl interprets her husband's behavior in light of subsequent events, which are recounted in the following text.

153. This was true up to this point. Later, they did have more children (see Book Seven, p. 292, n. 17).

154. The role of the godparent (Yiddish *kvater*) at the circumcision ceremony is to carry in the baby and/or hold him during the circumcision. For more information, see *Language and Culture Atlas* 2000, map 92; Pollack 1971, pp. 23–24.

155. A Spanish-French gold coin, worth sixty-six marks (see Feilchenfeld 1913, p. 273, n. 23; Freiherr von Schrötter 1930, pp. 158, 163–164; North 1995, pp. 103–104).

156. See "It was the third day from Abraham's circumcision" (b.Bava Metzi'a 86b); and cf. Minhagim de-k"k Wermaiza (1988–1992), II, p. 79, n. 1.

Elia[157] fell ill with recurring violent seizures that continued for more than eight days; as we watched the beloved boy suffer so, woe is me, sometimes I would pray in my heart to God, blessed be He, to shorten the beloved boy's agony, for no doctor or any other person believed he would survive. But blessed Heaven took pity on him in the blink of an eye and sent him a cure, which goes to show that God, blessed be He, can help when all human resourcefulness is at a loss, in His deliverance making a fool of all the physicians and learned men, as is written: *"For I the Lord am your healer"*[158] — my everlasting praise and thanks to Him. May the good kind Lord enable his father and mother, may they live long, to raise him for Torah, the *marriage canopy, and good deeds,*[159] amen.

It is easy then to imagine my daughter's joy and all the things she did both openly and covertly to redeem the life[160] of the beloved boy, since my son-in-law and many others of his kind pursue base money over-avidly, until perhaps they embody the man to whom *his wealth is dearer than his person*:[161] never satisfied, as in the story of Alexander the Great.[162] He traveled all over the world, as is well known, and conquered it. He was thinking to himself: "I am such a hero and have come so far that I am not far from the Garden of Eden" — he was at the Giḥon River, one of the four rivers flowing around the Garden of Eden.[163] So he built big sturdy ships and set sail in them with his men and was clever enough to find the spot leading to the entrance to the Garden of Eden. But as he approached, fire erupted and devoured the ships with all hands aboard, leaving only his own ship with himself and his men. King Alexander, seeing that only his own ship and the men aboard were left, entreated to be let into the Garden of Eden despite everything; he wanted to tell of its wonders all over the world.

157. The baby just born to Esther, Glikl's daughter, and her husband Moshe Krumbach. This grandson of Glikl became a rabbi in Hagenau (see Ginsburger 1907).

158. Exod 15:26.

159. B.Shabbat 137b.

160. That is, to save his life, referring to good deeds the mother did during her son's illness to save him from death. Chiefly, this refers to giving charity, as is the custom according to the popular understanding of Prov 10:2; 11:4—"charity" (not "righteousness") saves from death.

161. Cf. b.Pesahim 25a.

162. On the stories on Alexander the Great, see Book One, p. 54, n. 55. The version of the story that Glikl tells now is an enhanced, well-crafted version of the brief story in the Talmud (b.Tamid. 32b).

163. According to Gen 2:11–14.

But a voice came to him bidding him to get away from there, he cannot enter the Garden of Eden since *this gate — the righteous may enter through it*.[164] Alexander persevered in his entreaties that if he was not to enter the Garden of Eden, they could at least throw something from the Garden to him for him to show all over the world as proof that he had come so near the Garden of Eden. They forthwith threw him an eyeball. Holding it in his hand, he had no idea what to do with it or even start doing with it. They told him to take all his gold and silver and all his valuables, place them all on one side of the scales, and place the eyeball on the other; the eyeball would outweigh the rest, since the eye is heavier than all the rest. King Alexander, wise, a great philosopher, as is well known, who studied with Aristotle[165] as his teacher, wanted to know all branches of knowledge, and how one little eyeball could outweigh so much gold and silver and other things, so he started investigating the matter. He took a pair of good hefty scales, placing the eyeball on one side and several hundredweights of gold and silver on the other. But no matter how much he heaped on, the eyeball steadily outweighed the rest. Alexander, astonished, implored for an explanation of how one little eyeball could outweigh so much gold and silver and more besides, and what could be done to satisfy the eye so that it might not be so heavy. By way of reply, he was told to throw a handful of dust over the eye; that slight weight would tip the scales. King Alexander did so, throwing a handful of dust over the eye, and this slight thing tipped the scales against the eye. Seeing this, Alexander was even more astonished and requested an explanation. He was told: "Listen, Alexander, take heed: as long as the eye is alive in the human body nothing satisfies it, for the more a person has — the more he wants. That is why the eye outweighed all the gold and silver. But once a person dies and dust is thrown over his eye, he has enough. That is why, once you threw dust over the eye, you could tip the scales against it with that slightest thing. Now see, Alexander, you can see this in yourself. You were not satisfied with your kingship or with your conquest of the entire world — you sought also to go to the place where the sons of God and His servants dwell. As long as you live you will never

164. Cf. Ps 118:20 (JPS 1917). The verse also appears in the Talmud's version of the story (see this Book, p. 282, n. 162).
165. See this Book, p. 284, n. 167.

be contented, you never rest, you always want more. Now I tell you for certain that you will die in a foreign land in the near future, and once they strew dust over you — you will be content with your four cubits of earth,[166] whereas beforehand the whole world was too small for you. So beware, Alexander, speak no more and ask no more questions, for you will receive no answer and will only be banished from this place; heed lest your fate be like that of your men and your ships." The king thus returned to India with his ship, to die shortly thereafter, an untimely, bitter death after being given poison to drink, as described in detail in the chronicle of his life by his teacher and mentor Aristotle.[167]

Many pursue money avidly, as mentioned, never satisfied, which can often lead to disaster. Nor is it right to be too extravagant and spend what one has on useless things. Legitimate money honestly gained is acquired by dint of hard labor, but one must perceive how to act in every situation. There is a well-known proverb about that: "Stinginess enriches no one, moderate generosity impoverishes no one."[168] A time for everything, a time to spend money and a time to save money.[169] The Dutchman says: "Money spent in a timely manner yields a profit."[170] There are good descriptions of many of these things by learned men of other nations.

This then was the first storm I weathered in this place,[171] though — God have mercy — it did not end there; the same thing happened to me as to the man who tried to escape the angel of death by fleeing to Luz,[172] where

166. The size of the grave, according to b.Bava Batra 100b.

167. According to legend, Aristotle was Alexander the Great's "teacher who taught him wisdom." Alexander wrote many letters to Aristotle, telling him of his experiences (see Flusser 1981, pp. 462, 475), but nowhere is it told that Alexander wrote a chronicle of Aristotle's life.

168. I could not find this proverb in any sources. For a slightly similar proverb, see Wander, 1987, I, p. 1454, no. 32.

169. The sentence follows the form of Eccl 3:2–8, but I was unable to find a parallel in any sources. It may well be an original coining by Glikl.

170. I was unable to find this Dutch proverb recorded anywhere. There are similar proverbs in German (see Wander 1987, I, p. 1488, no. 477, and p. 1513, no. 1080). Glikl's use of a Dutch proverb indicates that she encountered the language on her trips to Amsterdam, and in commerce with the people there or with some of the many Dutch merchants then living in Hamburg (see Feilchenfeld 1913, p. 275, n. 24).

171. This apparently refers to her grandson Elia's illness, which she calls "the start of my despondency in Metz" (see this Book, end of p. 281).

172. The former name of Bethel (see Gen 28:19; Judg 1:23, 26). The name also appears in the Talmud (see next note).

people die only at a ripe old age. As soon as he reaches the gate, the angel of death says to him: "You have fallen into my hands at this very spot so that I may take your life. Nowhere else do I have jurisdiction over you except right here."[173] The same thing happened to me, alas. I left Hamburg, *the land where I was born*,[174] my children, my relatives, thinking: I'll put enough distance between them and myself so as not to hear anything bad about them. Yet You, just God, You have proven to me — and continue yet to prove to me — that I cannot flee the rod of your wrath.[175] *Where to go, where can I flee from Your presence?*[176] I realize that I have reached a place where I do have some little happiness and contentment, but I must endure much trouble and heartbreak on account of what I see and hear concerning myself and my dear children. I resign myself to my judgment as one should, for God, blessed be He, gives me forbearance so that despite all my troubles and calamities I am nevertheless still able to be like anyone else, for Divine retribution could have been much worse yet, God forbid, as the physician says in my story recounted earlier.[177]

Not long afterward I received the bitter news that my son Reb Leyb Segal was dead,[178] alas, a young person, not yet twenty-eight years old. Even though this son of mine caused me a great deal of worry and anguish,[179] I still took his death bitterly hard, as is only natural for parents. This can be learned from the late virtuous King David, who had so much ill and heartbreak on account of his son Absalom;[180] then, as the king's troops were about to go to battle against Absalom, he commanded all his men to be gentle with that same Absalom, and when the king heard that he had been killed — how the king grieved for his son Absalom, crying out seven times "Absalom, my son,"[181] thereby getting him out of the seven levels of

173. The story told here freely incorporates details from the Talmud (b.Sukkot 53a and b.Sotah 46b; also see Feilchenfeld 1913, p. 276, n. 25).

174. Gen 24:7.

175. Apparently an adaptation of the biblical phrase "his rod of wrath" (Prov 22:8; Lam 3:1).

176. Cf. Ps 139:7; and see this Book, p. 272, n. 100.

177. See the physician's statement in the story cited in Book One, pp. 48–49.

178. According to his gravestone in the Altona cemetery, Yudah Leyb Hamel, son of Chaim, died on July 23, 1701; see Simonsen 1905, p. 99.

179. See Book Five, pp. 213–223.

180. See this Book, pp. 263–269, for another version of this narrative.

181. David actually repeated the cry "son" eight times: five times in 2 Sam 19:1 and three more times in verse 5 (and see next note).

Gehenna and into the Garden of Eden.[182] In the same way I too have for-
given this son of mine from the bottom of my heart for all his mischief;
he let himself be led astray, alas. He was the best person in the world, he
studied well, had such a Jewish heart[183] for the poor, his good deeds are
known far and wide. The problem was that he was extremely careless in
his business affairs, unfortunately; evil people noticed this about him and
caused his financial ruin, alas. So I will let him rest, I pray God that he
benefit from his father's merit. What should I do, what can I do? I must go
to him — when Heaven wills it — he will return to us no more.[184] Almighty
God did not wish to take me before my time, before taking my virtuous,
upright husband Reb Chaim Hamel, who at his age could have lived longer. But *because of evil the righteous was taken away*[185] to spare him from
undergoing so much suffering and troubles in his lifetime. May he rest in
peace, he died prosperous and had only good from his children. But why
should I tell of this at length? I have told of it enough. With this I conclude
my Book Six, may almighty God spare my loved ones and all of Israel from
misfortune of any kind and in His great mercy and loving kindness pardon
us for everything we sinful human beings owe, and lead us to the Holy
Land, may our eyes behold the Temple rebuilt[186] in splendor to atone for
all our sins, as is written "I will sprinkle clean water upon you."[187]

END OF BOOK SIX

182. See b.Sotah 10b. There, some say that the first seven cries saved him from the seven levels of
Gehenna and the eighth got him into the Garden of Eden.
183. This phrase commonly connotes a person who is compassionate, good-hearted, empathetic,
and so on.
184. Cf. "I shall go to him, but he will never come back to me" (2 Sam 12:23); and cf. Book Three,
p. 144, n. 200.
185. See Book Five, p. 202, n. 28.
186. This apparently flawed rendering echoes the "Temple Service" benediction of the Eighteen
Benedictions prayer, which concerns the renewal of the service in the Holy Temple in Jerusalem
and includes the phrase "And may our eyes witness Your return to Zion" (see Siddur 2016, p. 126).
187. This echoes two dissimilar liturgical verses: (1) "and built the Temple for us to atone for our
sins" (end of the *Dayenu* passage in the Passover Haggadah; Tabory 2008, p. 99), and (2) "I will
sprinkle clean water upon you, and you shall be clean" (Ezek 36:25 and in the Yom Kippur prayers;
e.g., see Maḥzor Yom Kippur 2014, p. 158).

FIGURE 13

Interior of Metz Synagogue.

sdv.fr /judaisme/histoire/villes/metz/synagogues.

FIGURE 14

Ancient synagogue at Metz (engraving, English School).

Private Collection / Bridgeman Images.

BOOK SEVEN

I now begin the seventh book, with God's help, being a mixture of some disappointment together with some satisfaction, as is human nature in the order of the world, and I will resume where I left off. With this I begin my seventh book.[1] May God spare me any further sorrow from my beloved children in my lifetime, may I merit contentment in their joy and well-being in my old age.

I mentioned earlier[2] how I parted forever from my late son Reb Zanvl. God have mercy, such a talented young person forced so soon to chew the black dirt.[3] I had not yet been here in Metz two years when I received the bad news that he had departed the temporary and gone to the eternal, alas. What sorrow and grief I had — God knows, blessed be He. To lose such a beloved son at such a young age! What then should I do or say, should I lament at length? A short time after his death his wife gave birth to a baby girl, thank God she is a healthy, beautiful child, may God protect her. May it please God that she bring us many happy occasions, in every sense. She must be about thirteen now,[4] apparently a very talented person. She's with her grandfather, community leader and parnas Reb Moshe Bamberg.[5] My daughter-in-law, the late Reb Zanvl's wife, remarried but did not remain married for long — he too died — so this good young person's youth has been quite miserable for her till now, poor thing. What is there to say? *Who can say "What are you doing?"*[6] It is possible that I shall not mention this again, because it breaks my heart.

1. In Book Seven, Glikl's sentences become more convoluted and repetitious.
2. See Book Six, p. 273, n. 102.
3. An idiom meaning "to be dead" (cf. Book Four, p. 190, n. 79).
4. According to Glikl, the girl was born shortly after her father's death, which occurred less than two years after Glikl moved to Metz in June 1700. Thus, according to the girl's approximate age, it is reasonable to assume that Glikl began writing Book Seven in 1714 or 1715; cf. this Book, p. 297, n. 51.
5. Her mother's father (see Book Five, p. 238, n. 157).
6. Cf. Job 9:12.

Well then, I had been here about a year, believing I could live here comfortably as I had estimated, going to some extent by appearances. Had my late husband managed to hold out about another two years he would have succeeded in extricating himself, because two years after he was forced to turn over everything he owned to his creditors, there was a business opportunity in France that made our entire community rich, and he was a very shrewd, clever businessman, well liked among Jews and non-Jews. But that was not God's will, blessed be He; his creditors exerted such pressure on him that he was forced into bankruptcy and had to leave behind everything he had for them to repossess. Though they could not repossess even half of what he owed them, they were nevertheless quite lenient with him.[7]

While I could have had the full amount of my marriage contract from him, I could see for myself that there was nothing to be had. My daughter Miriam's funds,[8] may she live long, were all in the keeping of the departed, but I got them from him in other bills[9] endorsed by Jews, though God, blessed be He, knows how bitterly hard this was for me. My son Nathan Segal was also supposed to get several thousand reichstaler from him, and I took care of obtaining them for him too, and because of this I gave no thought to my marriage contract, accepting with love everything God, blessed be He, inflicted upon me, like the eagle who bears his young on his back, saying: "If they shoot, let them shoot me, not my young ones."[10] How I suffered! My late husband was forced to go into hiding. His creditors, when they found out, sent three rogues[11] over to take inventory; they listed every last nail in the wall, then sealed everything up, not leaving me *food for even a single meal.*[12] I remained in the heated room with the housekeeper;

7. For more information on Hertz Levy's bankruptcy, which occurred at the beginning of 1702, see Davis 1995, p. 18, and p. 229, n. 46.
8. This clarifies Glikl's previous mentions of her daughter Miriam's money (see Book Six, p. 262, n. 30).
9. That is, her daughter Miriam's money was returned not in cash or currency as Glikl had given it to her husband, but rather in bills that Glikl had to redeem from their endorsers.
10. Based on Rashi's commentary on Deut 32:11 ("Like an eagle who rouses his nestlings, / Gliding down to his young, / So did He spread His wings and take him, / Bear him along on His pinions"), which explains that unlike other birds, who carry their young under their wings because they fear the eagle, the eagle carries his young on his wings because he fears only arrows, thinking, better the arrow pierces me and not my young.
11. Glikl uses a derogative term for "bailiffs."
12. M.Shabbat 16:2; b.Shabbat 117b, 118a; and elsewhere.

the rogues were there too — they were the masters, no one was allowed to enter or leave the room. If I wanted to leave once during the day, they would search me to see if I had anything on me. We lived in this miserable situation for about three weeks.

Finally my husband reached an agreement with his creditors; they took inventory of all his property and left it all with him to sell at public auction. There wasn't a tin spoon in his house that went unlisted; he could not conceal a single thing nor did he want to, for he gave thanks to God that he emerged alive. When his creditors saw that he had given them everything he possessed, they actually felt sorry for him since he did not even have enough for half of what he had agreed to pay them. Despite this, they were lenient with him and did not act roughly. They could have thrown him in jail, but they realized that he was an honest man and had given them everything he had until he was left with absolutely nothing. He was a most accomplished man, and when his financial circumstances were good, everyone regarded him with affectionate respect. He was parnas and interceder with the authorities on behalf of the Metz community for about thirty years; he ran things smoothly and for this reason Jews and non-Jews liked him. Unfortunately, when he ran into bad luck our situation grew so miserable that during the steep price increase here a few years ago, we often literally had no bread in the house. I still had a little money of my own that I sometimes used to pay household expenses. As soon as my husband, of blessed memory, got some money, he'd reimburse me. My son-in-law the distinguished parnas and leader of the community Moshe Krumbach[13] did a great deal for him, though by doing so he himself lost over two thousand reichstaler. God, blessed be He, enabled my son-in-law to enjoy his reward for it:[14] he became quite the richest man in the entire community, an upright man given a new heart,[15] and he's very active in the interests of relatives both on his side and my daughter Esther's, may she live long; his house is wide open to the poor,[16] and at present he is parnas.

13. Husband of Glikl's daughter Esther.

14. That is, his success (described in following text) was his reward for the kindnesses shown to Glikl's husband.

15. That is, his stinginess and greed (at which Glikl hinted in Book Six, p. 282, n. 161) gave way to generosity.

16. Cf. "Let thy house be wide open, and let the poor be members of thy household (m.Avot 1:5).

All the important visitors from the four corners of the world are invited to his house; he treats everybody with honor and deference and the like. His wife, my daughter Esther, may she live long, behaves in similar fashion. In short, both of them have good hearts, and much goodness issues from their home. May God, blessed be He, reward them and keep them and their children[17] in good health, prosperity, and dignity to age one hundred.[18]

Around the beginning of Sivan 5472,[19] my grandson Elia,[20] may he live long, became engaged to be married. The wedding date was set for Sivan 5476[21] since both of them, bride and bridegroom, are still of a tender age, may God grant them long life. Together they bring to the marriage, including the presents, no more than thirty thousand reichstaler.[22] May Heaven grant them luck and success.

Now I will resume writing about my husband, of blessed memory, who could not grow accustomed to his distressed circumstances, for his children were at that time not yet in a position to help their father much. Still, they did what they could. My husband's son — his name is our master and teacher R. Shmuel,[23] a learned man, successful at everything, and shrewd — he lived in Poland for a long time studying and was ordained rabbi. When he returned from Poland I was not yet living in Metz, but when I arrived here a few years afterward, I found master and teacher R. Shmuel in a house of his own. My husband, as well as the distinguished and pious parnas and leader of the community our master and teacher R. Avraham

17. This indicates that the couple had more children after their son Elia (see Book Six, p. 281, n. 153; and later in this Book).

18. See Book Four, p. 181, n. 194.

19. May 1712.

20. The grandson was born in July–August 1700, eight weeks after Glikl's arrival in Metz (see Book Six, p. 281). He became engaged in 1712, when he was twelve.

21. That is, four years away. Elia, son of Moses Krumbach-Schwabe, appears in the 1717 census as newly wed (see Kaufmann 1896, p. 303, n. 1) to Karen Lemlen, daughter of Meyer of Mannheim (see Davis 1995, p. 229, n. 50).

22. Since thirty thousand reichstaler is a much larger dowry than any mentioned thus far in the memoir, Glikl's words "no more" are unclear. Perhaps the negative words are extraneous (as Feilchenfeld believes, 1913, p. 283, n. 7; and see Kaufmann 1896, p. 321, n. 2). However, it is entirely possible that Glikl is being ironic. The identical dowry sum appears in the following text, without any comment by the author (see this Book, p. 299, n. 62). On the dowry and the obligations of the groom's family, see Davis 1995, pp. 241–242, n. 108, and p. 251, n. 169.

23. Son of Hertz Levy, Glikl's second husband (regarding him, see Ginsburger 1907; for some additional details, see Davis 1995, index entry "Levy, Samuel").

Krumbach,[24] father-in-law of the aforementioned R. Shmuel, were extremely generous to him, enabling him to continue with his studies. They assisted him so much — the authority of the previously mentioned two parents was somewhat influential here too — that my stepson R. Shmuel Segal was accepted for the position of head of the rabbinical court in Elsass,[25] a position he filled very well in his cleverness. The entire community grew to like him very much, but *a handful cannot satisfy a lion*,[26] since his compensation was not adequate to the needs of his household, as our master and teacher R. Shmuel, head of the rabbinical court, and his wife, the Rebbetsn Knendele,[27] may she live long, both came from wealthy households that maintained a grand style and did much good, and they too aspired to the same situation, but a rabbi's salary was inadequate for that. R. Shmuel, head of the rabbinical court, therefore put himself at the service of the Duke of Lothringen,[28] whose court at that time was at Lunéville, since war had just broken out between His Highness the King of France and His Highness the Emperor[29] and his allies; no need to mention them by name since everyone knows who they were. At that time,[30] R. Shmuel leased the mint[31] from the previously mentioned duke. The enterprise required a large amount of capital, which R. Shmuel Segal was unable to raise on his own. Six months before R. Shmuel leased the mint he had opened a store, it too requiring a large amount of capital, as the duke and his entire court would buy everything from him, for the duke and his ministers were fond of him; indeed, he is the kind of person who finds favor *in the eyes of God and man*.[32] But R. Shmuel could not run the store properly on his

24. Father of Moshe Krumbach, who was the husband of Glikl's daughter Esther. He was also the father of Knendele, wife of R. Shmuel who is discussed here.

25. For a detailed description of R. Shmuel's rabbinate in Elsass and its problems, see Ginsburger 1907, pp. 488–500; Feilchenfeld 1913, p. 284, n. 9.

26. B.Berakhot 3b; b.Sanhedrin 16a.

27. Daughter of Avraham Krumbach, wife of R. Shmuel, and sister of Moshe Krumbach (husband of Glikl's daughter Esther).

28. Duke Leopold Josef of Lothringen, father of Franz Stephen (husband of Maria Theresa) and Karl von Lothringen (see Kaufmann 1896, p. 314, n. 2).

29. The War of the Spanish Succession between Louis XIV, King of France, and Emperor Leopold I, which lasted from 1710 to 1714 and ended after the Treaty of Utrecht.

30. The episode described here began in 1707 (see Schwarzfuchs 1971, pp. 15–16).

31. R. Shmuel leased the mint and the minting rights.

32. Cf. Prov 3:4.

own either, so he took on his two brothers-in-law who lived here in Metz; one was called Reb Ishai, a well-known householder married to R. Shmuel Segal's sister,[33] and the other was Reb Yakov Krumbach. R. Shmuel's wife was this Reb Yakov's sister;[34] he — a respected, talented person too — is the brother of my son-in-law parnas and leader of the community Moshe Krumbach. These three,[35] then, owners of three fine homes on Jews' Street, left them and moved to Lunéville, where they entered into partnership[36] with R. Shmuel Segal. In their store they had a large quantity of fabrics that sold well, and they had other lines of business too; they were doing very well there. Then R. Shmuel got the mint, which, though it did not yield a big profit, was nevertheless quite profitable too due to its scale.

When they entered the mint business, R. Shmuel wrote about it to his late father, but my husband, of blessed memory, did not like that line of business; being a shrewd businessman who understood the nature of business, he did not think such a thing could succeed, mainly because His Highness the King of France would never tolerate it, given that Metz is so close to Lunéville, not more than a day's ride, while all the monies[37] were intended for circulation here in Metz. My late husband thereupon weighed everything up carefully like a seasoned businessman and wrote in detail to his son R. Shmuel about the large amount of capital needed and what the consequences were liable to be. But the three of them were all young men, extremely eager for business, and ultimately they reached an agreement with His Highness the Duke to supply him with an enormous quantity of raw silver and be paid in coins of various denominations from the mint. The whole thing went well for a while, but — as will be told presently — for some of them it ended up not too well, but for R. Shmuel it proved his utter ruin, as will be told.

33. Reb Ishai Wilstadt was brother-in-law to R. Shmuel; he was married to his sister Hendele, daughter of Hertz Levy, Glikl's second husband. For additional details about him, see Kaufmann 1896, p. 314, n. 6.

34. He was the brother of Knendele, wife of R. Shmuel, son of Hertz Levy (Glikl's second husband), as well as being brother to Reb Moshe Krumbach, Glikl's son-in-law, through his marriage to her daughter Esther (see following text).

35. That is, Reb Ishai Wilstadt, Reb Yakov Krumbach, and R. Shmuel Segal (see next note).

36. That is, Reb Ishai Wilstadt and Reb Yakov Krumbach became partners with R. Shmuel Segal.

37. That would be minted at the Lunéville mint.

About six months after the three partners had been running their fabrics business and other lines of business with bills of exchange or other means as Jews do, there lived here a certain householder by the name of Reb Moshe Rothschild.[38] He too was very wealthy and had been engaging in commerce with Lothringen[39] for several years, so he was well known there among officials and merchants. Hearing how well their business was doing, he moved there too with his son, R. Shmuel's son-in-law, having arranged it with His Highness the Duke's[40] ministers, and settled not far from Lunéville; he had much influence with His Highness the Duke and his ministers. In short, this Reb Moshe too put himself at the duke's service to supply raw silver to the mint; this went on for a while, and they were satisfied with the way their business was going. R. Shmuel Segal accomplished much in every area, including helping his father, my late husband, so that he lack for nothing. The monies would be sent from there over here; sometimes the monies were delayed, sometimes they never arrived at all.

Meanwhile, my husband was constantly anxious, perceiving the heavy responsibility and danger involved. Although he wrote many times to his son R. Shmuel, it was of no use, for what is done cannot be undone. Now, as the war grew fiercer between His Highness the King of France and the Emperor,[41] the king issued an edict prohibiting any transfer of monies into or out of France. Moreover, the king, via his chief minister, ordered a proclamation dispatched here to Monsieur Latandy[42] for him to pass on to the community and have it read aloud to them; it mentioned by name the five Jews,[43] the partners who used to live here before moving to Lothringen, stating that if they wished to remain in Lothringen — well and good; however, they were forbidden on pain of sundry punishments to set foot anywhere in France ever again. The choice was theirs — to come back to

---

38. Reb Moshe Rothschild was also an in-law to R. Shmuel Segal (regarding him, see following text, as well as Ginsburger 1907, pp. 486–487; Kaufmann 1896, p. 316, n. 1).

39. This refers to the Lothringen region in general. The continuation clarifies the people with whom he engaged in commerce.

40. See this Book, p. 293, n. 28.

41. See this Book, p. 293, n. 29.

42. Apparently then the governor of Metz (see Feilchenfeld 1913, p. 288, n. 11).

43. That is, Reb Ishai Wilstadt, Reb Yakov Krumbach, R. Shmuel Segal, Reb Moshe Rothschild, and his son.

live in Metz or to stay in Lothringen. They now had a few months to weigh their decision.[44]

When the partners received notice of this they were greatly alarmed, not knowing what choice to make since they all had fine homes here, nor did they look forward to giving up their municipal residency permits. On top of that, they had a heavy commitment to the duke in the mint and stood to pay a stiff fine. Hence, they were in a grim situation indeed. His Highness the King had also written: If these five Jews remain in Lothringen, it shall be entered in the community records that they no longer have municipal residency permits in Metz. In short, they were in a terrible situation. Eventually time was up and they had to return their decision. In short, Reb Ishai Wilstadt was the first to make the choice to come here.[45] Yakov Krumbach did likewise; I know not how they arranged matters with His Highness the Duke. They divided among themselves what fabrics they still had in their stores, then came here with wife and children and everything they owned, and returned to their respective homes. However, R. Shmuel and Reb Moshe Rothschild and his son decided to stay there, which sorely grieved my husband; he took it so hard that he could no longer bear the sorrow and anguish. He was not strong to begin with and suffered badly from the gout, with these extra afflictions depressing him terribly. His son R. Shmuel Segal saw to it that he lacked for nothing and sent over anything he needed, instructing his proxies to give my husband anything he requested, but it was all no use. R. Shmuel Segal also sent over a physician, a specialist, to treat his father with various medicines, and he stayed a few days administering treatments but declared immediately that he was dying, which indeed proved true, for God, blessed be He, took him to be with Him for all eternity.[46] He is certainly in the world to come, since for a long time — many years — he was a parnas, to the utmost satisfaction of the community; he literally risked his neck for them, much could be written

44. On the proclamation and its background, see Davis 1995, pp. 18–19, and p. 229, n. 49, especially her reference there to *Les Juifs de France* by Robert Anchel.

45. His signature as member of the community appears on one of its documents as early as Wednesday, June 6, 1714 (see Kaufmann 1896, p. 317, n. 1).

46. Glikl's husband, "R. Naftali Hertz son of R. Isaac Avraham Ephraim Halevy passed away in the evening after the Sabbath on July 24, 1712, and was buried the same night" (for the full inscription on his grave, see Turniansky 2006a, p. 574, n. 104).

about this, but I see no need for it. He went to his rest leaving me needy and in distress. I received a meager sum for my marriage contract, not even a third of what was rightfully mine. Still, what is there to do? I entrusted all into God's hands. At that time I was still living at Reb Ishai's, whose house belonged to my husband, of blessed memory,[47] thinking I'd be able to remain in his house for the rest of my life, as indeed Reb Ishai had promised me. But when my husband died, Reb Ishai came here with his wife and children and with furniture too, and I had to leave his house without delay, not knowing where to go. Nor could I stay with my son-in-law parnas and leader of the community the distinguished Moshe Krumbach, since at the time he had not yet finished building,[48] as he has done in the meantime, with God's help. I was therefore in a terrible situation indeed. In the end a certain householder, Yakov Marburg, built for me a little cubicle where I had neither stove nor fireplace, but I stipulated the conditions that I could cook in his kitchen and stay in his winter house. But whenever I wanted to go to bed or just go to my room, I had to climb up twenty-two stairs, which was extremely difficult for me because I was not well most of the time, God preserve you. My previously mentioned son-in-law Moshe paid me a visit when I was sick — it was around Tevet 5475[49] — and said I should come to his house; he'd give me a ground-floor room so I would not have to climb steep stairs, but I refused this as well because I had never wanted to live with my children, for several reasons. However, as time went by, I could bear it no longer. That year there was a steep price increase, I did have to keep a maid, and it cost money by the community,[50] so finally I agreed to do what I had steadily refused for a long time and went to live in the house of my son-in-law parnas and leader of the community Moshe Krumbach. That was around the month of Iyyar 5475 — I am writing this in Tammuz 5475.[51] My son-in-law and my daughter, may they live long,

---

47. No doubt the house came into the possession of Reb Ishai as a result of his marriage to the daughter of Hertz Levy, Glikl's husband (see Davis 1995, p. 251, n. 168).

48. On the enlargement of Reb Moshe Krumbach's house, see Kaufmann 1896, p. 318, n. 3.

49. December 1714–January 1715.

50. The nature of the payment to the community (or perhaps by the community) is not clear, nor whether it is connected to keeping a maid, as Abrahams (1962, p. 175, n. 1) believes.

51. Thus, Glikl moved in with her daughter in April–May 1715, three years after her husband's death (see this Book, p. 296, n. 46) and about five months after she refused her son-in-law's invitation to do

and the children, may God protect them, were very pleased with me. Shall I write how my son-in-law and daughter treat me — I could never write enough about it. May God reward them for it. They show me the utmost respect, give me the best of everything, from the serving bowl I am offered more than I want or wish for; I worry it will be deducted from my merits, God forbid, if of these I have a paltry few.[52] If I am not here for lunch — served punctually at noon, the very hour Psalms are recited in the synagogue for the soul of the late Yachet,[53] my son-in-law's pious mother; this has been going on for a long time[54] and may quite possibly continue until the coming of the Redeemer — and this lasts a full hour. Afterward, when I come home from synagogue, I find my meal ready, three or four different dishes, delicacies all, that truly I don't deserve, till often I tell my daughter: "Please just leave me a little something," to which my daughter retorts: "I don't cook any more or less because of you," and it's true. I've traveled far to many communities but never have I seen such well-run housekeeping. They give generously and in good taste to all comers, guests by "tickets"[55] just the same as the most illustrious guests. May God preserve them so that they continue in this way in peace and good health, prosperity and dignity, for another hundred years.

Shall I write at length what else is happening here, or whether the community is following the right path? If so, I can only say that when I first came here this was a very fine, decent community; there was a fine community building, and all community parnasim, literally all of them, were learned men,[56] a real enhancement to the community building. In those

---

so (see previous note). The time Glikl states for the writing of this passage (June–July 1715) matches her previous statement (this Book, p. 290, end of n. 4), but does not define when the earlier or later passages were written.

52. Glikl worries that because she is receiving return on her merits (if she has any) in this world, she will not receive such return in the "World to Come."

53. It is customary to recite Psalms in the synagogue to benefit the souls of the departed. Glikl's in-law, Yachet, passed away on Thursday and was buried on Friday, November 22, 1709 (see Memorbuch Metz 1971, p. 61, no. 676). Among her many good qualities mentioned there, during her life, she "sustained a burial society's recital of Psalms every afternoon."

54. When Glikl wrote this (June–July 1715; see earlier), five and a half years had already passed since Yachet's death (see previous note). It thus seems to me that Glikl's next words are slightly ironic.

55. See Book Four, p. 162, n. 91.

56. Lit. "elderly men," meaning sages according to the Talmud (b.Qiddushin 32b).

days no man ever wore a peruke[57] in the community building, and it was unheard of to litigate in the non-Jewish courts of law[58] outside the Jewish quarter. If disputes arose, as happens unfortunately among Jews, it would all be resolved quietly by community institutions or rabbinical judges,[59] nor was there such ostentation as today. Neither were people accustomed to such expensive foods then as they are now. People took pains to give their children an education and always employed the most important rabbis.

In my time the righteous gaon our master and teacher R. Gavriel[60] served as head of the rabbinical court and head of the yeshiva, may God preserve and save him. To write of the righteous and charitable deeds of this man would be too much for me, and since it is all very well known, it is not for me to write of his outstanding qualities, for I could not succeed in describing even a fifth or a tenth of them. In short, the previously mentioned head of the rabbinical court and our master and teacher R. Shimshon of Vienna[61] betrothed their children to each other: the son of R. Gavriel married the daughter of R. Shimshon. Dowry and presents together came to more than thirty thousand reichstaler.[62] So R. Gavriel went with his wife and his late son our master and teacher R. Leyb[63] and the excellent bridegroom our master and teacher R. Berish[64] to Vienna, where they held a lavish wedding of such splendor never before seen among Jews. But why

57. The style during Louis XIV's reign of wearing wigs began taking hold among the important Jews of Metz during this period (see Feilchenfeld 1913, p. 219, n. 436).

58. This apparently hints to the case fought by Yakov Krumbach (see p. 294, n. 34) and others against the Metz community and its rabbis in non-Jewish courts (see Kaufmann 1896, p. 320, n. 3, and p. 314, n. 7; Feilchenfeld 1913, p. 292, n. 15; Davis 1995, p. 258, n. 220). The case began as a result of the event that Glikl recounts in the following text (see p. 310, n. 129).

59. It is reasonable to assume that "community" here refers to the various bodies governing the community, which included the rabbinical judges.

60. Gavriel, son of Yudah Leyb Eskeles, was rabbi of Metz from 1695 to 1707–1708. He was then appointed rabbi of Moravia and became head of the Nikolsburg yeshiva. He died in 1718 (see *Encyclopedia Judaica* 1972, vol. 6, cols. 893–894; and cf. the contradictory details in Cahen 1884, pp. 258–260, and Glikl's statements that follow about him leaving his Metz position).

61. R. Shimshon Wertheimer (see Book Five, p. 328, n. 159); regarding his son-in-law, the son of R. Gavriel, see this Book, n. 64.

62. See this Book, p. 292, n. 22.

63. See Kaufmann 1888, p. 89, n. 2.

64. Regarding him, see "Issachar Berush" entry in *Encyclopedia Judaica* 1972, vol. 6, cols. 894–895.

should I go on about it? Given that I cannot write of the whole thing in its entirety, it is best to be content with this little bit, since the matter is sufficiently well known.

The head of the rabbinical court, our master and teacher most learned righteous R. Gavriel, may God preserve and save him, had been given a year's leave of absence by the community institutions, though it was not believed here that he would be away only one year. That one year became nearly three. At the end of the year the community officers, may they live eternally, wrote to him most respectfully to kindly return and resume his rabbinical position here in Metz, since the community here is *like sheep without a shepherd*;[65] a community such as this cannot run itself properly without the head of the rabbinical court, although there certainly are talented people here, great scholars, wise and learned men, notably the old gaon our master and teacher R. Aaron,[66] a great scholar, for many years also head of the rabbinical court of Mannheim and of the region, and of Elsass too. This same elder R. Aaron and R. Gavriel's son-in-law were relatives by marriage: his daughter married the son of R. Aaron,[67] head of the rabbinical court in Elsass. Hence, R. Aaron sided with R. Gavriel's camp and several times had already proclaimed that his in-law R. Gavriel was coming here, for this gaon R. Aaron is a very capable man and people heed what he says; he is altogether successful and extremely shrewd in higher matters as well as in practical things. The community calmed down for a while. Eventually the community leaders, may they live eternally, found out that R. Gavriel had in fact been appointed head of the rabbinical court in the holy community of Nikolsburg; much could be written of all the quarreling that ensued. R. Gavriel's son came here thinking he could persuade the community leaders to keep waiting. However, once they found out here that R. Gavriel had accepted that position, the leaders of the community, joined by a majority of its members,[68] sought to appoint someone else as head of the rabbinical court, thereby instigating a great quarrel, be-

65. Cf. "like sheep that have no shepherd" (Num 27:17; 1 Kgs 22:17).
66. R. Aaron Worms (see Book Six, p. 275, n. 114).
67. R. Gavriel's granddaughter (his daughter's daughter) was married to R. Aaron's son.
68. This terminology is common in community minute books and indicates that the community leaders and most of the community members backed the decision.

cause R. Gavriel's followers such as R. Aaron with his followers were very active, and there was a huge quarrel because they sought to prevent the appointment of anyone else as head of the rabbinical court; nothing else would satisfy them but to wait for our master and teacher the righteous R. Gavriel. But when this did not happen, a great quarrel erupted, no need to write about it. Finally the community leaders, joined by a majority of householders, solemnly undertook, adding threats of severe penalties, that if the previously mentioned righteous head of the rabbinical court failed to return immediately, they would appoint someone else as head of the rabbinical court, which in fact was done, and a rabbinical appointment writ was prepared with the utmost respect due such a scholar, addressed to the gaon our master and teacher R. Avraham,[69] may God preserve and save him, who at that time was the highest rabbinical authority and head of yeshiva in the holy community of Prague; the letter was then dispatched by special courier. A short while later, once certain conditions pertaining to the head of the rabbinical court had been stipulated by the community institutions,[70] may they live eternally, and approved by a majority, the previously mentioned head of the rabbinical court duly notified the community leaders of his acceptance: he would come.

Whether it was because our master and teacher R. Gavriel found out about this or because he really wanted to come back here to resume his rabbinical position — R. Gavriel came here with the intention of keeping this rabbinical position,[71] with the help of his followers — I will not write of what happened here, there were many quarrels. May God, blessed be He, forgive the sins of each one. For me as a simple, lowly woman, it is not correct that I push myself right between towering mountains.[72] May God

69. R. Avraham (son of Shaul), born in Bohemia, was first a rabbi in Lichtenstadt and Raudnitz. In 1693, he was appointed head of a yeshiva in Prague. In 1709, he was appointed rabbi of Metz, and in 1713 rabbi of Frankfurt, where he lived until his death in 1717 (see *Encyclopedia Judaica* 1972, vol. 4, col. 1390; *YIVO Encyclopedia* 2008, p. 241; and Glikl's statements that follow, which corroborate well the information there; cf. the contradictory details in Cahen 1884, pp. 260–261, as well as pp. 262–263 for a detailed description of the dispute discussed in the following text).

70. Although it is not stated explicitly, we may assume that it was R. Avraham Broda who suggested the stipulations in the contract (on the contract, see Kaufmann 1896, p. 323, n. 1).

71. R. Gavriel was still rabbi of Metz on June 7, 1708 (see Kaufmann 1896, p. 323, n. 3).

72. Cf. "Why should you," he said to them, "put my head between two great mountains, between two great groups of disputants?" (b.Yevamot 15b).

forgive whoever did anything wrong in his camp. An entire book could be written about what each camp did for its own justification. God grant us merit for the good deeds of them both.

Now, after the gaon our master and teacher R. Gavriel spent some time here and realized he would achieve nothing, since the community leaders could not renege on their word, righteous R. Gavriel left our city and went on his way, in great honor, for the members of the entire community were not enemies of his; quite the contrary: they were all his friends. The obstacle lay in that they could not renege on the writ of rabbinical appointment here that they had already sent, given that our great master and teacher R. Avraham, head of the rabbinical court, had written his acceptance. Well, I will restrain my pen and write only that said great rabbi our master and teacher R. Avraham arrived here safely. Words cannot describe the grand welcome shown him here upon his arrival, it is surely well known, so I do not think I need write of it. They built him a brand new house with a study where he had his chair; to the best of my limited knowledge this was done nowhere else. And all the members of our community — all, including those who had not sided with him before he came — all nevertheless got along with him in friendly fashion. Certainly one could write extensively about his personality, his learning, and his good deeds; the whole world knows very well of the learning the eminent scholar brought here to the community, asking for nothing except to devote himself to his learning day and night[73] and to *disseminate Torah in Israel*.[74] He took children who had learned literally nothing and studied with them until they became proficient. Well, why should I go on at length? His Torah learning is famed everywhere. Alas, our joy was short-lived because the previously mentioned gaon, head of the rabbinical court, accepted a rabbinical appointment in the holy community of Frankfurt, and although the community leaders, may they live eternally, implored him to stay, promising him *whatever his heart desired*,[75] he absolutely refused. Since the gaon left us, we have been through hard times, physically as well as financially, as I will set out in brief. Many respectable young women with untainted reputation died, alas.

73. Based on "recite it day and night" (Jos 1:8).
74. See b.Mo'ed Qatan 25b.
75. See b.Mo'ed Qatan 17a; b.Hagigah 16a.

There was great distress, may God have mercy on us in future and remove His wrath from us and from all Israel,[76] amen and amen.

I cannot refrain from writing about the event[77] that took place *in our community of Metz on the holy Sabbath during the Festival of Shavuot, in the year 5475,[78] when we were in the synagogue, men and women; the cantor, Reb Yokele, the great singer from the community of Rayshe in Poland,[79] had just begun praying the yotser prayers[80] and was chanting from "God, in Your mighty powers . . ." to the blessing "maker of the luminaries." Before he could reach the blessing, many of the men and women* heard sounds as of something breaking, and there was a very loud noise. The women in the synagogue's upstairs balcony thought the entire roof was caving in on them. *Men and women were seized with fright and terror* because of the noise of an awful crash, as of rocks, as though a large building were collapsing; they were terrified. The women in the synagogue's upstairs balcony rushed to get downstairs, each one desperate to be first, *to save her own life, one said this, another said that*[81] — men and women. *The women, hearing the commotion in the men's section,[82] rushed out in urgent haste,[83] believing that an enemy was upon us, God forbid, each one of them, trying only to save her own life and her husband's,* all the women in the synagogue, *each and every one bravely left their section*[84] and reached the stairs. In their haste to precede one another, they toppled over each other, God preserve us, trampling each

76. For this particular combination of sources (also mentioned in Book Five, p. 249, n. 208), see Turniansky 2006a, p. 474, n. 589.

77. Two passages of Glikl's description of the event that follows — the one beginning here and the one beginning later, on p. 306, "After that people went up to the women's section" — are notable for being written partially or totally in Hebrew. For more details see Turniansky 2006a, p. 586, n. 187. For more on Glikl's knowledge of Hebrew, see the Introduction to this English edition. pp. 21–22.

78. This incident, which occurred in Metz on Saturday, June 5, 1715, the second day of the Shavuot festival, was registered in various official community records and related in several Hebrew or Yiddish works (for details, see Turniansky 2006a, p. 587, n. 188).

79. R. Yokele of Rzeszów (which the Jews called Rayshe or Reyshe) in Galicia was a wandering cantor famous throughout Europe during 1715–1725 (see *Encyclopedia Judaica* 1972, vol. 12, col. 627).

80. This apparently refers to the liturgical poems recited during the morning prayers before the *Shema* (Hear O Israel) prayer.

81. Cf. 1 Kgs 22:20.

82. That is, in the main hall of the synagogue (as opposed to the women's section on the second story).

83. Cf. Esther 8:14.

84. That is, the women's section, which was on the second story.

other to death underfoot. In about half an hour, six women were killed and more than thirty injured, some fatally; these remained in the doctors' care for over a quarter of a year. Had they descended in orderly fashion, no one would have been hurt. A blind old woman sitting upstairs in the synagogue, poor thing, could not run and remained seated there *until the indignation should pass*;[85] she was unharmed and reached home safely. But because of the loud noise the women heard, they were seized with fright that the roof of the synagogue was caving in on them.

What a terrible situation it was—impossible to tell or write. Most of the women who escaped emerged from the crush with head bared and clothes torn. One woman, and several more, who had actually been sitting in the synagogue's upstairs balcony, told me that they too had intended to run downstairs but their way was blocked. Since they could not get through, they went back into the synagogue, saying "If we must die, we might as well stay inside the synagogue and die here instead of being trampled on the stairs." More than fifty women were sprawled on the stairway all entangled, as if stuck on top of each other with tar, the living with the dead—*He who separates the living from the dead*[86]—all sprawled together. The men all came running. Each was anxious to rescue his own loved ones, but it was only with great difficulty and effort that they succeeded in disentangling the women heaped on the stairs from each other. All this took a good half hour, no longer. The men were a great help. Many people, gentile burghers, came into Jews' Street bearing ladders and axes to attempt to get the women down from the upper story,[87] since the situation upstairs in the women's section was not known. The men inside the synagogue also heard the sound of a crash, and they too thought the ceiling was caving in on them. That's why they shouted to the women to hurry downstairs. This made the women hasten even more until they fell over each other and could not extricate themselves and remained sprawled there on the stairs, alas. Easy to imagine the sorrow as they separated the live women from the six corpses that had been alive and well only an hour before.

85. Cf. Isa. 26:20; and cf. Book Two, p. 67, n. 53.
86. For details, see Turniansky 2006a, p. 591, n. 220.
87. That is, the women's section on the upper story. Later Glikl mentions that there was also a women's section on the lower story.

Heaven have mercy on us in future and remove His wrath from us and all of Israel.[88]

The exit from the downstairs women's section was also jammed. I, the mother, was in my seat in the downstairs women's section, praying. Suddenly I hear women scurrying around. I asked: "What's all this scurrying around?" My neighbor replies: "What could it be? Some pregnant woman must be feeling nauseous." That scared me, because my daughter Esther, sitting about eight seats from me, was pregnant. So I went to her in the crush where she was also trying to get out, asking her: "Where are you going?" She replies: "My God, the roof is caving in!" So I propelled my daughter before me, motioning with my hand for the others to let me through so that I could get my daughter out of there, may she live long. Now, in order to exit the women's section you have to go down five or six steps. As I reached the bottom step with my daughter, I fell and knew no more, I could not move, I did not call for help. I was lying right where all the men had to pass through as they rushed through to rescue the women in the upstairs women's section; in another moment I would have been trampled underfoot. Finally the men noticed me and helped me to my feet. Out in the street I began shouting, not knowing where my daughter Esther had disappeared to. On being told she was at home, I sent someone over to see if she was there, but the report came back that she was not home. I ran around frantically like one who has lost his mind, heaven forfend. Just then my daughter Miriam[89] came running up to me, so happy to see me, poor thing. I ask her: "Where is my daughter Esther?" She replies: "She's at her brother-in-law Reb Reuven's[90] house — who lives not far from the synagogue. So I run as fast as I can to Reb Reuven's to find my daughter sitting there literally with no clothes on or head-covering, with several men and women standing over her reviving her from her faint. Well, why should I go on at length? Thank God for helping her and keeping her healthy and thank God she and her baby were unharmed. May almighty God, blessed

88. Glikl brings here, as well as earlier in this Book (p. 303, n. 63), a Yiddish translation of the Hebrew phrasing she quoted in Book Five, p. 249, n. 208.
89. In none of her mentions of her youngest daughter Miriam does Glikl recount whether she married.
90. Reb Reuven Krumbach, brother of the husband of Esther, Glikl's daughter (see Kaufmann 1896, p. 328, n. 4).

be He and His name, remove in future His wrath from us and all of Israel and keep us safe from such tragedies.

After that people went up to the women's section to investigate if anything had fallen from the ceiling or the building in the women's or the men's sections, but nothing was found, nor can we know whence came this tragedy. We can attribute it to nothing else but our sins. *Woe unto us*[91] *that such a thing has come to pass in our time, when our ears hear it, our soul is sick,*[92] *that the verse has come to pass "I will cast a faintness into their hearts. The sound of a driven leaf shall put you to flight. Fleeing as though from the sword, they shall fall though none pursues."*[93] *Because of this our hearts are sick, our eyes are dimmed,*[94] *because of the desecration of the Sabbath and holy day and because of prayers suspended, in the words of the prophet "Who asked that of you"*[95] *on that holy day of the giving of our holy Torah*[96] *and He has chosen us from among every nation and tongue,*[97] *had we been deserving we could have rejoiced on the day of the giving of the Torah, a sacred occasion.*[98] *And now "We have become the butt of our neighbors, the scorn and derision of those around us,"*[99] *as though the Temple had been destroyed in our time.*[100] *And because poor wretched women were killed our eyes shed streams of water.*[101] *Most of these women had just given birth, alas, and one was pregnant.*[102] *For them — rest, for us — sorrow and anguish and sighs. The*

91. From here, up to the end of this paragraph ("Amen"), the text is in Hebrew. The wording of the first part (up to "a sacred occasion") is quite similar to that of a manuscript *Kinah* (Lamentation) entitled *Ma'aseh Metz* (see Turniansky 2006a, p. 587, n. 188, source C). Language echoing lamentational rhymes occurs in both, as well as in Glikl's version up to the end. It is likely that the mentioned *Kinah* (or a longer version of it) reached Glikl somehow (after all, her husband and his parents were pillars of the community), and that she copied from there into her memoir.

92. See Turniansky 2006a, p. 595, n. 241.

93. Lev 26:36–37 with two changes: the phrase "in the land of their enemies" is left out, and "put you to flight" appears instead of "put them to flight."

94. Cf. Lam 5:17.

95. Isa 1:12.

96. The incident took place on the Shavuot festival, which celebrates the giving of the Torah.

97. Cf. "who has chosen us from all peoples and raised us above all tongues" (from the blessing over the wine for holidays and Rosh Hashanah; Maḥzor Rosh Hashanah 2014, p. 105).

98. Cf. "These are the set times of the Lord, the sacred occasions" (Lev 23:4).

99. Ps 79:4.

100. Cf. "as if the destruction of the Temple had taken place in his days" (b.Sanhedrin 22a).

101. Cf. "My eyes shed streams of water" (Ps 119:136).

102. The sources cited earlier in this Book (p. 303, n. 78) confirm these details.

*day after the festival the Burial Society men go early to the cemetery, the six
dead women are buried next to each other in a row.*[103] *Henceforth, all must
examine their conduct,*[104] *every man according to his ways,*[105] *and with the
proper fruit of their deeds, attesting that the Lord is upright,*[106] *a faithful God,
never false,*[107] *but He, being merciful, forgave iniquity and would not destroy
and did not give full vent to His fury and wrath,*[108] *and said to the angel who
was destroying, "Stay your hand!"*[109] *etc. May the Master of Compassion*[110]
*grant our request, the Lord will guard our going and coming to life and peace,
now and for evermore.*[111] *And there will be no more breaching and wailing
in our streets*[112] *among our brethren, the whole house of Israel, in all their
dwelling places, and let us say Amen.*[113]

It is true that talk of this incident continues unabated, but who can
write it all down or believe it all? Despite this, I, the mother, will write
something in the name of a woman called Esther. Her husband's name is
Reb Yakov; he is a householder[114] and teacher here. Well, this woman and
her little boy, about five years old, were sitting on the stairs to the women's
balcony when the incident began. She saw six very tall women wearing
small head-coverings;[115] these women then went and pushed this Esther

103. Up to this point, all details of Glikl's description of the incident (except those relating to her
personal experiences) that have parallels in the sources cited in Turniansky 2006a, p. 587, n. 188, are
fully corroborated. However, the sources do not mention most of the events related in the text that
follows here, from the paragraph beginning "It is true that talk of this incident continues unabated"
through the paragraph ending "I, the mother, heard nothing either."
104. Cf. b.Berakhot 5a.
105. Cf. Jer 32:19.
106. Ps 92:16.
107. Cf. Deut 32:4; the end of this verse — "true and upright is He" — connects to the former
mention: "the Lord is upright" (see previous note).
108. Cf. Ps 78:38.
109. Cf. 2 Sam 24:16.
110. A common appellation for God in the liturgy (e.g., see "You are a God slow to anger, you are
called the Master of Compassion" in the *Selichot* prayers (Siddur 2016, p. 924).
111. Cf. "The Lord will guard your going and coming now and for evermore" (Ps 121:8). The insertion "to life and peace" is a common blessing formulation (see Siddur 2016, p. 632).
112. Cf. "There is no breaching and no sortie, and no wailing in our streets" (Ps 144:14).
113. For "our brethren, the whole house of Israel," see Maḥzor Rosh Hashanah 2014, p. 195. For "in
all their dwelling places," see Siddur 2016, p. 166.
114. "Householder" refers to a community member obligated to pay community taxes.
115. The vision of six women also appears in *Ḥelkat Binyamin* (see Turniansky 2006a, p. 587, n. 188,
source E).

down a few steps. The woman screamed: "Do you want to kill me along with my little boy?" So they seated the boy down in a corner and departed. The woman and her little boy were saved. It was in that very blink of an eye that the terrifying commotion started, when all the women in the balcony scrambled downstairs falling all over each other until they could not move and ended up squashing each other, sprawled on the stairs as if stuck together with tar. My son-in-law parnas and community leader Moshe Krumbach wanted to get out too and asked the women why they weren't coming downstairs. The poor things replied they couldn't come down because the staircase had collapsed underfoot, although actually nothing at all was broken on the stairs; nothing but the terrifying horror made them imagine it, alas. The woman Esther with her little boy were rescued; it took great effort to extricate her and her boy from among the other women, since this woman was closer to death than to life, for it emerged that she fell and was so badly bruised that the doctors had to treat her for more than three months. I spoke to the woman myself, I, the mother, and she swore to me that everything happened exactly as she had told me. Her husband and her father and mother also testified that she had immediately[116] recounted everything as described. Distinguished people came to her as well, learned men, and she recounted her story to them under oath. She and her husband, like her father and mother, are upright, decent people; never has a falsehood or slanderous word been heard from them in our community.

It chanced once again, one night around the time of that incident, that the wife of a respected householder here, the distinguished Yakov Krumbach, whose house is right by the synagogue, heard a loud commotion in the synagogue as though there were thieves inside taking everything out of there and as though candelabra were falling inside the synagogue. The woman woke her husband, saying: "My God, can't you hear the racket in the synagogue? There must be thieves in there emptying the whole place out." Thereupon they sent for the shammash, asking him to open up the synagogue — *but there was no sound, and none who responded;*[117] not even the smallest object had been moved from its place, no one knows alas *on*

---

116. That is, immediately after the incident, such that her evidence was reliable and not influenced by later events. Further tests of the reliability of her evidence are recounted in the following text.
117. 1 Kgs 18:26.

whose account this misfortune.[118] There was a huge tumult, God save us. The women thought that the men's section was collapsing, and the men thought that the women's section was collapsing. That is why the men shouted to the women to get out of the synagogue. In short, impossible to say or write wherefore came this blow, alas. Most of the men and women heard a loud explosion resembling thunder or the firing of a large cannon. Most of them heard it, many heard nothing; I was among these, I, the mother, heard nothing either.

And so we spent the holy day *in sorrow and anguish.*[119] Instead of rejoicing as one should on that pleasant holy festival of the giving of the Torah, it passed amid *sorrow, anguish and sighing.*[120] Cantor Reb Yokele left the synagogue and went home in the middle of the most important prayer and another cantor got up to lead the prayers, but he sang very little or not at all. Several righteous women of the community formed a society and hired ten learned men to go to the synagogue every day at nine o'clock to recite Psalms and study there too for about an hour so that the new orphans could recite the mourner's prayer.[121] May God willingly receive their souls and may their death, such an unnatural one, be atonement for their sins, *may their souls be bound in the bundle of life*[122] in the Garden of Eden, may they forgive all those who injured them and caused their death, alas; may they also pray to God to forgive everything.

I would not be writing of this in my book were it not that the like of it has never been heard of or known to happen — may it never ever happen again. Everyone, *man or woman, married or unmarried,*[123] must now heed this well and pray to God, blessed be He, not to inflict such a punishment on any Jewish person ever again; may Heaven show us mercy and deliver us from languishing in exile, amen and amen.

---

118. Cf. "on whose account this misfortune has come upon us" (Jon 1:7).
119. See Turniansky 2006a, p. 373, n. 56.
120. See Turniansky 2006a, p. 373, n. 56.
121. According to the custom of studying a Mishnah, legend, or Talmud after the prayers so the orphans or other mourners can recite the kaddish (mourner's prayer) afterward (see Lewinsky 1975, p. 652).
122. Plural of the inscription used on tombstones: "May his/her soul be bound in the bundle of life."
123. This detailed wording is common in community minute books and in similar records indicating permissions or prohibitions and their punishments.

I cannot, alas, attribute it[124] to anything other than the sins committed on the holy day of Simḥat Torah of 5475,[125] when all the Torah scrolls
were raised aloft, as is the custom.[126] Even with seven Torah scrolls placed
on the table, a fight broke out among the women, who started tearing the
kerchiefs from each other's head, woe is me, and stood bareheaded[127] in
the women's section. As a result, the men, in the men's section, also started
brawling and quarreling, despite the reverend gaon our master and teacher
R. Avraham[128] who was shouting at them with threats of excommunication to be silent and stop the desecration of the holy day. But all this was to
no avail. The aforementioned gaon, head of the rabbinical court, hastily left
the synagogue with the eminent officers of the community to determine
punishment to be meted out to each individual.[129]

In Nissan of 5479[130] a woman was standing on the bank of the Moselle[131] at night, washing dishes. At about ten o'clock light shone out as
clear as day. As the woman gazed heavenward, the sky was open like ***,[132]
with flashing sparks, then the sky closed up again as though a curtain had
been drawn over it, and once again there was darkness. May God, blessed
be He, let this bring good, amen.[133]

END OF BOOK SEVEN[134]

---

124. That is, the incident just mentioned. Glikl tries her hardest to find a reasonable explanation for
it and understand its cause.

125. On October 20, 1714, about eight months before the Shavuot tragedy just recounted.

126. According to the custom of raising the Torah in the synagogue in order to honor it by displaying it so that it can be seen by all the worshippers.

127. Thus violating the commandment for a married woman to cover her head.

128. R. Avraham Broda; see this Book, p. 301, n. 69.

129. For details about the incident and the reactions of those punished, see Davis 1995, p. 258, n. 220.
The events must have been known to Glikl too, but she does not recount them.

130. That is, between March 21 and April 19, 1719, more than five years before Glikl's death (on
September 19, 1724; see Introduction). However, the point in time after March–April 1719 when
Glikl wrote these lines that conclude her book is unknown.

131. Metz is one of the French towns along the Moselle River.

132. A word is missing here.

133. Glikl chose to end her memoir with this incident (if in fact the closing "End of Book Seven" in the original, now lost manuscript, was hers), which, according to Davis 1995, p. 62, records a vision by a woman, probably Glikl herself, washing dishes at the banks of the Moselle River. The description fits that of a meteor disintegrating in the air, and indeed a meteor that was seen on March 29, 1719, in England, Scotland, and Ireland, disintegrated over the shores of Bretagne, France. It was reported by Sir Edmond Halley and registered by Hone 1838, cols. 373–374 (for this information I am most obliged to Reuven Gvaryahu of Philadelphia; for more details, see Turniansky 2006a, p. 605, n. 314). It is reasonable to assume that knowledge of the unusual astronomical event spread and reached Glikl.

134. For the copyist's note that appears here in German written in Hebrew characters, see Turniansky 2006a, pp. 604–605, and nn. 313–314 there.

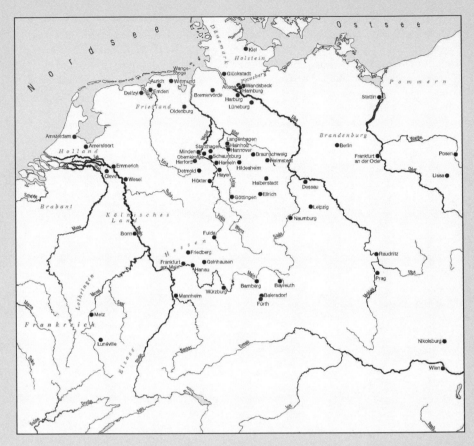

FIGURE 15

Map of places mentioned in the memoirs.

APPENDIX

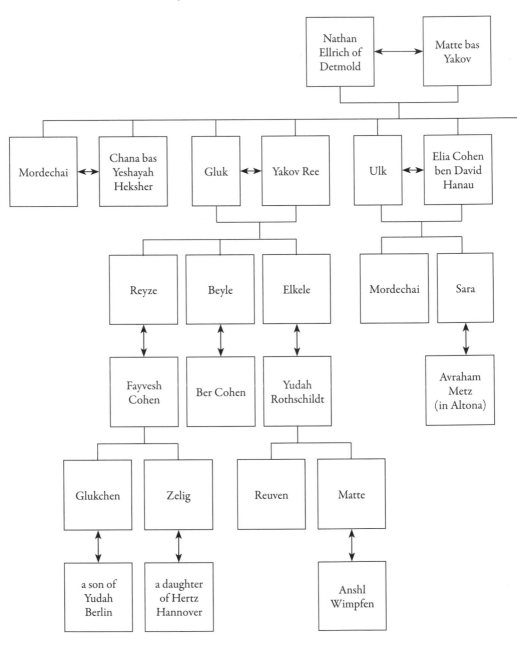

*ben: son of
bas: daughter of

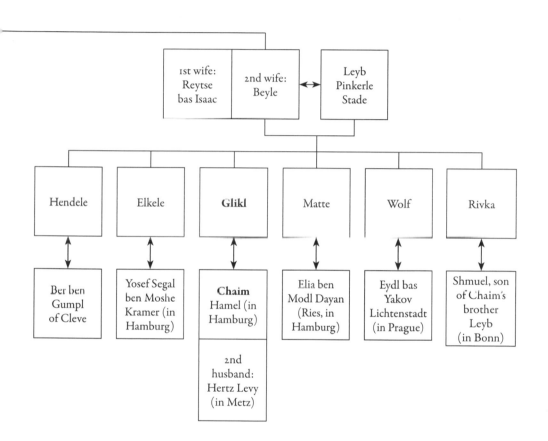

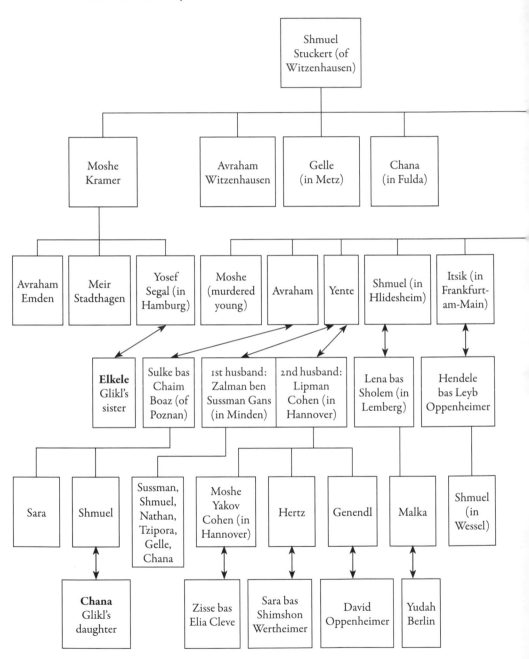

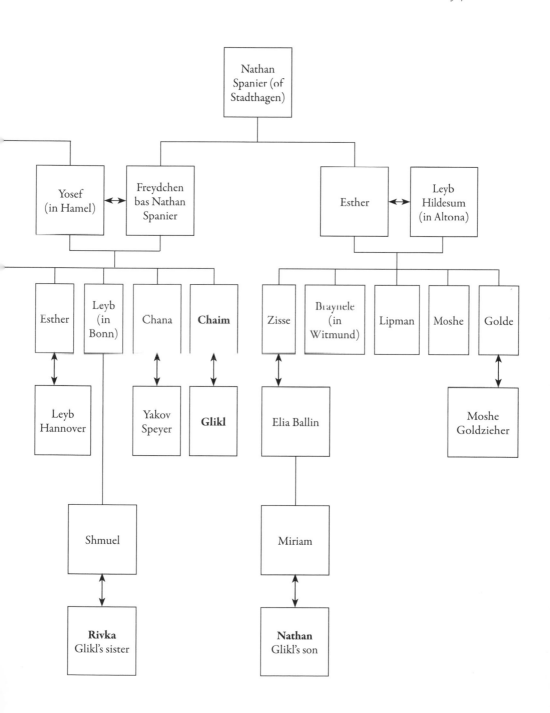

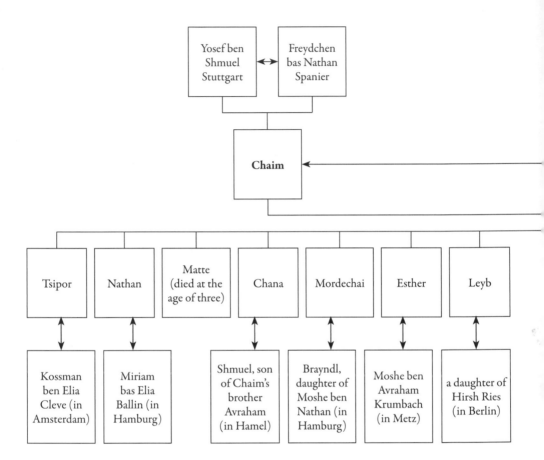

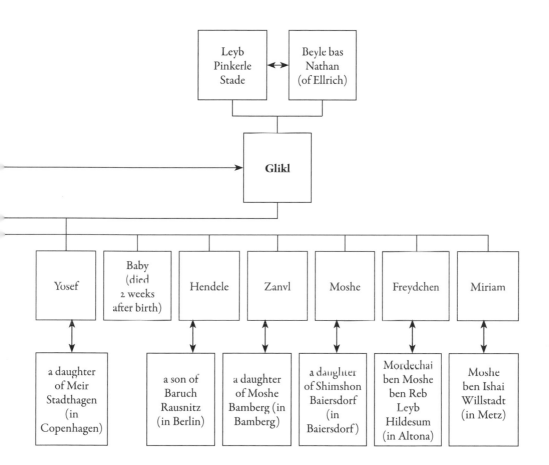

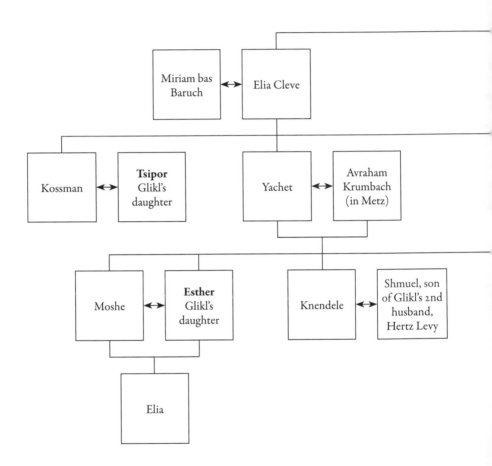

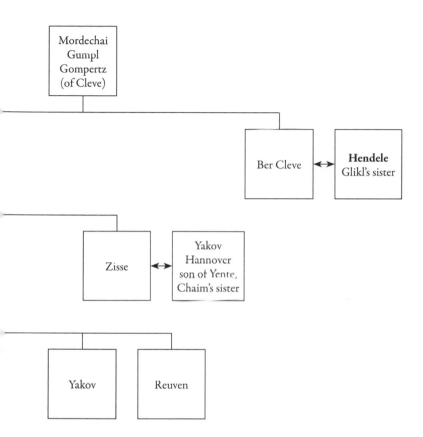

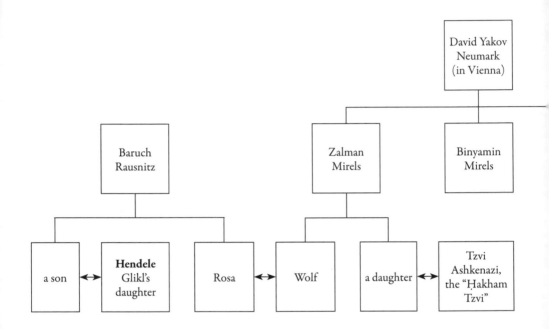

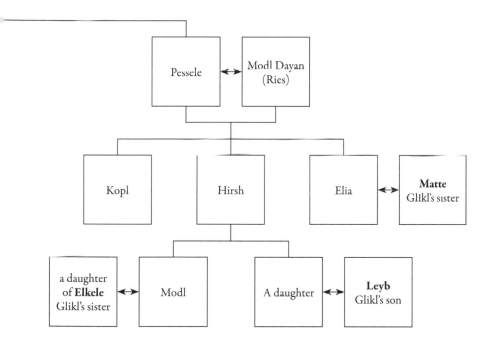

REFERENCES

Aarne, Antti, and Stith Thompson (1987). *The Types of the Folktale: A Classification and Bibliography*. Folklore Fellows Communications 184. Helsinki: Academia Scientiarum Fennica.

Abrahams, Beth-Zion (1962). *The Life of Glückel of Hameln (1646–1724). Written by Herself.* Translated from the original Yiddish and edited by Beth-Zion Abrahams. London: East and West Library, Horowitz Publishing (2nd ed. 1963. New York: Thomas Yoseloff).

Abrahams, Israel (1969). *Jewish Life in the Middle Ages*. New York: Atheneum.

Alphabet of Ben Sira [Alpha Beta de-Ben Sira] (1544). Venice: Giov. dei Farri et fratr.

Arrian (1971). *The Campaigns of Alexander*. Translated by Aubrey de Sélincourt. Harmondsworth, UK: Penguin Books.

Ashkenazi, Shmuel, and Dov Jarden (1966). *Ozar Rashe Tevot: Thesaurus of Hebrew Abbreviations*. Jerusalem: Rubin Mass.

Avron, Dov (1967) *Pinkas hakshoirim shel kehilat Pozna, 1621–1835*. Jerusalem: Mekize Nirdamim.

Awerbuch, Marianne (1980). "Über das Lebensverständnis der Glückel von Hameln." In Peter von der Osten (ed.), *Juden in Deutschland: Zur Geschichte einer Hoffnung, Historische Längsschnitte und Einzelstudien*, pp. 127–142. Veröffentlichungen aus dem Institut Kirche und Judentum 11 [Publications of the Institut Kirche und Judentum 11]. Berlin: Institut Kirche und Judentum.

Balaban, Majer (1962). "Die Kracauer Judengemeinde-Ordnung von 1595 und ihre Nachträge." In *Jahrbuch der jüdisch-literarischen Gesellschaft* 10 (1912), pp. 308–360; 11 (1916), pp. 88–112.

Bar-Levav, Avriel (1997). *Tfisat hamavet besefer haḥayim lerabi Shimon Frankfurt*. Dissertation, Hebrew University, Jerusalem.

——— (2002). "Ritualisation of Jewish Life and Death in the Early Modern Period." *Leo Baeck Institute Yearbook* 47 (2002): 69–82.

Ben-Sasson, Chaim Hillel (1959). *Hagut vehanhagah: Hashkafoteihem haḥevratiot shel yehudei Polin beshilhei yemei habeinaim*. Jerusalem: Mossad Bialik.

Bernfeld, Yosef (1967). *Glikl Hamil, Zikhroynes*. In hayntikn yidish fun Yosef Bernfeld, araynfir un redaktsye fun Shmuel Rollansky [Translated into Modern Yiddish by Yosef Bernfeld, introduction and edition by Shmuel Rollansky]. Musterverk fun der yidisher literatur 26. Buenos Aires, Ateneo Literario en el IWO.

Bernstein, Ignaz (1908). *Yidishe shprikhverter un rednsartn*. Collected and explained by Ignaz Bernstein. 2nd edition with the collaboration of B. W. Segel. Frankfurt a.M.: J. Kauffmann.

Bilik, Dorothy (1992). "The Memoirs of Glikl of Hameln: The Archaeology of the Text." *Yiddish* 8, no. 2 (1992): 5–22.

Böhm, Günter (1991). "Die Sephardim in Hamburg." In Herzig and Rohde 1991, pp. 21–40.

Braden, Jutta (2001). "Luthertum und Handelsinteressen — Die Judenpolitik des Hamburger Senats im 17. Jahrhundert." In Richarz 2001, pp. 159–194.

Brocke, Michael, ed. (2009). *Verborgene Pracht. Der jüdische Friedhof Hamburg-Altona. Aschkenasische Grabmale.* Dresden: Sandstein.

Buber, Shlomo (1895). *Anshei shem [. . .] ba'ir Levov bemeshekh 400 shanah 1500–1890.* Cracow: Yosef Fisher.

Cahen, Abraham (1884). "Le rabbinat de Metz pendant la période francaise (1567–1871). *Revue des études juives* 8: 255–274.

Carlebach, Elisheva (2001). "Die messiansche Haltung der deutschen Juden im Spiegel von Glikls *Zikhroynes*." In Richarz 2001, pp. 238–253.

Cassuto, Alfonso (1927). *Gedenkschrift anlässlich des 275 jährigen Bestehens der portugiesischen jüdischen Gemeinde in Hamburg.* Amsterdam: M. Hertzberger.

Chayes, J. H. (2003). *Between Worlds: Dybbuks, Exorcists, and Early Modern Judaism.* Philadelphia: University of Pennsylvania Press.

Chovav, Yemima (2009). *Alamot ahevukha: Hayei hadat veharuah shel nashim bahevrah haashkenazit bereshit ha'et hahadashah.* Jerusalem: Zalman Shazar Center for Jewish History and Carmel Publishing House.

Davis, Natalie Zemon (1995). *Women on the Margins: Three Seventeenth-Century Lives.* Cambridge, MA: Harvard University Press.

——— (1996). "Riches and Dangers: Glickl bas Judah Leib on Court Jews." In Vivian B. Mann and Richard I. Cohen (eds.), *From Court Jews to the Rothschilds: Art, Patronage and Power 1600–1800*, pp. 45–57. Munich: Prestel.

——— (2001). "Glikl bas Judah Leib — ein jüdisches, ein europäisches Leben." In Richarz 2001, pp. 27–48.

Duckesz, Eduard (1903). *Iwo lemoschaw, Enthaltend Biographien und Grabstein-Inschriften der Rabbiner der drei Gemeinden, Altona, Hamburg, Wandsbeck.* Annotated by Salomon Buber. Krakow: Fischer.

——— (1908). *Chachme AHW: Biographien und Grabsteininschriften der Dajanim, Autoren und der sonstigen hervorragenden Männer der drei Gemeinden Altona, Hamburg, Wandsbek.* Ins deutsche übertragen von [Translated into German by] Salomon Goldschmidt. Hamburg: Goldschmidt.

——— (1915). *Zur Geschichte und Genealogie der ersten Familien der hochdeutschen Israeliten-Gemeinden in Hamburg-Altona.* Hamburg: M. Lessmann.

——— (1932). "Rabbi Salomon Mirels Neumark: Zum 225. Todestage." *Menorah* 10: 354–357.

Elkoshi, Gedaliah (1981). *Thesaurus proverbiorum et idiomatum Latinorum in linguam Hebraicam versorum. [. . .]* Jerusalem: Magnes Press.

Encyclopaedia Hebraica (1988). Jerusalem: Hevrah lehotsaat entsiklopediot.

Encyclopaedia Judaica (1972). Jerusalem: Keter Publishing.

Erik, Maks (1928). *Di geshikhte fun der yidisher literatur fun di eltste tsaytn biz der haskole-tkufe.* Varshe: Kultur-lige.

Faustini, Pascal: *Aaron Worms, Rabbin de Metz, sa famille, origines inédites à Metz et à Worms (1640–1722).* http://judaisme.sdv.fr/histoire/rabbins/worms/worms.htm.

Feilchenfeld, Alfred (1898). *Aus der ältesten Geschichte der portugiesisch-israelitischen Gemeinde in Hamburg.* Hamburg: M. Lessmann.

——— (1899a). "Anfang und Blütezeit der Portugiesengemeinde in Hamburg." *ZVHG* 10: 199–240.

——— (1899b). "Die älteste Geschichte der deutschen Juden in Hamburg." *MGWJ* 45: 271–282, 322–328, 370–381.

——— (1902). *Die jüdischen Besucher der Leipziger Messen in den Jahren 1675–1699.* Offprint from the periodical *MGWJ*, 1901. Frankfurt a.M.: J. Kaufmann.

——— (1913). *Denkwürdigkeiten der Glückel von Hameln.* Aus dem jüdisch-deutschen übersetzt, mit Erlauterungen versehen und herausgegeben von Alfred Feilchenfeld [Translated from Judeo-German, with explanations and edited by Alfred Feilchenfeld]. Berlin: Jüdischer Verlag. Following editions: Berlin 1915, 1920, 1923; Darmstadt 1979; Königstein 1980; Frankfurt a.M. 1987; Bodenheim bei Mainz 1999.

Feiner, Shmuel (2017). "Tmunot miḥayei nisuin: Glikl bat Leib bein Hamburg le-Metz." In Shmuel Feiner, *Et Ḥadasha: Yehudim be-Eyropa bameah hashmone esre, 1700–1750.* Jerusalem: Zalman Shazar Center, pp. 57–69.

Flusser, David (1981). *Sefer Yosifon, yotse laor sadur umugeh al pi kitvei yad belivyat mavo, biurim veḥilufei girsaot.* Jerusalem: Mossad Bialik.

Frænkel, Louis, and Henry Frænkel (1999). *Genealogical Tables of Jewish Families, 14th–20th Centuries: Forgotten Fragments of the History of the Frænkel Family,* I–II. Edited by Georg Simon. Translated from Danish by Malene Woodman. München: K. G. Saur.

Fram, Edward, and Verena Kasper-Marienberg (2015). "Jewish Martyrdom without Persecution: The Murder of Gumpert May, Frankfurt am Main 1781." *AJS Review* 39: 267–301.

Freiherr von Schrötter, Friedrich: (1930). *Wörterbuch der Münzkunde.* Berlin: W. de Gruyter.

Freimark, Peter (1970–1972). "Zum Verhälteniss von Juden und Christen in Altona im 17./18. Jahrhundert." *Theokratia: Jahrbuch des Institutum Judaicum Delitzschianum* 2: 253–272.

Freudenthal, Max (1928). *Leipziger Messgäste: Die jüdischen Besucher der Leipziger Messen in den Jahren 1675 bis 1764.* Schriften der Gesellschaft zur Förderung der Wissenschaft des Judentums. Frankfurt a.M.: J. Kauffmann.

Friis, Astrid, and Glamann Kristoff (1958). *History of Prices and Wages in Denmark 1660–1800,* I. London: Longmans Green.

Furman, Israel (1968). *Yidishe shprikhverter un rednsartn.* Tel-Aviv: Hamenorah.

Gaster, Moses (1981). *Ma'aseh Book: Book of Jewish Tales and Legends Translated from the Judeo-German.* Philadelphia: The Jewish Publication Society of America.

Ginsburger, Moses (1902). "Elie Schwab, Rabbin de Hagenau [1721–1747]." *REJ* 44: 104–111.

—— (1907). "Samuel Levy, ein Stiefsohn der Glückel von Hameln." *MGWJ* 51: 480–500.

Grabbücher Altonaer Friedhof, Königsstrasse (1874). Copies kept in Staatsarchiv Hamburg (JG 82 STA) and CAHJP, Jerusalem (AHW 82). (The ordinal number corresponds to the alphabetical order of the surnames of the deceased, and is followed by the number of the grave in my notes to the memoir.)

Graboïs, Arie (1967). "Dmuto shel Karl hagadol bamekorot ha'ivriim shel yemei habeinaim." *Tarbiz* 36: 22–58.

Graupe, Heinz Mosche, ed. and trans. (1973). *Die Statuten der drei Gemeinden Altona, Hamburg und Wandsbek*. Hamburg: Hans Christians Verlag.

Great Dictionary of the Yiddish Language [*Groyser verterbukh fun der yidisher shprakh*]. (1961). Edited by Judah A. Joffe and Yudel Mark. New York: Yiddish Dictionary Committee.

Grossman, Avraham (2004). *Pious and Rebellious: Jewish Women in Medieval Europe*. Translated from the Hebrew by Jonathan Chipman. Waltham, MA: Brandeis University Press.

Grunwald, Max (1902). *Portugiesengräber in deutscher Erde*. Hamburg: A. Janssen.

—— (1904). *Hamburgs deutsche Juden bis zur Auflösung der Dreigemeinden 1811*. Hamburg: A. Janssen.

—— (1915). "Beiträge zu den Memoiren der Glückel von Hameln." *MGJV* 18: 68–63.

Güdemann, Moritz (1880–1888). *Geschichte des Erziehungswesens und der Cultur der abendländischen Juden während des Mittelalters und der Neueren Zeit*, I–III. Wien: Hölder.

—— (1892). *Quellenschriften zur Geschichte des Unterrichts und der Erziehung bei den deutschen Juden*. Berlin: Hofmann.

Halpern, Israel (1968). *Yehudim veyahadut bemizraḥ Eyropa, Meḥkarim betoldoteihem*. Jerusalem: Magnes Press.

Herodotus (1956). *The History of Herodotus*. Translated by George Rawlinson. Edited by Manuel Komroff. New York: Tudor Publishing.

Herzig, Arno, and Saskia Rohde (1991). *Die Juden in Hamburg 1590 bis 1990: Wissenschaftliche Beiträge der Universität Hamburg zur Ausstellung "Vierhundert Jahre Juden in Hamburg."* Hamburg: Dolling und Galitz.

Hirsch, Erika (1994). "Glückel von Hameln, eine Hamburger Theateraufführung als Stadtgang." *Jiddistik Mitteilungen* 11 (April): 21–24.

Hone, William (1838). *The Every-Day Book and Table Book* [. . .], I. London: Thomas Tegg and Son.

Horovitz, Marcus (1969). *Frankfurter Rabbinen: Ein Beitrag zur Geschichte der israelitischen Gemeinde in Frankfurt a.M*. Ergänzungen von Josef Unna. Jerusalem.

Hummel, Hildegard (1990). "Die 'Memoiren' der Glückel von Hameln, Das Schicksal einer jüdischen Frau um die Wende des 17. Jahrhunderts." In Norbert Altenhofer and Renate Heuer (eds.), *Jüdinnen zwischen Tradition und Emanzipation*, pp. 7–26. Jahrbuch des Archivs Bibliographia Judaica 2–3. Bad Soden: A. & V. Woywod.

Idelson-Shein, Iris (2010). "'What Have I To Do with Wild Animals?' Glikl bas Leib and the Other Woman." *Eighteenth-Century Studies* 44, no. 1: 57–77.

Israel, Jonathan I. (1989). *European Jewry in the Age of Mercantilism 1550–1750*. Oxford: Clarendon.

Jancke, Gabriele (1995). "Die Sichronot (Memoiren) der jüdischen Kauffrau Glückel von Hameln zwischen Autobiographie, Geschichtsschreibung und religiösem Lehrtext: Geschlecht, Religion und Ich in der Frühen Neuzeit." In Magdalene Heuser (ed.), *Autobiographien von Frauen: Beiträge zu ihrer Geschichte*, pp. 93–134. Untersuchungen zur deutschen Literaturgeschichte 85. Tübingen: Niemeyer.

—— (2001). "Glikl's Autobiographie im Kontext frühneuzeitlicher autobiographischer Schriften." In Richarz 2001, pp. 91–122.

Jelinek, Estelle C. (1986). *The Tradition of Women's Autobiography from Antiquity to Present*. Boston: Twayne.

Katz, David (1993). "Arum dem toytn-tants in di zikhroynes fun Glikl fun Hameln." In Katz, *Der motiv fun "toytn-tants" in der traditsye fun literatur bay yidn*. Dissertation, Bar Ilan University.

Katz, Tuviah ben Moshe (1707). *Ma'aseh Tuviah*. Venice: Bragadin.

Kaufmann, David (1888). *Samson Wertheimer: Der Oberhoffaktor und Landesrabbiner (1658–1724) und seine Kinder*. Wien: F. Beck.

—— (1896). *Zikhronot marat Glikl Hamel mishnat taf-zain ad taf-ayin-tet* [*Die Memoiren der Glückel von Hameln 1645–1719*]. Frankfurt a.M.: J. Kauffmann.

Kaufmann, David, and Max Freudenthal (1907). *Die Familie Gomperz*. Frankfurt a.M.: J. Kauffmann.

Kayserling, Meyer (1897). *Die jüdische Frauen in der Geschichte, Literatur und Kunst*. Leipzig: Brockhaus.

Kellenbenz, Hermann (1958). *Sephardim an der unteren Elbe*. Wiesbaden: F. Steiner.

—— (1989). "History of the Sephardim in Germany." In Richard David Barnett and Walter Manfred Schwab (eds.), *The Sephardi Heritage*, II: *The Western Sepharadim*, pp. 26–49. Grendon, Northants, UK: Gibraltar Books.

Kinot (2011). *The Koren Mesorat HaRav Kinot / The Complete Tisha B'Av Service*. Commentary by Rabbi Joseph B. Soloveitchik. Jerusalem: Koren Publishers.

Klayman-Cohen, Israela (1994). *Die hebräische Komponente im Westjiddischen am Beispiel der Memoiren der Glückel von Hameln*. jidische schtudies 4. Hamburg: Helmut Buske.

Kossoy, Edward, and Abraham Ohry (1992). *The Feldshers—Medical, Sociological and Historical Aspects of Practitioners of Medicine with Below University Level Education*. Jerusalem: Magnes Press.

Landau, Alfred (1901). "Die Sprache der Memoiren Glückels von Hameln." *MGJV* 7: 20–68.

Landau, Alfred, and Bernhard Wachstein (1911). *Jüdische Privatbriefe aus dem Jahre*

1619: Nach den Originalen des K. u. K. Haus-, Hof- und Staatsarchivs. Quellen
und Forschungen zur Geschichte der Juden in deutsch-Österreich 3. Wien:
W. Braumüller.

The Language and Culture Atlas of Ashkenazic Jewry (2000). Edited by Marvin I.
Herzog. Vol. III: *The Eastern Yiddish — Western Yiddish Continuum.* Tübingen:
Niemeyer.

Le Brase, Herve (1991). "Glückel Hameln, une paysanne de l'Allemagne du Nord."
In Daniel S. Milo and Alain Boureau (eds.), *Alter histoire*, pp. 169–184. Paris: Les
Belles-lettres.

Lev Tov (1620). Yitzḥak ben Eliakum of Pozna, *Sefer lev tov.* Prague: Sons of Yaakov
Bak.

Lewinsky, Yom-Tov (1975). *Entsiklopedia shel havay umasoret bayahadut.* 2 vols.
Tel-Aviv: Dvir.

Liberles, Robert (2001). "Die Juden und die Anderen — Das Bild des Nichtjuden in
Glikl's Memoiren." In Richarz 2001, pp. 135–146.

Lowenstein, Steven (2001). "Weltlichkeit und Jenseitsorientierung in den Memoiren
der Glikl." In Richarz 2001, pp.223–237 .

Lowenthal, Marvin (1978). *The Memoirs of Glückel of Hameln.* Translated with notes
by Marvin Lowenthal. New introduction by Robert S. Rosen. New York: Schocken
Books.

Luschin von Ebengreuth, Arnold (1926). *Allgemeine Münzkunde und Geldgeschichte des
Mittelalters und der neueren Zeit.* München: R. Oldenbourg.

Maḥzor Rosh Hashana (2014). *The Koren Rosh Hashana Maḥzor.* Introduction,
Translation, and Commentary by Chief Rabbi Jonathan Sacks. Jerusalem: Koren
Publishers.

Maḥzor Yom Kippur (2014). *The Koren Yom Kippur Maḥzor.* Introduction,
Translation, and Commentary by Chief Rabbi Jonathan Sacks. Jerusalem: Koren
Publishers.

Marwedel, Günter (1976). *Die Privilegien der Juden in Altona.* Hamburger Beiträge zur
Geschichte der deutschen Juden 5. Hamburg: Hans Christians.

——— (1982). *Geschichte der Juden in Hamburg, Altona und Wandsbeck.* Vorträge und
Aufsätze, Verein für Hamburgische Geschichte 25. Hamburg: Hans Christians.

——— (1983). "Glückel von Hameln und ihre Familie in den Steuerkontenbüchern
der ashkenasischen Gemeinde Altona." In Peter Freimark, Ina Lorenz, and Günter
Marwedel (eds.), *Judentore, Kuggel, Steuerkonten*, pp. 70–97. Hamburger Beiträge
zur Geschichte der deutschen Juden 9. Hamburg: Hans Christians.

——— (2001a). "Die aschkenasischen Juden im Hamburger Raum (bis 1780)." In
Richarz 2001, pp. 41–60.

——— (2001b). "Probleme der Chronologie in Glikl's Memoiren." In Richarz 2001,
pp. 123–133.

Memorbuch Metz (1971). *Le "Memorbuch" de Metz (vers 1575–1724): Un obituaire
Israelite.* Traduit de l'hebreu, avec une introduction et des notes par Simon
Schwarzfuchs. Metz: Société d'histoire et d'archeologie de la Lorraine.

Minhagim de-k"k Wermaiza (1998–1992). Juspa Shammash, *Minhagim de-k"k Wermaiza*. Edited by Shlomo Hamburger, Yitshak Zimmer, and Israel Mordechai Peles. Jerusalem: Mifal torat chachmei Ashkenaz, Machon Yerushalayim.

Minhagot Wermaiza (1987). *Minhagot Wermaiza* le-R. Juda Löew Kirchheim im he'arot umarei mekomot [...] umavo raḥav meet Israel Mordechai Peles. Jerusalem: Mifal torat chachmei Ashkenaz, Machon Yerushalayim.

Minkoff, Nokhem Borekh (1952). *Glikl Hamel (1645–1724)*. New York: M. Vexer.

Moseley, Marcus (2006). *Being for Myself Alone: Origins of Jewish Autobiography*. Stanford, CA: Stanford University Press.

Munck, Thomas (1990). *Seventeenth Century Europe: State, Conflict and the Social Order in Europe 1598–1700*. London: Macmillan.

Muter, Silke (1999). "Zu Bildung und ökonomischen Aktivitäten jüdischer Frauen im Hamburg der Glikl Hameln." *Zeitschrift für Religions- und Geistgeschichte* 51: 217–237.

Naḥalat Shivah (1992). Shmuel ben David Moshe Halevi, *Sefer Naḥalat Shivah*, im hagahot mimahadurah batra ... kolel divrei ha-Tur E[ven ha]-E[zer] ve-Sh[ulḥan] Arukh be-inyenei gitin vekidushin [...]. Bnei Brak: Frenkel.

Neubauer, Adolf (1886–1906). *Catalogue of the Hebrew Manuscripts in the Bodleian Library*, I–II. Oxford: Clarendon.

Netter, Nathan (1938). *Vingt Siècles d'Histoire d'une Communauté Juive (Metz et son grand passé)*. Paris: Librarie Lipschutz.

North, Michael (1995). *Von Aktie bis Zoll: Ein Historisches Lexikon des Geldes*. München: C. H. Beck.

Noy, Meir (1968). *Sipur umanginah bo: Shishah sipurei-am mimizraḥ Eyropa*. Haifa: Municipality of Haifa, Museum of Ethnology and Folklore.

Ornan-Pinkus, Ben Zion (1986). "Die portugiesische Gemeinde in Hamburg im 17. Jahrhundert." *Ost und West* 5: 7–51.

Ozment, Steven (1986). *Magdalena and Balthasar: An Intimate Portrait of Life in 16th Century Europe Revealed in the Letters of a Nuremberg Husband and Wife*. Illuminated by Steven Ozment. New York: Simon and Schuster.

Pach-Oosterbroek, Hilde (2014). *Arranging Reality: The Editing Mechanisms of the World's First Yiddish Newspaper, the Kurant (Amsterdam, 1686–1687)*. PhD Thesis, Amsterdam School for Culture and History, University of Amsterdam.

Pappenheim, Bertha (1910). *Die Memoiren der Glückel von Hameln, geboren in Hamburg 1645, gestorben in Metz 19. September 1724*. Autorisierte Uebertragung nach der Ausgabe des David Kaufmann [Authorized translation of David Kauffman's edition]. Wien: Verlag von Stefan Meyer und Wilhelm Pappenheim. Later editions: *Die Memoiren der Glückel von Hameln*, Aus dem Jüdisch-Deutschen von Bertha Pappenheim, Mit einem Vorwort von Viola Roggenkamp, Weinheim: Beltz Athenäum 1994; Weinheim und Basel: Beltz Verlag 2005.

Paul, Hermann (1966). *Deutsches Wörterbuch*. 6th ed. Edited by Werner Betz. Tubingen: Niemeyer.

Perles, Joseph (1865). *Geschichte der Juden in Posen*. Breslau: Schletter.

Pinkas Kehal Tiktin (1996). *The Minutes Book of the Jewish Community Council Tykocin 1621–1806*, [. . .]. Annotated and edited with introduction, appendixes, indexes, glossary by Mordechai Nadav [. . .]. 2 vols. Jerusalem: Israel Academy of Sciences and Humanities.

Pinkas Lita (1925). *Pinkas hamedinah* [. . .] *1623–1761*. Edited by Simon Dubnow. Berlin: A'yanot.

Pinkas Metz (1770). *Pinkas ḥevra kadisha shel Metz 1575–1770*. Ms. 5396 in the Library of the Jewish Theological Seminary, New York.

Pinkas Metz (1829). *Pinkas hazkarat neshamot shel kehilat Metz 1721–1829*. Ms. 3670 in the Library of the Jewish Theological Seminary, New York.

Pinkas Va'ad Arba Aratsot (1945). Edited by Israel Halpern. Jerusalem: Mossad Bialik.

Plutarch (1932). *The Lives of the Noble Grecians and Romans*. Translated by John Dryden. Revised by Arthur Hugh Clough. New York: Modern Library.

Pollack, Herman (1971). *Jewish Folkways in Germanic Lands 1648–1806*. Cambridge, MA: MIT Press.

Rabinovitz, Alexander Siskind (1929). *Zikhronot Glikl*. Translated by Alexander Siskind Rabinovitz. Tel Aviv: Dvir.

Rafalowicz, Mira (1987). *De Memoires van Glikl Hamel (1645–1724) door haarzelf geshreven*. Nederlandse vertaling Mira Rafalowicz. Amsterdam: Feministische Uitgeverij Sara.

Rapoport-Albert, Ada (2015). "Glikl Hamel ke'almanah." In Rapoport-Albert, *Ḥassidim veshabtaim, anashim venashim*, pp. 492–504. Jerusalem: Zalman Shazar Center for Jewish History.

Rashi Commentary: Sefaria.org/person/Rashi: *A Living Library of Jewish Texts . . . in Hebrew and English Translation*. https://www.sefaria.org/person/Rashi.

Rashi Commentary on Torah (1998). *Sapirstein Edition Rashi: The Torah with Rashi's Commentary Translated, Annotated and Elucidated*. Vols. 1–5: Genesis, Exodus, Leviticus, Numbers, Deuteronomy. New York: Artscroll, Mesorah Publications.

Reiner, Elhanan (1993). "Hon, ma'amad ḥevrati vetalmud torah: hakloyz baḥevrah hayehudit bemizraḥ Eyropa bameot 17–18." *Zion* 58: 287–328.

Richarz, Monika, ed. (2001). *Die Hamburger Kauffrau Glikl: Jüdische Existenz in der Frühen Neuzeit*. Hamburg: Christians.

Richarz, Monika (2001a). "Einleitung." In Richarz (2001), pp. 9–26.

Riemer, Nathanael (2008). "Some Parallels of Stories in Glikl's of Hameln 'Zikhroynes.'" *PaRDeS. Zeitschrift der Vereinigung für Jüdische Studien e.V.* (2008) 14: 125–148.

Rivkind, Itzhok (1960). *Yidishe gelt in lebnsshteyger, kultur-geshikhte un folklor, leksikologishe shtudie*. New York: American Academy for Jewish Research.

Robert, Paul (1989). *Dictionnaire alphabétique et analogique de la langue française*. Rédaction dirigée par A. Rey et J. Rey-Debove. Paris: Le Robert.

Sadan, Dov (1975). *A vort bashteyt*. Vol. 2. Tel-Aviv: Y. L. Peretz Farlag.

Schechter, Solomon (1908). "The Memoirs of a Jewess of the Seventeenth Century." In Schechter, *Studies in Judaism: Second Series*, pp. 126–147. Philadelphia: Jewish Publication Society of America.

Scholem, Gershom (1973). *Sabbatai Sevi: The Mystical Messiah, 1626–1676*. London: Routledge and Kegan Paul.

Sefer Hamafteah (1971). Nissim ben Jacob of Kairwan, *Sefer Hamafteah leman'ulei hatalmud: Tractates Berakhot, Shabbat, Eruvin*. Introduction by Rabbi Nissim. Edited by Jacob Goldenthal. Jerusalem: Makor.

Sefer Hayashar (1986). *Sefer Hayashar, hehedir vetseyraf mavo*. Edited with introduction by Joseph Dan. Jerusalem: Mossad Bialik.

Sefer Maharil (1987). *Sefer Maharil, minhagim shel rabeinu Yaakov Molin*. Yotse laor [. . .] al yidei Shlomo J. Spitzer. Jerusalem: Mifal torath chachmei Ashkenaz, Machon Yerushalayim.

Shevet Yehuda (1947). Shlomo Ibn Verga, *Sefer Shevet Yehuda*. Edited by Azriel Shoḥet and Yitzḥak Baer. Jerusalem: Mossad Bialik.

Shmeruk, Chone (1961). "Baḥurim me-Ashkenaz bishivot Polin." In S. Ettinger, S. Baron, B. Dinur, I. Halpern (eds.), *Sefer yovel leYitzhak Baer bimlot lo shivim shanah*, pp. 304–317. Jerusalem: Haḥevrah hahistorit ha-isre'eilit.

——— (1978). *Sifrut yidish, prakim letoldoteha*. Tel Aviv: Mifalim universitaim.

——— (1981). *Sifrut yidish be-Polin, Meḥkarim ve'iyunim historiim*. Jerusalem: Magnes Press.

——— (1985). "Hakadosh Reb Shakhne: Krakow 1682 — Rishum bapinkas shel haḥevra kadisha leumat shir 'histori.'" *Gal-Ed* vii–viii: 57–69.

Shnei Luḥot Habrit (1649). Yeshaya ben Avraham Halevy ish Horowitz. *Sefer Shnei Luḥot Habrit*. Amsterdam: Immanuel Benveniste.

Shoḥet, Azriel (1960). *Im ḥilufei tkufot — reishit hahaskalah beyahadut Germania*. Jerusalem: Mossad Bialik.

Siddur (2016). *The Koren Siddur*. Introduction, translation, and commentary by Rabbi Lord Jonathan Sacks. 2nd Hebrew English Edition. Jerusalem: Koren Publishers.

Silverman-Weinreich, Beatrice (1988). *Yiddish Folktales*. Translated by Leonard Wolf. New York: Pantheon Books.

Simonsen, D. (1905). "Eine Confrontation zwischen Glückel Hameln's Memoiren und den alten Hamburger Grabbüchern." *MGWJ* 49: 96–106.

Stanislawski, Michael (2004). *Autobiographical Jews: Essays in Jewish Self Fashioning*. Seattle: University of Washington Press.

Steinschneider, Moritz (1852–1860). *Catalogus Librorum Hebraeorum in Bibliotheca Bodleiana*. Berolini: Typ. A. Friedländer.

Stern, Selma (1950). *The Court Jew*. Philadelphia: Jewish Publication Society of America.

Studemund-Halévy, Michael (1991). "Sprachverhalten und Assimilation der portugiesischen Juden in Hamburg." In Herzig and Rohde 1991, pp. 283–298.

——— (2000). *Biographisches Lexikon der Hamburger Sefarden*. Hamburger Beiträge zur Geschichte der deutschen Juden 22. Hamburg: Christians.

Studemund-Halévy, Michael, and Peter Koj (1994). *Die Sefarden in Hamburg: Zur Geschichte einer Minderheit*. Hamburg: H. Buske.

Stutchkoff, Nahum (1950). *Der oytser fun der yidisher shprakh* [Thesaurus of the Yiddish Language]. Edited by Max Weinreich. New York: Yidisher Visnshaftlekher Institut (YIVO).

Tabory, Joseph (2008). *JPS Commentary on the Haggadah: Historical Introduction, Translation, and Commentary*. Foreword by David Stern. Philadephia: Jewish Publication Society.

Takanot Medinat Mehrin (1952). *Constitutiones Congressus Generalis Judaeorum Moraviensum (1650–1748)*. Edicit et explanavit Israel Halpern. Jerusalem: Mekize Nirdamim.

Teller, Issachar Baer (1988). *The Wellspring of Living Waters: A Medical Self-Help Book*. Translated from the Hebrew and Yiddish with introduction and notes by Arthur Teller. New York: Tal Or Oth.

Tendlau, Abraham (1860). *Sprichwörter und Redensarten deutsch-jüdischer Vorzeit, Als Beitrag zur Volks-, Sprach- und Sprichwörter Kunde: Aufgezeichnet aus dem Munde des Volkes und nach Wort und Sinn erläutert*. Frankfurt a.M.: J. Kauffmann.

―― (1864–1865). "Aus dem handschriftlichen Tagebuch einer Frau aus dem 17. Jahrhunderts." *Der Israelit* 5 (1864): 53–54, 89–90, 107–108, 117–118; *Der Israelit* 6 (1865): 461–463, 476–477.

Timm, Erika (1999). *Matronymika im aschkenasischen Kulturbereich, Ein Beitrag zur Mentalitäts- und Sozialgeschichte der europäischen Juden*. Tübingen: Niemeyer.

―― (2001). "Glikls Sprache vor ihrem sozialhistorischen und geographischen Hintergrund." In Richarz 2001, pp. 49–67.

―― (2006). "Leshonah shel Glikl." In Turniansky 2006a, introduction pp. 61–74 (Hebrew numbers).

Tsene-rene (1622). Yaakov ben Yitshak Ashkenazi of Janów, *Ḥamishah ḥumshei torah beloshn ashkenaz, tsena urena bnot tsiyon*. Basel (or Hanau): No publisher.

Turniansky, Chava (1987–1989). "Zum Charakter der Memoiren der Glückel von Hameln." *Hebräische Beiträge zur Wissenschaft des Judentums deutsch angezeigt* 3–4: 80–89.

―― (1988). "Yiddish Song as Historical Source Material: Plague in the Judenstadt of Prague in 1713." In Ada Rapoport-Albert and Steven J. Zipperstein (eds.), *Jewish History, Essays in Honor of Chimen Abramsky*, pp. 189–198. London: Peter Halban.

―― (1989), "Yiddish 'Historical' Songs as Sources for the History of the Jews in Pre-Partition Poland." *Polin: A Journal of Polish-Jewish Studies* 4: 42–52.

―― (1992). "Bashraybungen fun gesheenishn in Glikl Hamels zikhroynes." *Di goldene keyt* 134: 35–40.

―― (1993). "Vegn di literatur-mekoyrim in Glikl Hamels zikhroynes." In Israel Bartal, Chava Turniansky, and Ezra Mendelsohn (eds.), *Keminhag Ashkenaz u-Polin, Sefer yovel le-Chone Shmeruk*, pp. 153–178. Jerusalem: Zalman Shazar Center for Jewish History.

―― (1994a). *Beyn kodesh leḥol: lashon, ḥinukh vehaskalah bemizraḥ Eyropa*. Course unit 7 of Polin, The Jews of Eastern Europe: History and Culture. Tel Aviv: Open University of Israel.

———— (1994b). "Tsu voser literarishn zhaner gehert Glikl Hamels shafung?" *Proceedings of the Eleventh World Congress of Jewish Studies*, Sect. C, Vol. 3, Jerusalem, pp. 283–290.

———— (1994c). "Hasipurim bitsirata shel Glikl Hamel umekoroteihem." *Jerusalem Studies in Jewish Folklore* 16: 41–65.

———— (1996). "Hadrasha ve-hadrasha bikhtav kimtavekhet bein hatarbut hakanonit vehakahal harahav." In Benjamin. Z. Kedar (ed.), *Studies in the History of Popular Culture*, pp. 183–196. Jerusalem: Zalman Shazar Center for Jewish History.

———— (1998). "Dmut haisha bezikhronoteha shel Glikl Hamel." In Israel Bartal and Isaiah Gafni (eds.), *Eros erusin visurim, miniut umishpahah bahistoria*, pp. 177–191. Jerusalem: Zalman Shazar Center for Jewish History.

———— (2001). "Glikls Werk und die zeitgenossische jiddische Literatur." In Richarz 2001, pp. 68–90.

———— (2002). "Der loshn-koydesh komponent in Glikl's verk vi an eydes af ir bildung." In Jürgen Jaehrling, Uwe Mewes, and Erika Timm (eds.), *Röllwagenbüchlein, Festschrift für Walther Röll zum 65: Geburtstag*, pp. 433–441. Tübingen: Niemeyer.

———— (2004). "Die Erzählungen in Glikl Hamelns Werk und ihre Quellen." In Christiane E. Müller and Andrea Schatz (eds.), *Der Differenz auf der Spur: Frauen und Gender in Ashkenaz*, pp. 121–148. Berlin: Metropol.

———— (2006a). *Glikl, Zikhronot 1691–1719* [*Glikl, Memoirs 1691–1719*]. Edited and translated from the Yiddish by Chava Turniansky. Jerusalem: Zalman Shazar Center for Jewish History, Ben-Zion Dinur Center for Research in Jewish History, Hebrew University of Jerusalem.

———— (2006b). "Glueckel of Hameln." In *Jewish Women: A Comprehensive Historical Encyclopedia*, ed. Paula E. Hyman and Dalia Ofer. Jewish Women's Archive Inc. https://jwa.org/blog/jewish-women-a-comprehensive-historical-encyclopedia.

———— (2009). "Tfilah uthinah besefer zikhronoteha shel Glikl." *Massekhet* 8: 11–27.

———— (2010). "Halimud baheder ba'et hahadashah hamukdemet." In Immanuel Etkes and David Assaf (eds.), Uriel Gellman (asst. ed.), *Haheder—Mehkarim, te'udot, pirkei sifrut vezikhronot*, pp. 3–35. Tel Aviv: Tel Aviv University.

———— (2015). "Zikhroynes, Glikl bas Leyb Pinkerle." In *Enzyklopädie jüdischer Geschichte und Kultur*, Im Auftrag der Sachsischen Akademie der Wissenschaften zu Leipzig, herausgegeben von Dan Diner, Vol. 6, pp. 556–559. Stuttgart-Weimar: Verlag J. B. Metzler.

Verdenhalven, Fritz (1968). *Alte Masse, Münzen und Gewichte aus dem deutschen Sprachgebiet*. Neustadt an der Aisch: Degener.

Wander, Karl Friedrich Wilhelm (1987). *Deutsches Sprichwörter-Lexikon*. Vols. I–V. Augsburg: Weltbild.

Weinreich, Max (2008). *History of the Yiddish Language*. Edited by Paul Glasser. Translated by Shlomo Noble, with the assistance of Joshua A. Fishman. New Haven, CT: Yale University Press.

Weinryb, Ber (1928). "A pekl briv in yidish fun yor 1588 Kroke-Prog." *Historishe Shriftn* II: 43–67.

Wiedemann, Conrad (1986). "Zwei jüdische Autobiographien im Deutschland des 18. Jahrhunderts: Glückel von Hameln und Salomon Maimon." In Stéphane Moses and Albrecht Schöne (eds.), *Juden in der deutschen Literatur: Ein deutsch-israelisches Symposion*, pp. 88–113. Frankfurt a.M.: Suhrkamp.

Winston, Richard (1954). *Charlemagne: From the Hammer to the Cross*. New York: Vintage Books.

Wolfsberg-Aviad, Oskar, et al. (1960). *Die drei Gemeinde: Aus der Geschichte der jüdischen Gemeinden Altona-Hamburg-Wandsbeck*. München: Ner Tamid.

Yaari, Abraham (1946). "Shnei kuntresim me-Eretz Israel." *Kiryat Sefer* 23: 149–155.

Yassif, Eli (1985). Tales of Ben-Sira in the Middle Ages: A Critical Text and Literary Studies. Jerusalem: Magnes Press.

——— (1987). "The Man Who Never Swore an Oath: From Jewish to Israeli Oikotype." *Fabula* 27: 216–236.

Yesh Noḥalin (1615). Avraham ben Shabtai Halevy ish Horowitz, *Sefer Yesh Noḥalin*, with glosses of his son R. Yakov. Prague: Abraham Lemburger.

The YIVO Encyclopedia of Jews in Eastern Europe (2008). Editor-in-chief Gershon Hundert. New Haven, CT: Yale University Press. www.yivoencyclopedia.org.

Yoḥasin Hashalem (1963). Abraham Zakut, *Sefer Yoḥasin Hashalem*. Edited by Herschell Filipowski and A. H. Freimann. Jerusalem: Vardi Printing House.

Yosef Ometz (1965). Yosef Yospa Hahn Neurlingen, *Sefer Yosef Ometz, kolel dinim uminhagim lekhol yimot hashanah*. Jerusalem: Dfus ofset haomanim.

Yuval, Israel Yaakov (1989). *Ḥakhamim bedoram, hamanhigut haruḥanit shel yehudei Germania beshilhei yemei habeinaim*. Jerusalem: Magnes Press.

——— (1995). "Hahesderim hakaspiim shel hanisuin be-Ashkenaz bimei habeinaim." In Menachem Ben-Sasson (ed.), *Dat vekhalkalah: yaḥasei gomlin*, pp. 191–207. Jerusalem: Zalman Shazar Center for Jewish History.

Zinberg, Israel (1972–1978). *A History of Jewish Literature*. Translated from the Yiddish and edited by Bernard Martin. Cleveland: Press of Case Western Reserve University.

INDEX

Note: Photographs and illustrations are indicated in italics.
Page numbers with "n" or "nn" indicate footnotes or endnotes.